RETURN
with
ELIXIR

T0355955

"Miles Neale masterfully weaves this universal quest with alchemical lore, Buddhism, Gnosticism, mythology, Western and Eastern esoteric knowledge, astrology, Balinese traditions, and more into a deeply heart-felt personal biography of rebirth. His work is invaluable to seekers on the journey to find the elixir of the True Self."

TJOK GDE KERTHYASA, BHSc (HOM.), ADHOM., FOUNDER OF
TIRTA USADA HOLISTIC HEALTH

"Miles Neale's brilliant account of the inner quest brings together the compelling voices of mystical Christianity, esoteric Buddhism, shaman-ism, Jungian depth psychology, alchemy, and the cries of pain in living an authentic life right now. The reader will not only find a set of maps for the journey but also a guide to learning the taste and texture of what truly heals the human spirit as it attends, moment to moment, the pas-sage from death to life."

REV. CANON DR. FRANCIS V. TISO, AUTHOR OF
RAINBOW BODY AND RESURRECTION

"*Return with Elixir* is a thoroughly engrossing journey. This book is for everyone. In a time where we're all asking questions, this book will give answers and have us concentrating on what really matters."

DAMIEN ECHOLS, AUTHOR OF *HIGH MAGICK*

"Miles's account of his inner and outer pilgrimage through the dark depths of angst and into the light of the sacred is one that can motivate us all to embark on a journey toward meaning and wholeness. *Return with Elixir* illustrates the basic human need for authentic and embodied spiritual experience that has existed throughout time and across cultures and encourages us today to join the great heroes, yogis, and seekers of the past in facing adversity to heal our soul and find freedom."

CHRISTIANA POLITES, DIRECTOR OF PURE LAND FARMS AND
SOWA RIGPA INSTITUTE OF TIBETAN MEDICINE

"*Return with Elixir* is far more than a manual for rebirth, blending esoteric traditions East and West; it is a deeply personal and relatable story of transformation. With this map of the inner landscape in hand, led by such an expert guide, you too can embark on the sacred pilgrimage to face your worst fears, taste the nectar of compassion at your heart, and return home for the benefit of others. It reveals the secret path of converting obstacles into opportunities and making meaningful whatever miseries arise along life's unpredictable journey."

GESHE TENZIN ZOPA, TEACHER AT THE FOUNDATION FOR THE
PRESERVATION OF THE MAHAYANA TRADITION

"Miles Neale embarks on a bold journey to resurrect what has been lost in the West, reminding us of a time when medicine was experiential and deeply connected to our inner landscapes. Through visualization, pilgrimage, and psychedelics—practices that modern standards might find suspect—Miles offers a transformative process of healing that arises from within and is not reliant on external authority. He is an exceptional guide, one with whom I have walked into the darkness and for whom I am deeply grateful"

JOHN W. PRICE, PH.D., LPC, FOUNDER OF CENTER FOR THE HEALING
ARTS AND SCIENCES AND HOST OF *THE SACRED SPEAKS* PODCAST

"*Return with Elixir* is a wonderful literary pilgrimage, taking the reader through the channels and chakras of the Tantric subtle body to taste the nectar of immortality. It is both an excellent example of comparative mysticism and a gripping personal tale of transforming human adversity into spiritual awakening."

GLENN H. MULLIN, BUDDHIST AUTHOR, LECTURER, AND TEACHER

"Miles dives deeply into the nature of pilgrimage, traversing the universal and time-tested path for self-inquiry, healing, and purpose that is born from our innate desire to go home, to find our way back to our true, human nature. For the life-affirming pilgrim en route to this sacred destination, this is more than a book; it is a spirit guide."

JAKE HAUPERT, COFOUNDER AND CONSCIOUS CEO OF THE
TRANSFORMATIONAL TRAVEL COUNCIL

"This heartfelt exploration of the possibilities for personal and planetary healing through a fusion of ancient esoteric traditions and modern psychotherapy is itself an elixir, one that can help bring about the transmutations we need during this turning of time's wheel."

JOHN MICHAEL GREER, AUTHOR OF *THE TWILIGHT OF PLUTO*
AND *THE OCCULT PHILOSOPHY WORKBOOK*

"A fascinating exploration of cosmic, societal death and rebirth. The author's traumatic journey of self-discovery is the compelling thread that skillfully weaves together Jungian psychology, mysticism, astrology, and Tibetan Buddhism into one cohesive pilgrimage of the soul. It provides a map for seekers of meaning and purpose to navigate not only the big issues of life and death but also the fears and beliefs that prevent us from realizing our full potential. A wonderful modern addition to a genre that is as old as humanity itself."

TONY STEEL, OAM, DIRECTOR OF THE VAJRAYANA INSTITUTE

"Hearing the drumbeat of universal spiritual teachings and the wisdom song of the sacred feminine, Miles Neale offers himself into the reservoir of omniscient, timeless awareness. *Return with Elixir* is a deeply personal and inspiring account of the awakening path and finding freedom from a world of mass delusion. It shares the extraordinary magic and meaning that occurs when we melt into the clearlight network of the Dakini and reemerge as a sublime avatar of compassion in the world. It gives us practical tools to access this most valuable treasure within us all."

MICHELE LOEW, COAUTHOR *THE YOGA OF NIGUMA* AND
FOUNDING DIRECTOR OF VAJRA YOGA SCHOOL

"My teacher said: 'One should not discard his maps until the destination is within sight.' At this point in history, most people don't even know they need maps! Miles is a mapmaker and guide who has seen the rocky shoals. Read this book!"

WALTER CRUTTENDEN, AUTHOR OF *LOST STAR OF MYTH AND TIME* AND PRODUCER OF *THE GREAT YEAR*

"A masterful synthesis of Eastern and Western esoteric teachings. Miles beautifully weaves together disparate threads from various sources— including mythology, Jungian psychology, and Tibetan alchemy—to focus on the growth of the soul. This will be of great interest to anyone on the perennial search for meaning. For them, this book will be a revelation."

RAY GRASSE, AUTHOR OF *THE WAKING DREAM*

"Amidst the collapse of civilizations past, ancient cultures once turned to cosmology and mysticism to illuminate the journey from darkness to light. In *Return with Elixir*, Miles revives these sacred teachings—from circumambulating the Borobudur mandala to channeling the serpent energy within our subtle body nervous system—guiding us on the soul's pilgrimage from crisis to clarity. For those seeking a manual of rebirth and ready to heed the revolutionary call to consciousness awakening, this book offers life-affirming nectar to savor."

PATRICK VANHOEBROUCK, RESIDENT ANTHROPOLOGIST AT AMANJIWO, JAVA

"Miles Neale takes us on an extraordinary odyssey of exploration and transformation born out of his own inner call to awaken through misfortune. This fascinating synthesis of Eastern and Western wisdom illuminates a profound and ancient mystery of transformation still alive and relevant today."

ROB PREECE, AUTHOR OF *THE WISDOM OF IMPERFECTION* AND *TASTING THE ESSENCE OF TANTRA*

"Miles Neale offers readers a series of maps to help them successfully navigate their own inner states of being and thus overcome their fear, anxiety, and apathy. Learning to 'die before you die' is one of the primary pathways emphasized in the book as a way to triumph over yourself. Conquering oneself is the first act of every aspiring warrior of light."

ROBERT BREEDLOVE, HOST OF THE PODCAST *WHAT IS MONEY?*

RETURN
with
ELIXIR

Four Maps for
the Soul's Pilgrimage
through Death and Rebirth

MILES NEALE, Psy.D.

Inner Traditions
Rochester, Vermont

Inner Traditions
One Park Street
Rochester, Vermont 05767
www.InnerTraditions.com

Cataloging-in-Publication Data for this title is available from the Library of Congress

ISBN 978-1-64411-843-6 (print)
ISBN 978-1-64411-844-3 (ebook)

Printed and bound in India at Replika Press Pvt. Ltd.

10 9 8 7 6 5 4 3 2 1

Text design by Debbie Glogover and layout by Virginia Scott Bowman
This book was typeset in Garamond Premier Pro with Artifex used as the display
typeface

To send correspondence to the author of this book, mail a first-class letter to the
author c/o Inner Traditions • Bear & Company, One Park Street, Rochester, VT
05767, and we will forward the communication, or contact the author directly at
milesneale.com.

Scan the QR code and save 25% at InnerTraditions.com.
Browse over 2,000 titles on spirituality, the occult, ancient
mysteries, new science, holistic health, and natural medicine.

To my boys Bodhi and Pema for your pilgrimage into the labyrinth and beyond. When I'm gone look for me in Bodhgaya, you'll always find me there.

The dark night of the soul comes just before revelation.
JOSEPH CAMPBELL

My friends, it is wise to nourish the soul,
otherwise you will breed dragons and devils in your heart.
CARL JUNG, *THE RED BOOK*

Oh noble-one, when your body and mind were separating,
you must have experienced a glimpse of the Pure Truth,
subtle, sparkling, bright, dazzling, glorious, and radiantly
*   awesome,*
in appearance like a mirage moving across a landscape in
*   spring-time*
in one continuous stream of vibrations.
Be not daunted thereby, nor terrified, nor awed.
That is the radiance of your own true nature.
Recognize it.
TIBETAN BOOK OF THE DEAD,
TRANSLATED BY ROBERT A.F. THURMAN

If you die before you die, you won't die when you die.
DOORWAY INSCRIPTION, SAINT PAUL
MONASTERY. MOUNT ATHOS, GREECE

Contents

Foreword Ambrosia: Elixir of Immortality   xi
          By Robert A. F. Thurman, Ph.D.

          Acknowledgments   xvii

PART I
Ground

1 Visions: Third Eye Intuitions   2

2 Panorama: As Above, So Below   32

3 Soul: Imbibing the Elixir   68

4 *Solve et Coagula*: Dying to be Reborn   88

PART II
Path

5 Pilgrimage: There and Back Again   104

6 Departure: Fall from Grace   137

7 Initiation: Rite of Passage   170

8 Ordeal: Taming the Dragon   206

PART III

Fruition

9 Treasure: Claiming the Sword   238

10 Return: Bestowing the Boon   278

11 Therapeia: Pilgrimage & Psychedelics   319

12 Reunion: End of Separation   346

Afterword Nostos: The Return of Longing   377
           By Phil Cousineau

           Notes   384

           Bibliography   394

           Index   403

Ambrosia

Elixir of Immortality

Robert A. F. Thurman, Ph.D.

Profound, peaceful, clear-light, nonproliferating, uncreated—
Like the deathless elixir, this one reality I've become.
SHAKYAMUNI BUDDHA'S FIRST WORDS IN THE
PRE-SUNRISE DAWN UNDER THE BODHI TREE.

Miles reminds me of Neo in the first Matrix movie, especially in the beginning, when he is sitting in his office in front of his computer, doing okay in his corporation and city life, but nevertheless feels like something is wrong; he's living in a falsity, an unreality. Neo has no clue why that could be, so when Trinity and Morpheus and company come for him, he is too excited and terrified to be able right away to make the leap. After capture by agents, followed by escape with the rebels, he resists intensely at first, refusing the call to adventure. Soon after however, he goes with them wholeheartedly and begins his odyssey with his training under Morpheus!

What is the real reality Neo lives in? Who is he himself? Why do they think he is "the one"—the messianic person capable of saving humanity from the domineering machine robots who have taken over the planet? Why should he believe that? How does his falling in love with Trinity affect the mission? The Matrix saga goes on and on, getting better and better after four blockbuster adventures, and still there's no final conclusion, no definitive end to the saga.

Here in our own "real" world, Miles has made his own Hero's Journey, going through breakdown, descent into the dark night of the soul, discovery, and ascent back into joy on an island paradise. In this dynamic book *Return with Elixir*, Miles bestows for the rest of us a boon, encouraging us to embark on our own grail quest for the ambrosia of inner peace and spiritual attainment.

I have known Miles for nearly twenty-five years. During this time I have watched him grow steadily from a young, wide-eyed volunteer at Tibet House, US, into a compelling teacher in his own right in New York City and around the world. I'm happy to have played a role in his development, and to witness how those early seeds have come to fruition for him, and through him, for others. Miles was doing very well as an effective psychotherapist with a thriving clinical practice, helping clients from his glass-walled skyscraper office in New York City, in a loving relationship with his true partner Emily Wolf on a shared spiritual basis, raising a cheerful family, and still studying the codices of his life and craft—Eastern scientific wisdom and Western psychological research. He was providing healing and counseling while also teaching Eastern philosophical and yogic methods, serving as a popular Dharma and psychology teacher creating modern ways of accessing the traditions of ancient India's Nalanda University, preserved and refined for us by the Tibetan sages and adepts. All of this was accompanied by his research and teaching of serious studies and practices of the philosophical/scientific complexities of the world as revealed by the Buddhist Indo-Tibetan "inner" or "spiritual" sciences viewed through the lens of a dawning awareness of the limitations of the scientific materialism of our limited consensus reality. Miles also pushed himself and his students past mere conceptual knowledge, daring to burn away with the gut-borne fury-fire that can be yogically manipulated to arise from the navel chakra, sending it surging upward on a subtle body pilgrimage to melt down the lunar bliss energy that transforms the constricting, low-energy lifestyle of rigid ego-identity habits and complacent materialist social identity. He gradually melted down the ego-controlling structure of our American conventionalities and ventured to explore the inner subtle body and mind, and the super-subtle soul-continuum that transmigrates through the ever-spiraling stages of life, death, and rebirth until it reaches the farthest shore of self-actualized emancipation in Buddhahood.

Miles and his intrepid partner Emily, his "Trinity," then courageously broke away from the sham security of his office, income, status, and profession geared to helping people not fitting well into our materialist culture merely to cope, yearning to lift them even higher, toward the meaningful realization of our awesome human potentials. Miles renounced his world like spiritual adepts of the past, driven by his searing honesty of self-investigation and enabled by the courageous integrity and daring energy of his wise and loving partner. He dared to embark on a new life-pilgrimage to discover the nectar of wisdom, love, and compassion, the ambrosia of the experience of truth, the higher reality that is the only experience that makes life worthwhile and conquers the subjugation by death.

Physically, Miles left the United States and took his family with him. They hopped from the bustling island of Manhattan to Homer's serene island of Ithaca in Greece, eventually landing on the tantric island of Bali. Along the way, Miles devotedly followed his intuition, Green Tara herself, just as the Indian sage Atisha Dipamkara Srijnana did in the eleventh century before him, when he ventured on a perilous pilgrimage from India to Sumatra and Java, Indonesia, on a twelve-year odyssey to receive transmissions of the nectar of bodhicitta from master Serlingpa. Atisha eventually returned to bestow his own boon upon the

Tibetan civilization during a period of fragmentation, a blazing lamp to light the path that continues to burn brightly, inspiring us today during our own civilization's dark night. Similarly, Miles emulates the seventeenth century Japanese Buddhist monk, Haiku poet and pilgrim, Bashō on his "journey to the deep north," aiming to face death and not return unless he had something revitalizing to share with his fellow humans.

After leaving New York City, Miles continued his study of scientific, reality-seeking philosophy and practice of the yogic science of self-examination of both mind and body. He started with the time tested mind science disciplines of Indo-Tibetan Buddhism and then added a marvelous array of teachings to help him integrate his sophisticated and beautifully woven Elixir tapestry, incorporating Western mystical traditions, Eleusinian psychedelic mysteries, Christian and hermetic yogic traditions, ancient astronomy and astrology, and—using the insightful help of modern mythonauts and healers Joseph Campbell and Carl Jung—brings them all into conversation with the wisdom and compassion enlightenment quest.

I very much enjoy the way Miles has mastered these various threads of Western disciplines and succeeded in weaving them together with their Eastern counterparts using what he calls the universal, esoteric loom of *solve et coagula*, and of course inspired by the mandala, a cosmic womb of integration. Reading this book, one can now clearly appreciate how the Indo-Tibetan psychologies, transcendent compassionate ethics, alchemical inner tech, and secret yogic pilgrimages of the East, aimed towards imbibing *amrita*—the elixir of immortality innate within the subtle mental continuum and held within the chalice of the heart chakra—dovetails seamlessly with the ancient Greek mystery schools, with their outer pilgrimages and healing purifications, temple incubation and dream analysis, ecstatic feasts, and imbibing of ambrosia and *kykeon*—ergot-infused wine held within kantharos vessels—instantly dispelling existential mortality fears in order to provide direct, personal access to the deathless state, allowing us to behold reality nakedly, live more virtuously, and fulfill our human purpose. *Return with Elixir* inspires a deep awe and reverent gratitude for the amazing achievements, exquisite mythologies, and refined inner and outer technologies developed into proven efficacy by adept sages East and West, from India and Tibet to ancient Greece, preserved and bequeathed to us through unbroken lineages of ear-whispered, master-student transmissions, secret texts and commentaries, sacred sites of pilgrimage, and devoted esoteric communities. But mere armchair admiration of history and legacy is insufficient.

We should make no mistake about it, we meet in Miles, through his sharing of his life and escapades with his intrepid partner Emily, his lama Geshe Tenzin Zopa, his merry band of travel companions Tjok Gde Kerhtyasa and other wisdom keepers of Bali, and his work of sharing his golden elixir with us all, a provocative and reliable guide for our own life's epic master work of discovering who we really are. As Miles has shown us, this knowledge is not achieved by unquestioningly adopting a simplistic answer or label, but by opening our minds and hearts, through trial and terror, to the gnosis treasure of what we can become—what we have to become—to make truly meaningful our amazing lives in the midst of the cosmic planetary catastrophic crisis we chose to be born into! We should not fear to rise up from our comfort zones, or face tyrannical foes, which are mostly based on the false ground of the spiritually unexamined and unvirtuous life unknowingly projected outwards, nor cease to be trapped in the obviously false scientific materialist delusion that nothingness is the ground and destiny of all meaningless life. This is our chance to open our exquisite human soul-intelligence centrally processing supercomputer of a subtle nervous system sensitivity to channel the infinite bliss energy of empirically discoverable ultimate reality known to all enlightened sages and adepts of all cultures throughout all history.

Now is the unique moment of planetary emergency at the end of history, the so-called apocalypse or revelation, both of the grotesque underbelly as well as elevated triumphs of humanity, when we must not just passively outsource leadership to others, but ourselves all arise—like Miles—to break free from the matrix of collective egocentrist delusion. With this excellent pilgrim's guidebook in hand, its multidimensional, interdisciplinary cyclic maps beckoning us on our own circumambulation to the sacred center, we can make our lives worth living infinitely for others. As we venture forth with what Miles calls our "mythopoetic third eye" wide open, I trust we shall renounce self-imposed blindness and misery, face courageously the collective dark night, rediscover the elusive soul, humbly accept atonement, realize we are already free, and return with amazing grace to our own loved ones and the planet, each having tasted the immortal life-affirming ambrosia for ourselves.

TENZIN BOB THURMAN

ROBERT A. F. THURMAN, PH.D., is an authority on spirituality, mind science, philosophy, and Tibetan Buddhism. Named one of *Time* magazine's 25 most influential Americans, he cofounded Tibet House US—a nonprofit dedicated to the preservation and renaissance of Tibetan culture—with Tenzin Tethong, Richard Gere, and Philip Glass as well as the Menla Mountain Retreat and Healing Center with his wife, Nena. He is the author of more than 20 books on Tibet, Buddhism, art, politics, and culture.

Acknowledgments

Many kind and skilled people offered technical expertise to birth *Return with Elixir* into this world. My gratitude extends to my agent Linda Lowenthal; for transcriptions, Colonel Christopher Biggs; elegant diagrams and design, Karen Meneghin; citations, Putu Yudiantara; the entire Inner Traditions publication team; and most especially my friend and master editor, Alice Peck, for our second tour of duty together.

There are also those who inspired the pilgrimage: Asclepius god of Healing; the renegades of the Contemplative Studies Program, now the Gradual Path; magician Damien Echols; mystic Carl Jung; filmmakers Phillip O'Leary and Matthew Freidell; the oracle Lynn Bell; Belgian anthropologist Patrick Vanhoebrouck; Javanese Tantric master Mangku Jitho; and the many wisdom keepers of Bali, notably Pak Ketut Sedana and Jero Ning.

Homage to my mentors, the one-eyed Tibetologist Robert Thurman for his foreword and transmission of the *Bardo Thodol*, and poet-mythologist Phil Cousineau for his afterword and transmission of Joseph Campbell's monomyth.

Nothing would be possible without my new, old friend the Wizard of Bali Tjok Gde Kerthyasa, the sacred island sanctuaries of Ithaca and Bali that harbor secret portals; my beloved wife, Emily Wolf, who pushed me off a cliff when I was convinced I couldn't fly; my outer guru, the incomparably virtuous Geshe Tenzin Zopa; and my inner guru and animus, the Diamond Queen Tara. All ignited and tended to the fire of my soul.

Finally, I extend my respect to those who betrayed me and thus made me stronger, and to all those nascent heroes, yogis, psychonauts, and psychedelic wayfarers that will seek the Elixir, aspiring to die before they die.

I raise a chalice of wine transformed ambrosia in each of your names and blissfully imbibe.

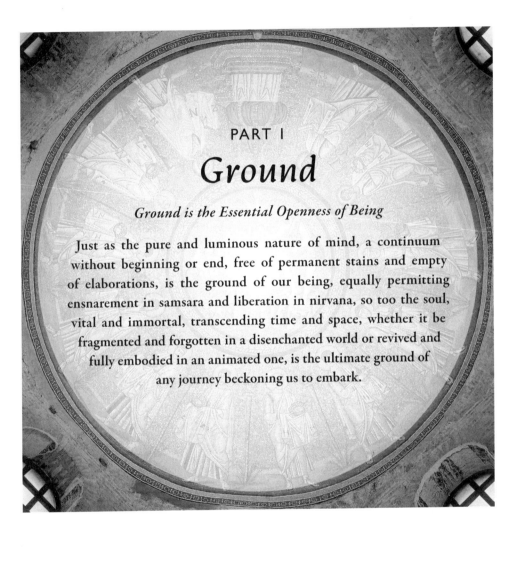

PART I

Ground

Ground is the Essential Openness of Being

Just as the pure and luminous nature of mind, a continuum without beginning or end, free of permanent stains and empty of elaborations, is the ground of our being, equally permitting ensnarement in samsara and liberation in nirvana, so too the soul, vital and immortal, transcending time and space, whether it be fragmented and forgotten in a disenchanted world or revived and fully embodied in an animated one, is the ultimate ground of any journey beckoning us to embark.

1
Visions
Third Eye Intuitions

I've never considered myself a visionary, but I do have visions. By this I mean full images appearing in my waking state seemingly out of nowhere, offering a message to decipher and prompting me to begin a discovery process. I'm no longer apprehensive about sharing these visions because they are more common than we think. Most of us have intuition, premonitions, or even extra-sensory perceptions, yet we've been conditioned by our culture to dismiss them outright or keep them private for fear of being labeled an attention-seeker, lunatic, grandiose, or worse. As I will explore in depth in this book, that's part of the prob-lem: our culture fails to acknowledge and connect us with the dimen-sions of non-ordinary states of consciousness like the unseen world of spirit or the Dreamtime. The deeper our separation from Source, or what the ancients called the awe-inspiring mystery becomes, the more profound our symptoms of dis-ease.

For centuries Western culture has cast skepticism on our innate capacity for expanding consciousness. While we have made strides toward understanding the material world through quantum physics, cognitive neuroscience, and molecular biology—even sending people into space and manipulating genetic code—we have done so at the expense of our innate psychological abilities, the evolutionary advantage of awareness, the healing capacity of the subtle, energetic, nervous system, and the potential for meaning derived from fulfilling our soul's purpose.

In the months preceding the pandemic of 2020, I had a series of revelations that directed my students and me on a path of sacred wisdom intertwining ancient cosmology, Joseph Campbell's mythopoetics, Carl Jung's archetypal psychology, and the Tibetan alchemy of rebirth. Departing home I followed these threads deep into a foreboding labyrinth where I faced a terrifying minotaur and eventually came through the other side, not alone, but with a group of fellow pilgrims, seated atop the Borobudur, largest mandala in the world, and together broadcasting a message of hope to you and future generations. The tapestry woven from those threads and their relevance to the "meaning crisis" humanity now faces during this seismic epoch shift became this book— *Return with Elixir.*

Visions like mine mark an odyssey as ancient as time itself and led to me reclaiming something vital that is so often lost in modern culture. The particulars may not have global relevance, but my visions were part of my conscious metamorphosis, and by extension, an invitation for us each to embark upon on a collective journey and shared mythos. My journey is my own, but I followed the path of mystics and heroes, validating and reaffirming the larger enterprise we human beings can—and I would add *must*—undertake in a pursuit of truth, meaning, and fulfillment. As Campbell wrote, "We have not even to risk the adventure alone; for the heroes of all time have gone before us; the labyrinth is thoroughly known; we have only to follow the thread of the hero-path."[1] This is especially true nowadays, when we find ourselves on the cusp of an extraordinary paradigm shift toward the expansion of consciousness, societal regeneration, structural reorganization, and a renewed spiritual connection with nature. In this way, sharing my story is a call to action, a leap of faith, and a reunion of reason with intuition.

This book is an invitation to you, in which I encourage you to go deeper into the mythological mysteries—the shadow world—to listen to the whispers of your embodied wisdom, the echoes of your ancestors, the prophecies of mystics, the forecast of astrologers, and even the noetic silence of God. No matter where you are in your journey, never underestimate the power of your soul to teach and guide you, even if it appears in unrecognizable guises, communicates in unsuspecting ways, or leads you into territories of hardship and loss; learn its language, become a servant to its mission, and be willing to take risks to receive its boon. Challenge the status quo of globalist propaganda and materialistic culture that has zombified us into a dissociative servitude, deprived of meaning, and instead embark upon an adventure into the netherworld.

For me, it was visions of the Greek god Asclepius that prompted me to begin an odyssey to reclaim my soul.

VISIONS OF ASCLEPIUS

In 2017, I was working as a psychotherapist and Buddhism teacher, when the panic attacks I'd had when I was young returned. The irony of being a psychotherapist plagued by anxiety before seeing my patients is not lost on me. They mainly occurred on Monday mornings. I felt suffocated, like the walls were closing in. The collar of my button-down shirt choked me. My high-rent Manhattan office, once a source of pride, evidence of my so-called success, had become an ornate birdcage—pretty from the outside, but a trap, nonetheless. The windows looked out on façades of enormous buildings that typified the concrete jungle. Piles of garbage stacked neatly in those iconic black bags lined the streets below obscuring flowers and trees. Day after day, building after building, floor after floor, office after office, for as far as I could see, workers buzzed, clutching their to-go coffee in one hand while sedated by their smartphones in the other.

As Annie Dillard famously wrote, "How we spend our days is, of course, how we spend our lives."[2] Where were their lives going? How was living like this accepted, even sought after? How did we get there? How did *I* get here? In those mornings of panic, I felt like I was the only person witnessing how humanity had devolved. In this unnatural landscape, caged and barely able to glimpse the sky, a consistent but confusing drip of stimulants and anesthetics delivered through digital IVs, the pace of life has hit warp speed. Yet, we persistently run around in circles, exhausted and going nowhere, living what the Buddha described as a cycle of suffering without end—*samsara*—on steroids. Although my vocation was to heal this suffering, I myself had become symptomatic. The view from my office revealed the communal symptoms, my panic attacks the private ones—messages from my soul alerting me that we had lost our way.

I had reached the limit of my ability to offer the care my patients deserved, so something had to change. I felt like a fraud. For decades, I'd trained in and practiced conventional talk therapies and took seriously my aspiration to be of service to those in pain and for whom the manifestations of the outer world were the causes of problems in their inner worlds. I counseled the working well, what Freud called "ordinary neurotics," about their job stress, relationship difficulties, low-grade depression, and the all-too-common meaninglessness, apathy, and unworthiness that plague us modern humans. These were well-intentioned and mostly high-functioning people struggling with the symptoms of our post-industrial civilization, best characterized as fragmentation between body and mind, self and other, humanness and nature.

While my consistency, presence, and attunement often helped people in their time of need so that they could keep putting on *their* button-down shirts and heading to *their* offices, something was missing. Something vital was not being addressed during our weekly sessions. *Could people even get well when our world has gone so utterly mad?* How could we treat a dis-ease that had become so normal, its symptoms so well blended, they dissolved in the everyday currents of life? I constantly recalled the words attributed to Indian philosopher Jiddu

Krishnamurti: "It's no measure of health to be well-adjusted to a profoundly sick society."[3]

THE LAMENT OF HERMES

My vitality, patience, and capacity for delight atrophied as I slipped toward the precipice of my existential self-doubt. *What the fuck was I doing?* According to the mandates of my training as a psychologist, I was following protocol. According to the benchmarks of my culture, I had achieved all measure of success. Yet nothing could have felt more misaligned. Was I *really* helping people? My Monday morning anxiety persisted as the answers evaded me. Was I going to put myself on medication, spend more hours with *my* therapist in his concrete box on the other side of the city, or was there an alternative?

Those questions raced through my mind as I listlessly searched the internet for answers. By chance, but more likely synchronicity, I saw a video by British author Graham Hancock reading the "Lament of Hermes," an ancient Greek and Latin text interpreted by Saint Augustine in the first century CE. Like a piercing arrow, the words emanating from my computer screen bypassed my linear, left brain and dove deep and directly into my soul.

Of thy religion, nothing will remain but an empty tale, which thine own children in time to come will not believe; nothing will be left, but graven word and only the stones will tell of thy piety. And that day, men will be weary of life, and they will cease to think the universe worthy of reverent wonder and worship. And so religion, the greatest of all blessings, for there is nothing, nor has been, nor ever shall be, that can be deemed a greater boon, will be threatened with destruction; men will think it a burden and will come to scorn it. They will no longer love this world around us, this incomparable work of God, this glorious structure which He has built, this sum of good made up of things of many diverse forms, this instrument whereby the will of God operates in that which he has made, ungrudgingly favoring man's welfare, this combination, and accumulation of all the various things that can call forth the veneration, praise, and love of the beholder.

Darkness will be preferred to light, and death will be thought more profitable than life; no one will raise his eyes to heaven; the pious will be deemed insane, and the impious wise; the madman will be thought a brave man, and the wicked will be esteemed as good. As to the soul, and the belief that it is immortal by nature, or may hope to attain to immortality, as I have taught you, all this they will mock at, and will even persuade themselves that it is false. No word of reverence or piety, no utterance worthy of heaven and of the gods of heaven, will be heard or believed.[4]

The words Hancock shared are described as a "lament," which is precisely what I felt toward our culture. The message conveyed in this passage could not have been more relevant to my plight. After a moment of profound awe, I dug deeper and discovered this wisdom was based on a mythological prophecy attributed to Hermes, the Greek messenger of the gods, describing the fall and rebirth of the Egyptian civilization. Addressed to his student Asclepius, it was part of a text of the same name—*The Asclepius*—found in the *Corpus Hermeticum* containing the ancient foundational teachings of Egyptian magick, alchemy, astrology, and other esoterica. Hermes's Lament was a message transmitted through the ages, which fortunately for me, reached my soul's antenna.

I'd been a student and teacher of Tibetan Buddhism for more than twenty years, so my first encounters with Asclepius and his serpent-entwined staff via synchronicities such as this one—and later, in dreams—took me by surprise, because they originated from a culture I knew little about. I came to learn Asclepius was the Greek god of healing. His name means to "cut open" because, according to myth, he was delivered via cesarean section by his father, the god Apollo, from his mortal mother's womb as she lay on her deathbed. For me, this was profoundly symbolic because it was Asclepius who would excise me from the bondage of my culture-bound prison.

Apollo entrusted young Asclepius to the centaur and physician Chiron, archetype of the wounded healer, who raised and trained him in the secret arts of natural healing. One day, Asclepius killed a snake with his staff, then observed another snake revive the dead one by regurgitating medicinal herbs into its mouth. He deduced which herbs were used and began resurrecting patients from the dead. As his gifts as a healer grew, Asclepius antagonized the gods, deprived Hades of souls for the underworld, and disrupted the natural order of things to the point of provoking the ire of Zeus, who killed him with a single thunderbolt. After his death, Asclepius spent a short time in the underworld, but because of his acumen and virtue, Zeus placed him among the stars as the constellation Ophiuchus—the Serpent Holder—elevating his status from demi-god to god.

Asclepius is often depicted as a healthy, bare-chested, bearded man dressed in a toga, holding his iconic staff. Many will notice the similarities to the caduceus—the staff with not one but two intertwined, winged, and ascending serpents wielded by the Greek god Hermes and the Egyptian goddess Isis—which still today represents medicine and is depicted on modern hospital and pharmacy logos. In most Indigenous cultures, the serpent is a potent symbol of rejuvenation and rebirth because the snake sheds its skin to become anew. The snake is also a compelling symbol because its poison, if administered appropriately, can be transformed into medicine becoming—according to the Asclepius myth—the elixir of immortality. Poison, which ordinarily kills, with esoteric wisdom, liberates.

Citizens of ancient Greece and Asia Minor made pilgrimages to their nearest Asklepion—healing temples and sanctuaries, sacred places to resolve physical and mental diseases. Ruins of more than 300 Asklepion still exist in the Mediterranean and the Middle East. These include the most well-preserved and famous sites at Athens, Kos,

Pergamon, and Epidaurus in modern Greece and Turkey. They were our hospitals' precursors, but their healing modes were holistic and spiritual. The locations for these healing sites weren't arbitrary; they were remote places of natural beauty, far from the bustle of the cities and of commerce; quiet, serene, and restorative. They were places where natural elements featured prominently as part of the healing matrix.

This isn't limited to the Mediterranean. Ancient and Indigenous peoples have customarily considered location and environment to be as important as action and process—*and it's universal*. Consider how Chief Joseph of the Nez Perce peoples famously said, "The earth and myself are of one mind. The measure of the land and the measure of our bodies are the same."[5] The Greeks understood this; as part of the therapy, the Asklepion incorporated the power of the sun, geothermal radiation, hot and cold natural springs, medicinal herbs, fresh air, and perhaps even magnetic fields called ley lines.

As for protocol, based on inscriptions on stela that have survived the centuries, we know pilgrims and patients made their way to the sanctuary entrance where they underwent two phases of healing. The first—*katharsis*—involved a strict diet and ritual bathing—practices of purification sometimes lasting several days. This had a twofold purpose: cleansing the body and priming the mind. Offerings were made to Asclepius himself at the inner temple, along with prayers and other rituals recommended by the temple priests according to the patient's symptoms. Again, I imagine these actions of reciprocity with the divine allowed the soul access to what we would now call the placebo effect, or what famous Harvard cardiologist Dr. Herbert Benson redefined and coined "remembered wellness."[6] There was a keen awareness that, in addition to the natural environment, a patient's belief, worldview, and lifestyle were critical in the restorative process. Consider all we have lost along the path of industrialization.

Patients were led to a sizeable open dormitory called the *abaton* for the second phase—*incubatio*. You read that correctly; the main form of healing at the Asklepion was incubation or "temple sleep," which was more than mere rest and perhaps the earliest known precursor of psychoanalytic dream interpretation. In the abaton, patients may have been given hallucinogenic plants to facilitate deep hypnotic slumber and initiate them into the therapeutic dream journey not unlike the current therapeutic use of psychedelics.[7]

At some Asklepion, hundreds of beds filled the central dormitory. Along with the patients, supine on low mattresses on the marble floor, host animals—dogs, roosters, and of course, non-lethal snakes—roamed among the sick, occasionally biting or licking the wounds of the injured who, in their dream journeys were visited by Asclepius or his daughters Hygeia and Panacea, who might spontaneously heal or directly diagnose and prescribe treatments. At other times, dreams were more cryptic, and upon awakening, patients would receive counsel and interpretations from temple physicians we might call the first psychotherapists, literally soul healers. When healing wasn't immediate, patients were prescribed holistic treatments and remained on the sanctuary grounds for days or weeks to recover and rejuvenate. In some cases (as evidenced by the array of surgical implements uncovered on-site at Epidaurus by modern archeologists), surgeries were performed, or patients were sent to the gymnasium for exercise and rehabilitation. Finally, they could attend the outdoor amphitheaters—the one at Epidaurus held 15,000—for music and performances that elicited catharsis or emotional release. The origins of Western theater used now for entertainment likely came from these early forms of therapy, allowing onlookers to access the shadow world of their unconscious and, through active imagination, identify with the heroes and antagonists in classical drama and comedy, which allowed for emotional integration.

Testimonials of patient recoveries were inscribed in stone at Epidaurus for future generations. Along with the Oracle at Delphi and the summoning of mystical or non-local agencies for healing and guidance, the Asklepion served the sick throughout Greece and Asia Minor for centuries before being phased out toward the end of the Roman period. Despite their success, these natural healing centers, and the remedies they delivered, accomplished perhaps what was most threatening to the late-stage Romans and early Christians: they empowered citizens to heal themselves. As in the mythology of Asclepius, destroyed by a threatened Zeus because of his power to heal, successive civilizations would require unquestioning and unflinching allegiance to the state or dominant religion and could not afford the competition posed by the empowering wisdom of the great mystery schools and bastions like the asklepia.

MY DEPARTURE

This potent symbol of the Asklepion was a stark contrast to my sterile office in Manhattan. This vision of more natural and integrated healing inspired me to break out of the suffocating status quo. After years of meaningful psychoanalysis, I left my therapist and deepened my work with astrologer Lynn Bell, who encouraged me to follow my intuition, to engage my dreams and daytime visions of Asclepius, and to more broadly turn myself over to a mythological way of life. With her, I reconceived how I could deliver therapy in ways that fed rather than starved my patients's souls and mine. Lynn challenged my attachment to long-held dogmas in psychotherapy and Buddhism—organizing systems that were instrumental in my development but began to stagnate the growth of my psyche just as my Manhattan office confined me. As you shall soon see, every step forward arrives not at a sought-after destination but at a new way station on the soul's journey. Lynn helped me connect with a fire that was destroying me from within, one representing my soul's pushback against the restrictions of professional conventions, and she coached me on how to channel that fire to incinerate those limitations to make way for a new, more creative work with my clients. Just as one may ironically slash-and-burn to make fields more fertile for new crops, Lynn helped me confront rigid, long-standing allegiances to external institutions I cherished, so a new, inner authority could emerge.

Along with the button-down shirts, gone was the neck-up therapy approach. As Lynn guided me, I gave myself permission to employ and blend techniques I had gathered over the years but lacked the confidence to implement. I introduced my clients to guided visualizations from the Buddhist tradition, the mythological dimension from Joseph Campbell, somatic therapy for root-cause trauma, shadow-work from Swiss psychoanalyst and mystic Carl Jung. More important than any method, I trusted our intuitive processes and spontaneous interactions.

To truly accomplish this shift in therapeutic practice—and, as the ancient Greeks had done in the Asklepion—mindset and setting needed to be considered as part of the treatment, and for *that* to happen, the right brain had to come online, and the conversational, analytic left brain integrated with the right's embodied sensations, dreams, rituals, poetry, and art—all serving as highways into the soul. To connect right brain with left—reason with intuition, executive prowess with creative genius—I recognized that mythology and astrology needed to be incorporated into my psychology practice along with Tibetan alchemy.

As I journeyed in this new direction my panic attacks subsided because something within me was being attended to and acknowledged. I was breathing deeply again. The dormant serpent of vitality and creativity had been roused from its depressive slumber. Had I consulted a conventional psychiatrist instead of Lynn Bell, perhaps medications would have been prescribed, suppressing my panic attacks, and drowning out the faint call to adventure of my soul. Panic may not always be a symptom of pathology after all, but an intuitive push against stagnation and conformity. In many cases when we suppress the symptom in its early stages, when a tremor, it can magnify becoming a volcanic eruption—a midlife crisis, manic episode, depressive relapse, psychotic break, or suicide attempt.

During this metamorphosis I exchanged my network of over-medicating psychiatrists and cognitive therapists for natural healers of various disciplines: astrologers, Tibetan doctors, reiki practitioners, herbologists, and sound bowl experts. This meant incorporating the missing mythological dimension of healing. If I had dreams, saw images, or felt sensations in my body during or between sessions with my clients, I interpreted these not as pathologies to be feared or distractions to be dismissed but as messages to be interpreted. Whenever I felt resistance or blocks, or if something felt incredible, extraordinary, or altogether unknown, I leaned in with curiosity and allowed the process to unfold. I instructed my patients to do the same—to attune to their bodies, attend to their dreams and synchronicities, and be intrigued by imagery, myths, music, and literature as they followed the path into their psyches, braving the unknown, and trusting that together, we could revitalize a sacred relationship with the unconscious. For example, some clients selected myths that resonated strongly with their presenting problems, and we enacted the narrative themes in their lives. Others used paintings or mandala drawings, and we tracked, metabolized, and integrated emergent material from their unconscious. Dreams were not minimized as flights of fancy and dismissed, nor were they overanalyzed as Freudians do, privileging reason, but by deeply attending with reverence, as archetypal psychologist James Hillman said, "the dream has nothing to do with the waking world but is the psyche speaking to itself in its own language."[8] The power of healing comes not from eliminating symptoms through cognitive-behavioral reframes, but by restoring the broken lines of communication with the soul.

Soul, Buddha nature, mystery, God, Self (as opposed to self) . . . whatever you name it, is ceaselessly communicating messages from subtle realms—where what Carl Jung referred to as the *collective unconscious* and personal unconscious meet. Although our culture has tried to destroy these invaluable relay lines through skepticism, the need for rational control, or because wisdom does not engender profit, occasionally, the messages slip past the barricades. The question becomes: Do we listen to whispers, decipher encoded messages, and allow the intuition to guide us deeper into the netherworld for a chance at discovering something new? Can we surrender hyperrationality, to liberate the soul?

I chose to listen, and as I did, something happened. Beyond my panic attacks subsiding, my existential doubt about the plight of our modern culture did as well. I believe the same can happen for humanity if enough of us listen and learn from what lies hidden within us. Our global symptoms are likewise a call of the collective soul to adventure, to disrupt the status quo of rigid conformity, to salvage our sovereignty, and begin again anew.

FROM KNOWLEDGE TO WISDOM

In the months before the pandemic of 2020, I had a series of three more visions that became the impetus for this book. The first occurred while I was visiting the island of Ithaca in Greece, made famous as the home and primary destination of Odysseus. I learned an incredible new word while I was there: *nostos*. Lexicographers may refer to this as an acquaintance or something known, but in the epics of Homer, nostos refers to the love for and longing to return home. After the Trojan War and what we will see was his Hero's Journey of separation, initiation, trial, and treasure, Odysseus persisted for ten years before he returned to Ithaca and his beloved wife and son.

The power of myth is that it allows us to walk in a hero's footsteps, so think about what home means to you—the place, people, and state of mind. If you were separated from them for a long time, what creature comforts would you surrender, what unimaginable challenges might you face, in order to return? Put in the context of the soul, we've been on a journey since beginningless time, yearning, seeking, but not arriving home. Yet, against unfathomable odds, we have earned this precious human life endowed with liberty and opportunity, and all the internal resources and external conditions are ripe for us to return to the headwaters from which we sprang. Every myth, religion, philosophy, or story throughout time and culture has this archetype of nostos at its thrust: to return home, to return to our spiritual source.

If you visit the Greek island of Ithaca, you'll find the ruins of Agios Athanasios or Homer's school, a place of higher learning during antiquity built on the remains of the Odyssean Palace that sits below a more recently constructed Byzantine Church. Within a crumbling third-century BCE stone chamber overlooking Afales Bay, I had my second vision, one that inspired me to shift direction from the two-year curriculum of Buddhist studies I had recently launched. As I was recording a video there to include in our program, I experienced a powerful intuition that caused me to change course, pivoting on a dime. It was the call of the mythic dimension of life. I realized then and there that myths are the archetypal narratives that underlie our rational experiences, connecting us with transpersonal, ancestral, and universal realms, nourishing the soul with symbols and wisdom, which, if applied skillfully, can transform the everyday muck of human misery into the mulch of spiritual maturity. Without the mythological dimension, the soul is trapped behind a perceptual filter, reducing a spectrum of reality into a narrow band of matter that we can only perceive with our five senses—in the same way human eyes see only a fraction of the spectrum of light.

I realized I had been omitting a crucial element from my teaching and—in the video I was recording—I articulated to my students how important it was to include mythology in their studies. Consequently, I rebuilt my Contemplative Studies Program (CSP), changing the curriculum by integrating three seemingly disparate threads of knowledge: 1) Tibetan Buddhism, 2) the mythological perspective of Joseph Campbell, and 3) the analytic psychology of Jung.

First, the Tibetan Buddhist alchemical art of rebirth, which involves mastering the cycle of three phases: *conscious death, sublime liminality,* and *altruistic rebirth.* This Buddhist framework follows the transmigration of consciousness across lifetimes and dovetails with a distillation of Campbell's mythological cycle, called the monomyth or Hero's Journey, which offers a neophyte a rite of passage through the three phases of *separation, initiation,* and *return.* Both models align with the psychological process of individuation articulated by Jung, which can also be condensed into three phases: from *ego,* deepening into *shadow* of the personal unconscious, to the *Self* in the collective unconscious. These three distinct systems—each divided into three phases—would guide my students and me in a natural progression from the ordinary into the magical world from which we can all return as transformed beings, each a map for navigating the human landscape from delusion to awakening—and it was my hero's call, a concept I will explore in depth in this book, to synthesize them.

I wasn't pursuing this convergence of ideas as artifacts of passive interest in the same way people might amuse themselves in an art gallery or museum. What drove me wasn't knowledge for knowledge's sake, but creating a practical, unified map that could help us all navigate the actual terrain of life's struggles, chaos, and uncertainty.

INITIATION INTO THE MANDALA

Despite the consternation of a quarter of my students (who had rightfully expected the original Buddhist course direction) dropping my class, I continued to follow my intuition, a lesson for anyone caught at the crossroads between comfort and uncertainty, loyalty and independence. If we betray our passion to meet the fickle expectations and needs of others, we send ourselves to the cross for crucifixion. As I learned the hard way, we must be willing to disappoint, even disobey, others to follow the never-before-tread path of authenticity. Throughout my teaching career, I had been well-acquainted with the topic and prepared before class, but for this new version of the course, I gave myself over to the unconscious and allowed intuition to be my guide in realms hitherto unfamiliar. I was following the hero's thread into the labyrinth, and being summoned by some mysterious force from the depth of my psyche towards revealing.

Normally I began each class with a traditional Buddhist visualization, but on the evening before the first course resuming the new term, while alone in my Manhattan office gazing down onto the rush hour streets congested with pedestrians mindlessly circumambulating the concrete towers of financial institutions, I had my second vision. There I saw a mandala—which I later crudely sketched as a series of concentric circles, one within the other, surrounding a central axis and representing the relationship between the cosmos and the psyche. The outermost circle was the ouroboros, the universal motif of the serpent eating its tail, a Chinese, Mayan, and Greek symbol of infinity, the timeless nature of ultimate reality. Within that was the zodiac, with its twelve archetypal symbols and the water bearer Aquarius strategically positioned at six o'clock. Puzzlingly to me was how the zodiac unveiled over time, mysteriously began rotating counterclockwise, yet I persisted in flowing with the vision. This is how the journey of the soul goes—no neat and well-tread passageways to follow. No familiar roadside neon signs.

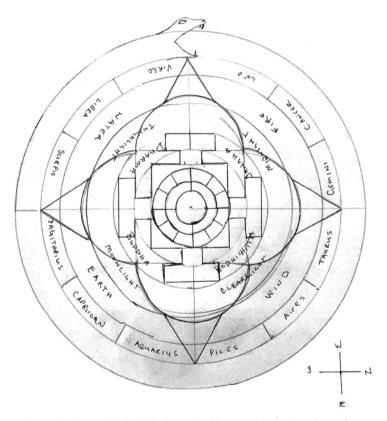

Fig. 1.1. Original Mandala Sketch: Circumambulation through astrology, stages of dissolution, and Buddhist refuge.

Within this series of circles was a topical view of the Mahabodhi temple in Bodhgaya, India, the site of the Buddha's enlightenment. The temple is built in the classical Buddhist style, structured like a mandala or cosmic palace with four gateways in each cardinal direction surrounded by a series of three concentric square walkways descending toward the inner sanctum at the center. There we find what is known as the Diamond Throne, both a physical site and a universal symbol. The diamond thrown is positioned within the sanctum sanctorum of the Mahabodhi Stupa flanked by the Bodhi tree to commemorate where the young prince Siddhartha Gautama sat and discovered the nature of reality, the actual seat upon which he claimed Buddhahood. As a metaphoric symbol the diamond throne represents the innate potential within each of us to awaken at any moment, reclaiming our royal sovereignty from the tyranny of samsara.

In the vision, I saw the procession of the equinoxes (the zodiac) in its rotation of the Great Year (an approximately 25,800-year cycle—I'll talk more about this later) spinning counterclockwise. Within the cycle of the Great Year I saw myself walking with pilgrims, circumambulating the Mahabodhi temple three times as we descended together into the inner sanctum. During our first circumambulation we experienced the dissolution of the four elements, one element and phase of dissolution occurring in each of the four directions respectively: earth dissolving into the East, water into the South, fire into the West, and air into the North. As the elements dissolved, our physical bodies died, releasing free-floating consciousness from the binds of material form.

The second circumambulation was a dissolving of the three mental afflictions expressed in Buddhism, the instinctual drives, which contaminate consciousness and distort perception—grasping, aggression, ego-centrism and transforming these base instincts into luminance, radiance, and imminence, and culminating in the pure, clear-light nature of mind known as transparency or *dharmakaya*.

During the final circumambulation, we took refuge in the three jewels of Buddhism—Buddha, Dharma, Sangha—and generated altruistic intent (bodhicitta) as we continued circling each of the four directions, before entering the final threshold of the Mahabodhi Temple. After making extensive offerings to the Buddha sitting on the Diamond Throne in the inner chamber—reconceived as an alchemical crucible or pregnant womb—we took his nectar blessing in the form of rainbow lights that entered our crown, throat, and heart, purifying body, speech, and mind, transforming us into the future Buddha.

After this coronation ceremony, and assuming the divine pride and pure view of the Buddha, the pilgrims and I turned 180 degrees away from the altar and the Bodhi tree to face the Eastern gate through which we entered, now flanked at our back by the tree and the lineage totem of deities, protectors, and master sages. There at the horizon, on the dawn of a new day, we witnessed the turning of The Ages, from Pisces to Aquarius.

From the Diamond Throne, the pilgrims and I actualized our potential, donning our crown, sending a wave of nectar lights coalescing the union of wisdom and compassion, or what Jung called the *coniunctio,* the conjunction of masculine and feminine energies, emanating from our hearts outward, past the mandala gates and walkways, rippling out across the planet as a harmonic resonance calling all beings home to their true nature.

This mandala vision became the mainstay meditation practice for my students and myself at the beginning of each class in the new course. I led them through the circumambulations of elemental dissolution and royal coronation, as we collapsed and rehearsed the entire span of evolution towards becoming a Buddha in a single session. Following the tantric methodology of assuming the goal, interspersed with Jungain, Campbellian, and astrological archetypes, we tried our divine dignity and destiny on for size, internalizing the insights gleaned from active imagination just as a fighter pilot gains invaluable learning experience in a virtual reality flight-simulation. What we think repeatedly, we become.

I later asked my astrologer Lynn why the zodiac I had seen in the vision was rotating counterclockwise. She said functionally when we look down at a birth chart it rotates clockwise. But from the point of view of us looking up at the night sky, and because of the rotation of the earth, the constellations have the deceptive appearance of rotating around us in a counterclockwise manner. Synchronistically, when I showed my mentor Phil Cousineau—a direct disciple of Joseph Campbell—a drawing I had made of the Hero's Journey map, he also told me that the direction of the stages should be depicted counterclockwise. In an email Phil wrote me during my initial mapmaking, he explains:

> Your drawing of the Hero's Journey is fine stage-wise, but it is backwards. The journey is not clockwise; it is counterclockwise. That was Joe's [Joseph Campbell's] innovation and it is critical to understanding the depth of it. So many people get it wrong these days, I'm in despair about the original message getting lost. . . . All adventures and all stories go counterclockwise, which is why they feel . . . timeless.[9]

THE MAGICIAN DAMIEN ECHOLS

The third vision occurred two weeks after the first class guiding my students through this mandala visualization, when I had the pleasure and fortune to meet with my friend Damien Echols. He is a teacher of ceremonial magick and has written extensively on how this ancient occult practice sustained him for eighteen years in maximum security prison for a crime he didn't commit, enduring torture at the hands of guards and long stretches in solitary confinement. Upon his release, one of the first places Damien went for solace was to the Metropolitan Museum of Art in New York City, particularly the exhibit of the Assyrian and Sumerian artifacts, which he describes as his second home.

Several years after his release, Damien started giving private tours of the exhibit and using the artifacts as an energetic source to draw upon for talks and guided experiences of his magick practices. Continuing to follow my intuition, I decided this was a perfect opportunity to meet him in person. Upon encountering Damien in the museum lobby, what struck me was how he had a timelessness about him. He was dressed in black with his ever-present tinted sunglasses to protect his eyes after incarceration-induced retinal damage. Heavily tattooed, with a long black beard, he seemed to emerge as a modern-day manifestation of the Nimrud, from among the carvings of the man-headed, lion-bodied Assyrian temple guardians around us. I gifted him a *phurba*, a Tibetan ceremonial dagger symbolically used for the decimation of the ego, but also, uncoincidentally, in the shape of a magic wand. It had been in my possession for a long while, but I never felt it to be mine. In Damien's hands, it was returned to its rightful owner.

We wandered the galleries discussing history, astrology, and mysticism, until arriving at a fountain at the center of the museum. Damien asked if I wanted to do a short meditation practice with him. We made an offering of coins into the fountain and synchronized our breath. He asked me to draw energy from the periphery of my body toward my heart chakra and to hold my breath to coalesce the energy before releasing. Then, to my amazement, on the third round of breath-holding, a vision appeared! For a few minutes, time stood entirely still. The museum and even New York City disappeared, and all that remained was the magician and me in the courtyard of a Babylonian temple. Then, as I looked where my heart was supposed to reside, I saw a single planet orbiting through a sea of stars. Saturn was clearly distinguished by its concentric rings undulating and pulsating as the universe's heartbeat. I inhaled, Saturn expanded; I exhaled, it contracted. Then, suddenly, Saturn exploded in my chest! *Boom!* The seemingly solid planet fragmented into millions of particles of dust before completely dissolving. Although Damien and I never spoke about my experience, I sensed we'd shared something profound beyond words. We left the museum as if what needed to be seen had been seen. Our meeting had served its purpose, and as quietly as the magician appeared, he disappeared into the chaotic sprawl of Manhattan's evening streets.

I was perplexed and enthralled by my vision of Saturn. I discussed it with my reiki healer, who directed me to explore the archetype of Hermes, perhaps because of his gift for moving and communicating between realms and worlds. This turned out to be another synchronicity, one that reconnected me to the Lament of Hermes. Again, I searched for answers in the dark, traveling through labyrinth corridors, towards an unknown destination. Was I unsettled? Yes. Was I enthralled and alive? Absolutely. Opposing states like paralyzing fear and mobilizing vitality, shame and confidence, are often tethered in a secret relationship, but because we often disavow one aspect to the shadow, we are bereft of the other.

My search for the meaning of the exploding rings of Saturn led me back to astrology, which turned up an article by evolutionary astrologer Maurice Fernandez entitled "The Saturn Pluto Conjunction and the Transits for the Year 2020."[10] Maurice and several astrologers predicted that as the major planets of Saturn, Jupiter, and Pluto align in their long and complex cosmic dance, a cataclysmic event would unfold, the likes of which had not been seen since World War I and would usher in a historic period of transformation—particularly of structural and institutional change. Little did I know that we were only a few months away from the coronavirus pandemic. Astonishingly, Fernandez's article was written in 2016! The precision with which he wrote, coupled with the vision of Saturn I experienced with Damien, led me to take the predictions seriously. I integrated the article, along with some of the guidance from Lynn Bell, into my teaching and shared the insights with my students so we could prepare for whatever might come next. The power of astrology lies not in passively enduring fatalistic facts, but in navigating predicative possibilities with greater preparation and agency.

CYCLIC TIME

These visions following my discovery of Asclepius allowed me to connect the intuitive wisdom of the psyche with the predictive science of cosmology. I rekindled long-held fascinations—ancient cultures from

Egypt to Greece, alchemy to astrology and recalled something I'd read about during college. In 1901, a fisherman looking for sponges in the reefs along the coast of a Greek island retrieved a wooden box from an old shipwreck. It's not entirely uncommon to find earthen jars and bits of pottery from antiquity in this region, but his discovery was unexpected, even baffling. The contents of the box came to be known as the Antikythera Mechanism, a surprisingly old and sophisticated mechanical model of the solar system called an *orrery*—dubbed the oldest analog computer in the world.

The instrument contained a series of gears that modern scholars determined were used to track astronomical movements of the sun and moon through the zodiac, calculate the positions of the five classical planets, make predictions about rare eclipses, and schedule events like the four-year cycle of the athletic games. The ancient orrery dates somewhere between the second and first century BCE, but its astrological and mathematical knowledge could have been significantly older because we can't know how long the device was lost at sea. To put it into perspective, sophisticated astronomical clocks like this weren't invented—or we might now say *reinvented*—until the *fourteenth* century CE in Europe.

The Antikythera Mechanism revealed ancient technology and knowledge older and more profound than we expected that once helped our ancestors navigate time and space. To the child's innocent imagination, this time machine is the stuff of legends, but to some dogmatic members of the scientific community, it's a complete nightmare, forcing them to defend long-held beliefs about history and culture. Interestingly, the Antikythera Mechanism was recently digitized and made into an app. For $1.99, you can appreciate the sophistication of this ancient technology, and more importantly, you can apply its practical wisdom to your current situation, locating yourself within time and space. If we can see the logic in using a weather forecast to plan our day, why not an astrological forecast?

Time is not linear; it's cyclic. Ancient cultures knew this and, millennia ago, built megalithic structures from Giza to Chichen Itza to

Stonehenge, as well as city complexes from Angkor Wat in Cambodia to Gobekli Tepe in Southern Turkey, shattering the long-held historical timeline of first civilizations by nearly 5,000 years. Yet, despite our first impressions of awe at the architectural marvels these represent, we now know that each functioned essentially as a celestial time machine. With them, our ancestors could analyze the past and predict the future. This precise knowledge ensured survival and helped find meaning and purpose within the cosmic order.

As humans evolved materially, in some ways, our consciousness devolved spiritually, and as Hermes described in his lament to Asclepius, our gaze at the vast celestial horizon shifted downward, our sense of time and possibility narrowed, these great time machines were abandoned and forgotten, and with them the sacred knowledge of our place and purpose in the universe. In the last few centuries of our human odyssey, most of us have become directionless, like a ship stranded in the currents of time. Blinded by our neon lights, mesmerized by our smartphones, we no longer look to the stars for answers; we scarcely even ask the perennial questions: Who am I? Why am I here? What is true?

THE GREAT YEAR

The Greeks, Mayans, Tibetans, and Indigenous peoples of each continent looked to the heavens as a predictor and context to understand themselves in time and place, taking heed of astrological patterns to guide their future actions. Jung recognized this, particularly toward the end of his career, using astrology to help understand his patients' unconscious, personality types, as well as making specific predictions about global affairs in his book *Aion* (1951). There, I came to see the connection between astrology and psychology—cosmos and psyche— through the steady decline in our lives of the experience of religion and esoteric knowledge, we have lost sight of our place in the grand cosmic, cyclic context.

Scientific astronomers define the Great (or Platonic) Year as the length of one complete cycle of the equinoxes—otherwise known as the *precession of the equinoxes*—around the ecliptic (the plane of earth's orbit around the sun) or about 25,800 years. Most ancient wisdom cultures articulate their own version of this grand planetary cycle, and tend to separate it into four Great Ages: Golden, Silver, Bronze, and Iron. The Vedic Yuga system describes four ages of humankind's spiritual evolution, each age defined by a unique set of characteristics. Human consciousness devolves towards blindness, destruction, and preoccupation with physical matter in the so-called Dark Age (kali yuga), and then rises again towards wisdom, harmony, and union with spirit in the Golden Age (satya yuga). An entire cycle of the universe evolves through death and rebirth, and lasts approximately 24,000 years, though in the Vedic Yuga cycle the length of each age differs slightly than in the Greek Plutonic year, the symbolic meaning and over all time expanse is roughly the same. The great ages (yugas) are further broken down depending on whether they are ascending or descending (whether we are in the phase of the grand cycle evolving towards its high point in civilization and consciousness, or descending to its low point). Plotting our current bearing on this cosmic map suggests we are in a transitional phase, on the ascension from the darkest Iron to the Bronze Age, which may account for the upsurge of popular interest in meditation, shamanism, divination, and the expansion of our global consciousness that has disrupted centuries of effort to control the material world. The Bronze Age and its equivalent in the Vedic system, the Dwapara, specifically on the upward ascension of the cyclic trajectory towards the Golden Age, are characterized by increased intelligence, and the rise of powerful technologies that exceeds our burgeoning human virtue as we are still largely dominated by corporal interest, base instincts, and fixation with the material world, residual vestiges of the dark age we have transitioned through.

Within the Great Year, we can benefit from considering the *precession of the equinoxes* and the astrological Zodiac comprised of twelve archetypal energies, each lasting roughly 2,150 years, tracking the so-called second hand of time, which, when combined, make up the approximately 25,800 years that comprise the Great Year. Think of this as a clock in the sky, with each increment representing powerful archetypal potentials, both positive and negative, lasting twenty-one centuries, before the hands of time move to the next aion. Here we can locate ourselves again at another "turning point," not only between zodiacal archetypes from Piscean to Aquarian for the next 2,150 years but also the influence of elemental signs as we transition from the earth to air signs for the next 200 years. Therefore, we are currently caught on the cusp of three major simultaneous transitions.* The first is a Great Age transition, somewhere early in the Bronze age (*Dwapara yuga*) lasting 2,400 years, the second is a zodiacal or aion transition from Piscean to Aquarian age lasting 2,150 years, and the third is an elemental transition from an earth to air sign lasting the next 200 years. Which begs the questions, what do these transitions, ages, and elements represent? How do the cosmos and our psyche interact? Could knowing where we are in time and space, the precise location in the Great Year and precession of the equinoxes help us sense-make and navigate life more effectively?

Following a series of powerful planetary conjunctions bookending the pandemic of 2020, Lynn Bell and Maurice Fernandez's forecasts show it's possible to apply ancient star maps of the Zodiac. The ancient Greeks might have used the Antikythera Mechanism as a celestial timekeeper to anticipate cosmic seasons and trends before it was lost at sea. Cosmologist Rick Tarnus proposes that the ancients understood two important principles that helped them use astrology in their daily lives. Firstly, everything is connected in the principle of *unus mundus*, (Latin, one world) a fundamental unity of reality, wherein everything relates above and below, within and without. And secondly, the world is enchanted, pregnant with vitality and meaning, just as we can experience animation and coded messages in the language of dreams, so too can we

---

*See figure 4.2 Great Year: The Pilgrimage of the Cosmos on page 101.

read the natural world and the stars. Can we revive and rely on ancient wisdom—like cosmology, mythology, and prophecy—to anticipate the next few centuries as a period of structural collapse, social unrest, institutional regeneration, and revelation of our collective shadow as we head toward greater equity, justice, and universal responsibility? That's what the astrological forecast may be predicting. Now, amidst the sunsetting of the Piscean Age of Christianity, having reaped first the benefits of monotheism, benevolence, then of humanism and rationality bequeathed by the Age of Reason, we are now confronted by their mirror opposite extremes, self-centeredness, deprivation, and lost enchantment, described by Jung as the collision of Christ and antichrist archetypal opposites— the spirits of virtue and vice, light and darkness, residing within each of us. As the dogma of scientific materialism dawns to displace religion, we will encounter its shadow during a necessary but painful revelation, having to contend with the opposing forces of all that we have gained. [11]

EMERGING FROM DEEP SLEEP

In the spring, when the snow melts, what is revealed? Lost artifacts of a prior season, perhaps a child's toy forgotten before winter fell. What if we extended the metaphor? What would emerge from an Iron Age of darkness thousands of years long? Could this transition account for why we are now unearthing lost cities, civilizations, and ancient knowledge all over the planet? Consider the City of Aten in Egypt or La Ciudad Blanca in Honduras, buried and forgotten for over a millennium. Could our celestial position explain these uncovered cities, our sudden shifts in collective interest, the growing disillusionment with scientific reductionism and materialism, and our gravitation toward quantum theory and spirituality? Perhaps our resurgent fascination with plant medicine is a symptom of a more subtle shift in consciousness connected with a grand cosmic turning of The Ages? Is the snow melting? Are we awakening from a deep sleep? Are we uncovering memories after a prolonged amnesia? Are we in the early, drowsy liminal phase of waking up? What might life look like in the future? And what if we reunited ancient wisdom with modern science and technology?

From a Buddhist perspective, we all undergo micro birth-and-death cycles within a single lifetime whenever we face the challenge of letting go of familiar identity and routine, experience the uncertainty between "worlds," and gather the energy and vision to rebuild a new life. Often, the forces of fear, karmic habit, and unconsciousness propel us back into near-exact approximations of our former life and self, no matter how traumatizing or dissatisfying, in an endless cycle of self-perpetuated recreation. With each iteration, we seem to forget that the nature of reality is constant change, and don't seem to realize the powerful lessons the soul has contracted to learn. As such, life remains a repeated struggle for survival instead of a gradual evolution toward awakening.

This book was conceived under the pressure of the circumstances of the 2020 pandemic: the deaths of innocent people, the destruction of our global economies, the breakdown in trust with governments, global leaders, and even science and facts, the collapse of social institutions, and despair wrought from isolation on a scale not seen since World War I. But even before the onset of the pandemic, we were in the grip of an even more insidious threat that cognitive psychologist John Vervaeke calls the "Meaning Crisis," which began in the late 1800s when Nietzsche proclaimed that "God is Dead."[12]

In my previous book, *Gradual Awakening*, I argue that most of the world's problems—ecological devastation, economic divide, social injustice—can be traced to a root I call the "sickness of paradigm," which I attribute to our materialism and nihilism. This underlying and pervasive worldview, the cultural shadow of killing God in favor of science, must be addressed if we want to go beyond rearranging the deck chairs on the Titanic. Similarly, Vervaeke points to a loss of existential meaning to account for increased rates of depression, anxiety, suicide, and isolation in our secular world and traces this to the abandonment of wisdom cultures and practices in our move toward secular modernization.[13]

We reached a cultural tipping point when the tsunami of the pandemic hit. With this symptomatic backdrop, *Return with Elixir* emerges as a response to and preparation for the next pandemic—be it biological or spiritual—and as a remedy to the deleterious effects of secular materialism which has cut us off from spirituality, myth, embodiment, and communion. Part of the alchemical methodology as we shall see is to not avert or waste the opportunity of fragmentation and collapse, but to seize it, to understanding the origins, confront the underlying shadow, discover our lost power hidden within, and to rise like a phoenix from its ashes. For as all wisdom traditions teach, death and destruction beget rebirth.

If we are going to reclaim the soul through the daunting and complex wilderness of the psyche, we'll need a series of maps:

The *cosmological* map of the terrain above us, its distinct increments broadcasting an archetypal signature that mirror our soul's shifting meaning context.

The *psychological* map of the terrain below our consciousness, which through complexes and archetypes structures the patterns and dispositions of our individual soul within a single life.

The *alchemical* map of the energetic terrain within our bodies, which through yogic manipulation can help access and liberate the soul across a multi-lifespan trajectory.

The *mythopoetic* or narrative map that reconceives external hardships as advantageous, providing the soul with meaning and purpose.

These perennial maps show us how to make a brave departure from ordinary stagnation or crisis, courageously reframing and facing any trial as a growth opportunity, reclaim the lost treasure of the soul, and returning home with the boon—the elixir—for others. There can be no new discoveries without leaving home, no treasure without trial, and no meaning without a connection to community. Because the maps offer distinctive perspectives, combining them gives us a comprehensive view to orient within the cosmos, our personal psyche, our energetic body, and a cultural mythos.

Life can be shifted from that not-so-merry-go-round struggle for survival to an ever-evolving, cyclic process of self-actualization upon which most ancient cultures created a science they attempted to preserve and transmit over time. What can we remember about the impacts of these cycles and traditions discovered in prehistory and their incremental shifts on us as individuals and societies? What did each system suggest about how best to live in relationship with these cycles? Was there an opportune moment, a symbolic stroke of midnight, in which innate genius could be realized? What happens when we consider the potential correlations between these cycles and maps?

The alchemical motto "As above, so below. As within, so without" points to sacred interrelationships between seemingly discrete phenomenon or dimensions of reality, governed by the so-called *principle of correspondences* in which the macrocosm of the physical universe mirrors and influences the microcosm of an individual's psyche, and similarly the inner intention of even a single individual can impact the outer manifestation of the entire universe. As you progress through this book, I hope you'll connect with *your* soul through its cosmic theater above, its structural architecture below, its visceral embodiment within, and its mythic narrative without. As you do, I hope you'll transcend attachment to any sacred tradition, map, or tool described throughout, bowing ultimately to your sovereign, inner guide. Together we can experience direct *gnosis* by following the hero's thread into the labyrinth to reclaim what has been lost and what is desperately needed—the soul—returning with its immortal elixir for our families, societies, and planet as we turn the page for a new cosmic chapter.

Before we set out on any journey, and that includes this book, it's important to survey the terrain, landmarks, and destination, even while accepting we must get lost. Therefore, I've divided the book into three parts, like Campbell's three acts—separation, initiation, and return—but drawn instead from the Tibetan meditative tradition known as ground, path, and fruition. Ground refers to the starting point or basis of the journey, the buddha nature, our innate potential, in this case the soul, pregnant with possibility, which has been lost or remains buried. Path refers to the process of searching for the soul, through our esoteric method of *solve et coagula*, subdivided into chapters comprised of the major stages of what Joseph Campbell calls the "monomyth." Fruition refers to the crowning achievement, reclaiming the soul and our integration back into everyday life in a grand reunion at the culmination of our odyssey—that is, finding the *elixir*, and creating a means to bring it back to benefit others. At the outset, we find ourselves surveying the ground, exposing the meaning crisis as symptoms of the soul we have lost. In the chapter that follows we look around, up, back, and within, capturing a panorama—the big picture view of how we lost our way.

I've structured this "big picture" orientation according to the Buddha's Four Noble Truths (discussed more in depth in chapter ten) which were based on an ancient medical model still used today to delineate the symptoms of a problem (*dukka*), determine the etiology or the cause (*samudaya*), assess a prognosis or solution (*nirudha*), and prescribe a treatment or plan of action (*ashtangika marga*). It's an elegant system, perfectly fitting our introduction. We'll look at the problem, its origin, and progress toward the solution and plan. Then we'll be ready for our pilgrimage through death and rebirth.

These vantage points of looking around, up, back, and within lay the conceptual ground to orient us before we depart, but they shouldn't be confused with the one vantage point the reader hopes to awaken: the mystical third eye of intuition, through which the soul sees and navigates the world as it exists beyond distortions. This book, all its maps, only point the way, but you must travel your own path.

2
Panorama
As Above, So Below

THE CONVERGENCE OF CRISIS: A LOOK AROUND

In chapter one, I shared my personal experience of panic attacks, stagnation in my profession, and my identity constraints about who I could be in the world. Together we are similarly experiencing an upsurge of cultural panic attacks—*symptoms* of an underlying problem.

When we hit the pavement and look around at our current world, we'll find the symptoms of a civilization that has lost its way from the soul, a syndrome cosmologist Rick Tarnas calls the "disenchantment" of Western culture, and what Vervaeke calls the "meaning crisis."[1] The symptoms may seem disparate, but they are interrelated and traced to a fundamental root cause.

I've identified a convergence of at least six crises, categories of symptoms, which comprise our current existential predicament.

Environmental Crisis
Economic Disparity
Civil Unrest
Technocratic and Memetic Warfare

Mental Health Crisis
Meaning Crisis

Environmental Crisis:
Disconnection from Nature

The U.N.'s International Panel on Climate Change's 2021 report points to faster temperature changes and the likelihood of the world reaching a climate tipping point sooner than anticipated.[2] Increasing temperatures from burning fossil fuels and other human activities mean water temperatures rise, causing the polar ice sheets to melt more rapidly, rising sea levels, displacing animals and people, and releasing more methane gas into the atmosphere, which reinforces an entire chain reaction of interrelated environmental contingencies. Meanwhile, we have cut down the forests and polluted, overfished, and destroyed the oceans coral reefs, which are the planet's lungs and heart. We are committing matricide of Mother Earth, suffocating her, and in a few short decades, have managed to bring the biosphere to the brink of possible irreversible collapse. We have done so out of willful blindness at the nation-state level, greed for profit and infinite economic growth at the corporate level, and convenience and apathy at the individual level.

Economic Disparity:
Unchecked Capitalism

Economic disparity is the second symptom. Never before in human history has there ever been such extreme wealth inequity, with such abundance in the hands of so few. Some speculate the top 1% of the global population owns roughly 50% of the planet's total wealth.[3] The same report suggests that during the pandemic, at our most economically vulnerable, the [global population] bottom half's wealth fell by 11%. At the same time, a few thousand billionaires saw their wealth increase by 12%. For example, the owner of Amazon, Jeff Bezos, alone gained $24 billion in a single year.[4] Most of us know what it's like to play the game of Monopoly and experience that sinking feeling when we pass

Go with nowhere to land but on our opponent's hotels. The zero-sum game of late-stage capitalism may be nearing its final act. It's conceivable that swaths of humanity will be wiped off the playing board through lack of access to basic needs of food, water, shelter, and medicine. At the same time, a precious few will enjoy lavish comforts and unimaginable privileges in their ivory towers.

Civil Unrest:
The Struggle for Power

Civil unrest and the resistance to authoritarian pressures are other apparent symptoms. The rise of totalitarianism, the iron fist of dictators and the nation-state is apparent from Trump to Putin, North Korea to ISIS. We see fascism disguised as conservative nationalism on the far-right vying for control against the opposition of communism and globalism posing as progressive liberalism on the extreme left in an ever-widening binary, where moderately inclined individuals seem to have been silenced, cancelled, or converted by the sword by public shaming, deplatforming, or freezing assets. Brexit, Trump's proposed border wall between the US and Mexico, Israel's missile strikes on defenseless Palestinians, and Buddhists murdering the Rohingya in Myanmar, examples of nationalism and isolationism, pose an equal and opposite extreme reaction to the hidden agendas of globalist institutions like the World Economic Forum, World Health Organization, International Monetary Fund, and the World Bank, where a small cadre of unelected bureaucrats conspire to impose economic, health, and social policy upon the entire world. Global expansionism and national contraction into isolationism are reciprocal reactions of one another, driven by the extreme polar opposite views of a minority with power. Both agendas, conquest or exclusion, rightly fuel dissent amongst the major populous who have grown weary of the lies, propaganda, and political power plays touted as being in the service of the greater good.

Meanwhile, people's liberation movements worldwide signal the growing mistrust of leadership, whether nationalist or globalist in persuasion, and discontent with perceived corruption and increasing inequities. From Arab Spring to Occupy, climate strikes to criminal and justice reform, we see grassroots movements of ordinary, disenfranchised people channeling their collective will for change against perceived repressive regimes. This is reflected not only in the drive toward structural change but in the call for individual rights, most recently represented by the #MeToo movement for gender equity and the Black Lives Matter movement against systemic racial injustice. Each represents a noble call for change, mobilized bottom up from the base of the pyramid of power. But few stop to look at these movements through the trauma lens; if core wounding is left unhealed, victims of each campaign can become tomorrow's abusers, repeating cycles of violence. The social justice warrior, who has not done their shadow work, can fall prey to self-deception, self-righteously justifying the very objectification and hatred of the "other" they condemn, furthering the polarization. In an eternal power struggle, today's marginalized fighting for freedom can become tomorrow's repressive regime. When will we recognize the pendulum of history's aggression swings between extreme views, that neither side acknowledge nor resolve the underlying trauma? As we shall see, the middle-way between these extreme views is not found by dismantling power structures and asserting external control, but by turning within, what I call an "inner about-face," acknowledging our own wounding, disarming our self-protective instincts such as anger that conceals core shame, clouds our better judgment, and forces us to project our insecurity on others, unconsciously acting out our own unresolved conflicts externally in the world. While civil unrest represents a symptom of dysfunctional societal power imbalances, we should not be confused about where their ultimate origins and resolutions lay.

Technocratic and Memetic Warfare: The New Battle Ground is in our Minds

Most of us no longer have God for a single organizing principle with a coherent narrative and unifying moral framework. Instead, corporations, governments, and technology collude to claim power, control narratives, subdue populations, and maximize profits. Now in play are fifth generation warfare (5GW) tactics, a term first coined by Daniel Abbot to describe non-kinetic military action, like social manipulation, psychological operations, misinformation, disinformation, cyberattack, the use of bots and trolls to manipulate narratives, stir up emotions, confuse, gaslight, and control the minds and behaviors of the populous.[5] When you throw in advanced technologies, AI, and smartphones, we are talking about the generation and delivery of narratives so subtle, so compelling, that most human beings don't even know they are being manipulated. Given the deluge of information, misinformation, and disinformation, we no longer know who or what to trust. The technological algorithms, programmed to detect and exploit our desires, fears, and biases, amplify our base passions, corralling us into silos, pitting us against one another, like lambs before slaughter. They don't have to slit our throats and bloody their hands; they leave the dirty work to the divided masses. In such a traumatized state, bombarded from all sides, our nervous systems fluctuate between states of overwhelm and shut down when we are all too willing to relinquish critical thinking, objectivity, and sovereignty to the dictates of our tribes.

Wars once fought on the battlefield to claim territory and secure resources for the victor, are now fought in our heads, for the economy of our attention. We no longer need to be threatened by tanks or dictated at gunpoint. As long as we are segregated along political, racial, economic, or religious lines, the rifts between "us" and "them," become vectors for exploitation by select elites who seek control. Here, our ally and our protection are critical thinking and discernment, the ability to analyze, sense-make and convert knowledge into wisdom, wisdom into action, and networks into movements.

Mental Health Crisis:
Depression, Trauma, and Suicide

As with the societal level, there are symptoms for the individual. Following the Four Noble Truths framework, we must face the so-called bad news if we are to isolate the symptoms by examining their causes. One recent literature review of mental health issues in the general population during the global pandemic reports 28.0% for depression; 26.9% for anxiety; 24.1% for post-traumatic stress symptoms; 36.5% for stress; 50.0% for psychological distress; and 27.6% for sleep problems.[6] The data included nearly 400,000 participants across 32 different countries. This could represent that almost 1 in 3 people on the planet struggles with clinical symptoms that compromise daily functioning. Even more alarming, the WHO now estimates that 700,000 people commit suicide yearly, that's one human being every forty seconds.[7] That's someone's child ending their life because they cannot cope with the prospect of living. An enduring and pervasive desperation, meaninglessness, and apathy has led to this.

Rates of suicide among active duty in the US military are even higher than in the civilian population.[8] They estimate that since 9/11, more than four times the number of servicepeople died by suicide than were killed on active duty in war operations. While several factors are involved, unresolved Post Traumatic Stress Disorder is among the significant contributing factors to suicide. But one needn't be exposed to war to be traumatized; not all those who are traumatized develop symptoms of PTSD.

What's going on? We can delineate between two traumas. "Simple" trauma involves a significant impact—some call it Trauma with a "T"— like war, near death, and rape—and if unresolved, can lead to PTSD characterized by events that *shouldn't happen but do*. Whereas "developmental trauma" or "complex trauma"—trauma with a "t"—refers to the slow and sustained exposure to multiple events like emotional neglect or abandonment, ruptures in safety and love, often in childhood or of an interpersonal nature, and characterized as the thing(s) *which should have happened but didn't* like consistent attunement and presence, and unconditional positive regard.

In clinical settings, trauma is characterized as blindsiding, a perceived near-death experience of oneself or another in which ordinary coping strategies are ineffective. Trauma is subjective; it's based on one's perception, which means it is conditioned heavily by past experiences, including childhood attachment—the ways we form or don't form nurturing bonds with our caregivers. There is a growing consensus among trauma researchers, including Dan Siegel, Bessel van der Kolk, and Gabor Mate, suggesting addiction and trauma are primarily the results of insecure attachments in early childhood development.[9] After exposure to traumatic events, adults with insecure attachments (anxious, avoidant, and disorganized styles) exhibit less mental health resilience and are prone to succumbing to PTSD. While we may be unable to stop traumatic events from occurring, by developing secure attachments we can create conditions for mental health resilience and recovery.

I consider the contours of trauma and how it can contribute to PTSD not only to justify how this may account for the alarming suicide rates but how it may impact the declining mental health of the general public in the modern world. I believe that our fragmented society, separated from nature in heavily industrialized urban centers, removed from extended family relations and collaborative networks like those more prevalent in agricultural communities of previous generations, where both parents in the nuclear family, due to economic pressures, must now focus on earning a living, leaves children in the critical years of their brain development with more strained and compromised attachments. It may be that modern urban life has left more of the population prone to complex trauma and depression because the fabric of our interpersonal lives, sense of safety, and connection with caregivers, extended family, community, and nature have been severely disrupted. There is no hard evidence to support this claim directly, but I'm laying it out as my intuitive hypothesis.

Meaning Crisis:
Cognitive and Neuroscientific Frameworks
Modern life within post-industrialized culture represents a dramatic and multileveled disconnection or fragmentation from our bodies, emo-

tional life, caregivers, communities, and nature, which contributes to insecure attachment, impacting brain development, and leaves growing numbers of people prone to trauma and post-traumatic symptoms like depression and suicide. By a similar etiology, Vervaeke suggests a useful construct he calls the "meaning crisis," loosely defined as the loss of meaning modern people struggle with, which contributes to their feelings of disconnection, apathy, loss, anxiety, and despair.[10] "Many people are talking about the meaning crisis, but I want to argue that these problems are deeper than just social media problems, political problems, even economic problems. . . they're deeply historical, cultural, cognitive problems."[11]

Vervaeke proposes the symptoms I've described in our "look around" derive from a pervasive cognitive deficit in our ability to make sense of our world and experience it. He introduces concepts like sensemaking, knowledge acquisition, and wisdom as critical mediating factors between our experiences of the world and our subjective understanding of our place in it. The loss of wisdom traditions and the mythopoetic maps that were cultivated through them must be addressed to resolve the meaning crisis. For example, in his popular YouTube lecture series, Vervaeke described four ways of knowing or sensemaking to demonstrate how, throughout history, we have atrophied our abilities to understand and navigate the world, leaving us in a state of prolonged confusion.

Propositional knowing or fact acquisition for increased conviction
Procedural knowing or skill cultivation for increased fluency
Perspectival knowing or perspective widening for increased presence
Participatory knowing or experiential deepening for increased attunement.[12]

Modern culture tends to focus exclusively on propositional knowledge, and with such limited perspective to navigate the world, we are now drowning in a deluge of information. We have failed to emphasize skills, meta-narratives, and visceral experiences that would help us meet the multifaceted challenges of our complex world and psyches.

In his book *The Divided Brain and the Search for Meaning,* psychiatrist Ian McGilchrist proposes a neuroscientific perspective supporting Vervaeke's argument: we've thrown the baby out with the bathwater by not taking seriously the fundamental role our bicameral brain plays in our lives. Understanding how the left and right hemispheres of our brains perceive reality provides essential insight into not only ourselves but our history and the development of the culture in which we're immersed. McGilchrist writes that civilization thrives when these two hemispheres are in balance. If the left hemisphere's perspective dominates, and we rely on rational, reductive knowing, civilization frays.[13]

According to McGilchrist, breaking the left and right hemispheres into discrete, localized functions of reason-versus-emotion is a simplistic and outdated notion. He claims both sides of the brain are involved in tasks of processing thoughts and feelings. McGilchrist prefers to call it the "left mode" versus "left brain" and "right mode" versus "right brain" assuming this mutual interaction between left and right. He determined that the left mode is oriented toward specific points of data, using pinpointed attention to focus on details and facts, to deconstruct, analyze, and refine the information, and does exceptionally well with concepts it already knows—or is holding/grasping in mind. In other words, the left is concerned with what is already recognized in consciousness (what is known). It uses narrow-focused attention and language to sense-make a picture of reality from a narrow band of facts. McGilchrist says, "the left hemisphere sees truth as internal coherence of the system, not correspondence with the reality we experience."[14] Therefore, the downside of the left mode is that it is prone to certainty, taking what it understands as a conclusion and not being receptive to feedback and revision. While the map is valid now, forgetting how to walk in the actual jungle can be dangerous. The left mode can easily cast us out of touch with real-world experience and block inputs we need to update our mental maps in real-time. Consequently, we can become prisoners of our biases and reified understanding.

However, the "right mode" supports a more open awareness, broad in its scope, receptive in its nature, responsible for putting pieces in context, and creating a big picture or gestalt. The right mode works with abstraction, symbols, and metaphors and is naturally more capable of tolerating uncertainty and ambiguity of the unknown. The right mode is associated more with a scanning awareness, looking for what is unfamiliar beyond focal attention, like the perception involved when one first walks into a room and gets nothing more than an eerie feeling. For example, "[T]he newness of the devil's advocate is always on the lookout for things that might be different from our expectations, to put things in context. It understands the implicit meaning, body language, emotional expression in the face, it deals with an embedded world, not a concrete one, it understands individuals not just categories, it has a disposition for the living rather than being mechanic."[15]

Therefore, the right mode is associated with the unconscious—what remains outside of conscious awareness—memories, fantasies, bodily sensations, and impulses. The downside of the right mode is that it can't verbalize and express what it knows. It is like a preverbal child filled with intense emotion and prone to acting out. As psychiatrist Dan Siegel put it in *The Developing Mind*, the verbal left mode must come online to help the emotional right mode process and synthesize energy flow into information.[16] However, the right is more engaged directly with the field of experience and less mitigated through concepts. McGilchrist explains, "Meaning emerges from engagement with the world, not from abstract contemplation of it."[17] Ancient cultures that embraced myths, the arts, theater, music, embodied spiritual practices along with language, science, and logical reasoning—*remember the Asklepion*—may have had greater hemispheric integration and, through its wisdom, more than we do today in our hyper data-driven and left mode leaning information age.

For our purpose, we can see that Vervaeke and McGilchrist employ cognitive and neuroscientific frameworks to account for the meaning crisis, cultural malaise, and symptomatic depression of our time. I will incorporate these frameworks into our plan of action. Reclaiming the soul will require a multilevel approach to knowledge acquisition, including all four types of knowing proposed by Vervaeke and the left-right brain hemispheric integration offered by McGilchrist.

Having looked around, we see we are up against human-created climate change that has reached a tipping point, a wealth gap unlike any other in history, political unrest and mistrust underpinned by technocratic mind control, and an alarming increase in mental illness facilitated by a pervasive rupture in our childhood attachments and social isolation. As we transition from the street view to the mountaintop to a look up at the stars, we should keep a keen eye on the origins of the blindness underlying our crises of morals and meaning leading to pervasive malaise and purposelessness.

THE GREAT YEAR: A LOOK UP

When we climb a mountain peak and wait until dark, we'll see the stars that tell us an ancient story spoken in archetypal language about where we came from, the predominant energies within us, and where we're going. Looking up (and later looking back), we'll understand the origins of the problem of our moral and meaning crisis and answer the question of how we lost the soul. Good students of astrology and history learn from their mistakes and fare better in their evolution.

For thousands of years, this is where our ancestors turned for answers to essential questions, both mundane—like when to sow and harvest—as well as profound—like where they came from and where they were going. While delving into astrology in any meaningful depth is beyond my expertise and this book's scope, I pose the following questions: What is the character of The Ages or eons? Where are we exactly in the cosmic trajectory and what does this location say about our symptoms? What can we expect to see in the emerging, new aion?

Our cosmic clock called the Great Year provides answers. On March 21, an hour before dawn, if we look East on a clear night from somewhere in the northern hemisphere, on the point on the horizon where the sun will rise, we will find a pattern of stars. Twelve prominent visible constellations comprising the ancient astrological zodiac; each represents distinct archetypal energy that will rule an age or aion, shape our collective conscious, and represent meaning to our personal psyches.

Because of its position in the heavens over the past two thousand years, the primary constellation and ruling archetype of our time has been Pisces, symbolized by two fish swimming in opposite directions and implicitly suggesting a duality between worldly and spiritual realms and accounting for the rise of monotheistic religions that sought salvation from the world of misery to a transcendent heaven above. Jung felt the two fishes represented good symbolized by Christ, and evil, characterized by the anti-Christ, (materialism), that we must each reconcile within us. Water in which fish swim is an archetype of the unconscious and emotions, so we see a strong emphasis on social emotions of love and guilt, charity and greed, for better and worse.

Because of a wobble on the axis of the Earth called axial precession due to tidal forces and planetary interactions, the Sun, as our main pointer against the zodiac, tracks backward against the heavens at the precise increment of one degree every seventy-two years. Because the Earth rotates forward on its axis against the fixed constellation in the sky, the constellations deceptively appear to the naked eye to be spinning backward. Therefore, my vision of the mandala described in the introduction in chapter one, which appeared on the second week of my new course, curiously had the zodiac turning counterclockwise. There are 30 degrees for each Age of the Zodiac, so it takes precisely 2160 years (30 degrees × 72 years) to complete a single age based on the vernal equinox on March 21, moving through the sidereal zodiac.* Think of it like a cosmic clock

---

*Apparent backward movement of fixed stars or constellations of about 1 degree every 72 years.

with twelve hours, each increment represents a zodiac sign, and each hour lasts roughly twenty-one centuries. Magnificently, each period has unique signature and marks the rise and fall of distinctive civilizations and the development of what Jung referred to as our "collective consciousness" in the archetypal tides of time. Within the Great Year, Jung referred to each incremental age as a Plutonic month.[18]

The precise estimate differs between astrologers, but it takes about 25,920 years (2160 years × 12 Ages) for the cosmic clock to complete a cycle, passing through all twelve ages in a phenomenon known as the *precession of the equinoxes*. According to various traditions and interpretations, there is no exact date marking the beginning or end of The Ages, nor when a complete precession cycle begins. However, some astrologers like Ray Grasse assert that within the last 10 degrees of each age (roughly 72 years), we see the signs of the decline of the passing age and the symptoms of the new age emerging, likening the transitions between ages more to a cosmic tide than a fixed point.[19] Grasse also observes that when the Sun crosses one constellation in the northern hemisphere's spring equinox on March 21, it will cross its opposite constellation of the zodiacal sign on the spring equinox in the Southern Hemisphere on September 21. What can we learn about the signature of each Plutonic month within the Great Year?

THE TWELVE ASTROLOGICAL AGES

Each astrological age is distinguished by a prominent archetypal energy—a signature—and complemented by its opposing astrological sign. This is why we see astrologers like Grasse refer to the Piscean Age as the Age of Pisces-Virgo. As I review and synthesize the significant ages of the zodiac and their archetypal energies, I've drawn inspiration from astrologers Robert Fitzgerald and Ray Grasse.[20]

The Age of Cancer-Capricorn:
8640–6480 BCE

According to Fitzgerald this age symbolized by the crab (with its shell), is archetypally defined by agriculture, settlements, family, and community, and the mother goddess. The Age of Cancer coincides with the Neolithic revolution, when our ancestors began to transition from nomadic hunter-gatherers into more settled collaborative networks with domesticated animals, building settlements near bodies of water in the Near East, Mediterranean, and central China, and Yucatan Peninsula.

The Age of Gemini-Sagittarius:
6480–4320 BCE

This age is symbolized by twins or companions and according to Fitzgerald are archetypally defined by communication, movement, trade, increased social interaction, craftsmanship, and trade across large distances. [21] As brain, mind, and fine motor skills evolve through representational art, the development of root languages defines this period from Indo-European to Chinese.

The Age of Taurus-Scorpio:
4320–2160 BCE

This age is symbolized by the bull, and according to Fitzgerald, is archetypally defined by money, wealth, megalithic structures, a sense of solidity, and permanence.[22]

We have arrived at the period conventionally considered the dawn of civilization. Hunter-gatherer tribes who settled into organized communities have refined their skill in agriculture, trade, and exchange of knowledge and created conditions for the first large cities with surpluses of stored energy. In and around the fertile crescent in Mesopotamia, large bodies of water from the Tigris and Euphrates Rivers to the Nile are technologically harnessed to help grow larger crops with more yield than ever, helping to establish the Sumerian and Babylonian, and later the Egyptian civilizations as well as the Harappan in the Indus Valley.

With surplus and wealth, money was created—a form of stored energy combining an abstract representation, the technical innovation of the first copper coinage, and consensus social agreements—and from there, the rise of banking and economies, which improve and hasten trade, allowing for large-scale civic projects and empire building.

The Scorpio opposite energy of Taurus manifests as an emphasis on death and rebirth. The Pharaohs were often buried in extravagantly designed tombs, along with their wealth, possessions, and attendants, in preparation for their afterlife in the heavens, a return to the stars. Ray Grasse speculates that death-and-rebirth initiations may have occurred while Pharaohs and kings were still alive.[23] I bring this up because we will be rehearsing a death-rebirth practice in this book, linking our activities with our ancestors some four or five millennia ago. Regarding recently discovered evidence at the Tomb of Osiris, Grasse speculates that "the sarcophagus was empty [and unadorned], which suggests its function may have been more symbolic than practical, a ceremonial site than an actual tomb. It may have served as a secret place for initiation, a ritual re-enactment of the death by drowning, burial, and resurrection of Osiris."[24]

The Age of Aries-Libra:
2160–0 BCE

This age is symbolized by the ram and according to Fitzgerald archetypally defined as war, fighting, individuality, and independence.[25] Every age marks a dramatic shift in consciousness. As the Age of Taurus wanes, so does the long-standing reverence toward the mother goddess, representations of the divine feminine, living in intuitive connection with nature, and the vast pantheon of gods or polytheism, characteristic of ages before. The rise of the masculine, the patriarch, and the solitary warrior emerges in the celestial transition and its influence on the collective psyche. But perhaps the biggest shift is the introduction of monotheism as the collective mythos, the consolidation of power and energy into a single religious archetype represented by the emergence of the Jewish tradition. The archetype of the single ruling God above, his chosen people, their holy mission, and their promised land are all emblematic of the trend toward individuality from plurality and the emergence of the dark shadow of exclusivity and competition with it.

We see vital elements of judgment and wrath by God in the Old Testament of the Bible, which then translates across humans's psyches. Moses returns from the mountaintop to find the Israelites worshiping a golden bull (the old sign of Taurus), which incurs his wrath. Anger and ferocity are Aries energies, while law, order, judgment, and punishment are emblematic of its opposing sign Libra. In Judaism is the story of Abraham sacrificing a ram instead of his son, Isaac; the ram became a symbol of redemption—the undoing of judgment. Regarding our energy principle, the Age of Aries sees the innovation of more sophisticated weapons, military strategy, and the rise of warring empires, represented by Sargon of Akkad, credited as history's first ruler of a kingdom with his defeat of Sumerian city-states. The energy innovation of this age— military prowess and technology—allows empires to steal and hoard the surplus, money, and energy stores of other tribes and to justify this with the mythos of divine providence. Therefore, war and conquest supported by religious dogma became the norm.

The Age of Pisces-Virgo: 0 BCE–2160

This age is symbolized as two fish swimming in opposite directions and archetypally defined as transcendence, spirituality, dreams, delusions, duality, and the unconscious. The Age of Pisces coincides with the period termed by German philosopher Karl Jaspers as "the Axial Age" and the rise of world religions with human prophets or messengers at their center, like the Buddha and Mahavira in India, Loa Tzu in China, Jesus and Mohamed in the Middle East, and Socrates in Greece.[26] Some of these figures arose during the transitions between late-stage Aries prefiguring the Piscean age as the tides and cultural zeitgeist shifted. The imprint and repercussions on the collective unconsciousness of the humanity of these religions and philosophies were widespread and persist. One common feature they all share is the duality or distinction between a wordily, sinful life of sorrow and a heavenly, blissful one. They each promise the possibility of transcendence or liberation for the common person, not just religious or political elites; this lateral shift allows the masses to rise above misery and meaninglessness and swim against the stream of human suffering as the Piscean symbol represents.

A hallmark of the process of transcendence is strict adherence to a moral code. Looking through the lens of innovation or applying the energy conservation principle, a doctrine of moral principles and practices and their relationship to the promise of transcending human suffering not only helps individuals sublimate self-centered impulses and energies like greed and hatred into socially acceptable and mobilizing forces of love and empathy, but also provides sophisticated frameworks of personal meaning. People not only learn to live a "good" life of wholesome behaviors but derive a sense of purpose that enables them to structure order from chaos, find the strength to endure misery, create fundamental meaning when there is none, and orient their lives to some higher, transpersonal virtue like heaven or nirvana. From China, through the Middle East, and on through the holy Roman Empire across Europe, more than half the planet is attempting to become "civilized," its egoic impulses restrained, and its prosocial inclinations cultivated. But religion is based on a moral split, and so the shadow also swells.

CHRISTIANITY TO THE SCIENTIFIC REVOLUTION: A LOOK BACK

Before continuing to the emerging Age of Aquarius-Leo, it makes sense to look back into near history, during the Piscean Age, to ascertain how today's problems are accounted for.

While the Age of Aries-Libra began to consolidate disbursed energy from polytheistic veneration of many gods at the local level into a unifying regional God in Judaism, the Age of Pisces-Virgo expanded this approach across the known world. Similarly, while the Age of Aries-Libra saw the rise of militarization and conquest of external surpluses and resources of neighboring empires, the Age of Pisces-Virgo turned military conquest into an internal war over self-deception, hedonism, a battle between good and evil, and the salvation of the soul. Consequently, monotheistic religions with socially sensitive moral values became de facto political institutions governing populations across the most extensive territories in history. No age is without its shadow, so as the pagan, militaristic Roman Empire gave way to Christianity and Islam, aspiring for moral high ground, their darker natures of political power and dominion produced the Crusades and centuries of conflict and bloodshed. The irony and hypocrisy of monotheistic religions trying to spread a doctrine of love by the sword that travels through their evolution is part of their eventual demise.

According to Jung the most emblematic archetype of the Piscean Age is Jesus Christ, who is often symbolically depicted as or in conjunction with the Piscean symbol of the fish. In the New Testament, Christ is baptized in water, is considered a "fisher of men," his disciples are fishermen by trade, he walks on water in the sea of Galilee, and his miracles include turning water into wine and multiplying fish and bread to feed the masses. There is a deep mythological and astrological significance here that often gets overlooked. The influence of the cosmos and zodiac above that for centuries in prior ages—explicitly expressed in religious doctrines, mythologies, art, and architecture—is maintained in a less obvious form during the Axial Age. For example, there is a beautiful mosaic floor of the 4th-century CE synagogue at Hamat Tiberias, Israel (see plate 2) that features a Hellenistic zodiac fused with traditional Jewish imagery, and a distinctive Aries Age signature. Like the Asklepion, this site was built near hot springs known in antiquity for healing properties. The central figure of the mosaic is the Greek sun god Helios, surrounded by a mandala of twelve zodiacal archetypes, a depiction of the Temple in Jerusalem takes prominence above Helios, and in the four corners are figures representing the four seasons. The composition matches perfectly one of my favorite mosaics found in the dome of the Arian Baptistery in Ravenna, Italy, (see plate 3) dating to the 5th century CE, a hundred years later. There you see a beautiful scene of Christ's baptism flanked by John the Baptist and an anthropomorphized figure of the River Jordan. The Holy Spirit descends in the form of the dove. Surrounding the central figure are the twelve disciples forming a mandala, bringing their crowns to be laid in respect at the throne of God. Between the two mosaics, we see the same archetypal scene revealed in evolving historical and cultural contexts, the sun God Helios surrounded by the twelve constellations of the zodiac, slowly morphs into the son of God, Jesus Christ, surrounded by twelve apostles, with a distinctive Piscean Age signature. Scholarship pointing to the pagan origins of Christianity argues that powerful astrological knowledge was encoded within Christian art, keeping it alive yet hidden in plain sight.[27]

As the Ages turn from Aries to Pisces, there is an attempt to sublimate the force of aggression and dominance into love and compassion. Christ comes to symbolize *agape* or transcendent love and asks us to turn the other cheek, whereas the Old Testament calls for an eye for an eye. Similarly, Buddha's teaching on liberation cultivated through attention, virtue, and introspection, is echoed in the principles espoused by Socrates, who, at his trial before being put to death, reminds us that the unexamined life is not worth living.

The world is an illusion; the goal is to awaken to break free of suffering. Wisdom is the key. Wisdom is Sophia, in India Prajna, the divine feminine, intuition leading to gnosis. Virgo represents discernment or a clear view allowing the ascension from the Piscean waters of delusion. The fish swims in emotions and underwater—symbolizing the unconscious—so while religions of this Age promote love, empathy, and heaven above, guilt, hatred, and shame lurk below consciousness. Beyond representing discernment, Pisces' opposing companion is Virgo, the virgin associated with service. The archetype stretches back to the

Babylonian goddess Shala, Egyptian Isis, and the Greek Demeter, representations of fertility, harvest, and renewal. Christ and Buddha are said to have miraculous conceptions and births from a virgin, compassion emerging from the untainted womb of Wisdom, a divine human on earth mirroring Pisces-Virgo in the sky.

Christianity to the Dark Ages:
The Pendulum Swings Right

As we look back at history beginning with the Piscean Age and the birth of Christ, we see how monotheism creates, to that point, the world's most compelling, effective, and far-reaching meta-narrative, not only to help individuals create meaning and purpose from an existence fraught with suffering, but also to provide a moral compass structuring and mobilizing the collective energies of large societies and empires from the Mediterranean to Europe to the Middle East.

For the next 1,500 years, Christianity and Islam emerge as dominant pillars of faith that serve to unify most of the Western world. During the Middle Ages (500–1500 CE), however, we see a possible indication of a decline in what McGilchrist called the left mode of inquiry, as the Church began to eschew the disciplines of science, mathematics, astronomy, and astrology inherited centuries ago from Mesopotamia, developed in the Golden Age of the Greeks, preserved by the Romans, and instead emphasized critical analysis of the natural world. While these disciplines go underground in the West, they are picked up and refined by scholars of the Islamic world; and we can ask ourselves what happens to the collective consciousness as it shifts to the primarily right mode during this time?

The decline of the Roman Empire is attributed to interrelated causal factors that resemble those we see today in America; the expansion of its territory and its military, government corruption and political instability, erosion of core values into hubris, debauchery, and hedonism, and the rise of an empirical threat, with the Goths in the North and Byzantium in the East, perhaps the equivalent in our day of China's rise as an economic and military threat to America's global power. The end of the Roman Empire may well be a clear example of the rift between brain hemispheres in the collective psyche; as the pendulum of Christianity swings predominantly toward the extreme right mode, and we enter the Dark Ages (5th–10th century CE).

This is characterized by a marked decline in intellectual, economic, scientific, and cultural achievement. Rather than seeing human evolution as a linear progression of ever expanding human achievement, some, like Renaissance scholar Petrarch looked back in time for inspiration, and considered Greece and Rome as the Western world's cultural golden age to emulate.[28]

By the time we approach the thirteenth century, however, we see a return of the left mode and scientific inquiry in Europe. Ironically, this return occurs at a time when the major universities and research funding were religious—it was primarily monk scholars, men of faith—that are entrusted with the pursuit of truth via religion and science in tandem. Think of these literally and metaphorically as our brain hemispheres.

Renaissance:
The Pendulum Finds its Mid-Point

By the time we arrive at the Renaissance (1400–1500 CE), Christians conducted most scientific pursuits. I say this to challenge the erroneous notion the relationship between science and religion has always been at odds or mutually exclusive. Thirteenth-century Franciscan friar Roger Bacon is considered one of the earliest European advocates of the modern scientific method, the fifteenth-century physicist and Catholic Cardinal Nicholas of Cusa first proposed an infinite universe, and Nicholas Copernicus wasn't only a mathematician and astronomer but a Catholic canon. In India and Tibet, we find a similar synthesis, where religious luminaries like Nagarjuna and Patanjali were equally adept at linguistics, philosophy, and medicine, as they were meditation, yogic alchemy, and art. Just as the end of Rome saw the decline in the left mode and the predominance of the right mode triggering the Dark

Ages, the Renaissance may represent a period in Europe where the two hemispheres were attempting to recalibrate to function in unison again.

As a result of this symbolic reintegration during the Renaissance, we see an absolute explosion of innovation across all disciplines from philosophy, science, medicine, and technology, especially art, architecture, music, and literature. Funded by the philanthropic family, the Medici, the likes of creative visionaries Botticelli, Michelangelo, Leonardo da Vinci, and Raphael successfully fulfilled their explicit mission to establish an ethos of humanism, transforming the mundane life on earth through increases in beauty, efficiency, prosperity, and discovery of truth in the material world.

Accordingly, with the pursuit of truth, there is a revival of interest in the classical disciplines of Greece and Rome that were lost during the Dark Ages, driven by the emergence of humanism, the belief in the power of human beings to advocate for their freedom, autonomy, and progress. The humanistic method of learning that remains prevalent relies on reason and empirical evidence, in contrast to divinity and the religious study of the previous centuries, which relied on faith and adherence to scripture. What unites these seemingly disparate disciplines—science and religion—in their pursuit of the truth, and where they both falter, is in calcification into dogma.

During the Renaissance, humanist education was based on a well-rounded, secular liberal arts curriculum known as *studia humanitatis*, which combined grammar, rhetoric, poetry, history, moral philosophy, and ancient Greek and Latin studies.[29] Without this comprehensive education, it would be difficult for scholars to advance in their training and research but, more importantly, develop the cognitive capacities, perspectives, and skills to navigate the world and become productive members of society. The curriculum was based on the *trivium* and the *quadrivium*, an approach to learning devised by the Greeks that used three primary subjects of grammar, logic, and rhetoric as a foundation for four additional subjects: arithmetic, geometry, music, and astronomy. Sister Miriam Joseph, in her 2002 book *The Trivium*, describes the importance of each, "Grammar is the art of inventing symbols and combining them to express thought; logic is the art of thinking; and rhetoric is the art of communicating thought from one mind to another, the adaptation of language to circumstance."[30]

Buddhist monastic universities in India (and later Tibet) preserved a similar curriculum comprised of five classical subjects, including wisdom (Prajnaparamita), critical reason (Madhyamika), ontology (Pramana), psychology (Abhidharma), and ethics (Vinaya) that complemented their meditative study and served as a foundation for advanced study of the tantra, which included astrology, ritual, dance, subtle body science, art, and medicine. I imagine Vervaeke would qualify these approaches as optimal for cognitive development, comprised of all four ways of knowing.

Scientific Revolution: The Pendulum Swings Left Again

By the time we reach the late fifteenth and early sixteenth centuries, we see several polymaths develop the heliocentric cosmology and make inroads that would lead to the Scientific Revolution. While remaining entirely committed to his Catholic faith—and although originally proposed by the Greek astronomer Aristarchus of Samos in the third century BCE—Copernicus is credited with postulating the heliocentric model of the universe. What makes Copernicus's findings so critical is that putting the sun, and not the earth, at the center of our universe conflicted with religious notions of truth, and created conflict between the method or means by which truth is derived.

Copernicus's *On the Revolutions of the Heavenly Spheres* (1543), credited by some as the onset of the Scientific Revolution, may well be the hairline fracture that led to compounding incidences like Newton, Darwin, and Freud that resulted in the all-out rupture of left and right mode, and the split between science and religion. Still, at this time, science and religion were united, the German astronomer and astrologer Johannes Kepler built on early work with his discoveries of precise planetary orbits, and the Italian astronomer Galileo Galilei is credited with innovations in astronomy, engineering, and physics earning him the title "Father of Modern Science." Both were religious men. Unfortunately, Galileo's refinement of Copernican heliocentrism was met with disdain from the Catholic Church. By the Roman Inquisition of 1615, it was concluded that heliocentrism was heretical since it contradicted scripture.

Enter Isaac Newton (1643–1727), theologian, astronomer, and physicist, who built upon the earlier work of Galileo's heliocentrism and Kepler's planetary orbits, and was directly influenced by Rene Descartes's epistemology and hyper-rationalism. Francis Bacon's scientific method delivers a compelling and unabashed retort to the Church's claim of Galileo's heresy. With his opus *Philosophiæ Naturalis Principia Mathematica* (1687), Newton's oedipal confrontation with the symbolic father of religion shows psychic maturity in the collective unconscious. It establishes classical mechanics, not contemplation, as the new modus operandi. His interests in calculus, optics, and gravitation all relied on the scientific method based on induction and deductive reason, which made the study of external phenomena objectively observable and verifiable by others.

In contrast, faith was confined to subjectivity, mandate, and speculation. How truth is known begins to shift the power dynamic and domain of preference from right to left mode, faith to reason. As we begin seeing the world as mechanical—although God created the clock, human beings can understand its inner workings—we see a preference for propositional (fact acquisition) and procedural (skill acquisition) ways of knowing. In contrast, religion ideally would have maintained the balance between perspectival (situational) and participatory (experiential) ways of knowing. For example, Newton was still spiritual in his leanings. A devout but heterodox Christian, he refused to take holy orders from the church. Instead, Newton received a notable exception from Charles II to avoid ordaining as a priest as was customary for fellows at Trinity College. Instead, he wrote several religious texts with a more symbolic interpretation.[31]

Western Enlightenment:
The Age of Reason

It wasn't until the eighteenth century that we saw a more fundamental schism between science and religion. In the hyperrational climate of the Enlightenment, philosophers like Immanuel Kant and Jean-Jacques Rousseau argued the two domains should be kept separate, neither of them being particularly inclined toward personal practices of religion; both men were likely more agnostic-leaning scientists in contrast to their forebears in decades and centuries before them. Perhaps the most critical figure in this era is naturalist and biologist Charles Darwin, whose revolutionary book, *On the Origin of Species* (1859), articulates theories of natural selection and evolution that represent the final coup de gras to the religious establishment and the demise of a way of seeing and living in the world that had persisted since the dawn of civilization. We cannot underestimate its impact, for better and for worse.

The Age of Reason—as the Enlightenment is also called—marks another critical juncture in our human story that leads to an unleashing of ideas that continue to permeate the way we see and live. Building on renaissance ideals of humanism, the principles of reductionism and empiricism developed in the Scientific Revolution, domination of the material world, and increased questioning of religious orthodoxy capstoned by Darwin's book, we see the advancement of human ideals including individual liberty, progress, and separation of church and state. Perhaps the greatest legacy of this period is the impact these values had on political developments from the American (1765) and French Revolutions (1789) to the Declaration of Independence (1776) and the drafting of the United States Constitution (1787). Science helps put humanity in charge of their destiny, but it does so by reminding them of their relative insignificance in an increasingly mechanistic world devoid of enchantment. Whereas religion and mythology had the fortune to mirror humanity's divinity, they also saturated the shadow with intolerance, rigidity, irrationality, control, and abuse of power. Copernicus, Darwin, and later Freud each revealed how humanity was not the center of the universe, not beyond the natural order, and not even the master of their own mind.[32]

God is Dead:
The Pendulum Hits its Left Extreme

Within just a few short decades of the publication of Charles Darwin's book *On the Origin of Species*, we see the emergence of another critical thinker who helps illuminate the cultural shadow of our pendulum swing from religion to science, from the right to the left mode of inquiry. While most observers of the early nineteenth century are brimming with confidence and optimism at the unbridled power of science and technology to harness steam and electricity, giving rise to the unprecedented expansion of travel and communications through the steam engine and telephones, Friedrich Nietzsche (1844–1900), a German philosopher, offers his cultural critique at what is threatened or lost with our hemispheric imbalance.

Harkening again to the Greeks, particularly in their mythologies and theater used for centuries as a method of unconscious emotional catharsis, Nietzsche points to the necessary interplay between two timeless dialectical principles in our psyche: that of chaos and order, for which he used the Greek terms Apollonian and Dionysian. Apollo represents harmony, progress, reason, and the individual, and perhaps we could add McGilchrist's left mode of inquiry, as well as the shadow of rigidity and the stifling of creativity. At the same time, Dionysius represents disorder, intoxication, the passions, ecstasy, and unity, McGilchrist's right mode of inquiry, and the shadow of the dissolution of boundaries, recklessness, and endangerment. Though he did not use the word integration, what is implied by Nietzsche is that for cultures and individuals to thrive, there must be a constant balance between these two opposing forces. Order stabilizes chaos, but chaos drives progress. Too much order in civilization leads to stagnation, causing creativity to atrophy. Too much progress can lead to chaotic instability and the degradation of core values.

Although Nietzsche celebrated the Greeks as high culture, he was critical that Socrates and Plato were too Apollonian and contributed to over-emphasizing reason to the detriment of mythology, planting the seeds of the Scientific Revolution. Conversely, Nietzsche was critical of Christianity as being too Dionysian, leading to the Dark Ages. Reason is required to structure chaos, but if it becomes predominant, it can stifle the passions that fuels progress and innovation, the likes of which were apparent in the Renaissance. However, suppose the passions and mythos underlying them are left unchecked to flame without reason. In that case, they can overwhelm the individual and society, as in the religious crusades between Islam and Christianity and during the Inquisition.

If we extrapolate and look at the United States, we see a hyperpolarization between two predominant political parties—the right and the left. Normally these parties work to counter balance each other, just like the Senate and the House, so there are appropriate checks and balances to guard against over representation. For example, conservatives value sovereignty and less government involvement to protect individual rights and property, while progressives tend to value community and welcome more government intervention to support the marginalized. Without any way to relate to the other party, to respectfully disagree within a greater understanding and tolerance of the other, division grows ever deeper and more contentious, with most people not recognizing the shadow result of the split is a descent of each into their respective extremes.

Nietzsche is perhaps most well-known for his proclamation that "God is dead." Still, it wasn't delivered in a celebratory tone. The statement is found in the "Parable of the Madman" in his book *The Gay Science*, and is often not cited in full, but it is revealing:

God is dead. God remains dead. And we have killed him. How shall we comfort ourselves, the murderers of all murderers? What was the holiest and mightiest of all that the world has yet owned has bled to death under our knives: who will wipe this blood off us? What water is there for us to clean ourselves? What festivals of atonement, what sacred games shall we have to invent? Is not the greatness of this deed too great for us? Must we ourselves not become gods simply to appear worthy of it?[33]

The meta-narrative of Christianity that provided a map of meaning and a moral compass for the Western world for nearly two millennia was dismantled in short order between the Scientific Revolution and the Enlightenment. Nietzsche recognized the impact this would have on the individual and collective psyche. Since science is essentially amoral, he felt the absence of a meta-framework would lead individuals searching for a new orienting principle in one of two possible directions or worse to a combination of both: nationalism and nihilism. Like children, society's collective psyche needs a parental figure to admire and a story to be molded as part of its development. Throughout history, Europe was ruled by monarchy and papacy, each calling on allegiance and its people's collective energies to support the empire's mandate. With the fall of feudal kings and religious oligarchs in the Ottoman and Russian Empires, the undercurrent of liberty, self-expression, and determination and the rise of secularism, a new wave of power consolidation emerged from the vacuum left by religious dethronement. The rise of nationalism across Europe in the early nineteenth century provides a pseudo-mythology that stratifies the urge of the human unconscious devoid of religion, channeling the energy and allegiance of the people towards the nation-state rather than God, but with no less religious fervor. One can imagine in this context what it looks like when a population's Dionysian passions become unbridled, fermented by charismatic political leaders, and charged with the mission of furthering the cause of the nation evidenced in the 20th century by the rise of Hitler and the Third Reich in Germany.

The other consequence of the loss of religion anticipated by Nietzsche was our descent into nihilism, defined as the absence of objective truth leading to a lack of meaning. Nothing makes sense or has intrinsic value, so life has no purpose. Nihilism not only leads to amorality but aimlessness and apathy, or worse, self-destruction and a death wish. Although we suffer under God, religion provides avenues for redemption and liberation. Without either, there is only darkness or despair. Nietzsche despised nihilism, and argued in *Will to Power* that under its withering scrutiny, "the highest values devalue themselves. The aim is lacking, and 'Why' finds no answer."[34] Inevitably, nihilism will expose all cherished beliefs and sacrosanct truths as symptoms of a defective Western mythos. This collapse of meaning, relevance, and purpose will be the most destructive force in history, constituting a total assault on reality and nothing less than the greatest crisis of humanity."[35]

From these two dire consequences, nationalism and nihilism, Nietzsche provided some hope for a resolution in the symbol of his Übermensch, meaning higher-man or superman, presented in his book *Thus Spoke Zarathustra* (1885). Superman is an archetype of the ideal human of the future, a replacement for mythic heroes like Christ in the archetypal vacuum left by the overthrow of religion by science, a figure that emerges more self-actualized from the existential trial of unavoidable human suffering.[36] In contradiction to the evolutionary picture painted by Darwin, Nietzsche proposed that humankind did not passively nor inevitably evolve in a linear fashion, but that certain individuals throughout different periods in history cultivated specific qualities or traits that made them exceptional standouts. Human beings therefore had an innate capacity to self-actualized, to become exceptional through their own efforts, not by divine intervention, nor genetic evolution, and thus Nietzsche's Übermensch was proposed to replace our idealization and dependence on abstract notions like god, without falling into the nihilistic abyss that no optimization is possible for humankind. Walter Kaufmann, a scholar of Nietzsche, extrapolates some of the most revered charismatic leaders from history, may have embodied these diverse ideal human attributes, like Goethe, DaVinci,

Shakespeare, Michelangelo, Napoleon, Caesar, and Socrates, and discusses at length how Nietzsche may have conceived and developed the notion of the Übermensch as the ideal human of the future.[37]

Beyond Übermensch

What can we presume if we take Nietzsche's cultural critique as a lens for the etiology of the problems we face today?

The environmental crisis, economic disparity, political instability, mental health suffering, and the existential loss of morality and meaning are all interconnected and can be traced to this recent period in history in which we "killed god" and failed to consider a replacement urge in the psyche. The rise of nationalism and nihilism are the shadow consequences of the loss of a coherent mythology and represent the collective unconscious's best attempt or failure (as the case may be) to cope with such a traumatic loss of psychic needs for structure and orientation. Furthermore, many symptoms represent failures of integration between the Apollonian left mode and the Dionysian right mode, both mythologically and neurobiologically.

The answer is not a return to prior ages or to reactively swing to an opposite extreme of the pendulum, but a synthesis evidenced during the Renaissance, uniting reason, science, and technology with intuition, religion, and mythology—avoiding rigidity of dogmas by seeking a middle way. The Übermensch not only represents Nietzsche's compelling critique of our culture's shadow, but also presents a secular, humanist orientation for optimization that avoids the pitfalls of passive reliance on superstitious religion in which only god can be exceptional, and an equally passive reliance on our genes for slow adaptation as presented in the science of evolution.

Following Nietzsche, to summarize the archetypal gestalt of the twentieth century, we can see how an explosion of scientific, philosophical, and technical advancements completely transforms life on the planet. Yet because of the absence of moral grounding and meaning, many of these developments express their unchecked shadow side of greed, aggression, ignorance, and divisiveness contributing to deleterious impacts on society. In communications, we see the advent of radio, television, personal computer, and the internet, which connect and inform us. They are equally used to hypnotize, mislead, terrify, isolate and control us. As transportation expands to interstellar travel, we secretly breed a lack of accountability and responsibility for the earth we rely upon. As medicine improves through advancements in surgery and the discovery of antibiotics, we lose sight of the holistic capacity for the body to heal itself and become dependent like drug addicts on expensive procedures and synthetic compounds made by Big Pharma and accessible only to a few. As economic innovations in capitalism raise the quality of life for many worldwide, the free-market ideal that should be grounded in secular or human ethics sinks into depravity and greed; without checks and balances, it creates the most significant wealth disparity ever known. The splitting of the atom and developments in Newtonian physics that could have powered the entire world led to nuclear weapons threatening our survival. What will happen as Artificial Intelligence (AI) develops absent a moral underpinning? Perhaps we need to reread the myth of Pandora's Box. With every advance we knowingly make as a species, there is a shadow cost unbeknownst to us until it's too late, the hedonic and unchecked drives for more power, pleasure, fame, convenience, and narcissistic aggrandizement deplete the planet's resources, pollute the oceans, and draw countries into never-ending wars over scarce reserves.

The world is out of balance and tipping toward an extreme. From a mythological perspective, we have arrived at a critical near-death phase in what some have conceived as a global initiatory rite of passage.[38] Yet without the prospect of redemptive transformation and rebirth, death is only pain and trauma. Are we willing to learn from the darkness to make our ascension toward the light, or will we perish in the belly of the beast of our ignorance? The choice we make right now, either to continue living blindly or to awaken and change, will make all the difference for the survival of future generations and the expansion of collective consciousness.

RETURNING TO THE AGE OF AQUARIUS

From this granular recounting of history we return to the zodiacal ages to see how the incoming archetypal signature will influence our collective unconscious in the future. According to Fitzgerald the Age of Aquarius-Leo (2160–4320 CE) is archetypally defined as freedom, unity, information, knowledge, empowerment, revolution, technology, and electricity.[39] The symbol of Aquarius is of Zeus's youthful pre-pubescent cup bearer Ganymede, pouring water from above into a stream below. However, Aquarius isn't a water sign; it's an air element, so Ray Grasse suggests the symbol instead as ether or energy, being poured from on high and merging below.[40] Whereas the Piscean Age is a water element associated with emotions and featuring seafaring civilizations, the Aquarian age is about expansive ideas, energy-harnessing technologies, represented by air and interstellar travel, the transition commencing with the Wright brothers, the first man on the moon, the Hubble telescope, and in our lifetime landing on Mars and beyond. While we expand outward through space travel, perhaps we'll never forget the iconic image of the earth seen from the moon that allowed us to see ourselves as one single family with a common home for the first time in human history.

The energy of the Age of Taurus, an earth sign, manifested as the conquest of the material world and the building of monolithic structures, best represented by Egypt's enduring pyramids. The energy of the Age of Aries, a fire sign, manifested as cultural expansion and conquest of other empires through military advancement best represented by Rome. The energy of the Age of Pisces, a water sign, manifests as conquest of the inner world—the emotions—through monotheism with social ethics represented best by Christ. The character of the Aquarian Age, an air sign, might well constellate around mind control and mind expansion, the polarization and unification of the ordinary masses, the unleashing and harnessing of subtle energies in the body, and the creation and destruction posed by advanced technologies like AI. While air signs make technologies and tools more agile and seem to accelerate time, they are particularly amorphous and challenging to control, predict, or pin down. Information, for example, is both quick and fluid but can be confusing and misleading.

According to Dan Seigel, mind regulates the flow of energy and information, and integration is achieved when each distinct brain region expresses their unique complexity while linking with other regions.[41] Seigel uses a church choir as a metaphor, each singer representing their unique voice and talent, yet the collective harmony is greater than the sum of its parts. The Aquarian Age coincides with our self-anointed "information age." With the advent of the internet, we merged the power of a single mind into an interconnected web of collective minds, and shortcomings. That's what the internet is—a digital ecosystem, a collective mind—with each node contributing to advancing or polluting the unitary stream. We have faster access to more information at the touch of a button than could have ever been obtained in the Library of Alexander in the prior age.

Access to information has a disadvantage, for anyone can pour anything—factual data or toxic waste—into the collective stream, leaving us in a confusing deluge of information, misinformation, and disinformation. The Age of Aquarius will continue to see innovations in storing, accessing, and spreading data in the service of good and ill. Heeding Vervaeke's advice, we must be careful not to conflate knowledge with wisdom, exercising all four ways of knowing. The Aquarian Age will require each of us to cultivate a high level of discernment, yoking intelligence with intuition to navigate the information deluge to avoid being misled. Heeding McGilchrist's advice, we'll need to be mindful of the left mode's tendency toward data fixation and certainty and exercise ways to bring the right mode online for tolerating dissonance long enough to generate new, higher order gestalts or synthesis. Heeding Nietzsche's advice, we will need to preserve our Apollonian sword of critical analysis to cut through the pressures of groupthink and Orwellian-style mind control, while at the same time freeing our

Dionysian inclinations toward beauty, art, nature, enthusiasm, and ecstasy without guilt and shame, and all that distinguishes us from AI and robots.

DECENTRALIZATION

Another defining characteristic or signature of the Aquarian age, according to Grasse, is decentralization.[42] Ganymede is pouring energy from above into a stream below. We can take this to symbolize a shift in power from vertical hierarchies, symbolized by the pyramid, that have dominated the planet since the dawn of civilization, to horizontal or distributive structures, symbolized by the mandala, that return power to the masses of ordinary and even marginalized people. Nowadays, with technology and a good idea, almost anyone, regardless of race, class, strength, or education, can disrupt long-standing institutions in an instant. Look at how Amazon, Airbnb, and Uber—all disruptive technologies—changed the commercial landscape by creating more access, choice, social linkages in peer-to-peer networks.

However, what tends to happen after a power play to depose the status quo hierarchy, is the newcomers form their own centralized power structure. Coup d'états and regime change can usher in new dictatorships. The young, dynamic, and innovative Silicon Valley tech-savvy geeks of the early 1980s, like the founders of Apple, Microsoft, Google, and later Tesla, are now the current apex predators, capable of wielding tremendous economic power to dominate the global economy and censor information. The struggle to decentralize is renewed, until the power resides with the masses of ordinary people. Innovative alternatives to vertical hierarchies—think mandala versus pyramid formations—will need years of experimentation and refinement.

Suppose we take the dialectical tension between individual and collective to a more macro-level. In that case, we needn't look further than our smart devices and ask ourselves if being more technologically connected on social media translates to feeling more connected as human beings. While technology creates some avenues for unity on a vast and nearly instantaneous scale, it also creates silos and can lead to despairing levels of alienation and eventually transhumanism. There is a shadow side of this constant connectivity worth considering because malevolent influences are also entering these portals of exchange. Just ask any one of the many teenage girls with a smartphone, the demographic most at risk for suicidal ideation as a direct result of the deleterious consequences of social media engagement.[43] While smart technology and the internet dissolve boundaries and allow unprecedented access to unimagined amounts of information, they also invade privacy, allow coercion, fester malice, and can lead to Orwellian thought control.

How will we find a balance between our urge for unity, access, and harmony, and the very real need within us to protect our privacy, express our individuality, and defend sovereignty? That is perhaps the central koan for us to contemplate during the emerging aion.

Our panorama—which had us looking around at the problems of the world today, up at the stars for the broader context, and back through history for the genesis—has hopefully given us the clearer, wide angle view we need to understand who we are as a culture in space and time right now. Civilizations that kept good astrological records knew that we weren't traveling linearly without the need to remember the past, but cyclically, affording them the opportunity to accrue and store knowledge of past experiences that would help them predict challenges and evolve their collective consciousness as the world turns through repeating aions. A close examination of the Great Year (see figure 4.2 on page 101), the cosmic clock, reveals we are amid a significant sea change between three transitions, from Iron into early Bronze Age, between Piscean and the Aquarian Ages, and between earth and air elemental signs.

What's more, the convergence of crises we are now experiencing is not random, it has a distinctive predictable signature attributed to the celestial archetypes we are influenced by from above and can be represented by the pendulum swing between the dominance of our brain hemisphere's shifting to the left extreme. The left mode is not in search of embodied meaning, it seeks mechanical or disembodied certainty at all costs; our psyches remain fragmented, disenchanted, and fragile in the face of change.

With this analysis of our collective predicament, and just like a competent doctor, we have identified the symptoms and delineated the origins or causes, determining the bad news first, so now we're able to move to the prognosis and treatment.

3
Soul
Imbibing the Elixir

Now that we have seen how Western civilization lost the soul, progressing into spiritual blindness and materialism during our current Great Year's decent into the Dark Age, and accounting for our recent evolution into rationality, science, and secularism, we can now define the soul and position its revival as our collective mission. The soul, however, is not easily defined. Despite being a primary focus of religious traditions since their inceptions, and academic and psychoanalytic traditions more recently, a standard definition does not exist. As psychotherapist and former Trappist monk Thomas Moore, wrote:

> It is impossible to define precisely what the soul is. Definition is an intellectual enterprise anyway: the soul prefers to imagine. We know intuitively that soul has to do with genuineness and depth, as when we say certain music has soul or a remarkable person is soulful. When you look closely at the image of soulfulness, you see that it is tied to life in all its particulars—good food, satisfying conversation, genuine friends, and experiences that stay in the memory and touch the heart. Soul is revealed in attachment, love, and community, as well as in retreat on behalf of inner communing and intimacy.[1]

Given there is no shared definition, a historical and philosophical survey of the concept of soul from a cross-cultural perspective can help us draw out major defining properties and a list of common principles to help us approximate the nature of the soul as distilled through time, place, and culture. This working model can serve as a basis for our inner exploration while remaining flexible enough to engage a variety of perspectives.

ETYMOLOGY OF THE SOUL

The modern English word soul is derived from the Old English *sawel* and is cognate with the Germanic *seula*. The Germanic root means "coming from the sea" because the belief that souls would arise out of and return to the sea, reaffirming the soul is distinct and continuous from the body. The sea is a common metaphor for a universal mystery, an expansive and unknown place where things can be dissolved and re-merged. It is believed that seula is a translation of the Greek word psyche, which connotes "life" and "consciousness" but literally refers "to cool or to blow" as in the breath.

The Hebrew word for soul is *nephesh*, meaning "breath" and in the mystical tradition of Jewish Kabbalah there are least five words for soul. Of note are two in particular: *ruach* refers to wind, and *yechidah* refers to oneness with God. The attribution of the meaning of immortal soul with the Jewish word *nephesh* may have been influenced by Hellenistic philosophy; prior, the word may have meant something closer to living, sentient being, or breathing body. Not surprisingly, a similar motif of dual and interchangeable definitions occurs in Islam between *ruh* and *nafs*, whereas the former refers to a divine spirit or breath of life, pointing to the universal principle. In contrast, the latter refers to the cognitive aspect of the individual that can recognize or realize God.

The word soul is commonly used interchangeably with the word spirit, meaning an animating or vital principle in man and animals, derived from Anglo-French and Old French *espirit* and directly from

Latin *spiritus* meaning to breath, respiration, and wind. This is how we get to the word "inspiration"—to lift like the wind—and usage like "spirited" to describe someone's character as invigorated, animated, or courageous. The word animated comes from *animus*, Latin for soul, derived from the root *ane*—to breath.

THE LEGACY OF THE SOUL

Paleolithic Era

Our odyssey to trace the legacy of our understanding of the soul begins in the Paleolithic period, around 2.5 million years ago, when homo sapiens, with their growing brains, take a giant leap forward in tool making and abstract thinking. While we have no definitive evidence to suggest a coherent belief in the soul, we can surmise a notion of the afterlife from intricate burial practices that only develop in sophistication as time passes. Why else would members of hunter-gatherer tribes bury their loved ones with tools and other essential artifacts that could be more useful to the living than the dead unless there was a sense the deceased might need them after death? The conception of adorning burial sites with objects that would ensure continued wealth, power, status, and sustenance for the dead beyond life became more widespread in the Neolithic period, as evidenced by sculptures and jewelry discovered across China, Africa, and the Middle East.

Greece

Due to their geographic proximity to the Eastern Mediterranean and the extensive bilateral trade extending deep into the Bronze age, the Egyptians influenced early Greek conceptions of the soul, afterlife, and propitiations of gods. However, they did not posit the soul as having multiple interrelated aspects; for the Greeks, the soul was a unidimensional, nonphysical, vital essence that separated from the physical human body at death and was relegated to the underworld Hades, governed by the god of the same name. Meanwhile, the gods enjoyed immortality in divine abodes with the ability to intersect at will with the human realm.

In Homer's *Odyssey* Book 11, the hero Odysseus journeys to the underworld, and there we get the sense from its descriptions of souls described as shades or phantoms languishing for eternity without emotion or purpose. With this inevitable fate as a disembodied spirit in Hades, early Greeks may have been appropriately oriented toward heroism within their lifetime, as Edmonds suggests:

> This bleak vision of death and afterlife is fundamental to the Homeric idea of the hero's choice—only in life is there any meaningful existence, so the hero is the one who, like Achilles, chooses to do glorious deeds. Since death is inevitable, Sarpedon points out, the hero should not try to avoid it but go out into the front of the battle and win honor and glory. Such glory is imperishable, the only meaningful form of immortality since the soul's persistence after death is so unappealing.[2]

While this dreary characterization of the early Greek view of the afterlife is drawn primarily from Homeric sources, Edmonds contends it is a gross overgeneralization and that in sources outside the epics of Homer, there was a greater multiplicity of perspectives regarding the soul's experience of the afterworld, including retention of a variety of emotions, purposes, social hierarchies, and both pleasurable and painful consequences of past actions from worldly life.[3]

Be this as it may, the concept of soul and its cosmology takes a pervasive shift in ancient Greece between the sixth and fifth centuries BCE. The philosopher Pythagoras (570–495 BCE) is often attributed with the first notion of a soul that transmigrates and reincarnates, in a process known in Greek as *metemphyschosis*. A frequently cited passage of Pythagoras reveals not the grim fate of the soul in the afterworld for eternity but his anticipation of an eternal return in various forms to this world. "Once, they say, he [Pythagoras] was passing by when a puppy was being thrashed, and he took pity on it and spoke the following words: 'Stop! Do not beat the dog! It is, in fact, the soul of a friend of mine. I recognized it when I heard its voice.'"[4]

This shift in the conception of the soul from a linear progression ending interminably in the afterworld to a cyclic return is accompanied by a new mythos altering the purpose of human life and influencing the works of Socrates and Plato. Once we have the notion of the soul's cyclic or eternal return, the emphasis shifts from bitter fate to gradual moral education and consequential learning. Socrates (470–399 BCE) said: "If the soul is immortal, it demands our care not only for that part of time which we call life, but for all time; and indeed, it would seem now that it will be extremely dangerous to neglect it."[5] From this passage, we can deduce the individual nature of the continuity of the soul, each responsible for the consequences of their actions in life.

Later, Socrates's student Plato (428–348 BCE) develops the notion of the soul in several of his masterworks, including the *Phaedo* and the *Republic*, which have had a major impact as the foundation for Western philosophy. In book X of Plato's *Republic*, he discusses the *Myth of Er*, an account of a soldier's descent into the afterworld, to be judged by the gods according to virtue or vice of their human life, and, importantly, *sent back* to inhabit a new human form on earth to continue spiritual development.[6] By contrast, Aristotle (384–322 BCE) did not assert the doctrine of metempsychosis as Socrates and Plato did. Instead, he saw the soul as the animating or vital force present in, and more importantly dependent on, the body, which gives life its meaning, thus the soul ceases when the body dies. According to Aristotle, immortality was achieved through the transgenerational impact of virtuous deeds on culture and the legacy of one's progeny, not through actual transmigration of the soul.[7]

Whereas the Homeric conception may have offered but a single life fated for Hades, placing emphasis on maximizing heroism in a relatively short lifespan to please the gods, the Pythagoran, Socratic, and

Platonic conceptions of the *eternal return*, or what Indic cultures call *cyclic existence*, extends the timespan of the soul's evolution to infinity. Consequently, each human being had a chance at continuous learning and improvement, a redemption, though that word wasn't used in the Greek vernacular of the time. Rather than being fated, the soul is in the process of awakening across time, according to moral actions and their consequences.

In parallel with this new view of the soul, we see the articulation of the tripartite theory of the soul, or its three characteristics, as found in Book 4 of Plato's *Republic*. These three characteristics are *reason*, *spirit*, and *appetites*. Reason is the faculty of discrimination that can know truth from deception and ultimately discover one's true nature and purpose. Spirit refers to intense emotions like love and hate, whereas appetites are the base impulses like sexual gratification or fear of death. Centuries later, Sigmund Freud's structure of personality and drive theory would draw on Plato's tripartite theory of the soul with the executive function of the *super-ego* corresponding to reason, the *ego* with spirit, and the *id* with the appetites. From the interrelationship between the three, we see how man's soul evolves according to meta-principles in pursuit of wisdom, moral justice, and self-mastery.

Much of what we know, even intuitively, about the soul in Western culture derives from the legacies of Socrates, Plato, and Aristotle. For example, their usage of the Greek word *psyche*, soul, versus *soma*, or body creates an early version of mind/body dualism. Centuries later, this mind/body distinction would be reaffirmed, most notably by the 16th-century French philosopher Rene Descartes, with the soul being the providence of religion and the body that of science. The thrust of the neoplatonists was how to live a good, morally just life and cultivate the psyche over time.

This gradual contemplative approach of slow but systematic cultivation of wisdom over lifetimes is contrasted with the more radical or mystical approach offered to initiates of the so-called Greek mystery cults of Orpheus, Dionysus, and Eleusis between 1600 BCE–392 CE. Through intensive ritual activities, including, most likely and but still controversially among todays scholars, the use of powerful psychedelic sacraments, *mytes* or initiates, could have profound, breakthrough revelations that may have fast-tracked a direct encounter with soul or divinity called *apotheosis* (apo = make and theos = god), hyper-motivating and hastening their spiritual development.[8] While I will describe these rites in more detail later in this book, suffice to say here that these sudden breakthroughs in consciousness could happen within a lifetime or even a single initiatory experience, rather than the gradual approach requiring innumerable lifetimes. Anticipating future comparison, I'll note here the possibility of fast-tracking enlightenment the Tibetan tantras propose in contrast to the gradualism of Mahayana Buddhism.

Cultural Confluence: Greece and India

There are further parallels between the gradual and radical paths of ancient Greece, India, and Tibet, both in their notions of the immortal soul trapped in unconscious cycles of rebirth, repeating the karmic consequences of negative actions, and in their notion of seeking liberation or apotheosis through wisdom, meditation, and virtue.

The title of this book, *Return with Elixir*, with the foreword by Buddhist scholar Robert Thurman, offers a point of synthesis between the mystical cults of two great cultures—Greece and India. The Greek word *ambrosia* and the Sanskrit word *amrita* share a common proto-Indo-European source and mean a divine substance that grants immortality. Similarly, a synonym for elixir, nectar, also shares this meaning, derived from the Greek nek (death) and tar (overcome). Throughout Greek mythology, ambrosia is an intoxicating substance drunk by the gods, granting them immortality. According to Brian Muraresku, ambrosia might be more than mythopoetic; perhaps also an actual psychedelic sacrament brewed by priestesses, shared with initiates of the Greek mystery cults, and capable of life-changing revelations, including conquering the fear of death.[9]

While the tantric systems of India and Tibet used ritual psychedelic sacraments like *soma* during initiations, the divine substance amrita is—through the process of yogic biohacking—reconceived mainly as a neuro-chemical drop of elixir, accessed and enjoyed within the symbolic chalice of the subtle anatomy. The tantric method is uniquely characterized as an art form of recognizing oneself as already enlightened, a fully actualized deity within a perfect mandala, one's sense of being ordinary, temporal, and incapable reflect a case of mistaken identity. The tantras rely first on visualization and vibration in the so-called generation stage of practice, to "reimagine" and "reacquaint" oneself with divinity, and later incorporate the completion stage of practice when the subtle body and inner winds underlying the physical body are recruited to blissfully support one's exalted self-perception. Rather than an external potion producing ecstasy and divine union, amrita is recast as an internal state of embodied inte-gration derived through yogic manipulation of identity formation, per-ception, and subtle energy in the nervous system, which we will explore in more depth as we proceed. Briefly, it is the process of consciously drawing contaminated energy down the two main side channels of the subtle body nervous system, shared in common with ancient Chinese medicine and acupuncture, into a metaphoric crucible resting upon a ritual fire at the navel juncture in a practice called *chandali*, inner heat, where the energy is alchemically purified like base metals into gold, then drawn up the cen-tral channel into the heart nexus. Along the way, the energy melts cal-cified drops of dopaminergic neurotransmitters, stationed at main axial hubs or *chakras*, producing ecstatic openness.

During this tantric visualization, heavily reliant on mythopoetics to overlay and consciously manipulate the energy within the subtle body, the so-called white father-drop (archetypal masculine energy) melts at the crown complex and is drawn down the central channel, while the red mother-drop (archetypal feminine energy) melts and its elixir is drawn up from the base complex, until both meet like twin streams at a conflu-ence at the heart nexus and merge inseparably with a third drop—a holy trinity forming a unity—the third is the ever-present or indestructible drop of pure consciousness variously referred to as Dharmakaya, clear-light, or Buddha nature. This secret pilgrimage of sacred union between father-mother drops and buddha nature, results in symbolic rebirth of a new being called a bodhisattva or master altruist, thus fulfilling the alchemical transformation of an ordinary egocentric being into a embodied deity. Accessing the clear-light nature of one's soul and the neural chemistry of bliss to reboot as Vajrayogini, the Great Bliss Queen, through tantric meditation is synonymous with the actualization of the deathless state, becoming one with Dionysus, the Divine Madman, achieved by consuming the Greek mystery potions.

My teacher, Robert Thurman, professor of Indo-Tibetan Buddhist Studies at Columbia University, explained in our training classes at Tibet House that this subtle drop of pure consciousness is indeed the soul released from its bondage of forced alienation and delusion by the alchemical transformation of neural energy that binds it. It's fascinating how outer and inner alchemical traditions, East and West, can converge to go beyond the terminal life predicament and its legions of fear to embrace gnosis or awakening to our infinite nature.[10]

Early Christianity and The Greek Mysteries

Brian C. Muraresku's book *The Immortality Key* uses an interdisciplinary approach of classics, theology, archeology, chemistry, botany, and technology to establish how the early Greek cults of Dionysian and Eleusinian mysteries had a direct influence on the development of Christianity. Following the bread crumb trail of the controversial *pagan continuity hypothesis*, Muraresku traces the through line of universal wisdom connecting Egypt, Greece, and early Christianity, implying figures like Osiris, Hermes Trismegistus, Dionysus, and Jesus may, in fact, be different cultural manifestations of the same archetypal psychopomp, a rebirth guide for what Muraresku calls the "religion with no name."[11] Strikingly, all these archetypes bear in common a miraculous birth, are known as "twice born," performed miracles, died and were resurrected, and initiated their mortal followers into secret cults that promised spiritual immortality. All promise to make mortal humans into gods. Central to all esoteric cults, argues Muraresku and others, is a psychedelic sacrament blended with wine, which allowed initiates to experience for themselves the wisdom (gnosis) of the deathless and direct union with the divine (apotheosis).

One could speculate that before Christianity formalized as the de facto religion of the Roman Empire under Constantine (306–337 CE), which led to the banning of the mysteries by Theodosius I in 392 CE, early Christian cults may have shared a similar worldview to the earlier Greeks, believing in an immortal soul that transmigrates in a multi-life span based on the consequences of our actions. With secret initiation leading to direct wisdom (gnosis), early Christians too could become twice-born; in other words, they could themselves become Christ or God-like and reach the deathless state, unthinkable heresy to later Church doctrine.

As political control established itself in the centralized early church of the Holy Roman Empire, Christianity continued its philosophical development, influencing what millions of people around the world today still believe—there is a soul that will be judged at death, those who accept Jesus as the one true God and savior are granted eternal life in heaven, while those who don't, receive eternal damnation in hell. There is but one life as a human being, only one chance at salvation or to "get it right." Redemption for one's sins in this life is critical and only possible through belief in Jesus as the savior. The archetype of Jesus as a direct experience of gnosis available to all initiates of the mysteries—including women and even slaves, without mediator or priest, was replaced by Jesus the symbol—eventually accessed only by blind faith, adherence to scripture, mediated by the hierarchy of priestly gatekeepers. At the same time, the ancient sacraments of ergot-infused wine that created ecstasy were replaced by a Eucharist comprised of ordinary bread and wine, rendered impotent by contrast. Apparently, no centralized authority wants its population to usurp its power, not least by knowing their divinity directly.

Swat Valley Nexus Point

I wonder if and how the pagan continuity hypothesis might possibly extend into the Indian subcontinent to influence, and be mutually affected by, the tantric cults of Hinduism and Buddhism, which arose around the sixth and seventh centuries CE. Are the Hindu god Shiva and the adept tantric Padmasambhava (the Indian Buddhist attributed with the revelation of the *Tibetan Book of the Dead*) merely an extension of this lineage of "twice born" initiates into the deathless state stretching back through Jesus, Dionysus, to Hermes Trismegistus and Osiris? There is evidence of Indo-Greek influence through trade routes along the Silk Road linking India, Persia, and the Ionian cities of Asia Minor two centuries before Alexander the Great's colonization of the Hindu Kush in the spring of 329 BCE.[13]

One possible nexus point linking Greek mysteries with Indic tantric cults is the Swat Valley in modern-day Pakistan. The earliest record of the region comes from the Rig Veda, which refers to Indo-Aryan settlements in this region around 1500 BCE. Described as lush and fertile, Alexander the Great later conquered the regional kingdoms, crossing the Kush in 327 BCE on his way to expanding his empire into modern day Afghanistan. In 305 BCE, the Mauryan Emperor Ashoka conquered the Greeks and introduced Buddhism, building several stupas (shrines) and other religious monuments. Then came the Greco-Bactrian rule, which reestablished Indo-Greek Kingdoms, led most famously by the Greek king Menander 1 (140 BCE), who converted to Buddhism. The later Persian Parthian Empire (around 50 BCE) is credited with the rise of a long legacy of Hellenistic-inspired Buddhist art, including the first portrayal of the Buddha in human form. Until this time, the Buddha in India was only represented symbolically as the Wheel of Dharma (*dharmachakra*) or a pair of feet, but the first waves of statues depicting the Awakened One iconically wearing flowing togas in the classical style of the Greek gods emerge from the Gandaharan civilization in the Swat Valley. By 403 CE, Chinese pilgrim Fa-Hsien visited the Swat and reported a thriving Buddhist community with 500 monasteries. Over these nearly 2000 years, we see the waxing, waning, and co-mingling of two cultures, Greek and Buddhist, both interested in the soul, rebirth, and liberation, and containing esoteric and exoteric approaches to immortality.

Following the collapse of the Mauryan Empire, the cultural synthesis known as Greco-Buddhism—forged by the legacies of Alexander the Great and Buddhist Emperor Ashoka—continued to flourish under the Greco-Bactrian Kingdom, Indo-Greek Kingdoms, and Kushan Empire. Mahayana Buddhism spread from the Gangetic plains in India into Gandhara, then Central Asia during the Mauryan Era, where it became the most prevalent branch of Buddhism. It was later transmitted via the ancient Royal Road and Silk Road from the Aegean in Greece east through Asia Minor and Persia, reaching the Hindu Kush, west of the Himalayas, in modern-day Afghanistan and Pakistan.

The most famous offspring of the Greco-Buddhist union is the Gandhara art style, as mentioned the first to depict the Buddha in human form, with hallmark Hellenistic features. Of note is that Hercules was often depicted alongside the Buddha, muscular, bearded, and holding a club. Some scholars believe Hercules transitions iconographically into Vajrapani, holder of the Diamond, a central archetype of tantric Buddhism. My research on extensive viniculture in the pristine Swat Valley, along with evidence of wine drinking and sculptures of Dionysus suggest the Greek mysteries may have traveled along the trade routes to this region and possibly fused with esoteric Buddhist practices, the tantras, only just emerging at this time.[14] The Swat Valley is, debatably, the location of the ancient country of Oddiyana, the birthplace of master psychonaut and tantric Buddhist Padmasambhava, and ground zero for the genesis of disseminating Buddhist tantras. An alternative view by Tantric scholar Keith Dowman suggests Odisha formerly Orissa, in Bengal East India as the birthplace of Buddhist tantra, and while there is archeological evidence of early Buddhist tantric sites, and co-mingling with the goddess cults of Tantric Hinduism, there is a paucity of cross-cultural exchange between Buddhists and the Greeks in this region.[15]

There is an interesting mix of variables in the Swat Valley that might account for the Indic mystical traditions of "dying before you die." There is evidence that the Swat Valley is home to one of the oldest vinicultural regions of the world. With the Silk Road serving as a highway for the influx of ideas and cultural practices from Greece and Rome—and evidence of the cult of Dionysus, bacchanalia or orgasmic feats depicted in stone reliefs—and this fertile and thriving wine-producing region, already home to Gandharan Buddhist art with evidence of tantric iconography such as Vajrapani, I agree it is a plausible location for the birthplace of tantra.[16] From the Buddhist side, the spread of the so-called Vajrayana or Diamond Vehicle, the esoteric form of Buddhism, is usually attributed to Padmasambhava hailing from a place called Oddiyana or Uddayana, which is debated to be among other places in either the Swat Valley or Odisha.[17] Art historian and ethnologist Max Klimberg explains it shouldn't surprise us, therefore, to find Buddhist Gandhara reliefs showing non-Buddhist images of wine drinking, revelries, and eroticism, as already commented on in 1992 by M.L. Carter.[18] He focused on the Dionysian features of the popular folk religion of the region. More recently, Anna Filigenzi, a long-time member of the Italian Archaeological Mission to Swat, Pakistan, similarly noted the wine cultures of Great Kafiristan flourished near Buddhist monasteries in the region, where she observes, "In the rich repertoire of the Buddhist art of Gandhara a special place is occupied by what we usually call 'Dionysiac scenes' [involving] . . . drinking, dancing, performing more or less explicit erotic gestures as a prelude to sexual intercourse or social ceremonies of unknown nature."[19] This would have been anathema to orthodox Buddhism, but seems uncannily analogues to the esoteric beliefs and practices of the Vajrayana such as *ganachakra* or tantric feasts and ecstatic, erotic ceremonies that may have been mutually influenced by Dionysian *orgia* or Roman *bacchanalia*.[20]

I suspect just as the cults of Dionysus and Eleusinian mysteries met with resistance and eventual suppression under the emerging anti-pagan, patriarchal establishment of the Roman and early Byzantine church, likewise the tantric lineages of Shivism and Vajrayana Buddhism enjoyed stretches of flourishing before they were considered threatening to more orthodox schools within each tradition. Just as their twin mystery schools in the Mediterranean, Indo-Tibetan tantras were largely a secret, orally transmitted or "ear whispered" lineage until being formalized and incorporated into the monastic universities of India like Nalanda (427–1197 CE), and later in Tibet, particularly under the renaissance figure Je Tsongkhapa in the fourteenth century. The mainstreaming and "monasticizing" of Buddhist tantra may have contributed to the replacing of psychedelic substances (soma) with contemplative methods for subtle body manipulation, and of actual partnered sexual practices (karmamudra) with visualized versions of deities with consorts, to prevent monks from breaking their vows.

Tantric Buddhism

We now reach the Buddhist contribution to the notion of the soul. You may already recognize the Buddha countered the pervasive Vedic notion of *atman*, eternal soul, with a concept of *anatman*, literally "no soul" or sometimes rendered "no self." Some may wonder how we can include a Buddhist perspective with others when the Buddhists don't believe a soul exists. As with Thurman, I propose that a literal interpretation of anatman as "no soul" is misleading, based on poor initial translations in the late nineteenth and early twentieth century. More precise would be that the Buddha objected not to the existence of a soul per se, but to an emphasis on the soul as eternally unchanging, nonrelative, or absolute.

The assertion that the soul is absolute contradicts *trishiksha* or "three marks of reality" doctrine in Buddhism, suggesting that all phenomena are impermanent and therefore have no lasting basis for fixed, unchanging identity, be it the self or soul, and that clinging to anything that changes results in suffering. If we understand anatman as a Buddhist critique of any sense that things—whether they are tables, bodies, personalities, or souls—contain an absolute, eternal, and unchanging essence, then we are free to continue to use the term *soul* as a relational process used to describe the continuity of consciousness, and the immaterial container, if you will, that carries karmic imprints across beginningless lifespans.

Fundamentally, how can things be absolute and unchanging, yet, one can relate to or realize them? This is the age-old Buddhist question. The act of realizing something means it is relational and therefore defies the language of absolutes. For Buddhists, a soul does exist. It's just not a permeant, fixed, independent entity outside some relationality matrix.

Rather than get fixated on the word "soul," consider what the Buddhist commonly uses as an alternative to determining its character and nature. The Buddhist posit *mind* (chitta) as the substratum of reality that is discrete from, yet interrelated with, the body. It continues after death. In Buddhist psychology, mind is defined as "merely clear and knowing." *Clarity* refers to the mind's natural capacity to reflect reality like a mirror, naturally spacious and uncontaminated. It is often likened to the openness of the sky that contains but remains unaffected by weather.

Mind is not a thing but an ever-changing process or series of mental events strung together like beads on a rosary in which cognizing occurs. The *knowing* aspect refers to the mind's capacity to recognize and discern between objects, analyze them, create meaning from them, and ultimately discover their ultimate or empty nature beyond appearance. For example, knowing (an English word derived from gnosis) refers to insight, and the non-conceptual or intuitive understanding (*prajna*) critical to the soul's liberation. The *mere* aspect of the Buddhist definition of mind is that just like all objects the mind perceives, the mind itself is a relative construct, impermanent, insubstantial, ever-changing, interdependent, merely labeled, and unfindable as an absolute unity in itself. In other words, because the mind is empty, it can discover its emptiness through self-reflective analysis and insight. The mind or consciousness that flows across time with these three attributes of spacious clarity, discernment, and insubstantiality, is often called a *mindstream*. According to the *sutra* or public, exoteric level of the Buddhist teaching, we can say that this (mindstream) is the soul.

According to the secret or esoteric teachings associated with the tantric approach of Tibetan Buddhism, the mind has three substrates each increasing in subtlety: *gross*, *subtle*, and *extremely subtle*. The *gross* level of mind relates to the gross layer of wind, circulating course sensory information within the subtle nervous system, and acting metaphorically as a horse (wind) that carries a rider (consciousness). Everyday thoughts, emotions, perceptions, and memories are associated with this level of mind, all of which break down during the death process, and as such are related more with mental functioning and less with the soul. The next layer is called the *subtle mind*, which is the awareness that perceives and cognizes objects at a subtler level of awareness, including during sleep and dream, where images and sounds are holographic compared to their coarse counterparts in the actual world perceived by waking consciousness. Again, this subtle awareness is contaminated with distorting associations and imprints, and dissolves during death. Until this point, there is a duality and a binary transaction between mind and body, information or sensory data, and wind or energy, the causal interrelationship of which accounts for illness and health.

The final level is the *extremely subtle mind*, also known as the *indestructible drop*. Difficult to access without advanced mental training, the indestructible drop represents the foundational substrate of the other two levels of the continuity of mind. It remains obscured by the gross and subtle fluctuations of awareness and energetic winds, which act as distractions (much like a hall of mirrors) and react to the appearances of phenomena, external and internal, as if they possess substantial reality. Moreover, through the natural death process or simulated death visualization in a tantric practice, the gross and subtle fluctuations are subdued, and access to the highly subtle mind becomes possible, even if briefly.

The extremely subtle mind resides in the central channel of the subtle nervous system within the heart chakra and requires specialized conscious manipulation of the subtle winds, purifying them and drawing them in, to gain access to it. It is considered indestructible because it remains undefiled by karmic imprints, like the unaltered sky containing all weather patterns. It perfectly follows the definition of the conservation of energy in the first law of thermal dynamics. It is neither created nor destroyed and can only be transformed from one moment to another. The indestructible drop, along with the stream of subtle, impersonal, karmic imprints, continues after death between lives and is what merges with sperm and egg to animate and influence the next rebirth. The indestructible drop doesn't achieve enlightenment, it is enlightened potential, Buddha nature, awaiting recognition.

At this level of subtle mind, the energetic wind is the "body" housing karmic imprints and qualities; mind and body are inseparable. Tantric Buddhist practice—specifically the subtle-body alchemy preserved in the Tibetan tradtion—resolves any dualistic notion of separation between mind and body, information and energy, which occurs at the grosser levels. The extremely subtle mind doesn't "ride" energy—it *is* energy. Subtle mind and subtle body are one. Through tantric visualization practice and the manipulation of the subtle winds, one trains to subdue the fluctuations caused by delusion and karma, generate tremendous psychic heat (tummo) experienced as blissful flow states, gain momentary access to the indestructible drop, variously known as the clear-light (prabhasvarata in Sanskrit), truth body (dhamrmakaya), Buddha nature (tathagatagharbha), and pure consciousness (rigpa in Tibetan), and achieve profound wisdom or gnosis capable of liberation. We would consider this process the tantric method of directly experiencing the soul's innate divinity, perhaps an Indic corollary of the Greek apotheosis, merging with the deity. While there are three levels of mind, in tantra we might equate soul only with the extremely subtle mind that transmigrates over lifespans, containing karmic imprints that can be resolved and the seed of enlightenment, Buddha nature, serving as the ground of being.

CARL JUNG AND THE SOUL

From this overview of characteristics of the soul, we make a historical leap forward from antiquity to the Dark Ages and from there into the Renaissance and Enlightenment, when our connection with religion as a basis for the soul loses its mooring and the value placed on the inner exploration is replaced by the outer exploration of materialism. For roughly 300 years post Enlightenment, as the pendulum swings from religion to science, the soul is disparaged as superstition, and only a faint memory of it remains in our collective consciousness.

A few contemporary seekers like William James and Sigmund Freud tended those embers long enough for them to rekindle. These early psychologists defied the trend at the advent of modern Western psychology to reduce soul to mind (thoughts and emotions) and then mind to the brain (chemistry and electric activity). Occupying his own niche was psychoanalyst Carl Jung, who broke with Freud, who valued the unconscious, but was invested in establishing psychoanalysis within the more mainstream scientific reductionist paradigm. Jung's departure was motivated by his interest in exploring more esoteric dimensions of the mind beyond the surface aspects of mental function, thoughts, emotions, and behaviors, and even beyond the personal unconscious with its hidden fantasies, wishes, drives, and impulses. Jung's significant contribution to the field and to this book comes from his willingness to venture into the further reaches of the unconscious beyond which any modern exploration had gone, transcending the event horizon of the personal, and discovering the realm of the collective unconscious and its archetypes, including the transpersonal Self.

What did Jung say about the soul? According to a comprehensive literature review of his collected works, Jung posited dozens of definitions of soul across his vast career, making it difficult to identify a single working definition. For example, he does state the soul has a "highly numinous character," is a "kind of life force" or "healing force," is "timeless" and "eternal," and in agreement with Greek and Buddhist notions, suggests the soul's "discriminative function separates opposites of every kind, and especially those of the moral order personified in Christ and Devil."[19] As elusive as it might be, Jung knew a connection with our soul was essential to human flourishing, and disconnection from it underlined many of the psychological symptoms pervasive in modern culture.

Jung warns us that our denigration of the soul has left us "alone and you are confronted with all the demons of hell," showing up as "anxiety neurosis, nocturnal fears, compulsions," and all of this because our souls have "become lonely;" they have no spiritual support system. Jung regarded religions as "the great healing systems for the ills of the soul," but he recognized that we are living in a time when the dogmas of many religions are questioned, to the point that they have lost their "healing power." This situation has left people "prey to their weakness," and when they seek out therapists, they get labeled "neurotic."[21]

Jung remains largely a fringe anomaly in modern psychology, the mainstream development of psychological theories after him grew mainly in the direction of scientific reductionism. From psychoanalysis, we see the birth of behaviorism, which led to cognitive science resulting in cognitive neuroscience. Today radical materialism and scientism essentially dismiss the construct of the soul. While they use the term "mind," it is still equated largely with cognition, emotion, and volition, and reduced to an epiphenomenon of the brain because science cannot objectively study it mechanistically or quantitatively. Although Dan Siegel and Richard Davidson offer functional constructs, today terms like "awareness" and "consciousness" still have no coherent agreed-upon definition; the study of consciousness it seems cannot compete with pharmacology and funding for neuroscientific research. [22]

SOUL-PLASTICITY

What could be more profound, more worthwhile of our precious human life than to be reacquainted with our most essential nature—the soul? To cut through the centuries of cultural denial and reexperience its numinous nature, allowing it to reanimate us, while reenchanting the world? What the ancients knew is that "soul" is an immaterial phenomenon that transmigrates after the death of the physical body. It has a vitalizing or animating function, without which physical life cannot exist. The soul is capable of gnosis and liberation; death can be conquered, and life itself—though rife with challenge—made exceedingly meaningful.

The soul is a subtle substrate of mind, operating in relation to the body, thoughts, emotions, and behaviors. The soul remembers, contains subtle imprints or memories—we can call it information—accumulated based on experience and driven toward familiarity with virtue and vice. These impacts form compulsive actions and network associations, color, and predetermine perception, laying deep grooves of learnings—I call them "soul contracts," Jung calls "complexes," and the Tibetans call "karmic tendencies,"—that bind us, to repeated habits, personality dispositions, subjective experiences, and even specific relationships and environments. Come what may, the soul always remains, in its nature, totally open, luminous, indestructible, and indescribable, and therefore the information or karmic accumulation it maintains is always relative—revisable and ever-changing. According to Buddhism, this quality of essential openness, or emptiness (*shunyata*), is precisely the condition that makes the soul interdependent, relational, malleable, transmutable, and transformable based on learning and insight. Emptiness is our buddha nature, the soul's innate potential to change and evolve necessarily includes the seed of enlightenment.

I coined the term "soul-plasticity" to capture the essence of this transformational quality and process, drawing on the term neuroplasticity from cognitive science, which represents the brain's innate capacity to learn, change and grow based on experience. By extension I also created terms like "soul-sculpting" a psychological corollary to body-building, and the inner "soulscape" in contrast the outer landscape. Once you establish the soul's existence, understanding its empty, luminous nature, you then become familiar with who you really are, how you should live and relate, and what your purpose in life is. To answer these perennial questions is to blissfully imbibe the elixir.

So, are you ready to reclaim the soul we have lost?

4
Solve et Coagula
Dying to be Reborn

Throughout this book I use a single Latin phrase drawn from the Emerald Tablet of Hermes Trismegistus, itself part of the broader *Corpus Hermiticum* of Western alchemy, as a loom or framework to unify distinct threads of knowledge to produce a tapestry for the process of spiritual transformation. The phrase is *solve et coagula*. There is perhaps no more profound way to distill and describe the art of the mystical experience, the pilgrimage of reclaiming the soul, found cross-culturally than these three words. You might recognize the Latin word *solve* as a cognate to the English term dissolve, *et* means and, and *coagula* as a cognate of coagulate—a process of disintegration and reintegration. In literature, this process is represented by the analysis and synthesis of ideas, critically breaking down principles, assumptions, and premises to extract their core value, then integrating them to propose a new understanding. On an exoteric level, the slogan typifies the thrust of the mystical experience, from Eastern versions like Tibetan tantra and Taoist alchemy to Western versions like hermeticism and magick rooted in the Sumerian, Egyptian, Greek, and Jewish mystery cults. The entire body of esoteric world literature and oral traditions includes this method of dissolution of the rigid ego, rediscovering the soul, and reconfiguring a new life in the world.

Considering our slogan in context from the Emerald Tablet, notice (in the quote below) how it opens with as above, so below, a reference to the dual mirror between the macrocosm of the universe and microcosm of the individual mind and body. But later the lines read "Separate the earth from the fire, the subtle from the gross, gently and with great skill. It ascends from earth to heaven, and again it descends to earth, and receives the power of the superiors and of the inferiors."[1] Here we have the two movements, first the dissolution or death, where the subtle soul is extracted from coarse ego and corporality of the body, and the second movement, a reconfiguration and rebirth of the soul from heaven to earth with a new power or embodied wisdom. From this verse is born the phrase *solve et coagula*.

> That which is below is like that which is above, and that which is above is like that which is below, to accomplish the wonders of the one thing. And as all things are made from one, by the meditation of one, so all things are born from this one thing by adaptation. The father of it is the sun, the mother the moon, the wind carries it in its belly, its nurse is the earth. It is the father of every complete work in the world. Its power is perfect, if it is turned into earth.[2]

While there is a distinction between physical alchemy and its psycho-spiritual counterpart, both employ the same metaphor of breaking down and being remade. Physical alchemy accomplishes this by melting down metals like sulfur and mercury under tremendous pressure and heat, reconfiguring them, and reconstituting them, to make a purer substance like gold. More commonly in botanical alchemy, plants are similarly distilled through a process incorporating the four elements. First, a solid (earth) is added to the solution (water), then boiled under high heat (fire), then their vapor (air) is cooled and collected as a solid again, this time as a highly potent extract or essence. In psycho-spiritual alchemy, the same process is employed, distilling, refining, and reconstituting energies of body and mind through meditative rituals and contemplative insights. The seventeenth-century Swiss alchemist Paracelsus called the process of physical alchemy *spagyric*, claiming that medicines could be improved by separating them into primal elements and recombining them, and that even poisons could be transformed into medicines. This was more than a powerful metaphor. The process of psycho-spiritual alchemy, which is the corollary to spagyria, is called spiritual resurrection and is well articulated by modern scholar Freddy Silva.[3]

METHOD OF UNIVERSAL METAMORPHOSIS

Our phrase *solve et coagula* is the key metaphor underlying every heroic journey and is captured succinctly in the subtitle of Tolkien's classic *The Hobbit*, otherwise known as *"There and Back Again."* As we know, the origin of our phrase has its roots in Hermeticism, the purported system of teaching of Hermis Trismegistus, the so-called "thrice great," and preserved in a corpus of text collectively known as the *Corpus Hermiticum*, Trismegistus is a cultural amalgam of the Egyptian God Thoth and the Greek god Hermes. Thoth was the scribe of the gods in Egyptian cosmology, the wisdom keeper of arts, science, astrology, and magic. Thoth is considered the judge of the dead and the revealer of the so-called Egyptian *Book of the Dead*.

Similarly, Hermes was the messenger of the gods, an intermediary between worlds, a revealer of higher states of consciousness, and the archetype of eloquence or communication. With his winged sandals, Hermes was employed to aid in literal and spiritual travel and was, therefore, the central deity or psychopomp guiding souls on their journey into the afterlife.

Hermes Trismegistus is considered the source of the Hermetica (a broader collection of texts that contains the *Corpus Hermeticum*) roughly dating to the third century BCE with some of the Greek and Egyptian texts dating as far back as the fifth century. The Hermetica is broken into two areas, technical and spiritual, the former involving astrology, medicine, alchemy, and magic, and the latter covering philosophy, cosmology, and morality. According to occultist John Michael Greer, the cultural exchange between East and West in general, and between Greece, India, and China along the Silk Road in particular, means there were several centuries of cross-pollination of ideas, including mystical teachings from disparate sources.[4] For this reason, we see a method of universal metamorphosis underlying most cultures and no way to account for a single original text or source tradition that can claim ownership of *solve et coagula*. We can speculate that as long as there have been cults of secret oral transmission offering direct and personal access to the numinous, from the Jewish Kabbalah and Taoist Secrets of the Golden Flower to Vajrayogin tantra and the Philosopher's Stone, there has been the practice of *solve et coagula*.

Consequently, all four of the maps and methods we will incorporate in this book follow this exact metaphoric process—the yuga cycle goes through a descending phase of 12,000 years into spiritual darkness, a transition, and an ascending phase of 12,000 years toward a golden age of spiritual awakening. This 24,000-year period is the longest pilgrimage of *solve et coagula*. Along the way, we see the archetypal energies of each individual zodiacal age in the precession of the equinox contribute to the fragmentation or disenchantment and reunification or revitalization of the collective unconsciousness. This is within the Great Year; the twelve increments each go through this mythic process, being born out of the death of the preceding zodiacal age, arising to a zenith, then following a descent into cultural collapse, from which the next aion is born in approximately 2150-year increments.

Though it's not explicitly one of our four models, the same motif of *solve et coagula* can be identified in the contemplative psychotherapy for healing trauma. We start with the left brain and waking consciousness in a period of certainty, metaphoric calcification, and narrow ego identification. With the introduction of sound, prayer, meditation, breath-work, or psychedelics, one transitions to the dream state of consciousness, quieting the left brain, activating more of the right brain, "dissolving" limited ego-identification and giving access to the chaotic swarm of the right brain with its imagination, emotions, memories and dreams. On this journey, one descends past the cortical regions and its defenses into the nether regions of the limbic system and the brainstem to access and reveal root trauma. Then we return from the shadow world of disintegration through dream state to waking state—where higher cortical functions and the left mode's linguistic capacity come back online to process emotions, create new expanded narratives and identifications, culminating in the heroic period of hemispheric integration or rebirth of a new mythopoetic sense of self. *As above, so below.* As the cosmos turns in a cycle from descent into darkness and ascent towards light in macro revolutions of contraction and expansion, so does the psyche undergo by fate of circumstance or voluntary effort, micro cycles of fragmentation and darkness, integration and rebirth.

THE LOOM:
WEAVING ESOTERIC THREADS

To represent the vast scope of material I synthesize in this book I use a chart I named simply "The Loom," a literal translation for the Sanskrit word tantra. On this loom I weave together the discrete threads of Campbell, Jung, Tibetan Alchemy, and Cosmology into the Elixir tapestry. One slogan, *solve et coagula*, unites all these esoteric traditions, just as Tolkien wrote "one ring to rule them all," in his epic the *Lord of the Rings*.[5] I conceive each system as a pilgrimage, comprised of twelve stages, like Jesus's apostles, subdivide into three phases, a holy trinity, demarcated above and below by a dichotomy or duality, heaven and earth, and completing its cycle with a grand culmination, a reset, only to begin again. The Loom allows you to cross-reference between systems, with surprising correlations. I also provide an individual, cyclic diagram for each system, containing all their distinctive features in illustrative form, for ease of learning and memorization.

The Solve et Coagula Loom: Weaving a tapestry of esoteric threads.

SYSTEM	Joseph Campbell	Carl Jung	Tibetan Alchemy	Cosmology
PILGRIMAGE	Monomyth	Individuation	Rebirth	Great Year
CULMINATION	Return with Elixir	Self	Awakening	Precession of the Equinoxes
DICHOTOMY	Ordinary World Special World	Conscious Unconscious	Relative Reality Ultimate Reality	Descending Ascending
HOLY TRINITY	I. Separation	I. Ego	I. Death	I. Silver Age
	1. Ordinary World	1. Persona	1. Moonlight	1. Cancer
	2. Call to Adventure	2. Ego	2. Twilight	2. Gemini
	3. Refusal of Call	3. Defenses	3. Midnight	3. Capricorn
	4. Meeting the Mentor	4. Personal unconscious	4. Clear-light	4. Sagittarius
	II. Initiation	II. Shadow	II. Bardo	II. Bronze & Iron Ages
	5. Crossing threshold	5. Collective unconscious	5. Admire	5. Taurus
	6. Test, Allies, Enemies	6. Archetypes	6. Offer	6. Aries
	7. Innermost Cave	7. Shadow	7. Disclose	7. Pisces
	8. Ordeal	8. Complexes	8. Rejoice	8. Aquarius
	III. Return	III. Self	III. Rebirth	III. Golden Age
	9. Reward	9. Coniunctio	9. Request blessing	9. Virgo
	10. Road Back	10. Unus mundus	10. Request presence	10. Leo
	11. Resurrection	11. Individuation	11. Dedication	11. Scorpio
	12. Return with Elixir	12. Self	12. Rebirth	12. Libra

Fig. 4.1. The *Solve et Coagula* Loom

THE PILGRIMAGE OF THE COSMOS:
THE GREAT YEAR

The Great Year has been observed by astronomers and used by astrologers across cultures for millennia, but its exact origin is debated. Researchers Graham Hancock, Robert Bauval, John Anthony West, and others contend that sacred knowledge, including the *precession of the equinoxes*, is part of a legacy of an ancient civilization predating any of those known in the mainstream accepted historical record, which was likely wiped out during the last ice age around 11,500 years ago.[6]

These authors hypothesize that our earliest known civilizations of the fertile crescent in Mesopotamia are, in fact, inheritors of this sacred knowledge from an older prediluvian civilization lost in time. This view is considered speculative and unfounded by mainstream archeologists despite the authors pointing out that two sites were recently discovered; the Nabta Playa, or so-called Stonehenge of Africa, was uncovered in the 1960s and is considered the oldest astronomical observatory on the planet, dating back 7,000–10,000 years or more. The second, more recent find is Gobekli Tepe in southern Turkey, which was uncovered and further excavated in 1995. It is a complex of monolithic stone structures dating to the Neolithic period between 9,500–8,000 BCE, older than our current record of civilization around 4,000 BCE. It is now considered one of the earliest examples of human-made monumental architecture, most likely a temple, as evidenced by animal remains used in rituals and extensive carvings of animals and therianthropes on huge monolithic pillars. Until his death in 2014, lead archeologist at the site was Klaus Schmidt, who believed the finding of Gobekli Tepe would rewrite history, specifically the long-held notion that hunter-gatherers transitioned to settled agriculture, creating cities based on surplus. Reversing this long-held belief, Schmidt said, "first came the temple, then the city."[7]

While the evidence at Gobekli Tepe extends further back than the current historical timeline on the rise of human civilization, there is, as of yet, no conclusive evidence to suggest astronomical or astrological knowledge from the site, although efforts to determine this are underway.[8] Furthermore, the uncovering of Gobekli Tepe does not prove Hancock and colleagues's hypothesis of a lost civilization. Still, it does remind us to keep an open mind, particularly considering McGilchrist's claim that our culture's primarily left mode tendency toward certainty can be a common liability. The scientific method should be one of open curiosity, continuous testing, collaboration, and flexibility to revise theories as new information becomes available, in contrast with scientific dogmatism, which like religious dogma, is closed off to novelties that challenge held convictions or threaten invested interests and power structures. One problem may be that our scientific paradigm is too reductionist and linear, whereas the ancients saw time, civilization, life, and the journey of the soul, as cyclic. Writes Walter Cruttenden, in *Lost Star of Myth and Time*:

> Written communication must precede any large engineered structures or populous civilizations. The problem with this widely accepted paradigm is that it is not consistent with the evolving interpretation of recently discovered ancient cultures and anomalous artifacts. In the last hundred years, major discoveries have been made in Mesopotamia, the Indus Valley, the Asian plains, South America, and many other regions that break the rules of the history theory and push back the time of advanced human development. Specifically, they show that ancient man was far more proficient and civilized nearly 5000 years ago than during the more recent Dark Ages just a thousand years ago. In Caral, an ancient complex on the west coast of Peru, we find six pyramids that are carbon dated to be 4700 years old, a date contemporaneous with Egyptian pyramids and rivaling the time of the first major structures found in the so-called "Cradle of Civilization" in Mesopotamia. However, Caral is an ocean away from the "cradle," and we find no evidence of any writing or weaponry, two of the so-called necessities of civilization.

At the same time, we find beautiful musical instruments, astronomically aligned structures, and evidence of commerce with distant lands. Clearly, such sites defy the standard historical paradigm. But what is stranger is that so many of these civilizations seemed to decline en mass.[9]

Whether or not there was a lost civilization before those in Mesopotamia, we know our ancestors were looking up at the stars and recording lunar phases in cave paintings, on mammoth tusks, and animal bones deep into Paleolithic times between 30–10,000 BCE. Their reasons were likely pragmatic rather than metaphysical at first; as nomads, they were keen observers of the seasons, animal migrations, and temperature changes to ensure survival. The earliest records written in cuneiform on clay tablets noting celestial movements of planets and stars are attributed to the Sumerians (2,100 BCE); their observations in the first settled communities helped plan agriculture and organize religious festivals. The Sumerians saw Sun and Moon as gods and combined sophisticated astronomy and mathematics with mythology to perform divinations and interpret omens. "By about 750 BCE, the Mesopotamians were master mathematicians and astronomers. They had mapped the entire sky, developed an 18-sign zodiac, and could accurately calculate the planet's future positions and eclipses. They had divided the ecliptic into 360° and attributed sixty minutes to each degree and sixty seconds to every minute of a degree."[10]

During the Greek and Hellenistic periods, we see rapid developments in astrology, that we rely on to this day. In his classic "Works and Days," Greek poet Hesiod (750 BCE) references auspicious celestial times for the kingdom and for individuals to start or complete projects.[11] Pythagoras (570–495 BCE) is perhaps the first to articulate the notion of the relationship between cosmos and psyche and how the macrocosm is reflected in the microcosm.[12] As the relationship between planets, the four elements, and the four humors is studied in unison, we see the advent of medical astrology for individual's diagnosis and

prognosis of diseases. Hippocrates (460–370 BCE) is credited with saying, "A physician who has no knowledge of astrology has no right to call
himself a physician." Plato (428–348 BCE) is credited with the term
Platonic Year, hypothesizing that the Sun, Moon, and planets, through
their orbiting cycles, would arrive at a set point in a complete revolution
lasting 36,000 years, though his calculations were off. By the second
century BCE, Hipparchus is attributed with the discovery of the *precession of the equinoxes*, which gives the more exact timing we know and
accept today, as it was used broadly for the first time to determine birth
charts for individuals and comes to underpin astrology until modern
day.

The conquests of Alexander the Great and the establishment of
trade routes for exchanging goods and knowledge contributed to fertile
East-West cross-pollination of ideas, including those on astrology and
astronomy, between Greece, Persia, Mesopotamia, India, and China.
During this time the library of Alexandria in Egypt becomes a center
for knowledge, attracting many from around the known world, availing
themselves of a trove of some 400,000 parchment scrolls from Assyria,
Greece, Persia, Egypt, India, and many other nations. Perhaps the most
famous Greek astronomer was Claudius Ptolemy (100–170 CE). His
writing includes his masterwork *Almagest*, containing a star catalog
of forty-eight constellations observed and collated over an 800-year
period, which served as a reference guide or almanac for astronomers of
antiquity from the known world to compute the positions of the Sun,
Moon, and planets, the rising and setting of the stars, and eclipses of
the Sun and Moon.

We see tremendous refinement under the Greeks using the patterns
of the stars to govern the empire and lateral distribution to predict and
navigate the individual lives of the common people. By the time the
Roman civilization came into prominence, astrology was a mainstay in
society, particularly as a horoscope; parents used it to understand the
destiny of children and emperors to gain an advantage over potential
rivals by knowing their individual character flaws. When the Goths

sacked Rome in 410 CE, astrology had begun a temporary period of decline in Europe, but during the Dark Ages, the Arab world continued to preserve and refine astrology. We see astrology come in and out of prominence over the centuries that follow, returning to vogue during the Medieval and Renaissance period along with alchemy and magick, but then falling out of favor again in the sixteenth century due to its heavily deterministic thrust being at odds with the Christian belief in a single god governing people's fate. By the time the Age of Enlightenment and Scientific Revolution emerged, astrology had lost favor as attention diverted—over a long period of time—our interest in cosmology replaced by mechanistic manipulation of matter, our intuitive sense of the cyclic eternal return replaced by rational, linear evolution. Later, with Blavatsky, Jung, and others, astrology would again find its way into cultural awareness through psychoanalysis and interest in the occult, only to become reduced a century later to tabloid horoscopes. Like cosmic tides ebbing and flowing along with the bidirectional emphasis on brain hemispheres, our attention and use of the symbolic nature of astrology have vacillated over history.

COSMOS AND PSYCHE: HOW DO THEY RELATE?

How does the large cycle of Great Year above effect the individual below? How should we understand the relationship between cosmos and psyche? How do we account for the impact of the signature of each zodiacal age on human culture as it evolves over time? *As above, so below.* Walter Cruttenden and Rick Tarnas offer two distinct perspectives, mirroring McGilchrist's left-right brain dichotomy.

Walter Cruttenden, author of *Lost Star of Myth and Time* and producer of the film *The Great Year*, is the Director of the Binary Research Institute in California. His explanation of the impact of the cosmos on the psyche during the Yuga Cycle, Vedic corollary to the Great Year (remember a "yuga,"—as mentioned before—consists of an infinite cycle of 12,000 years of contraction, followed by 12,000 years of expansion) aligns more with the scientific paradigm, proposing an electromagnetic and biochemical causality, with ultra-subtle emissions from the cosmos that has effects on human brain and perception. Our sun and a second hidden or lost star are in a so-called binary system, gravitationally bound to each other and orbiting a common center of mass. From opposite directions as the stars grow closer towards the center every 12,000 years human consciousness expands and reaches a Golden Age of civilizational harmony, and as they move apart every 12,000 years consciousness contracts reaching a Dark Age of moral deprivation and chaos, thus characterizing the seasons of the Great Year. [13]

Cosmologist Rick Tarnas, the author of *Cosmos and Psyche*, offers a different explanation, which sounds more quantum and Jungian than Newtonian. The two paradigms are, of course, not mutually exclusive. Tarnas proposes that astrology is not a fatalistic or deterministic science; we are not passive recipients of energy from above. Instead, for each of us there is an interdependence between archetypal influences resulting from planetary alignments at a specific time that constellate as our unique challenges and potentials for growth. The personal birth chart or horoscope of everyone represents their unique soulscape including life lessons, strength and weakness, and archetypal predisposition based on the stars on the horizon at the moment of their birth and factor into a complex equation about the cosmic context. We are born with an inner star map, an imprint of a set of specific constellations unique to the heavens at the time of our birth that will shape how we might respond to future planetary activities during our lifetime. This is not fixed in stone; the mutual influence is neither deterministic nor fatalistic but more a set of distinctive potentialities found on a vast horizon of possibilities that we can engage with as a conscious choice. This accounts for the variation of different individual experiences during the same celestial transitions and alignments during the Great Ages and their turnings. No one is impacted similarly because of our unique psychological constitutions. Accordingly, to get the most out of an astrological forecast, one needs to correlate the planetary alignments (above) with one's personal horoscope (below) creating a mythopoetic story to facilitate sense making.[14] While I will briefly describe the map above, I encourage you to seek counsel from a qualified astrologer for your personal chart.

ANIMA MUNDI

Quoting the Greek astronomer Platinus, Tarnas wrote, "The stars are like letters which inscribe themselves at every moment in the sky. . . . Everything in the world is full of signs. All events are coordinated. All things depend on each other; as has been said, everything breathes together."[15]

I resonate with Tarnas's metaphor of the universe as an extension of our living body, that we are part of a greater matrix of interconnectivity called *unus mundus,* or what Jung called the *anima mundi* or "world soul." As our consciousness expands, we disidentify from narrow or limited ego-boundaries, we experience others as an extension of ourselves, including the biosphere and cosmos. Ancient wisdom cultures have long taught, we are one in the many and the many in the one. This irritates classically trained scientists to no end because it starts to sound religious, superstitious, and New Age, has no quantitative basis, just as the existence of God can never be proven. Tarnas's book received tremendous praise and criticism; I suspect this rift represents the brain hemisphere readers are favoring. We are looking at a paradigm shift from Newton to quantum, and through quantum, a possible reunion with spiritual to create a new but old synthesis, reuniting both hemispheres, empiricism with mysticism, as we last saw in the Renaissance.

Can science reclaim spirit? Tarnas's metaphor essentially sees the cosmos as God or divine intelligence without using those words, and certainly not in a way that denies our humanity, agency, and choice in the interplay with cosmic forces. We are not passive actors or puppets, likewise the cosmos is not lifeless. So human beings participate with the cosmos just as relatives with distinct expressions do within a family system. We are not separate from cosmos, we are its partner, in a mirror-like dance. As science breaks through the event horizon of materialism, our reclaimed divinity will correspond to the re-enchantment of the universe.

Now that we've imagined expanding our horizons—seeing ourselves as part of a greater, living cosmos, reanimating each aspect from the individual to the biosphere to the planets, we can see synchronistic and symbiotic relationships requiring no direct, causal influence. Jung said, "astrology is one of the intuitive methods like the I Ching, geomantic, and other divinatory procedures. It is based upon the synchronicity principle, meaningful coincidence. . . . Astrology is a naively

Fig. 4.2. Great Year: The Pilgrimage of the Cosmos

projected psychology in which man's different attitudes and tempera-
ments are represented as gods and identified with planets and zodiacal
constellations."[16]

Jung noted the therapeutic value of astrology, just as the Greeks
understood the healing potential of mythology and propitiations to the
gods. We are not unitary beings, but are comprised of multiple inner
parts, sometimes even contradicting one another. Latent parts may need
activation; hidden parts, discovery; rejected parts, acceptance; overused
parts, support. Astrology, mythology, and the pantheon of gods represent skillful externalizations of these distinctive archetypal energies and
dynamics buried within us. Venus, love, Mars, aggression. As we exter-
nalize our inner worlds, our complexes and endowments alike become
more readily recognized for us to work with. Whether we look at an
astrological chart for a forecast, interpret a dream, relate to a myth, or
beseech a deity, we are consciously participating in a holistic story, sensemaking our own soul's projected fears and yearnings, conflicts, and
genius that would otherwise remain obscure. As Dan Seigel encourages, "name it, to tame it." For every part and dynamic within us, there
is active character and storyline without, beckoning recognition and
reintegration.[17]

Now that we have covered the Ground, the nature of our soul and
the soul of the world in their eternal return, let's proceed to the Path
and how we can reclaim what has been lost.

PART II

Path

Path is the Alchemical Process of Transmutation

Just as tantric visualization draws downwards psychic energy contaminated by egocentric greed and aggression into the sacred crucible fire at the base of the spine, transforming it into great bliss, and reverses its pilgrimage upwards through the central channel entering the womb-like heart chakra, where solar and lunar energies merge like sperm and ovum with pure consciousness to incubate a nascent Buddha embryo, so too does the hero's path call us to depart the naive safety and innocence of the ordinary world, descend into the dark night labyrinth of the foreboding shadow, wherein chaos subsumes order, the fire of regret forges redemption, the king of reason no longer reigns but concedes to the underworld queen of intuition's rule, where each maze misstep and impasse, each trauma and trial, necessarily summons forth dormant courage and compassion, elusive clarity and conviction, just as facing a terrifying dragon earns us a long sought after but buried treasure.

5
Pilgrimage
There and Back Again

THE PILGRIMAGE OF PURPOSE:
JOSEPH CAMPBELL'S MONOMYTH

Campbell (1904–1987) was an American author and lecturer on comparative mythology. He was raised Roman Catholic, but influenced by his early exposure to Native American traditions and the universality of themes among disparate religious and mythological traditions. After graduating from Columbia University, where he studied English and medieval literature, Campbell took up a two-year fellowship to learn French and Sanskrit in Paris and Munich and discovered the psychologies of Freud and Jung. This allowed him to apply the notions of universal archetypes and the collective unconsciousness to how mythic themes could be reproduced non-historically, a-culturally, and non-literally. He saw how myths were encoded with symbols that repeated themselves, despite their cultural trappings and diverse representations.

Perhaps the most significant breakthrough in Campbell's life came during the Great Depression; a biography reflecting *solve et coagula*. Due to the stock market crash and few employment opportunities, Campbell left Columbia University and spent the next five years in an alchemical crucible of relative isolation in a hermitage in upstate New

York. He lived like a monk and read voraciously, devouring myths and religious teachings from diverse sources.

For Campbell it was a period of incubation and fermentation of ideas, perhaps where his synthesis of his so-called monomyth was conceived. Later, he took a teaching position at Sarah Lawrence College, where he remained for the duration of his academic career, becoming popular on the American public teaching circuit during the 1970s and 80s. Despite publishing several books—his most successful being *The Hero with a Thousand Faces* (1949)—what made Campbell a household name came shortly after his death: the release of a six-part television interview hosted by Bill Moyers called *The Power of Myth*.

I watched the entire series as a high school senior in 1994 and was riveted by Campbell's command of global mythic literature and how he pulled themes from myriad sources, weaving them extemporaneously into a single tapestry. Even more, I was drawn to his infectious enthusiasm, child-like wonder, and eloquence. He spoke in poetic terms, his voice animated like the storytellers of old, as if around a tribal fire, before electricity, cinema, and internet. He was a living embodiment of world myth, and stories poured from him spontaneously and in ways that dazzled and delighted my imagination.

What Campbell's monomyth represents is a hero's rite of passage. He defined a hero as "someone who has given his or her life to something bigger than oneself."[1] A rite-of-passage is a special ceremony, ritual, or activity, used by traditional cultures for millennia to help individuals and small groups mobilize through developmental arrests and transition to a new phase of life. Each rite is designed to help ripen or mature an individual, expose and integrate their limitations, challenge them to discover new strengths and innate qualities, embolden them to develop new skills, attitudes, and outlooks, prepare them to successfully navigate the next phase of their life, and make a positive contribution to their community and planet.

On the Hero's Journey, we face our limitations and discover unknown strengths that will inevitably benefit society. The journey is primarily a personal grail quest involving two binary trajectories—succinctly captured as the second or alternative title to *The Hobbit* by author J.R.R. Tolkien rendered as *"There and Back Again"*[2]—which are consistent with the astrological descent of 12,000 years and ascent of 12,000 years forming the complete cycle or orbit of the Great Year. Within the binary movements—out (to the wasteland) and back (home)—or descent (into hell or shadow) and ascent (to heaven or Self)—there are three acts: *separation, initiation, and return.* Leaving one's familiar home, initiation into a sacred worldview, and experiencing an unimaginable ordeal form the descent arc and are equated with the dissolution aspect from our meta-framework of *solve et coagula.* Through the ordeal, inner resources are discovered—the elixir—and are integrated and shared, forming the second arc of the return home. The aesthetic of the homeward-bound leg of the journey is more communal, placing the transformation of the hero and the boon they've discovered into a transpersonal context of improving the society or world. I call Campbell's monomyth the *pilgrimage of purpose* because every individual must discover who they are and what they're meant to do or offer in life. It's rarely discovered or integrated without these efforts and stages.

THE CARTOGRAPHY OF MYTH

At the outset, we must understand why a mythological perspective is important or even relevant.

First, we should understand four types of myth:

1. *Rational* myths are stories that help us grasp natural events and unseen forces, like creation myths that represent the power of the gods to create and maintain our universe and structure order from chaos.
2. *Functional* myths teach moral codes to influence pro-social behavior and communal harmony. They're pattern-maintaining

in that they structure our thinking, speech, actions, and interactions.

3. *Structural* myths reflect the dual nature of the human psyche by depicting complexity—both darkness and genius—inherent within us, and how to work with contradictions—masculine and feminine, ego and Self—of our psyche.

4. *Psychological* myths present archetypes such as the mother, the warrior, the sage, and the trickster (to name a few), each representing projected aspects of the psyche to identify, resolve, and integrate.

In addition to the four types of myth, Campbell described four functions:

1. *Metaphysical myths* connect humans to the transcendent mystery of life, and engender a sense of awe and wonder of the unknown.

2. *Cosmological myths* connect humans to the hidden dimensions and rhythms of the universe, helping to create order out of chaos, and locating our place within it.

3. *Sociological myths* connect humans with their natural and social web of interdependence, impart moral and ethical codes of conduct, and engender prosocial capacities for harmony and justice.

4. *Pedagogical myths* connect humans to their purpose in life, helping to transform unavoidable hardship and create meaning.[3]

Myths are stories that prepare us to live and die well, meaningfully, and in harmony within ourselves and with others, including the environment and cosmos. Without a mythopoetic perspective, we stay mired in the rational, bound to narrow possibilities interpreted solely through the left brain of disembodied rationality. Instead, the world is a data field for collection, computation, and execution, and life is reduced to mechanics. As part of my introduction in chapter one I illustrated the symptoms of

our modern culture that result from our loss of myth and our disconnection from the unseen world of spirit. When reason is reunited with
intuition, and analytics with mythopoetics, our worldview and the horizon of possibilities expands beyond the immediate material reality to a
quantum universe that includes magic and meaning. The mythopoetic
dimension is a perfect complement to our rational and linear thinking.
The world of the intuitive, emotional, and metaphysical nuances brings
a more soulful, vibrant complement to the technical and functional
domain of reason.

In fact, we are making and living by (tragic) myths all the time,
often unknowingly. Mythic stories orient our worldview, how we filter and interpret data, how things move or compel us, and how we
respond or react. Maybe you're someone who can't remember a myth
from Greece or India, but that doesn't mean you're not living mythologically. There is the climate change-denying mythos, and its counter
climate-apocalypse mythos. There are Evangelical and Zionist hege-
monic myths. There is the myth promoted in the wellness space that
you can biohack your way to optimal, everlasting vitality. So be aware
of your myth and how it orients you, excludes others, defines good, evil,
and what to pursue. You may not know it as myth, but these stories
serve that function.

Since we jettisoned myth, astrology, and religion in favor of science and reason, we have rendered ourselves incapable of navigating the
complex and ever-changing landscape of life. Instead, the mythological perspective provides a time-tested lens that allows human beings to
see themselves from the broadest perspective, to not only analyze and
calculate, but to sense-make novelty, tolerate ambiguity, and navigate
complexity.

COMPONENTS OF THE MONOMYTH

Technically, Campbell's map comprises seventeen stages, but I've distilled them down to twelve:

1. *Ordinary World.* The hero is stuck in a mundane circumstance, safe, but not truly alive. Psychologically the ordinary world represents arrested development, being trapped in a child's idealization, or sleepwalking in a banal state of unconsciousness. This marks the persona, the narrow confines that trap and conceal the Self.

2. *Call to Adventure.* This is the initial impetus to change. Sometimes it comes as a quiet intuitive invitation to course correct one's life trajectory, but more often than not, "the call" is buried within an earth-shattering crisis, devastating news, an unexpected loss, or a monumental choice-point between the familiar and the unknown. It may not be obvious that one is being summoned for an evolutionary upgrade. It might be something unpleasant, a challenging situation or circumstance in which we find ourselves confronting a crisis of some kind in which we encounter shadow energy, either in ourselves or others, that makes it impossible to go on in the same way as before. Psychologically, this is the first time a message from the soul is received, the faint call of Self beckons us to remember who we are.

3. *Refusal of the Call.* The hero hesitates or resists. Fear of failure or loss of property, family, fame, or fortune, conceals the deeper fear of loss of identity and ego death. If it's not fear of failure, sometimes it's fear of success. The ego asserts its will over the Self.

4. *Meeting the Mentor.* The hero encounters remarkable figures and guides embodying the possibility of transformation and inspiring the hero's will to accept initiation. Psychologically, when the mentor within the student is ready, the teacher appears. The Self emerges in a form ego tolerates or admires.

5. *Crossing the Threshold.* The hero leaves the ordinary world of safety, familiarity, and identity and enters one of magic and wonder at the risk of uncertainty and vulnerability. Psychologically

the hero has left waking consciousness for dreamtime, the left brain of reason for the right brain of intuition, moving from the ego into the personal unconscious as defenses are loosened.

6. *Test, Allies, and Enemies.* A band of like-minded pilgrims joins hero and mentor for the adventure, hastening their development and supporting their mission. Simultaneously, adversaries appear, committed to challenging and disrupting their progress. Psychologically, we've entered the right brain of traumatic or implicit memories, self-defeating views and habits, and the outer enemies are merely projections of inner process designed to maintain arrested development.

7. *Approaching the Cave.* The hero travels on an outbound journey ever deeper into shadow, the dark forces at play in the world. Psychologically the hero grows closer to the center of the labyrinth where the Minotaur lurks; the hero's skills are tested and refined as they expose the insidious fear, shame, and traumatic narratives and identification that underpin their world. We've reached the shadow.

8. *Ordeal.* The hero must confront, slay, or tame the Minotaur, slay the dragon. They must face fear, that which the forces of denial and idealization in the ordinary world have served to protect him from at the expense of immobility and stagnation. The hero encounters the psychic tension of disintegration between over-identification or rejection of anima (feminine energy) or animus (masculine energy). We've encountered the archetypes of the collective unconscious.

9. *Reward.* In slaying (masculine) or taming (feminine) the dragon, the hero earns the treasure it protects. The energy of fear that was bound up in denial and self-protection has been released for transmutation, and the light of consciousness illuminates the darkness of unconsciousness. The boon of the wisdom of self-lessness, compassion, or confidence is earned. We've reclaimed the soul, integrated opposites.

10. *Road Home.* Having claimed victory the hero begins the journey home, undergoing a series of post-treasure trials that allow for the deepening of integration of the wisdom earned.

11. *Resurrection.* The post-treasure trials allow for insight to suffuse and transform the hero's way of being. The hero is fully reborn. The Self or soul, has become personal again, embodied in a more adaptable and capable ego.

12. *Return with Elixir.* The hero's new functional and relational ego can now find an authentic, personal way to transmit the elixir or boon in a meaningful way to family, community, and world. Self *and* others benefit.[4]

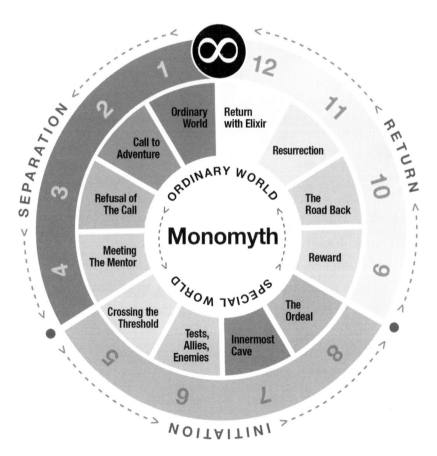

Fig. 5.1. Monomyth: The Pilgrimage of Purpose

These stages collapse into the potent trinity of *separation, initiation,* and *return*, containing four stages within each phase. A perfect clock with twelve-hour increments. Once we establish this trinity in the monomyth, we can use The Loom (see fig 4.1) to cross-reference maps over the same outlines by locating the trinity in Jung, Tibetan alchemy, and cosmology. We can also see this sacred numerology of the holy trinity in alchemy, Christianity, Hinduism, mathematics, geometry, and more.

The stages collapse further into a dichotomy or duality, the monomyth is divided into ordinary and special worlds, the former characterized by safety yet lifelessness, the later prospects of terror and treasure, mystery and magic, trial yet vitality. One must cross a threshold from ordinary to special world on the outbound adventure to receive the elixir but cannot remain there. Our encounter with the treasure—the soul—marks the return to our ordinary lives and world, transforming them.

CAMPBELL'S CRITICS

Every culture has a counterculture; for every innovation forward, there's pushback. As we enter the Aquarian age, we see the thrust of people's movements rightfully striving for greater recognition, equity, and inclusion. Within these, an influential feminist critique of the classic Hero's Journey has necessarily produced an alternative.[5] Mythologist Phil Cousineau who provides the afterword in this book, himself a direct student of Campbell, told me the Hero's Journey was primarily a male rite of passage motif and not always relevant to all genders or to all phases of life. This makes perfect sense; it places the significant contribution made by the monomyth in a particular context. Perhaps a masculine rite of passage or coming-of-age story involving a courageous confrontation and brutal slaying of a symbolic dragon is not as relevant to all people in all life phases. *At least not at first glance.*

What's more, there is a critique of the monomyth as too individualist; it lends too much credence to the accomplishment of the solitary seeker, and reinforces the assumption we must face life alone. This fails to inspire a collective vision that might address genuine social problems—racism, economic disparity, and xenophobia—of our culture's zeitgeist. For example, Campbell lived in a time when the United States prized its hyper-individuality and invested pride in its "pick yourself up by the bootstraps" mentality. Things have changed, and these critiques are valid. They appropriately illuminate limitations to Campbell's model.

However, I'm unsure these critiques fully recognize or value the universal application underlying the monomyth, requiring only a slight shift in emphasis to make it applicable to many demographics and contexts. There is a reason hero tales have endured. The solo journey involves asking for help from mentors and companions at the outset and is only successful when we return with a gift—the elixir—that improves the wellbeing of the collective. Who will come with you into the bardo when you die? Supporters may aid the death process, but we cross that threshold alone. There is no difference between actual, physical death, and mythological death. We face the dark night of the soul alone. Therefore, the journey is both individual and communal, its purpose is fulfilled when you make a personal breakthrough that impacts others. There is no need to throw the baby of the monomyth out with the bathwater of postmodern relativism.

Another vulnerability of Campbell's work is how his Hero's Journey motif has been co-opted by mass media, watered down into a trite trope, retold in nearly every animated film the Disney company has produced since Campbell's work was discovered, and consequently its relevance and potency as an archetypal narrative with mythological profundity has been overdone and diluted.[6] Just as my critique of the mindfulness revolution inspired me to coin the term McMindfulness, we are witnessing the deleterious effects of capitalism and marketing rendering the monomyth more of a McMonomyth.

If the story is retold often enough, on digital media, treated unceremoniously, and the participant is merely observing in a dissociative state, what impact beyond momentary entertainment can we expect?

The Hero's Journey is not meant to be fun or entertaining, although it can be. Its primary importance is to be lived, to be transformative, and by necessity it must bring its participant into an experience of their limits, fears, and vulnerability. It's not a passive experience.

When I say you must die before you claim the treasure and return with elixir, I mean a total death. It's not hyperbole, the journey assumes an utter shattering of self and world.

Everyone goes through ordeals, but not everyone is heroic. Heroes will always be rare, otherwise heroism would lose its meaning, no longer being something improbable and extraordinary.

The death Campbell talked about is losing everything and everyone—most significantly oneself. Every familiar structure that stabilizes and orients, every hope and dream that inspires, is obliterated. This is why they call it "the dark night of the soul." And it's not just dark for an hour or week. It can be an extended and excruciating episode of your life. Remember Odysseus was separated from family and home, lost at sea for ten agonizing years. Victory is costly and you can't buy the elixir. Wisdom is earned by struggling on the unpaved path of hell with no guarantees you will make it home alive. The journey is not for the faint-hearted.

The level of intensity and duration of ego death during the journey are the nonnegotiable price for the treasure of strength, clarity, and conviction that are the hallmarks of the heroine. Once you've been destroyed you must claw your way legless on your belly out of the abyss—that's where strength is earned. Once you've been at sea for years longing for shore, clarity dawns that you can be your own refuge. Once you've been betrayed by those closest to you and accepted the darkness that exists in us all, you fear no one, but have discovered wrathful compassion. The journey must slay you, just as you must slay fear. Only in the dark and dangerous spaces where the dragon terrifies you, can you find the treasure. Fear isn't only for young males to face and integrate, females and mature individuals should and can too—courage is a universal virtue.

What is problematic is the assumption we should throw the entire baby of Campbell's work out with the bathwater since a weakness or critique of his framework has been asserted. Remember, everything is relative and cyclic; what comes into vogue disappears and returns. An outright dismissal of Campbell is too extreme a reaction, for no matter what you replace, the monomyth will have its shadow and limitations. Every version that supplants Campbell's, be it male versus female, youth versus elder, individual versus collective, will inevitably possess relative limitations, although obviously not the same. Ultimately, we must look at the model from the universal perspective where it welcomes everyone into an opportunity for transformation, taking them into and back from the transpersonal domain.

THE PILGRIMAGE OF WHOLENESS: CARL JUNG'S PROCESS OF INDIVIDUATION

We know the work of Carl Jung influenced Campbell's monomyth. What follows will not be a comprehensive introduction to the life and work of Jung, which is available by many more adapt scholars of the subject elsewhere, but rather a taste of Jung's descent into hell, his mystical experience, and how he returned to the world with one of the most elegant and timeless psychologies.[7] Unlike the Buddha or Jesus, Jung represents an ordinary man with flaws and limitations—hopefully close enough to our human experience to emulate. If Jung can embark on the timeless quest, so can we.

Using our Loom (see plate 4.1), we see that the synergy between Campbell's Hero's Journey, Jung's process of individuation, and the Tibetan alchemy of rebirth, reveals points of convergence from all three maps's universal pilgrimage of *solve et coagula*. There are also essential differences between these epic systems. Whereas Campbell offers a longitudinal map for an external journey through a single life, Jung offers a structural model of the psyche, so we can navigate the terrain of the mind. The Tibetan alchemy of rebirth offers both a structural model of the mind (stream) and its journey across a multi-life span.

WHY STUDY JUNG?

As we ask what is so vital about myth, we should similarly ask the same about psychology. Why study Jung's version?

Not only is he one of the greatest synthesizers of science and eso-teric traditions of the last century—any work bridging psychology and Tibetan Buddhism would be remiss to exclude him—more than any-thing, it's Jung's emphasis on the soul. The history of Western psychol-ogy commencing with Freud proposed human beings were driven by primal instincts of self-gratification and fear of death, which were later supplanted by attachment theory which suggested love and connection oriented us. As the paradigm of materialism grew more entrenched, behavioral psychology emerged and proposed the idea that humans are driven like machines through mimicry and stimulus-response, whereas now, neuroscience reduces the human being down to nothing more than brain chemistry driven by epigenetics.

Here we begin our pendulum swing to center, aligning matter with spirit. Jung is on the fringe of many schools of Western psychology because he dared to propose we even have a soul and are driven toward wholeness in what he called the process of individuation (and what I call the pilgrimage of the Self).[8] Given this, each seemingly intolerable upsurge of shadow material disrupting our psychic equilibrium is a call of the soul from the collective unconscious—to widen parameters of the ego for a more inclusive and complete integration. From Jung's perspec-tive, the personal and collective unconscious are not adversarial to the ego but its ally—relaying information to expand consciousness forming greater levels of complexity within unity.

As the minute hand of the celestial clock shifts the cultural zeit-geist, something in our collective psyche is transforming. We are reach-ing the limits of materialism and beginning to break down and break through to the other side—the numinous. Our collective unconscious is activated, and interest in esoteric traditions, psychedelia, the mythic and mystical dimensions of life are seeing a resurgence. As we awaken the right brain from its slumber and allow the divine feminine to reclaim her throne alongside the patriarch of reason, Jung's emphasis on shadow work, universal archetypes, the soul, the quest for wholeness, and the mythological dimension of life will only grow more relevant in the years to come.

JUNG'S PILGRIMAGE

I'll offer more about his struggles and breakthrough dispersed through the chapters, but for now, we can say that Carl Jung's early childhood was fraught with disappointments and emotional deprivation that left him introverted and with an active imagination. He was destined to become a priest like his father and other family members. Instead, he became a psychiatrist. During his medical training, Jung joined the staff of the Burghölzli Asylum of the University of Zürich. Through his work with schizophrenic patients, he learned much about classic mental illnesses and what he called complexes—the manifesting symptoms of a constellation of underlying unresolved trauma.

Soon after his medical research, Jung began the most influential relationship of his life with his mentor Freud, from whom he unceremoniously split over substantive differences in theory of the psyche and the influence of sexual drives. This period from childhood to the golden years with Freud, culminating in their painful rupture, and his descent into near madness represent the dissolution arc of Jung's universal pilgrimage of *solve et coagula*. Meanwhile, his discovery of his soul, return from the brink of madness, encounters with Eastern esotericism and Western alchemy, development of his analytic psychology, and his final years as a scholar, mystic, and mentor all comprise the second arc—his reconstitution and return.

Trying to make sense of his mental breakdown and breakthrough, while confronting the limits of conventional psychology's absence of soul, led Jung between 1916–1926 back to religion and specifically the esoteric subject of Gnosticism. He pursued an understanding of his personal mystical encounters with the collective unconscious and his soul within the Christian framework of his upbringing. Yet, despite nearly a decade of research, Gnosticism failed to satisfy his yearning for a relevant and experiential path of transformation, although it did eventually lead him to alchemy.[9]

JUNG AND THE EAST

In the early 1920s, Jung met sinologist Richard Wilhelm, a Christian missionary who had lived in China, learned the language and culture, and who, upon his return to Europe, influenced Jung's thinking through translating two major literary works. The first was the I Ching or Book of Changes, a divination device used for predictive purposes that consumed Jung as he tried to determine how the mind and external events were related—the so-called "as above, so below." This inquiry convinced Jung of a causal parallelism he later coined as "synchronicity" and inspired him to write the foreword to Wilhelm's translation of the I Ching (1923).[10] The second work was an eighth-century CE Taoist inner alchemy or Chinese yoga text, *The Secret of the Golden Flower*, attributed to sage Lü Dongbin who supposedly lived for eight centuries having mastered his subtle body and directly tasted the elixir of immortality, which the golden flower represents.[11] The text is largely a lay meditation manual, its techniques presented as poetry and symbolic language, prompting Wilhelm to request Jung to make it more accessible to Westerners by writing a psychological commentary as the preface to his translation.

Although later translators offered their critiques of Wilhelm, the potent symbolic images of the mandala, flower, and tree are used as psychological prompts to orient the meditator to the inner landscape of their subtle body, provide instructions for directing awareness to harness and channel subtle energy (chi, prana) within the subtle nervous system, allowing for the purification and integration of opposing energetic forces—diversely and symbolically ascribed as unconscious and conscious, masculine and feminine, heaven and earth, fire and water, and personal and universal dimensions of human experience—and aims for embodied transformation of consciousness. [12] As Wilhelm wrote:

> Eternal is the Golden Flower only, which grows out of inner liberation from all bondage to things. A man who reaches this stage transposes his ego; he is no longer limited to the monad, but penetrates the magic circle [mandala] of the polar duality of all phenomena and returns to the undivided One . . . the goal is to preserve in a transfigured form, the idea of the person, the "traces" left by experience. That is the Light, which with life returns to itself, symbolized in our text by the Golden Flower.[13]

This last point made by Wilhelm is critical to our present study of the soul and deserves reiteration. Alchemy, no matter the tradition, East or West, is not about a Piscean escape from the world, but an inner transformation and Aquarian return, or relation, to it. Jung's karmic encounter with *The Secret of the Golden Flower* triggered an insight described in his psychological commentary on the text that allowed for a radical integration of conjectures and impressions about the psyche he had been developing through research and self-analysis.[14] It was as if *The Secret of the Golden Flower* was a catalyst for Jung's personal and theoretical rebirth, prompting an amalgamation in his theory of the psyche in general, for the process of individuation in specific.

Jung's process of individuation is the pilgrimage of becoming more of who we are—by differentiation or disidentifying from narrow egoic entrapments, then by liberation in the full totality of the Self, which permits an uncompromising, authentic, self-expression. In his words, "the experience of Self, is always a defeat of the ego," and later he adds, "Alchemy has performed for me the great and invaluable service of providing material in which my experience could find sufficient room, and has thereby made it possible for me to describe the individuation process at least in its essential aspects."[15] *The Secret of the Golden Flower* became a metaphoric gate into the numinous for the ensuing deep dive Jung took, lasting years, into the mystical traditions of the East, including Hinduism, Yoga, and Tibetan Buddhism.

Soon after *The Secret of the Golden Flower*, Jung read *The Serpent Power* by British Orientalist J.G. Woodroffe, leading him into the Indic subtle body nervous system, describing the arousing of the serpent-like kundalini life force coiled at the base of the spine through meditative manipulation and directing it through chakras or nexus points to achieve spiritual illumination. As he did with Chinese alchemy, Jung described the psychology of kundalini yoga as reliant on potent archetypal imagery used for the purpose not only of concentrating attention on a transformation of consciousness but serving as a symbolic landscape through which the immaterial world of the soul could be accessed and experienced along with the material world in a nondual, or integrative manner.[16] Symbols are the language of the soul, and dreams and active imagination, are its conversation.

FROM EASTERN TO WESTERN ALCHEMY

Between his commentary for *The Secret of the Golden Flower* in 1931 along with essays "Yoga and the West" (1936) and "The Psychology of Eastern Meditation," (1943), Jung went from arguing that the personal dispositions of modern Westerners were unsuited to the practice of alchemy or yoga, to appreciating the nuanced character of Indian philosophies and what they could offer.[17] This reconsideration was aided by his visit to India between 1938 and 1939, including the ancient Hindu city of Varanasi on the Ganges and other modern cities like Calcutta, where he toured sacred sites and lectured at universities. As his travels and understanding of Hindu and Buddhist culture deepened, Jung came to appreciate that Indic forms of spirituality were more naturally integrative. They lacked the binary split of the psyche typical in the West with its preferential leaning toward linear rational thought and suspicion of direct and personal numinous experience.

In his 1939 article "What India Can Teach Us," Jung praised India's integrative religion as a model for the modern Western world. India's religion embraced "the whole man from top to bottom," unlike the Western variety, which separated the rational from the natural human being. Jung appreciatively concluded that India had avoided the "fatal dissociation between an upper and a lower half of the human personality."[18]

Jung wrote four essays on Tibetan Buddhism and the "Psychological Commentary on *The Tibetan Book of the Dead* [Bardo Thödol]", which was first translated by his friend and colleague Walter Yeeling Evans-Wentz. Jung wrote, "For years, ever since it was first published, the Bardo Thödol has been my constant companion, and I owe not only many stimulating ideas and discoveries but also many fundamental insights."[19]

Some, like Buddhist scholar Donald Lopez have been critical of Jung's understanding of the text.[20] I agree with Lopez that Evans-Wentz's initial translation might contain inaccuracies, as did other translations during the tenuous years of first contact with Indic primary sources by European Orientalists.[21] The Evans-Wentz translation pales in comparison to the more recent version by Thurman—*The Tibetan Book of the Dead*—and that is the primary body of work I refer to throughout this book, a more sophisticated and accessible understanding of the Tibetan inner science of rebirth, it nevertheless inspired Jung greatly.

Jung was fascinated by the symbols in the Tibetan Buddhist tantric tradition, particularly the mandala, which represents the union of opposites in perfect integration. For Jung, the Buddha was perhaps the most potent archetype of his notion of the Self, the culmination of the individuation process. While Jesus was crucified for our sins, the Buddha discovered the elixir of immortality and the reality of bliss. The former is a gateway to salvation through self-sacrifice and unremitting devotion to God, the latter a mirror of our mind's potential awakening through ethical self-discipline, mental mastery, and insight. Jung saw the pervasive disillusionment among Westerners in the promise of the Christian path. He watched his father commit to a life of blind faith to dogma without much evidence of personal transformation.[22]

While Jung felt the Buddha was a more accessible symbol, he was nevertheless critical of all paths and philosophies that did not show respect for the power of the unconscious. In other words, more than God, Jung feared the unconscious if left unattended. Above any external divinity, Jung revered the power of the shadow—and its treasure, the Self—integrated into psyche. In his Essay "The Philosophical Tree," he remarked, "Filling the conscious mind with ideal conceptions is a characteristic of Western theosophy, but not the confrontation with the shadow and the world of darkness. One does not become enlightened by imagining figures of light but by making the darkness conscious. The latter procedure, however, is disagreeable and therefore not popular."[23] And in *Man and His Symbols*, Jung's final work, completed days before his death, he wrote,

> The Buddhist discards the world of unconscious fantasies as useless illusions; the Christian puts his Church and his Bible between himself and his unconscious, and the rational intellectual [scientist] does not yet know that his consciousness is not his total psyche. This ignorance persists although, for more than 70 years, the unconscious has been a basic scientific concept indispensable to any severe psychological investigation.[24]

Further to this, he added, "Modern man does not understand to what extent his 'rationalism' has placed him at the mercy of this underground psychic world. He freed himself from '"superstition"' (at least he believes so), but in doing so he lost his spiritual values to an alarming degree. His moral and spiritual traditions have disintegrated, and he is paying for this collapse with disarray and dissociation rampant throughout the world."[25]

The years of adventure into the mystical East were a period of ferment in Jung's theoretical formation of the psyche for what would become his most developed articulation of analytical psychology that would culminate with his return to Western mysticism. Like the pivotal point in the trajectory of a boomerang, Jung ventured from materialistic science with Freud to his psychic disintegration encounter with shadow—through the collective unconscious where he found his soul— then from there to Eastern spirituality for an explanation of alchemy and to the Western alchemy of his culture and lineage, and to a synthesis of them all. Late in his hero's quest, Jung began amassing and studying European alchemical texts, and like Campbell decades later, he was a voracious reader and synthesizer.

THE GREAT WORK: FOUR STAGES OF ALCHEMY

The Great Work or *Magnum Opus* of European alchemy became the primary interest of Jung between (1841–1896). As we've seen, the thrust of physical alchemy is to distill a substance down to its most essential substrate, called the *prima materia*, to create or extract gold from this distillation mythopoetically called the philosopher's stone. The process occurred in medieval laboratories and included identifiable substages correlated with chemically induced color changes as elements underwent transmutation. These four stages of alchemy become the hallmark character of the physical *solve et coagula* process and a corollary symbolic representation of psycho-spiritual alchemy Jung termed the process of individuation:

1. *Nigredo*, the blackening, burning away the dross, seeking the *prima materia*, the original, uncorrupted matter. It's equated psycho-spiritually with descent into the personal unconscious, psychological decompensation, the undermining of defenses,

regression, facing the shadow, direct exposure to the immensity of one's internal conflict as an ordeal, leading to ego death and the dark night of the soul.

2. *Albedo*, the whitening, is psycho-spiritually considered a crossing the threshold into the collective unconscious, characterized by bright white light, clarity, disembodied heightened awareness, and the first direct encounter with the archetypal elaborations of the soul.

3. *Citrinitas*, the yellowing, is psycho-spiritually equated with the dawn of amalgamation, represented by the golden rays of the rising sun. Now the soul or Self, not the ego, is realized at the center of the symbolic universe of the psyche, the opposing dualities can reintegrate and recalibrate on the conscious level.

4. *Rubedo*, the reddening, psycho-spiritually represents rebirth when the Self, inclusive of all the conscious dualities and opposing drives, is fully integrated and embodied as a creative, dynamic, functional ego capable of expressing self-mastery in the world.

PSYCHOLOGY AND ALCHEMY

Jung's fascination with European alchemy not only helped him navigate his psychological deterioration, but restore wholeness to his fragmented psyche providing understanding of the sophisticated mythopoetic, archetypal, and energetic maps needed to successfully traverse the process of individuation. It compelled him to consider how to apply his discoveries to the art of psychotherapy to make transformation accessible and practical for his patients. *In Memories, Dreams, and Reflections*, he remarked:

Only after I had familiarized myself with alchemy did I realize that the unconscious is a process and that the psyche is transformed or developed by the relationship of the ego to the contents of the unconscious. In individual cases that transformation can be read from dreams and fantasies. In collective life it has left its deposits principally in the various religious systems and their changing symbols. Through the study of these collective transformation processes and through understanding of alchemical symbolism I have arrived at the central concept of my psychology; The process of individuation.[26]

Obviously, access and integration of the unconscious occur through various means, including dream analysis, painting of mandalas, active imagination, art, and journaling. In its most concrete form, Jung developed a four-stage model for transformation applied to psychotherapy based on his observations of the stages of transmutation in alchemy. Instead of employing a laboratory, crucible, material substances, and heat, Jung envisioned the trust, mutual care, and introspection of a relational bond between analysis and analyzed in an office setting would produce the desired result. Trusting in the psyche's instinctual drive toward wholeness, Jung would only need to create the necessary conditions, the right container, for the natural unfolding of the process he called The Four Stages of Transformation:

1. *Confession*—Patients feel safe enough to release left-mode defenses to access the right-mode often painful, fragmented, and repressed associations, memories, and emotions bound up in the shadow.
2. *Elucidation*—The left-mode is re-engaged through dream analysis and interpretation, mythopoetics narratives and symbolic representations, relational transference, and countertransference analysis which help patients deepen their connection, tolerance, and acceptance of the hidden messages contained within and conveyed by those fragmented, unwanted aspects of the psyche.
3. *Education*—The left-right mode is reengaged by Socratic dialogue, critical thinking, objectivity, and analysis, forming new

associations, perspectives, and narratives that safely contain embodied pain, trauma memories, or lost fragments of the psyche or soma, leading to more profound learnings and insights.

4. *Transformation*—Through potent symbols, the client's learning, insight, and perspective shift reveal the original rigid ego formation or calcified trauma state was never as real or fixed as originally experienced. A new, more flexible, authentic, coherent identity is born through alchemy to embrace the shadow as strength.

PSYCHIC INTEGRATION

During Jung's pilgrimage of wholeness, it was the tremendous pressures of psychic disequilibrium in his confrontation with the unconscious and the awe of his mystical encounter with his soul that turned him to Gnosticism for an explanation of what he felt had become a lifeless edifice of the past without much relevance to modern people. As many of us in the West dissatisfied with our hallowed vestiges of spirituality do, Jung looked to the East, where his adventures into India and Eastern philosophies of Taoism, Hinduism, and Tibetan Buddhism revealed vibrant, still-living traditions that embodied, according to him, less split or fragmentation in the psyche.

The opposing forces of reason and intuition, masculine assertiveness and feminine receptivity, sacred and profane, order and chaos, spiritual and material, were conceived not as separate but as two sides of the same coin. And that coin, nondual in nature, was the archetypal mandala representing the full fruition of the path, or what Jung called the Self. You can't have one side without the other, or if you do it is short-lived and rife with consequences. While his early comments that Westerners could not benefit much from the spiritual practice of the East were tempered and nuanced, Jung was still hungry for a mystical system closer to his Western roots that expressed this integration, which led him ultimately to alchemy. It's in European alchemy that Jung not only found a resolution to his longstanding quest for a Western esoteric tradition to heal the psychic split through a symbolic process of transmutation, but this is where his synthesis congeals in an actual therapeutic technique that can be applied to the modern man in a clinical setting.

Ultimately, because the nature of the pilgrimage of *solve et coagula* is universal and archetypal, the process of individuation culminating in the Self—for Jung and for us—is an ever-present potential beneath our nose but that for which we need the long journey to help us discover. Arrival at a destination does not transform us; transformation is the result of the challenges and how we consolidate experiences along the journey. Jung had to undergo a direct experience with shadow to break through to his soul. He had to go *there and back again* to form analytical psychology. His insatiable pursuit led him through classical psychiatry to Gnosticism, Taoism, Hinduism, Buddhism, Alchemy, and astrology ushering in his process of psychic integration. And it's this relentlessness pursuit of truth that will guide us. As I often say, it is the journey, not the destination that transforms us. The journey and growth never end. We must trust our unconscious to lead us through the terrifying labyrinth from ego, through shadow, the personal and collective unconsciousness, to the Self and back to an expanded, more flexible, capable, and forthright ego, forged in fire, and primed to make a noble contribution.

I've selected twelve themes from Jung's analytic psychology to comprise the pilgrimage of wholeness, subdivided into three phases of ego, shadow, and Self, and demarcated by the dichotomy of conscious and unconscious. They are:

1. *Persona*—the mask or socially acceptable face we show others, concealing our unacceptable parts.
2. *Ego*—the center of conscious awareness, the organizer of conscious thoughts, emotions, sensations, impulses, and memories, maintaining continuity over time.

3. *Defenses*—largely unconscious strategies (projection, possession, inflation) that filter and protect the persona from the ego, and the ego from the world, maintaining psychic equilibrium, ego integrity, and continuity of identity, but also stagnate growth.

4. *Personal unconscious*—a layer of mind outside awareness containing those unacceptable aspects of the psyche, including personal trauma, base instincts, and fantasies.

5. *Collective unconscious*—a shared or collective layer of mind containing our common human legacy, universal archetypes, and complexes.

6. *Archetypes* (animus, anima)—thought formations and energies represented by universal symbols such as loving mother, wise sage, courageous warrior, or tree of life, to name a few. The anima and animus are a dualistic set of archetypes that represent the unactualized masculine aspect (rationality, assertiveness) for a female, and feminine aspect (intuition, receptivity) for a male, respectively.

7. *Shadow*—the psyche's emotional blind spot, containing split off parts of the personal and collective unconscious. The shadow is not always ominous or destructive, it is defined as the unknown, and therefore can include unintegrated self-love or confidence.

8. *Complexes*—unintegrated emotions, memories, perceptions, and behaviors, that cluster around a theme, such as power and subservience, which compel replication or repeated traumatic experience.

9. *Coniunctio*—the alchemical union of opposites, masculine and feminine, conscious and unconsciousness, virtue and vice, divine and human, ego and Self.

10. *Unus mundus*—the primordial, unified reality in which everything is ultimately interconnected, and from which everything corresponds and derives.

11. *Individuation*—the psyche's process of integration leading to wholeness and authenticity.

12. *Self*—the culmination of the process of individuation, the union of opposites (coniunctio), the resolution of duality. Whereas the flexible ego is the center of the conscious mind, the Self is the center of the entire psyche.

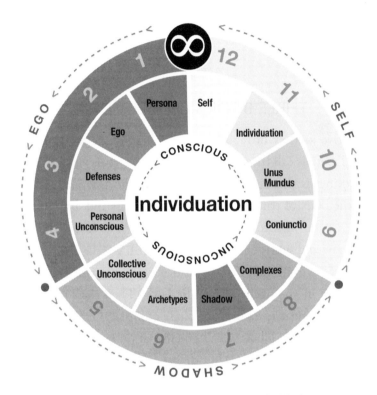

Fig. 5.2. Individuation: The Pilgrimage of Wholeness

THE PILGRIMAGE OF REBIRTH: TIBETAN BUDDHIST ALCHEMY

Campbell showed us that the journey of a lifetime traverses a route across identifiable milestones enabling us to create meaning from adversity and purpose from aimlessness. Jung turns the journey inward, as we become aware of the dimensions—or structures—of the psyche and attempt to reclaim lost fragments of ourselves—the unconscious, trauma, collective unconscious, and soul—into an expanded and unified conscious awareness. Both Campbell's cyclic journey across life's land-scape and Jung's deep dive into alchemical transformation were influ-enced by Tibetan Buddhism's pilgrimage of rebirth, the third thread I weave on the loom of *solve et coagula*.

As such, the pilgrimage of rebirth possesses both the narrative arc through multi-lifetime cycles and an alchemical transmutation of the mind and subtle body.*

THREE BODIES OF A BUDDHA

The narrative journey of rebirth follows three phases corresponding to what the Tibetans call three bodies of a Buddha, their version of the holy trinity, taking us through the death process and the *solve* phase enter-ing into the body of truth (dharmakaya), spacious and luminous soul or mind, then entering into a liminal phase known as *bardo*, the between, where the raw and subtle energies that support life—the *prima materia*—recently released from their toxic identifications now arise from the womb of compassion in an angelic or beatific body. Then the soul is reconfig-ured in the ensuing *coagula* or third phase of physical rebirth as an avatar, or *tulku,* in what the Tibetans call an emanation body (nirmanakaya) of seemingly ordinary appearance but divine origin.

I've synthesized these stages into a coherent mythopoetic narrative inspired by my teacher Robert Thurman's translation of *The Tibetan Book of the Dead,* his introductory material, and his translation of the Lama Chopa text in his seminal work, the *Jewel Tree of Tibet*.[27] It's in the latter where Thurman's innovation, that allows practitioners to sub-stitute the archetype or deity in their beatific or emanation body forms for religious and even secular role models. Thurman's rationale is based partly on his understanding of Jung's archetypes—Buddha, Christ,

---

*Although I cannot go deeply into it here, the model possesses the bioenergetic pilgrim-age into the subtle body nervous system so that a new consciousness is embodied in a new nervous system redesigned from the DNA and chemistry out, or from the *soul* level up through the material level.

Lao Tsu, and Krishna—each serving as culture-specific instantiations of universal qualities, combined with his knowledge of the precise psychological mechanism underlying the traditional tantric visualization liturgy. For these reasons, Thurman synthesized and innovated sacred text translations to a degree his predecessors could not. Although we owe those early pioneers a debt of gratitude for Western discovery and contact with Tibetan masters, it's Thurman's larger than life personality, erudition, and the historical context of his meeting the recently exiled young Dalai Lama that makes him an extraordinary preserver and innovator of the Tibetan Buddhist tradition.

REVERSING THE LIFE-DEATH CYCLE

The Tibetans long observed the pattern and conditioning of an unconscious life cycle, tracking it from compulsive birth in one of six realms of existence driven by karma, trapped in reactive patterns during a single lifespan, and blindly entering the death process with absolutely no preparation, ensuring a repeated cycle of misery the Buddhist call *samsara*, or aimless wandering through beginningless time. Compulsive birth, life, death, and rebirth. Until, in a stroke of genius and self-observation, the Buddha became the first human to disrupt the multi-life cycle with awareness and intentionality, gaining liberation from compulsive rebirth.

The Tibetan form of Buddhism with its blend of animistic and shamanic elements, paid particularly close attention to the life-death-rebirth process, beginning with Padmasabhava, an Indian tantric yogi of the eight century CE—the so-called second Buddha—credited with spreading the teachings to the Himalayan region. Padmasambhava is cited as the composer of the Bardo Thodol, *Liberation through Hearing in the Between*, popularly known as *The Tibetan Book of the Dead*. Based on his divine revelations, the material was transcribed by his chief disciple and rediscovered centuries later by Karma Lingpa in the fourteenth century. Just as the Mayans were known as astute observers of the stars and collected generational wisdom used for predictive power, the Tibetans were psychonauts, explorers of the soul-scape, and compiled an experiential or phenomenological, peer-reviewed science supporting and improving ordinary people's inevitable death process as well as guiding yogis in mastery of the process of reincarnation.

Learning to mindfully die disrupts the instinctual drives of perceptual distortion, aversion, and grasping from reiterating repeating cycles of compulsive suffering. For example, entering a between state, known as *bardo*, reconceived as a mandala or alchemical womb where sperm and egg can metaphorically merge with the buddha embryo of pure consciousness—Buddha nature or clear-light—to be soul-sculpted anew by proto-parents, deity-archetypes fused with the essence of one's mentor (guru). Here, based on the wisdom of emptiness or openness, one is reverse engineered as a deity through an optimal vision, altruistic impetus, and the skill to constructively awaken society. One then visualizes rebirth as a deity in the mandala, retaining that vision while rehearsing emanation in the world. What emerges because of reversing the compulsive life cycle starting with conscious death, entering sublime liminality, and concluding with altruistic rebirth as an avatar, not only radically reshapes one's mind in a single lifetime, but accelerates the attainment of enlightenment.*

Within the Tibetan holy trinity of death, bardo, and rebirth are eight stages of dissolution comprising the death process. The first four stages involve the dissolution of elements constituting the physical body:

1. Earth—solidity
2. Water—fluidity

---

*Inspired by Thurman's liberal use of mythopoetic language to describe the Tibetan stages of rebirth, I combined them with Campbell's Hero's Journey and intonations from Jung's process of individuation to create a unique, syncretic visualization, which I guided my students through in classes. One benefit of the tantras is they essentially collapse an entire lifetime—death, bardo, and rebirth—of experience into one single mediative session, so we can bank the mileage of the whole journey in less than an hour.

3. Fire—combustibility
4. Air—permeability

And the later four purify consciousness of afflictive instincts:

5. Moonlight/Luminance—grasping
6. Twilight/Radiance—aversion
7. Midnight/Imminence—delusion/separation
8. Clear-light/Transparency—pure consciousness

Phase 1:
Conscious Death and Dissolution

This first phase is conscious death and dissolution of the body (elements) and mind (afflictions) leading to what Jung called the *prima materia*, the Hindus call *Shiva–Shakti*, the Tibetan's call primordial awareness (*rigpa*), characterized as the nondual substratum of energy and awareness. The process requires an override of fear-based conditioning used for ordinary self-preservation. Just as fighter pilots train to remain calm during crash simulations, the meditative prescriptions in the *Bardo Thodol* habituate surrender, release, or a "trust fall," with the assumption that death is not a final abyss, but a doorway threshold.

From the final stage called transparency—pure consciousness— one enters without resistance into the bardo. Typically, the transition is terrifying, we encounter our unconscious projections appearing as demons, propelling us to grasp for the false security of the next compulsive rebirth. Following the advice of the *Bardo Thodol* one sees through the projections with the wisdom eye, avoids reactivity and immediate rebirth, and can, as in lucid dreaming, maintain conscious agency to travel deeper into the collective unconsciousness where, as Jung did, one recognizes one's own divine nature, even achieving liberation. The language here differs according to tradition, but we can interpret that recognizing *rigpa*, or clear-light, the pristine, transpersonal awareness, is akin to reclaiming the soul.

Phase 2:
Reverse Engineering in the Bardo

Once you reclaim the soul, ironically your purpose is not complete. One then trains consciousness to arise not in a physical body, but temporarily in a subtle, energetic, hologram body. From here one can reconstruct a body-mind in an exalted, virtual, reenactment. Although the reenactment differs across traditions and texts, in general one envisions a three-dimensional celestial palace, a mandala, protected by firewalls. At its sacred center appears the deity or archetype of your choice, fused with your mentor's presence, two becoming one, to role-model you like a proto-parent through a reenactment of evolution from gestation to maturation as a Buddha. This is the Tibetan meditative corollary of the alchemical crucible and process of transmutation which Jung synthesized in his clinical setting.

In *Gradual Awakening* I reiterated the seven relational steps of the mentor bonding process, taught to me by Joe Loizzo: steps (1) admiring the mentor's good qualities, (2) making offerings, (3) disclosing one's limitations, and (4) rejoining in one's merits.[28] These steps establish the awe, intimacy, safety, and gratitude representing stages of *idealization* and *identification* a child goes through naturally with a parent during development. They help to forge the uplink for a spiritual download along the same neural pathways evolutionary designed for mammalian mirroring and imprinting.

Phase 3:
Rebirth as an Altruistic Avatar

Once the uplink with the mentor is established, we enter the third phase, preparation for rebirth, concluding with mentor-bonding steps (5) requesting blessings, (6) requesting presence, and (7) dedication. Here, we request the teacher's blessing and guidance and visualize receiving them as nectar lights, like mother's milk, slipping from our crown into the heart. This represents the natural process of *internalizing* the mentor's qualities, just as teens do their parents over years of development.

Then we request their presence, so they can take up residence within us, activating our innate wisdom. The outer mentor and mandala and heavenly host melt into a drop of nectar that again proceeds from crown, throat, to heart, purifying body, speech, and mind, and impregnating themselves in our heart chakra. This represents the final phase of development, *integration*, when the outer parent is subsumed within young adult's personality. From a Jungian archetypal perspective this merger of the nectar drop symbolizes the point of conception, sperm and egg merging with our soul, the buddha nature, activating or fertilizing our innate potential of enlightenment. Now we are reconstituted as the mentor-deity ourself, perceiving, feeling, and acting just as they do.

Finally, one dedicates oneself to manifest perfect Buddhahood in the world to benefit others, taking rebirth as an avatar or emanation body to complete your pilgrimage mission. For those with the initiation into the highest yoga tantra, this visualization sequence, known as creation or generation stage tantra may then be accompanied by a profound redirection and amalgamation of bio-energetics in the subtle nervous system, in a second stage known as the completion or perfection stage tantra, offering an embodied accompaniment to the perceptual reframe achieved by way of the virtual simulation.

The key to this rebirth phase is to rebuild the self from the ground up, based on the new, altruistic rather than egocentric motivation—called the *bodhisattva vow*—the wish to awaken to free others. That becomes the new source code, or enlightened DNA if you will, what Thurman calls the spiritual gene, from which self and world are reconceived, and reboot, and the true purpose of life realized.

This dovetails elegantly with Jung's later stages of integration, with the Self expressed through a more fluid ego, and Campbell's return from the special world back to the ordinary bestowing boons for others. In sum, I've consolidated the Tibetan alchemical process of *solve et coagula* into twelve stages, and three phases to match coherently the models by Campbell and Jung. In phase one, I use the last four of the eight stages of death to dissolve the ordinary self and reveal the soul

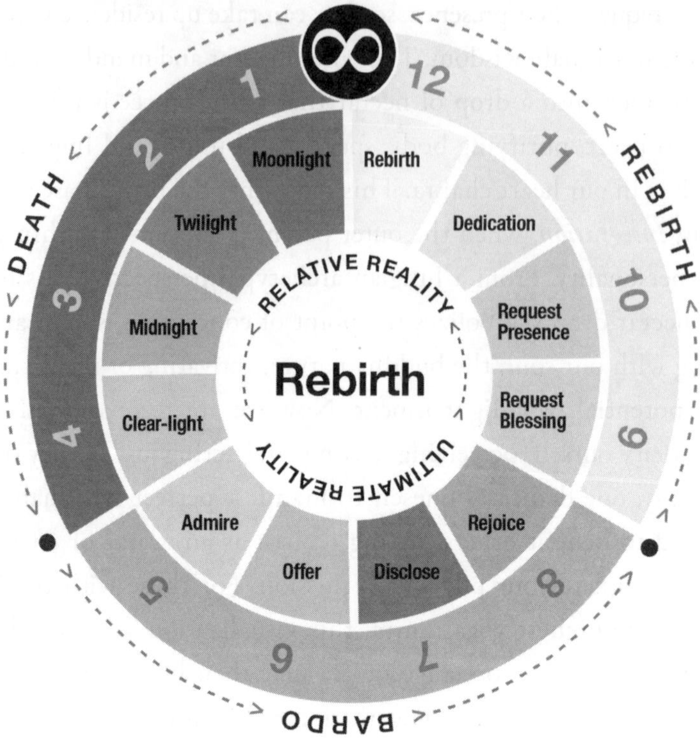

Fig. 5.3. Rebirth: The Pilgrimage of Rebirth

within the alchemical crucible, phase two comprises four (of the seven mentor bonding steps) intended to redesign the soul with archetypal mentors in the bardo, and the last three—of the mentor-bonding steps, plus rebirth—constitute the third phase priming the newly sculpted soul to reinhabit a body in the world. The demarcating duality between relative and ultimate reality, self and archetype-mentor, must be recognized as nondual. Having done a cursory tour of all three systems and maps, each a pilgrimage *there and back again*, now it's time to die . . . and be reborn.

6
Departure
Fall from Grace

FOLLOW THE MAGIC: DEPARTURE FOR BALI

We don't transition through the stages of the Hero's Journey once. It's not a linear process with a singular, spectacular arrival at a destination as if somehow, we make it, the movie credits roll to inspiring music, and our job is complete. But, like all the maps we are studying—and like the vision of the mandala I had, described in chapter one—they're based on a cyclic trajectory, a circumambulation around a sacred center. This is why I call each model a pilgrimage. Like the transition of the seasons there is no discrete beginning or end; the end is the beginning, just as the snake eats its tail. Fall begets winter, spring morphs into summer, and the earth rotates on its orbit as we evolve. Although we might wish it, there is no eternal summer. And although we might dislike it, winter is a necessary period for the incubation of dormant potentialities. Each unique phase works in perfect balance with the greater dance of life.

I learned this lesson firsthand. It began with a flight from New York to Jakarta, en route to Bali. I was threading the needle during all the Covid-related restrictions in the waning of the pandemic. Nations were still schizophrenic, unsure if the world was open or closed, whether vaccinations worked, whether we needed masks, or if we'd ever return to the old normal. Most people were holding their breath, treading water, praying for respite, and utterly spent after two years of severe losses and structural breakdowns. It's been surreal and pervasive; disbelief enfolding like a warm blanket, lulling us to sleep and paralysis.

For twenty-six hours of travel, I wore a mask unless I was eating or drinking. I clutched a dossier of documents permitting me to enter Indonesia, where they were now more concerned about my viral load and if I could pay for my Covid-related treatment than the possibility of concealed weapons. The new menace keeping us hypervigilant was a global virus, invisible and contagious, and an opportunity for governments to weaponize fear as a method of control.

The world had transformed, like the landscape after a tsunami. It was like living in a snow globe, having been upended and stirred up, and not knowing who we were or where we were going. Following my Sagittarius nature and thirst for adventure, I couldn't remain idle any longer. I seized the opportunity to ride the pandemic wave into a new world while others were frozen or imprisoned by their circumstances. For years I'd been looking for an inspiring place to relocate my family, raise my boys, and start my career anew. I'd been to Crete, Mexico City, and Costa Rica. All worked fine on paper, ticking the prerequisite boxes for my family's needs, but none of them generated an energetic alignment. Sound reason wasn't enough in these cases—my wife Emily and I needed that feeling of being lit up to know the place was right.

Being on a hero's quest is primarily an intuitive process. It's about aligning with the energy, following the magic, trusting in spirit guides, but being willing to feed demons. On my way to Bali, I was following the stars as well. I'd consulted with my family astrologer Lynn Bell, whom I affectionately call "The Oracle," who told me the current planetary alignments were good, a portal was open, and I'd experience a dream world that would fulfill my yearnings. She said, "you'll fall in love." I trusted her but remained quietly skeptical. Lynn is a no-bullshit astrologer, but even this bit of optimism was tricky for my nervous system to accept.

Speaking of falling in love, Emily, my wife of fifteen years, gave me the green light to explore new horizons—a break from my familial responsibilities for six weeks, while she cared for our sons at the height of the New York winter while I frolicked in the tropical sun of Southeast Asia, supposedly writing this book and avoiding yet another year of seasonal affective disorder. She encouraged me to answer the hero's call to adventure, this time looking for a new home for us all. I may never be able to repay Emily for her courage, strength, and generosity.

The decision to depart for Bali wasn't straightforward. Embarking on pilgrimage is never easy, the path is never clear, although I've done it more than a dozen times. It demands everything from you for a reason. You must pay a price, and make the ultimate sacrifice. There comes the point during the departure after you've consciously chosen your destination, and when preparations are complete, tickets bought, bags packed, arrangements made, that you must take that first step and leave home, as I did from my house in Westchester, New York, waving goodbye to my wife, kids, and dog through the window of the limo in route to the airport.

"Where are you heading?" the driver asked through his mask and sunglasses looking as if he just robbed a bank.

"Bali."

"That sure sounds exotic. Exotic, but far."

"It's the end of the world," I replied, literally and metaphorically.

When it's time for departure, it should feel like being on a fifty-meter diving board looking down. It all seems to make sense when ascending the ladder, but when you reach that place of no return, you freeze, on the verge of pissing yourself.

DEPARTING THE ORDINARY WORLD

The *departure phase*, as Campbell called it, has sub-stages: *ordinary world* or the world and life as you know it; the *call to adventure* when you get your first rude awakening that something's off here, or a subtle inkling that magic exists behind the veil of normality; the *refusal of the call* when fear draws you back from the edge and no price seems reasonable to pay to have a look behind the curtain; and *crossing the threshold* when you take the leap into the abyss and hope to hell the angels catch you.

The psychological essence of these sub-stages revolves around our relationship between the known and unknown worlds, specifically our confidence to navigate the shifting tides between certainty and uncertainty, ground and groundlessness. Our natures and brains drive us toward establishing safety and predictability—it's an evolutionary adaptation. Usually depicted in myth as a shire or meadow—a place of safety, idealization, and innocence, but also a place of comfort and familiarity which inevitably becomes a place to hide. Too little safety, and we can't heal the past, too much and we can't grow into the future. The "Garden of Eden" is a wondrous place, filled with verdure and delight, but it's also of place of stasis, of arrested development. Healing and growth, looking back and pushing forward, is a delicate process, which is why we must remember the journey never ends. It's a spiral of evolution. The end of any pilgrimage can become a new shire for stasis and sleepwalking unless we respond to the call anew. The mandala is constructed, consecrated, then deconstructed, only to be remade again. Crossing the threshold is about leaving our comfort zone, confronting the terror of uncertainty, and our utter loss of control. It's a micro death characterized by the unavoidable anguish of letting go as much as the thrill of anticipating new horizons.

Our ego is a self-appointed king of its domain, and it doesn't like change because that could spell its demise. The monarchy is risk averse. We are afraid to lose ourselves. Underneath the deliberation, "I can't leave my family, the flight is expensive, what happens if I get stuck in lockdown in Indonesia, what if something happens to my patients while I'm away, what about my loss of income," is the horror of losing the stronghold of one's identity.

On the edge of that diving board, our sense of self is tested, the status quo of our identity is so close it's basically a second, invisible skin, and it's so fragile it has created many subtle defenses to protect itself. Pilgrimages (and psychedelic journeys) are disrupters by design; they represent a conscious choice to allow one's castle walls to be dismantled, a coup d'état to replace the monarchy. The ego knows it, and it's holding on for dear life, sending up waves of resistance disguised as plausible horrors trying to convince you not to change. *It could all go so wrong. Who will you be if it all falls apart? What if you fail?* There is an ever-looming specter of failure, and for a few, the inverse of success, which is the most common and subtle internal obstacle standing in the way of our progress.

But there's another voice. The voice of the Buddhist diamond queen of intuition, Green Tara, the divine mother herself. She's already aligned with the astrology above and the energy within. She knows it's time to move beyond the shire, to extend past the comfort zone, to discover new outer worlds, and to develop new internal ones. She knows death is not terminal but a gateway to rebirth. And she is the one I've turned to with my devotion. I don't try to silence the inner critic deceiving me to remain stuck in the shire where it's warm, safe, and familiar. I pay more attention to Tara and put one foot in front of the other, trusting her where I cannot see.

There I was, a few hours into a twenty-six-hour-long flight, missing my boys, loving my wife, a little afraid and a lot alone. There were tears in my eyes, but also waves of excitement, the known world was behind me, and six weeks of the unknown world was ahead. Sure, I'd done this before, answered the hero's call, and crossed thresholds, but it's never easy, or the same, no matter how many times we embark. We just get better at reading the signs; perhaps there's a little less resistance or a little more willingness to perform what I call a backward trust fall into the open arms of reality.

When doubt arises, I look to the stories and biographies of those I admire most, and draw inspiration. Campbell said it best in his interview with Bill Moyers, "We have not even to risk the adventure alone, for the heroes of all time have gone before us. The labyrinth is thoroughly known; we have only to follow the thread of the hero's path. And where we had thought to find an abomination, we shall find a god. And where we had thought to slay another, we shall slay ourselves. And where we had thought to travel outward, we shall come to the center of our own existence. And where we had thought to be alone, we shall be with all the world."[1]

BUDDHA'S DEPARTURE

Supposedly the Buddha was born a human being, like you and me. Although human, Prince Siddhartha Gautama, of the warrior caste of the Shakya clan in what is now Nepal, did arrive through a miraculous birth from the side of his mother. King Suddhodana, upon receiving an astrological prediction that his son would be his royal successor expanding the empire throughout the known world or a spiritual leader, strove to keep Siddhartha close to the kingdom to preserve the lineage and his legacy. The king deliberately shielded him from the unpleasantries of life, and instead provided every comfort and advantage. And what goodhearted parent doesn't try this or wish for their child the same?

At age sixteen Siddhartha was betrothed to the princess Yashodhara following the king's wishes. Whose life was Siddhartha living? Was he aware his destiny was being curated, largely to fulfill the needs of his father? Siddhartha was unconscious, not in control of his life, although this would never have occurred to him at the time. He had *the illusion of choice*.

BEYOND THE PALACE WALLS

Siddhartha's dominion was comprised of many palaces, pleasure gardens, exotic experiences that tantalize the senses, build his confidence, boost his ego, and keep him entertained for years. Perhaps not to the same royal extent, but you too may have or had that experience, a loving partner, good friends, success and validation too. Life is good. But at a certain point it dawns on Siddhartha that, despite his comfortable life, high status, and loving wife, he is often surrounded by fortress walls. "What lies beyond them?" he wonders. That's when self-awareness dawns. It's as mysterious as any karmic moment and inconceivable to try to understand what prompts a syncretistic event like that. Perhaps it's unknowable until we become Buddha. Although it's short-lived and quickly returns to the drone of familiarity and creature comfort, this instance of awareness and curiosity represents an early tremor that leads to an explosion of Siddhartha's ordinary world.

QUESTIONING REALITY

As the days pass, that which normally resides outside of Siddhartha's awareness, beyond the fortress walls, began unsettling the prince, "like a thorn in the mind" says Morpheus in *The Matrix*. Despite the injunction against leaving the palace, Siddhartha's desire to explore the unknown world trumped his loyalty to tradition and his loving allegiance to his father.

One day, Siddhartha asked his charioteer to take him beyond the palace walls. It's a critical moment, the first of many departures in the Buddha's life story. The charioteer is a symbol too, transporting the hero between worlds, the ordinary and extraordinary, but also between states of consciousness, waking, dream, and vision. This is the shaman archetype, the ferrymen and messenger between hidden dimensions that we see in *The Mahabharata* as the lord Krishna in disguise facilitating Arjuna's expansion of consciousness; Quetzalcoatl, the Mesoamerican feathered serpent deity who can transition between worlds bearing the fruits of wisdom; and Hermes, the Greek messenger of the Gods, whose winged feet facilitate communication between the underworld, human world, and realm of the gods.

It's said on these secret successive excursions beyond the palace walls, Siddhartha came to observe four great sights that radically transformed him: a sick person, old person, dead body, and a yogi. The first three, represent our existential predicament as human beings, that until this point Siddhartha had been sheltered from and unaware of. Metaphorically these are images that shatter childhood's idealism. There is a disconnect, we call it cognitive dissonance. Suddenly there is the reality that life is not safe, predictable, or pleasant. We suffer, enduringly, and inevitably die. What's more, it's not others who suffer the human condition, as Siddhartha realizes, for the first time, despite all his fame and fortune, he is merely mortal, will suffer and die. It takes only a hairline fracture to eventually crack the dam. Consciousness is expanding, and as the dam breaks, a deluge of the darker aspects of life saturate Siddhartha's conscious awareness. However, the fourth sight, the yogi, offers Siddhartha an alternative to succumbing to suffering: inner contemplation leading to freedom. Like blazing an alternative neural pathway in the brain, the image of psychonaut or spiritual explorer primes the prince to consider leaving comfort and order, to embrace discomfort and chaos for the chance at liberation. Until now, the king wanted only one option for his son, and therefore amid the illusion of many choices, Siddhartha had none. In a state of unconsciousness, there is no free will.

We can only imagine the tension the four sights might have produced in the psyche of the prince as he reconciled his life inside the palace with the one he witnessed outside. Until now he was spoon-fed the answers, but his forays into the world left him with more questions. Questioning our reality is the necessary beginning of the spiritual path. Questions are a good way to start a heroic journey. A good scientific experiment starts with not knowing, but with asking questions, and the Zen master insists you sustain a "beginner's mind," no matter how unsettling, and for as long as you can.

One wonders how Siddhartha experienced his father's imposition upon him—as a sheltering gesture of care and compassion, as a narcissistic and controlling imposition, or something else? And what about his father's command over his empire, riches and reputation, but neither answer nor consideration for the problems of life? Was Siddhartha

disappointed, the way Jung was with his pastor father who lacked experiential authority or conviction about deeper dimensions of the soul? I
assume it was undeniable and so distressing, it compelled Siddhartha to
seek a solution for the human condition.

As he grappled with what we know was his eventual decision to leave
the palace and embark on a search, did he also, like most of us, refuse
his call, at least initially? With such a profound question, that of life
and death, I imagine he had a human reaction: *Who am I to answer such
a perennial question? How can I help with such an insurmountable problem? What good can I be?* And, most humanly: *What about my beloved
wife and son, how can I leave them for a journey into the unknown?* These
are classic expressions of the refusal of the call to adventure. Whether
it's a day or a year of deliberation, the refusal is paralyzing until an
insight dawns, like "If not me, who?" This ends the paralysis, and often
for the benefit of a loved one, (perhaps for Siddhartha, his only son), he
rises to the challenge and resolves to embark. That response implicates
us all, rippling over the centuries.

At twenty-nine, on the day of the birth of his only son, Rahula,
Siddhara Gautama, Prince of the Shakya clan, heir to throne of King
Suddhodana and the Shakya clan, husband of the admired Yashodhara,
took the biggest leap of faith into the unknown and renounced his
comforts and crown, family and fortune, and even his beloved son, to
embark on the spiritual quest for liberation. If you want it to be a true
hero's quest, it must involve this level of risk and sacrifice, otherwise it's
a Disney movie and you're kidding yourself. Could you sacrifice everything to follow the truth?

DEPARTURE AS DEFIANCE

There is an oedipal backlash that runs through the Buddha's origin
story. Common to the oedipal complex is young boys feeling competition with their father for their mother's love and attention, this settles
with castration anxiety, the fear of the authority figure's retribution,

which culminates in subservience. The young boy learns to obey, and seeks his gratification elsewhere, while the rage appropriately sublimates or incubates in the unconscious for a future explosion.

Siddhartha goes another route entirely, instead of subservience, he embodies defiance. His opposition to the rules is out and upfront; he makes a clear and contrary stand. The young prince defies his father's rules, risking his love and acceptance, by sneaking out of the palace, ultimately rejecting him and all he stands for, by renouncing the kingdom. Despite how painful it might be from the parent's side, having enough safety and inner confidence to defy authority respectfully and when appropriate, represents secure attachment and is a sign of healthy development. Although it's easier, we don't want overly compliant, accommodating children who don't know themselves or how to express their needs or values, especially in conflict with others.

One might say that Siddhartha also rejects his beloved son, abandoning him and his wife. He could have easily curated a comfortable environment and controlled his son for his own gratification as his father did for him, but perhaps he wanted to disrupt the transgenerational cycle of this royal imposition, which robs each generation of their precious process of individuation. Thus Siddhartha acts to leave the palace, reject his father, abandon his son, and accept chaos, to give himself, and through him the world, a chance of a deeper freedom. Defiance in this case is an unsuspecting, more long-term self-compassion. There are similarities between the Buddhist and the Christian myths, that God sacrificed his only son, Jesus, to be crucified, so that others may gain eternal life. Perhaps Siddhartha is sacrificing a predictable life for the chance that— through his efforts—his son, and others, might never suffer.

Ultimately, it's true; after his enlightenment the Buddha does return home to the kingdom with elixir, and both Rahula and Yashodhara become his students and attain the deathless state. But this wasn't guaranteed at the outset, so what we must recognize about the departure, and the defiance it represents, is that it involves the highest stakes of life and death.

Defiance is also about resisting cultural norms, familial expectations, internal beliefs, and impositions, which control us, preventing us from discovering who we are. Thus, the act of rebellion is also internal, the prince is not satisfied with creature comforts, a predestined legacy, or pat explanations, "We suffer and die, that's just the way things are." Think about all the external and internal impositions that confine and therefore define you, and what it would look like to have the courage to defy them, to lose your entire identity, to be found again.

THE KING OF REASON

Looking at the story through an archetypal lens, the king is a symbol for the brain's left mode, the executive function of the prefrontal cortex, rational thinking, which wants to be in control, wants to know, seeks predictability, certainty, and stability. It's focused on the details that are readily available, but not abstractions or uncertainty. How does the rational brain deal with matters of life and death that cannot be controlled or solved?

Perhaps this is what the palace represents: a place of denial, of unconscious comfort and familiarity, but also arrested development. Defying the king of reason, one pursues the queen of intuition, and enters the realm of the brain's right mode. By leaving the palace, we unfreeze arrested development, encountering all the bumps and bruises we need to grow. Perhaps the departure is also about states of consciousness, turning off autopilot, and awakening to the inevitable inputs of reality, uncertainties, and anomalies, along with life-affirming moments of awe and wonder at being alive. No risk, no reward. From a neuroscience perspective you must get out of the neural ruts and blaze new pathways, or they atrophy in predicative anticipatory patterns we call "survival mode." Media, perhaps even governments, are then all too ready to take advantage of us in this primitive state devoid of brain coherence, further hijacking our amygdala so we are primed to fight-flight-freeze, prone to coercion, and pitted against one another for distraction. Maybe the palace represents any status quo, safe but lifeless. When we disrupt the status quo, we may lose security but we expand our horizons.

END OF INNOCENCE

In pop culture we have a notion that a child should enjoy their adolescence, a period of exploration, when the brain can take advantage of the conducive conditions for optimal development, a phase that inevitably gets disrupted around ten or eleven years old, as the child is gradually confronted with, and thus relatively prepared for, the reality principal. As self-awareness grows, and identity forms, children realize they're not the center of the world, they can't have every need instantly gratified, and that they're surrounded by dangers, threats, and potential suffering. For some kids this happens naturally, and if they have secure attachment, the ability to self-regulate, access reliable support, it can lead to a gradual and successful transition we sometimes call "coming of age."

There is another, more traumatic version. Perhaps the result of the sudden death of a family member or childhood abuse, coupled with insecure attachments with caregivers, which shatters innocence but offers no rite of passage, keeps youth stuck in a bardo. Consider the Greek myth of Demeter and Persephone. However you experienced the end of innocence, I encourage you to revisit it as we reconceive and rewrite our story, giving it meaning and purpose. Some people carry that loss forever, hobbled by it, never coming to terms with the grief, stunted in their despair and resentment. Others hold on to the bubble of childhood safety—remaining indefinitely within the palace confines—way past its natural stage, we call this the Peter Pan syndrome, adult children, clutching their security blanket unwilling to grow up and face the world, to be rejected, hurt, or fail. All painful, but necessary.

The way to deal with failure, heal trauma, accept rejection, and to unarrest development, is never through avoidance, sanitizing one's world, or being over-protected, but through systematic, voluntary exposure to the things you fear most, or feel most overwhelmed by. Voluntary is key, like Siddhartha's series of chariot forays beyond the palace walls, and is a corollary to the incremental exposure of the twenty minutes when the child explores its surroundings alone, the mother having temporarily left the room, in the so called "strange situation experiments" by development psychologist Mary Ainsworth in the 1970s as she formulated her attachment theory. Life is unavoidably difficult, and we must strike a balance between fostering a safe place long enough for optimal brain development to unfold naturally, but not prolong the endeavor and remain in the comfort zone, and instead choose by free will to encounter unknown, harsher realities, so that one's own resilience and adaptive capacity can come online.

When we are resilient and adaptive, we can courageously venture anywhere, but when we are limited and fragile, we can go nowhere without terror. With low resilience and high fragility, we make unreasonable demands on the world to change and accommodate our limitations. To paraphrase the eighth century Indian Boddhisattva Shantideva, rather than covering the entire surface of the world with leather to protect yourself, it would be wiser to just cover your feet.[2] Volition is paramount, if you take the initiative to face your fear, step into the unknown, tolerate distress, or accept your fate by choice, rather than having it forced upon you, your ability to make a demon an ally, to grow from it, bears a much greater result than remaining sidelined. Your inner capacities are your best protection against the world's irreconcilable hardships and injustices. Siddhartha *chose* to end his innocence, abandon his comfort, face his family's rejection and retribution, and consequently he left on his terms, more empowered for it.

JUNG'S DEPARTURE

Consider Jung's biography in parallel to the Buddha's story. In 1908, Freud and Jung were invited to Clark University in Massachusetts to lecture on psychoanalysis and depth psychology. Freud came from Vienna, Jung came from Geneva, and they met in London to make the transatlantic crossing by ship. The journey aboard the vessel lasted seven weeks. Some of Jung's writings suggest that he and Freud had a morning ritual where they would meet on the ship deck to analyze each other's dreams from the night before.

The exchange of mutual dream analysis would go something like this: they would each bring up a vision and one element of a dream, and freely associate as the other listened attentively. During free association, you inhibit your mind's habitual way of filtering and narrating, and you let it become spontaneous and nonlinear. It's a right mode activity. This interplay allows aspects of the unconscious permission to break through into awareness. The relational rapport and attunement of the analyst creates a safe environment for dream reporter to risk take and explore. As repressed content emerges from the analysand in their receptive or regressive state, the left mode of the analyst continues to analyze, interpret, connect dots, and prompt inquiry, allowing the analysand to receive a more brain-integrated stroke of insight.

During one exchange in which Freud was freely associating with one of his dreams, a critical impasse was hit; Freud stopped associating. He paused. It appeared he had become too vulnerable in his free association while his mentee critically observed. According to Jung's journal, Freud refused to free associate further, stating, "I would lose my authority." [3] Jung later wrote that this single sentence which was burned into his memory spelled the end of their relationship—Freud placed personal authority over exploration and truth.

That night Jung had a dream that ends up foreshadowing the next chapter of his career, and reveals this dream to Freud the next day.

> I was in a house I did not know, which had two stories. It was my house. I found myself on the upper story, where a salon was furnished with fine old pieces of Rocco's style. On the walls hung several precious old paintings. I wondered if this should be my House. And I thought to myself, not bad. But then it occurred to me that I did not know what the lower floor looked like. Descending the stairs.

I reached the ground floor, and there everything was much older. I realized that this part of the House must date to about the 15th or 16th century. The furnishings were medieval. The floors were of red brick. Everywhere, it was rather dark. I went from one room to another, thinking now I really must explore the whole House.

I came upon a heavy door and opened it. And beyond it, I discovered a stone stairway that led down to a cellar. Descending again, I found myself in a beautifully vaulted room which looked exceedingly ancient. Examining the walls, I discovered layers of brick among the older stone blocks and chips of brick in the mortar. As soon as I saw this, I knew the walls dated from Roman times. My interest was now intense. I looked more closely at the floor. It was of stone slabs, and in one of these, I discovered a ring. When I pulled it, the stone stab slab lifted, and I saw a stairway of narrow stone steps leading into the depths. These too, I descended and entered a low cave. Thick dust lay on the floor, and in the dust were scattered bones and broken pottery. The remains of a primitive culture. I discovered two human skulls there. Obviously very old and half disintegrated. Then I awoke.[4]

The following day, the two men discussed the dream over breakfast. Jung felt Freud's energy was immediately invested in the two skulls. And he was insistent that Jung identify them by name. Jung reports in his memoirs that he felt pressured to conform to Freud's drive theory[5]. In 1908, the main drive theory underlying psychoanalysis wasn't the pleasure principle but the death instinct. Jung intuited Freud wanted to have those two parties named because he feared Jung harbored animosity toward him. Perhaps even a competitive or death instinct. Like the symbolic wish to displace or kill the father archetype represented at the conclusion of the Oedipal complex. In other words, Jung sensed Freud was insecure, and avoided confrontation by lying, saying he thought the two skulls were his wife and sister-in-law, whom he'd recently had some animosity toward. Jung throws Freud off the trail and from that day forward has confirmation of Freud's narcissism, insecurity, and lack of trustworthiness. Again, like Siddhartha, we see the archetype of necessary, yet painful, defiance.

JUNG'S DREAM INTERPRETATION

Jung's dream interpretation differed from Freud's. He saw the house as representing consciousness with its various domains. The top floor was waking consciousness in real time, or the ordinary world. As Jung descends into the different levels of the house, Jung regresses back in time. A stairwell leads to the second floor replete with furniture, art, and décor associated with the medieval period. Jung's taken a significant leap back in the time machine. There's something shamanic about Jung's dream descent into his unconscious. In fact, he's pleased with himself on the top floor. He is comfortable there, saying "not bad." The top level is the shire, where everything is orderly, safe, familiar, where you needn't confront complexity or horror. Jung then descends by curiosity to find himself into that second level which he would call the personal unconscious. He's crossed a threshold from the ordinary to special world, from ego to shadow. The second level represents the outer limit of Freud's paradigm.

For Freud, there are only two levels, the conscious and the unconscious. He had a precise way that these two related to each other, antagonistically. His drive theory suggested there are specific libidinal or instinctual impulses, sexual and aggressive, unbeknownst to us in the depths of our unconscious. Psychic defenses like repression are designed to keep these impulses restrained to maintain societal equilibrium. There is a war between the gratification of personal urges and civilized behavior. Freudian psychoanalysis attempts to modulate that tension, revealing the sexual and aggressive impulses from the unconscious so they can be consciously tempered and find expression in more socially acceptable ways, in a process called sublimation. For example, a young street kid born into poverty, homelessness, and violence, sublimates his justified pain, paranoia, and aggression through boxing, and becomes a world champion. We'll compare Freud's model with Jung's shortly.

A Cave with Two Skulls

Jung's descent into the unconscious doesn't end in the medieval level. He soon finds a stairwell leading to a Roman-era basement, and from there, a secret doorway that leads into yet another level of the house. There he discovers not a room, but a cave covered with earth, rocks, shards of pottery, and two skulls. He describes the descent through the rooms as a further regression through history to the prehistoric dawn of man. In contrast to Freud's interpretation of the two skulls as Jung's competitive or death instinct to overthrow him, Jung viewed the cave and skulls as universal archetypes of the collective unconscious. The trap door is a portal connecting Jung to a more ancient legacy and ancestry with little relevance to his individual identity, personal history, or private feelings. The process of unearthing the skulls lends itself to an archeology of the mind, Jung is reclaiming lost fragments of his past beyond memories of this lifetime, and certainly beyond his narcissistic insecurities or impulses. During his descent into the house, Jung moves from ego, to shadow, to the rediscovery of the collective unconscious, distinguishing his approach from Freud's.

Freud's drive theory is best characterized as an iceberg in which the personality or conscious world is just the tip above the surface, while the unconscious urges, impulses, and defenses are the wide base below the waterline. We must remain hypervigilant watching for disruptive forces from below. In contrast, Jung's model is best represented by the mandala, the sacred circle, with a spiral circumambulation towards wholeness and integration at the center. Consequently, the nature of Jung's method is less paranoid and hostile toward the unconscious and collective unconscious. Instead, we invite the lost fragments and exiles of our past, including the repulsive aspects, to be received and re-membered as a unity.

The portal to the cave is a link to our collective origins and represents the will to repair what has been broken, recover what has been lost, revive what is dead, and reunite what has been rejected. The identity of the two skulls is irrelevant from Jung's point of view. It's too limiting and self-referential. Distinctive to this endeavor is the more congenial relationship between conscious and unconscious. The unconscious is not there to overthrow or overwhelm us, but to beckon our attention for opportunities for growth and integration. According to Jung, the unconscious is not our adversary, but our ally because the soul speaks to us through the collective unconscious. The heroic journey reclaims a relationship with the soul from the outer reaches of the psyche, reinstates it as queen at the center of the mandala, and heeds its declaration to include and protect all that has been rejected.

Abandoning the Raft

The life story of Jung is emblematic of multiple forms of departure. Jung's dream was a symbolic catalyst for the departure from the personal to the collective unconscious, then there is the physical departure from his mentor. The split from the institution, parent, kingdom, or mentor is a profound archetype commonly found in the hero myths, and is critical in psychological development. After all, the mentor empowers the initiate to connect with a level of awareness and confidence that have, up to then, been hidden.

Unfortunately, Freud wasn't so gracious and self-secure to allow his pupil to transcend him, so Jung was forced to listen to an even deeper impulse, emerging from his soul. Not only does one need to find a mentor, but one must know when to disregard the mentor, teaching, or community for something even more authentic. They say when the student is ready the teacher appears, what they don't say as often is what happens when the student is ready to leave the teacher. That bit gets left out. My teacher Geshe Tenzin Zopa (Geshe-la) the young and charismatic Tibetan Lama featured in the *Unmistaken Child* documentary, taught us that the death of his beloved guru Geshe Lama Konchog was the "birth of his inner guru." The external one had to die, for the inner one to be born.

This is also exemplified by one of the Buddha's analogies of the Dharma—like a raft that helps you reach the other shore. Once you reach your destination, you abandon the raft. You don't carry it around on your shoulders, otherwise it becomes a burden and slows your progress. This is the point of the exercise: if we're not careful, the thing we've worked for or taken for granted, the lifeblood of our survival that keeps us comfortable, whom or what we might be dependent upon for our psychic or physical stability, can become an obstacle. This is why the monks during the Buddha's time were wanderers, they voluntarily sought out disruptive experience so they could not become complacent and too comfortable.

We can grow complacent, and forget that whatever feels like "home," even a mentor, is a waystation in an enduring process. In my case, I ignored signals—frustration and resentment—from my nervous system that it was time to move on. I was afraid I'd fail without my mentor or institution. I couldn't strike out alone. Frustration was my soul telling me it's time to evolve, while fear was my ego resisting, refusing the call.

We can all connect with our nervous systems. The body relays subtle messages from the soul. They may be irritation, boredom, resentment, anxiety, restlessness, or apathy. Whatever they are, these manifestations result from our inability to take the necessary leap of faith, our refusal to accept ego death of the inner child. Intuition says, "It's time to go" but reason replies, "No way, this is my home, job, identity." Connect with this dialogue, tracking who wins and why, so you don't prologue the inevitable like I did.

From the collective unconscious's perspective, your psyche provides healthy endorsements. Remember it's your soul whispering coded messages. Will you listen? The compensatory ingredient that Jung adds is that this message wouldn't be delivered unless the soul's wisdom deemed it an appropriate time. The unconscious is not your enemy; it's your sparring partner. It's a heroic instinct to push us out of the nest and forward to the next stage of individuation. If that's true, then a certain amount of trust must happen with messages of the unconscious, a willingness to let the process of separation unfold because there is some deeper appreciation that defies the intellect and says, this will hurt but it's good for you long term.

Jung heard that one phrase by Freud prompting his reluctance to disclose, and that was it for Jung; he listened as dutifully to his soul as he did his mentor, and he was gone. He listened to the soul that said, this guy is not interested in the truth, but you are. "I cannot risk my authority" was the coup de grace. We know this disappointed Jung like his father did with his shallow answers to spiritual questions. Freud broke Jung's trust and heart, along with his chains of dependency, freeing Jung to embark on his pilgrimage of individuation.

Jung's Descent into the Unconscious

As Jung parted ways with Freud, he embarked on an inward journey that would take him into the depths of his psyche. For a lengthy period of Jung's life, maybe fifteen years, he underwent a pseudo-psychotic break with consensus reality as he knew it although he could still function, receiving his clients for therapy, yet between sessions he would experience auditory hallucinations, of which he wasn't afraid. He was doing an inner exploration of the special world, while still living an ordinary life. Jung built a house with his own hands on the shore of Lake Geneva, while living in seclusion there he produced an outpouring of art, myth, and poetry based on the archetypal material discovered in his dreams, hallucinations, active imagination, and meditation. He meticulously documented these in an extensive volume of diaries and journals, which he then synthesized in his so-called *The Red Book*, released only after his death. It's an exquisite and vivid document capturing the heroic journey of a modern mystic. But Jung was clear that this was the map of his unique journey, his personal account, not one to be followed by anyone else. We need to find our own way, to allow our process of individuation.

Jung's willingness to explore the frontiers of his unconscious and the collective unconscious meant he had to give up psychic security and risk disequilibrium. Jung was pushing the boundaries of his cultural paradigm, veering from science and psychoanalysis, to alchemy, yoga, and Tibetan Buddhism, from the order of Apollo to the chaos of Dionysus. His departure involved the risk of losing family, livelihood, respect, and sanity, taking an all-or-nothing risk like Siddhartha.

THE FALL FROM GRACE

Looking at the cast of characters from Adam and Eve's departure story, the Garden of Eden—the Fall from Grace—we find God, the first man and woman, a snake, plus two trees: the Tree of Knowledge of Good and Evil and the Tree of Life.[6] The common rendition uses this as an explanation for why every terrible thing goes wrong in human beings's lives. We've fallen from grace, innate sinners in need of redemption, which comes only through Christ. We are bad children dependent on our parents, so it's best to obey or something terrible will befall us. Don't stray; follow the rules, not your heart. And since Eve was the original sinner, tempted by the snake, she was the weakest link, accepting the apple from the Tree of Knowledge, causing Adam's downfall, and launching the cascade of troubles with which we sinners still struggle.

This story demands an esoteric reading, adopting a mythological lens so we can interpret the signs along our journey, look for synchronicities and anomalies, which orient intuition to the profound mission that is uniquely ours, so let's return to that persuasive snake. The trickster is an archetype. In mythology and in any study of folklore and religion, it's a character, god, goddess, spirit, human, or anthropomorphized entity exhibiting intelligence or secret knowledge and playing with or otherwise challenging the rules of conventional behavior. Tricksters cross boundaries. They playfully violate principles of social norms and the natural order, disrupting everyday life and establishing new principles.

Further, in all esoteric traditions the snake symbolizes death and rebirth. Because of how they shed their skin, they represent transformation.

Usually however, the snake takes a lot of heat. Snakes are feared, evolutionarily speaking, they instinctively repulse us because they can kill us. In conventional religion we've been indoctrinated to mistrust the snake, but if the snake is a trickster, then its role in the story is more complex; it's not there to hurt Eve and Adam, to deceive them, but there to disrupt their ordinary consciousness and nudge them toward a rite of passage.

MASCULINE AND FEMININE ARCHETYPES

From an esoteric perspective Adam and Eve represent the masculine and feminine archetypes or energies within each of us. According to Jung the masculine archetype is action-oriented, assertive, aggressive, rational, left-brained, industrious, and orderly. The feminine is nurturing, receptive, emotional, passive, intuitive, creative, relational, compassionate, and chaotic. Eve is the intuitive one and can override her instinctual fear to communicate with the snake. Although Eve has been condemned by Christian patriarchy as causing the fall of man consider her instead as the more intuitive one, who accepted the fruit, and was the first to awaken and expand her consciousness. Intuition guided her journey, and like Siddhartha searching beyond the palace walls, Eve took the first step on the heroic path. Just as Siddhartha embodied courage, Eve embodied compassion—her sacrifice inspires our heroism. Eve's risk benefits the rest of us, because we now have an example of challenging authority, disrupting the status quo, and accepting the grave consequences, in order to align with an even greater truth—one's path of individuation. Eve and Siddhartha took a risk to lose it all, so that we might follow their example.

God told Adam and Eve they'd die if they ate the fruit from the Tree of Knowledge, whereas the trickster serpent said, "God knows that when you eat fruit from that tree, you will know things you have never known before. Like God, you will be able to tell the difference between good and evil."[7] What if the garden is a mandala with a periphery and center? The outer circumference is the totality of consciousness, encompassing everything, positive and negative, male and female, consciousness and unconsciousness, all in fragmented opposites. Meanwhile at the center of the mandala is the Self and perhaps the Tree of Life, the world tree connecting heaven, earth, and hell.

If you eat of the fruit of knowledge, you don't die, it's like the beginning of a psychedelic journey. Your third eye is now open to behold everything, joy and sorrow, ease and hardship, grace and grit, and you become like God. But to start the process, the gradual steps on the path to enlightenment, you must disobey your father, logic, order, ego, the rules that bind you, your self-identification, attachments to simplicity and comfort, and must be willing to shatter innocence and infantile narcissism. The verses say that once Adam and Eve tasted the fruit and their eyes open, "they realize their nakedness," this is the reference to the end of innocence as they now feel the shadow of shame and fear. Being unclothed is the symbol of defenseless and vulnerability as the ego submits to shadow.

What happens next? God punishes the serpent, Eve, and Adam, condemning them to endure hardships for the duration of their lives—the labors of pregnancy and providing for family. Basically, our entire life is condemned to struggle. Is hardship really a punishment, or is it a gift? Just after condemning Adam and Eve, God offers animal skins to clothe them—he is caring for them, supplying them what they need to go beyond Eden. Maybe he's not punishing them, he's preparing them?

Then it seems as if God gets concerned, if they have disobeyed and eaten of the Tree of Knowledge, perhaps they might also eat of the Tree of Life. Fearing they will live forever, he banishes them, and sets an angelic guard at the gates of Eden. The mainstream view is that as sinners the children don't get to eat the fruit of eternal life, but an esoteric view is that all of this has been a preparation, a test or "trial" so the Eve and Adam can embark on a grail quest of their own awakening. First, they must break the rules and disrupt the spell of unconsciousness to become more awake, then they must fall, struggle, and face their shadow. Only then, perhaps, can they rise again wiser, entering through gates past the guardians, who verify they're ready, so they can safely claim their right to eat from the Tree of Knowledge at the center of the mandala.

Only through pain and struggle can we grow; it's the anti-Eden, the anti-palace, *it's the harder choice to face the difficult realities of life that help us individuate and become our authentic selves.* For Jung the descent into the unconscious, the shadow, is necessary to discover the Self—risking it all to receive the reward, undergo trial to claim the treasure, dying to be reborn. We must fall from grace, face all our desires, fears, traumas in the unconscious. To leave we must discover free will, and learn how to wield it like a weapon, exercised through choices, facing consequences, and stepping up to responsibility. The first choice is to leave innocence, to become sovereign. Disappoint the king, reject God, suspend the left-brain. Otherwise, it's not a choice. There are lessons to learn from darkness that we never learn from the light, to see the full spectrum of reality.

Ultimately, you'll learn and grow more from your struggle having departed, than if you remain safe in the garden of ignorant innocence. You'll have the knowledge of the difference between good and evil. This is how to open your eyes, so you can act in the world as a sovereign individual, as an adult, free to make conscious choices, and equally free to take responsibility for your actions. With power comes responsibility, and with freedom comes the choice to be moral or immoral, and knowing the difference orients us in the world to consciously strive for the highest good. Although we may fail, at least we can endeavor, not from blind allegiance, loyalty, conformity, but through self-determination. Had they not known the difference between good and evil, death and life, Adam and Eve and Siddhartha would have lived out their days as unconscious dependent children, passive extensions of someone else's dream. God doesn't want to condemn us to a life of servitude, God wants us to become gods.

A TANTRIC FALL FROM GRACE

Once Eve and Adam are cast out of the Garden, what does God install there? A gatekeeper in the East. Every temple, every mandala, has guardians to ensure you're initiated into the secrets before being allowed to enter. And in Buddhism, we enter the mandala through the Eastern gate, the direction of the rising sun. If we switch the lens of our story from mythological to Tibetan alchemy, Adam and Eve are masculine and feminine energies flowing in the subtle body, a pair of binary opposites, cross-contaminated by grasping and aversion respectively, based on ignorance, and occupying the side channels of the subtle-body nervous system.

In tantric visuliazation practice, these energies are consciously brought down the side channels into an imagined skull cup at the base of the spine. Here one visualizes being decimated, consumed in the fiery caldron, so the energies of good and evil are separated and purified. *Solve et coagula.* Under the heat of the inner fire the poisons are transformed into medicines, pure energy, freed of delusion, hatred, and clinging, is then consciously prompted to ascend the center channel. We're now transposing the Eden mythology on the subtle-body nervous system. What is awoken at the base of the spine is the crucible of inner fire, an awareness represented by the snake of transmutation uncoiling and ascending the central channel. It reaches the heart chakra and merges with an indestructible drop—the soul—vivifying it. Once we've received the initiation of eating the first fruit of the Tree of Knowledge, descended into the underworld, undergone energetic purification, ascended the center axis mundi, the world tree, past the gate guardians, we're granted access to taste of the second fruit from The Tree of Life, the elixir of immortality.

The story contains multiple pairs of opposites that all come together, a trickster snake to initiate at the beginning of the journey, a cherubim gatekeeper confirming access at the end. We have Adam and Eve, the masculine and feminine archetypes that need purification and integration, during two movements, a descent into darkness, and an ascent into light, there and back again. We have two energies of good and evil, originally bound by ignorance or innocence, but through an initiatory trial, shadow-work, these energies are harnessed with discernment, allowing one to orient toward the good. We have two trees, one for knowledge and initiation, and one for integration and immortality. The Fall from Eden story retold, is not one of sin and condemnation, but of heroism and self-actualization.

MASTERING THE DEATH PROCESS

After setting the stage by identifying the three acts of Campbell's mon-omyth—departure, initiation, and return—and the Tibetan alchemical phases—death, bardo, and rebirth—we can prepare for the dissolution phase of our tantric visualization. Our culture doesn't prepare us for death, yet it's inevitable. Monks on Mt. Athos in Greece meditate fac-ing a wall of skulls and Tibetan yogis meditate at charnel grounds, to galvanize attention, because death is a motivating principle that allows us to fully live.

From the Tibetan point of view, it's not only facing the inevitabil-ity and uncertainty of death, but the quality of our awareness during the death process that is important. As we die, afflictions can stir up and cloud the mind, but with training the mind can remain clear and unafraid, allowing awareness to self-liberate in the bardo. If we don't rehearse and prepare well for death, our fears and past karmas will assail us like demons, compelling us to fall back on base instincts of grasp-ing and repulsion that will predetermine our next rebirth. Our base instincts will be in control, recreate our former life, and keep us stuck in a never-ending cycle of despair. But if we practice the death journey like a pilot clocking flight time, we can develop mastery of the transi-tion between death and rebirth, where consciousness is manyfold more powerful at recognizing itself as one with ultimate nature of reality. As the *Bardo Thodol* reminds us, recognition is liberation.

First, we must appreciate just how the spiritual worldview contrasts with the materialistic paradigm. When it comes to death, there is the terminal life perspective based on nihilism versus the multi-life per-spective based on the continuity of consciousness. We live in a modern culture where the moment we draw our last breath and brain activity and heartbeat stops, it's the end. We don't believe in consciousness in any given moment or the continuity of the soul. But remember, until three or four hundred years ago nearly every culture recognized the soul and its journey—the ancient Egyptians had their so-called Book of the Dead, so too the Mayans, the yogis of the Himalayas, the shamans from the Amazon to Java. Among these, it's the Tibetan culture that articulated perhaps the most sophisticated science for rebirth which persists today. The premise: death, bardo, and rebirth are part of the same continuity, like waking, dream, and deep sleep, in any of these states we can train to become lucid agents of reality construction.

You symbolically died when you were fired from your job, got your cancer diagnosis, discovered your spouse's affair, or were abused; the metaphoric rug was pulled out from underneath you, your higher cortical processes were disrupted, and your reality fell apart. In that moment of disorientation, everything you took for granted as real and reliable, both inside and out, crumbled, revealing a deeper truth as you slipped over a threshold into the bardo, the between. There, in a fit of panic, your memories and instincts, habituated over evolution, kicked up fantasies and nightmares, which appeared as real as the world did before your moment of trauma. What do we do under this assault? We fight, flee, or freeze, creating the karmic conditions for new life, based on the default scripts of the old. We left one unhealthy relationship in a past life but were compelled to find another in the next. We left one job in which we felt disenfranchised and disempowered, only to gravitate toward another just like it. We experienced betrayal in the past, but we attract, or at least play complicit roles in, disloyalty. Because we don't change, we don't upgrade the software in the reality-making mechanism of the soul. If that's true in our immediate experience, within a single life, then the same unconscious process governs our multiple-life continuity.

The key from the point of the Tibetan death science is that you can prepare in advance for the inevitable trauma and death, decrease your disorientation and resistance, retain your consciousness and recognition, override your automatic instincts and projections, and from the bardo, access the deep code, the spiritual DNA, for an optimal reprogramming and reboot.

When you hear about yogis in caves committed to tantric practice this is what they're doing, simulating death to be consciously reborn, *transforming themselves from the source code into angels.* Out of the urgency of compassion they aspire to do so in one lifetime and thus turn the tantric method is considered an evolutionary accelerator. The tantras collapse and reverse time to hasten a human being's psycho-physical development. We normally navigate through life unconsciously from birth until death. That arc averages around eighty years in real-time. What a tantric visualization does is collapse that eighty-year lifespan into sessions of 120-minute visualization. During retreat yogis are practicing in four intensive sessions each day. Thus, they rehearse dying and being reborn an angel four times a day for many years. Along the way this meditative process consolidates a vast amount of deep vis-ceral learning, embodied surrender during death simulation to resolve existential fears, internalizing the signs of dissolution to avoid confusion along the bardo sojourn, and recognizing the mind's natural luminance within hallucinatory projections to self-liberate from reactivity. What might ordinarily take the soul countless lives to learn experientially one literal death and rebirth iteration at a time, has been collapsed into a several-year period of high intensity tantric retreat, an ingenious feat of reverse bioengineering.

TANTRIC DEPARTURE

Given that general background let's get a bit more granular with the stages of dissolution in our visualization process. Rehearse and internal-ize the sequence as you read. There are four physical elements and four mental habits to dissolve. We'll look at the first four now. The earth element dissolves into water, into fire, into air, and finally, into space. These are physical and symbolic, so you encode each element with the subjective sense of their respective qualities. Earth—for example— would be materiality, solidity, substantiality, and structure. The elements dissolve from most coarse or gross level to most subtle, so you begin with earth, and you end with space. Got it?

Each element is also accompanied by a subjective sense. When my father was dying of pancreatic cancer, we were in our family home in Turkey. I had left my job to care for him along with my mum. The day of his passing was one of my greatest teachings. Nobody knew he was going to die that day. My dad woke up and brushed his teeth like he did every other day of his life, and my brother Julian went to get him a wet cloth to bathe. He was at the foot of the bed and gorgeous morning sunlight streamed through the window, flooding the room. It was just another day, you know.

As the morning light shifted into early afternoon his situation steadily declined, first he couldn't get out of bed, he lay down and never got up again. As the hours passed, more signs and symptoms of dissolution appeared. Two things helped me in the process of being prepared for his eventual demise. One was a frank and sobering conversation with the doctor. I demanded his prognosis. Most doctors in Turkey don't want to alarm patients or their families, so they reveal only the essentials. I went to see my father's doctor at his office at the hospital a few days before my dad's passing and he was giving me the update on one of his x-rays, and I could feel him tiptoeing around the situation, and so I was insistent. I said: "Just fucking give it to me straight, what's going to happen to him?" I pushed, and he told me the lung had deteriorated, that shortly it would fill with fluid, my father would then go hypoxic due to lack of oxygen, and he'd basically drown to death on his own fluids. I was speechless. I dissociated long enough to ask a few logical questions: *How long will it take? Will there be pain?* After getting the answers and leaving the hospital I collapsed sobbing in the streets of Izmir. I called my brother and we cried together. Although earth-shattering, the revelations were ultimately helpful; the end of innocence prepares you for reality. These aspects come together, rupture and break through. My brother and I had to swallow the red pill to gain the knowledge needed to support my father's passing.

The other preparation that helped me was the eight signs of dissolution I learned from my teacher Robert Thurman in his course on the *Bardo Thodol*. It's ironic because when I took his class, I had no pressing need to learn about death and dying, or so I thought. Now is a good time to study how to die well. The seeds were planted, and they ripened when the conditions were right.

Throughout the day of my dad's passing, I saw the stages of dissolution arise. As morning sun entered the room, there was a timeless quality, a strange, slow procession of the day. Emily was there, along with Julian and my mom. This was one of the most spiritual experiences of my entire life. As my father was in active dying, there came a point where I had no more fear. The quality of time and space shifted. I entered an altered state of consciousness. A flow state, the collapse of the time-space continuum, and the self/other dichotomy, just as it's described in meditative equipoise or psychedelic experiences.

The preparations freed me from feeling terrified by the unknown, and helped me ready my mind to be available, present, and I can say this: we gave my dad a good death. I'm proud of how my brother, Emily, and I were available, tender, and calm with him, so that he wasn't further burdened by our anxieties and needs. Any child wanting to repay the kindness of a parent for bringing them into this world, can do so by helping them transition out of it.

With the family was a local doctor attending to my father until his final breath. I'll never forget Dr. Tunjai. He arrived every morning, took my father's vitals, asked if we needed anything, and stayed for coffee and conversation. He was so sweet and cheerful, his mind clear; his energy kept us buoyant. Western medicine has lost some of these basic human qualities. We focus on the surgeries, medicines, and outcomes of prolonging life, but not the quality of care, relationships, experience of family and community. Tunjai was good medicine, you couldn't bottle it or sell it—but he was priceless.

I gave my dad a set of wooden Buddhist prayer beads (mala) with a single piece of turquoise collected from my travels to wear during his illness. Before cancer he would have preferred his Cartier gold watch; after cancer he wore the wood mala with pride. His illness terrified him, and he was comforted by my faith and what the mala meant to me. It's interesting how someone can borrow our faith, our refuge, when they have none. Remember: this is the bodhisattva's vow, to become a raft, a shelter, or medicine for others. When my dad passed, I gave his mala to Tunjai, along with tears of gratitude.

MY DAD'S STAGES OF DISSOLUTION

The stages of dissolution provide a roadmap to death, and by following it we can more effectively transition. The first sign was that dad lost weight in the weeks before, as the physical earth element deteriorated, he became even more frail, his eye sockets sunk, until he was immobile in bed, whereas two hours earlier he could stand to pee. That was the earth element dissolving. It's accompanied by a deterioration in the eye sense faculty, so sight is the first sense to be compromised. It's also inner sight, or insight, so memories can fade, leaving one disoriented and confused. The second element is the water dissolving, everything becomes dry. Here the sensation aggregate is deteriorating, pain and pleasure are dulled or muddled. His eyes, mouth, nose and other orifices, the fluids dry up like a dessert, sometimes the skin cracks and stings around these areas. The water element is associated with the ear faculty, so hearing is diminished.

Then the third sign, the fire element, dissolves. Notably this element fuels the digestive process, so as it wanes people lose their appetite or stop eating, triggering other system failures. As the metabolism slows, the body becomes cool, then cold. Dying people might request a blanket although the room is warm. Fire is associated with the perception aggregate, so the ability to recognize objects deteriorates, along with the sense of smell, leaving the dying unable to detect odor.

This is followed by the dissolution of the air or wind element, correlated with impulses or emotions, so motivations deteriorate, people lose control. It's observed as the loss of will, irritability, and laborious breathing, short and shallow. Wind relates to taste, which is the final sense to go. I had heard the word *death rattle*, but it's one thing to know this conceptually, and another to witness it with your family member. Witnessing and facilitating my father passing was a rare honor. The final dissolution of the air element was my dad's collapsed lung which had him gasping, helplessly chocking and sputtering, just as the city doctor had predicted. Rather than being alarmed, we remained calm and present, and reassured my father to surrender, let go. As Dad's struggle ceased, and consciousness lingered on a stream of shallow breaths, I whispered into his ear saying, "Everything will be okay. Everybody will be okay. I'll take care of Mom, we love you, you did great, Dad. You can let go." His eyes were open, and moving, but his inner gaze was cast on another world. The last words my dad uttered before he slipped away, were, "I see them." I believe he was referring to his long-deceased parents, who had come, like death doulas to collect him at the bardo threshold.

REFLECTIONS ON DEPARTURE

What is the purpose of this initial stage of the heroic journey? From the Buddha's biography we first learn that not everything that glitters is gold. We start with a problem, a thorn in the mind, something nagging at us, something is off. We learn about the need for defiance, to challenge the status quo of societal norms and parental expectations, external superimpositions that confine us, which are the external mirror of the de facto organizing principal of our reality, the cage of our comfort zone, the king of reason, and the ego. From there we must renounce, totally, give up our kingdom of comfort and certainty, to follow the hero's call to adventure, summoning us not from the left brain of reason, but from the right brain of intuition, and deep down beneath, the faint whisper of the soul.

Departure marks the end of innocence, of infantile narcissism, of idealization, yes, there is inherent sadness and grief involved, but better we strike out consciously, lest we wait for reality to give us a ruder awakening that could cripple us the rest of our days.

Jung's biography reinforces these themes. The departure is less about leaving house, status, and the world to embark on existential discovery, and more about disrupting and departing from social and interpersonal institutions. Jung's rebellion against materialistic science in favor of Eastern wisdom and alchemical traditions, his resistance against Freud's sexual drive theory in favor of the soul's impulse toward wholeness, and ultimately, his insistence on following his own path, seeking truth at the expense of his relationship with his beloved mentor, a relationship which had become like a bird cage, demonstrate that to spread our wings and fly, we must leave what is familiar and secure in order to discover who we truly are.

From the *Bardo Thodol*, we learn that with preparation, the macro letting go of this life through the death process or the micro surrender to attachments within this life can be handled with grace and confidence. Preparing for death and dissolution decreases fear and resistance, deepens recognition, facilitates self-liberation, leaves us with nothing to lose, and everything to gain. We need to become more familiar with the external signs, authority, institutions, or societal expectations that may be limiting us, and the internal signs like longing for adventure, curiosity, existential doubt, fear, or resentment. If we look closely, and listen intently, each of these is a sign of the soul beckoning us to move from order to chaos, encouraging us to embark toward metamorphosis.

Having departed with courage, let's begin our initiation.

7

Initiation

Rite of Passage

GUNUNG ABANG—MOUNTAIN OF BLESSINGS

It's about three hours until we touch down in Jakarta. It's been a long flight. Two days have elapsed during my journey in this tin can in the sky transitioning through time zones like a soul through lives. I'm flipping through the in-flight movie selection again, although I've done it a hundred times, somehow hoping to find something enticing to watch until we touch down. Nothing interests me. I take a stab at the documentaries. To my surprise, I find one about Bali called *Sacred and Secret*, and figure it might be good to learn about a place I've not been in more than thirty years. Finding this film was a life-changing synchronicity—we never know how karma ripens out of the mystery.

The documentary begins with what appears to be a cleric or priest dressed in all-white attire. He is regal and elegant as he walks Bali streets, greeting locals and tourists with a serene smile. He has a profound magnetism, and I'm thoroughly captivated. The scenes move through ceremonies with our enigmatic protagonist, amid exotic temples, praying in front of glorious deities, offering a rainbow stream of exotic flowers, sharing delicate sprinkles of holy water to devotees like drops of divine rain, all held within the distinctive sounds of the

Gamelan—the Balinese xylophone. This scene is why I'm heading back, to be immersed in this ancient culture with its living tradition of tantric Hinduism at its heart. Despite the crushing one-two punch of modernization and commercialization to the island of Bali, it has managed to preserve the ancient wisdom that we're losing across the planet as rapidly as endangered species.

Next scene, we see a massive crowd in a procession carrying an effigy from a temple high on a mountain ridge, down a steep cliff, apparently to be submerged in the waves as they break on the black lava sand and jagged rock shoreline. The deity at the center of the precession seems to float effortlessly by the harmony of voices chanting mantras on its pilgrimage from the mountain to the sea. It's a gripping spectacle, a symbolic reenactment of the death-rebirth process that every pilgrimage helps us embody. Leading the ceremony is our cleric, surrounded by hordes of people in prayer. The ritual is an orchestra and he the conductor, except the theater is nature herself, wind and waves, earth and fire, trees and flowers, breath and mantra, all the elements merging into a divine symphony to tantalize and rouse the soul from its slumber and from the doldrums of ordinary consciousness. It's psychodrama at its finest, something we've lost in the West.

A few hours later, I land in Jakarta. I am barely outside long enough to take in a last gulp of humid air before being escorted to my hotel room for six nights. I had splurged on a luxury hotel as I'd never experienced quarantine before. There was no leaving the room. No open windows. Meals are left at the door. It is a luxury prison I'd accepted as my price to get to Bali while the world stood still. Thanks to Emily, my time was my own. Flipping open my laptop, I look for the cleric who made such an impression.

It didn't take long to find his name in the documentary credits: Tjokorda Raka Kerthyasa, a royal family member. In fact, he's a high prince of Ubud, occupying positions that merge royalty, politician, and head of religious ceremony. I look further and find he has three children: one of them, Tjok Gde Kerthyasa, near my age, is a therapist like me.

Specifically, he's a well-respected homeopathic physician with a clinic in Ubud, the artisan heartland of Bali. I googled further and watched a lecture by Tjok Gde. He's dressed in ceremonial garb with a headdress, delivering in perfect English a topic known as Tri Hita Karana. I fall further down a rabbit hole for what seems like days. Between the jet lag and quarantine, I don't know what day it is.

Tri Hita Karana is exquisitely beautiful, a practical philosophy that seeks to optimize three-fold relationships between other human beings, mother nature, and the spirit realm. It does this through conscientiousness of our interrelatedness, interdependence, intentions, and acts of karmic generosity. It's aligned with my heart practice of Tibetan Buddhism. Both have Indic tantric origin, although I've never encountered a philosophy that so beautifully includes and reveres the natural world. More than that, I like Tjok Gde's eloquence, clarity, and grace. Like his father, he has a regal dignity and lovely energy about him, and I listen to everything he offers online.

I reach out to him for an interview. Initially, I don't hear back, so I persist. In the days after my quarantine, I leave Jakarta and finally make it to Bali, a meeting with Tjok Gde preoccupying me. Yes, the rice fields in Bali are beautiful, and there was this book to write, but I needed to meet the wisdom keeper, the spiritual representative of the island, and seek his counsel and blessing. The guy blows me off three times! Finally, I reach a staff member, introduced myself, and arranged an interview.

The day arrived. Tjok Gde was a half hour late and emerged from treating a patient in his clinic office. He looked tired, barely a smile on his face as we greeted each other. Not what I was expecting. We walked past his father's personal shrine and onto a beautiful veranda of a small traditional wood house called a *juglo*. The teak panels are a wonderful weather-beaten patina. Around us is a panorama of the raw and verdant jungle.

I began the interview asking him if there was a Balinese prophecy for our apocalyptic times. Unsurprisingly, there is one called the *Sabdapalon*. Tjok said the ancients knew well about the future precisely because they studied their past. They studied the stars. All ancient cultures did; they had to. They learned through observation, collected a database of knowledge across generations, and trusted that everything from the cosmos to the psyche rotates in endless cycles of ever-evolving experience. These cycles are so long that if you lose your oral transmissions, you lose your entire culture and the centuries of stored wisdom it contains.

The wisdom keeper's eyes widen as we discuss the prophecy for our present day, how everything will be "turned upside down," how people favor vice over virtue, "how men will become women," and how the righteous will be condemned. Simultaneously, the wicked will be celebrated, and we will become spiritually blind and disregard our traditions and venerate the material world and all its ephemeral pleasures. We will forget our ancestors and the spirits, and the power of prayer will become lost and confused. And we will destroy the planet and each other as a result. It echoes the First Nation's prophecy of the Seven Fires foretold by the Anishinaabe nation of North America, the Tibetan Shambhala prophesy, and the Lament to Hermes—a cross-cultural convergence of prediction. I see a spark in Tjok Gde's eyes now. He perks up as we banter; perhaps he senses this won't be an ordinary interview, and I won't just be another foreign ex-pat asking annoying questions about mindfulness or green juices, another impediment to his dinner plans and much-needed rest.

With each question and answer, more life is restored until we hit a natural flow of mutual synergy. At points, we complete each other's sentences, nodding intently and savoring the conversation as the afternoon mysteriously transitions to dusk, bringing the evening song of birds and wildlife that fill the cavernous jungle valley around us. To say the least, my "chance" encounter with Tjok Gde was unmistakably meeting a kindred spirit—a soul mate from a past life. This is a rare and remarkable encounter. You might go an entire lifetime and never be blindsided by an instant karmic connection. Lynn was right; I did fall in love. Not romantically, but in every sense of the Buddhist definition:

equally invested in the happiness of another as your own. The prince and I could have spoken for hours that night, and we did, meeting nearly every day during my six-week pilgrimage.

After several days of enjoyable conversations covering all our mutual interests from Buddhism and Hinduism, astrology and alchemy, Rudolph Steiner and Jung, with escapades to his organic garden where he grows natural medicines, to his clinic and its full-blown alchemy laboratory, I affectionately dub Tjok Gde the "Wizard of Bali," which he sheepishly accepts. During one of our early conversations, he asks me pointedly what I'm doing in Bali. I tell the Wizard I'm in a death and rebirth process, looking for a new home for my family, a place to reboot my career, I'm on a personal pilgrimage following the magic. I tell him about the panic attacks, that after years of one-on-one work confined in my Manhattan office, how I started leading spiritual tours that helped me heal and will help others heal from the root cause trauma of pervasive disconnection and disassociation. I want to bring groups here to Bali. He was keen to know more, and a light flashed in his eyes as we engaged. He asked if I'd join him on pilgrimage up a sacred mountain.

"Like a rite of passage?" I asked.

"Yes, everyone climbs a holy peak here."

The next night I arrived with my sneakers and water bottle. Clearly, I had no idea what I was in for. We didn't sleep; instead, we fell into another all-night discussion and, before I knew it, we were at the base of the mountain drinking strong black Sumatran coffee, thick as mud, with a local guide who couldn't have been taller than four feet, but who displayed heroic prowess as he led us into the thicket. Tjok Gde was decked in full trekking gear, boots, proper hiking pants, headlamps, and poles. "Oh shit," I thought. I gulped down a second cup of coffee with an extra spoon of sugar, "I'm going to need this."

The three of us set off from the mountain's base under the cover of darkness. At first, there was a trail, but soon I realized the trodden path merged into the raw jungle. Before I knew it, we were climbing through a thicket, treading over unstable rocks, desperate not to slip down steep slopes. Never mind the creepy crawlies and snakes, I couldn't even see my hand in front of my face. Then, after about an hour and at three other junctures ahead of us, we stopped in a clearing illuminated by moonlight, where I could make out the outlines of a small shrine with stone carvings. "Have some more coffee and catch your breath," Tjok Gde said, "then we'll make offerings and pray for the next leg of the journey." Yeah, we need to pray, I thought, that was brutal, and we're only a third through this thing. The next few hours were grueling as the incline increased and the route became more treacherous. I'm an active person, I run five miles a day and lift weights, but I wasn't prepared for any of this, and my body struggled with the landscape and the limits of my mind. There were moments when I was in full snake mode, slithering on my belly to reach the tree roots above me and pull myself up the slope. I struggled to keep up. The boys were often ahead of me, and I trailed behind in the dark.

The guide announced we were close, Tjok Gde translated, and I felt relieved. But we weren't done yet, and remember: the closer you are to your goal on pilgrimage, the more challenges will emerge. It's a purification, not a punishment. The mountain wants to know if you really want the summit. It wants you to be sure you're ready. It wants to know that you'll surrender everything. We approached a thick patch of jungle brush, and before I knew it, Tjok Gde fully disappeared into its tangled embrace. I went in after him, gasping for breath. Although I knew he was ahead of me, I felt utterly alone. It was a perfect tunnel shape, squeezing me with branches from all sides. Every step was labor. At one point, I fell and collapsed to the ground. I couldn't take another step. I was done. In fetal position, I was assailed by a barrage of self-criticism, *"You're weak, a failure."* Painful memories flooded me: times I blew up at my kids in frustration, said hurtful things to my wife, was arrogant and unkind. I felt selfish and guilty. I had tucked these memories in the recesses of my unconscious, yet the mountain activated them, summoned them for accounting, and I had nowhere to run. In a narrow passageway of thorns, I couldn't go back or forward. I was stuck in the bardo, drowning in my own karmic shit.

By some act of grace, the diamond queen of intuition appeared and spoke to me as an inner voice. She said two deceptively simple things. "Forget the summit. Think only about what is here and now." And "Take one step at a time, embracing the struggle." There is much profundity in these words, and I had no choice but to comply. What was here and now was an upsurge of regret and remorse. So, I made amends. Sobbing, I apologized to my kids, and most profoundly to my beloved Emily. *I vow not to take any of you for granted. I miss you all so much.*

I knew the guide and Tjok Gde might already be up on the summit enjoying the vista and a cold drink, but here I was. This was the only moment that was real. And I needed to be with my sorrow and regret. Then I thought of the second suggestion, to take one step at a time. I didn't need to get to the top. All I had to do was get up. As I stood up, I thought: *I don't need to catch up with the others. All I need to do is put one foot on that rock or grab that branch.* Green Tara reminded, "Don't think of anything else ahead. Just what's in your most immediate field of experience here and now. That's it." And that's all you'll ever need to do when confronted with any test or trial. Whether it's a mountain or leaving an abusive relationship, kicking an addiction, or facing your biggest fear, forget the summit, just focus on your most immediate, next step.

Through Tara's grace, I was moving again. Although I couldn't see him, I heard Tjok Gde ahead. I cried out, "Wizard, this is it, we're in the birth canal, and these are the labor pains before rebirth." He cried out, "You're right, brother, we're in the throes of labor now!" We emerged from the thicket no more than five minutes later. The Wizard and I fell into each other arms, tearful, muddied, and exhausted but filled with exhilaration and delight. It was magnificent. Later, he told me this climb was the hardest one yet, although he summited sacred mountains many times. Furthermore, while negotiating the thicket tunnel, he was also assailed by personal regrets as a father and human. It was as if we shared the same torment and awakening. Upon entering the clearing, I dropped to the ground for three prostrations at the main shrine on the summit although the real initiation had been done when the mountain tore down my defenses and activated the karma I needed to work through. The diamond queen appeared and taught me what I needed to learn, and there would have been no way for this to happen with my toes up sitting by the pool overlooking the Balinese rice fields at the villa. After a final round of offerings and a few well-deserved swigs of water, I caught a faint cell phone signal and called Emily and my boys. To my amazement, I got through from the summit! Through my tears and the broken cell reception, I shared my regrets and told them how much I loved them. From opposite sides of the planet, and dimensions of reality apart, I knew the message was received.

Then, the guide, the Wizard, and I all admired the vista. It was prehistoric. A thick blanket of cloud coverage obscured the land below us, and what remained was a panoramic view of the sacred mountain peak of Mount Batur in the near distance—staring from one sacred mountain to another, the active volcano on the island. The sun was at its apex now; only a clear blue sky was above. It felt like we were with all the gods on Mount Olympus, and perhaps we were. I asked the guide what the mountain was called, and he said Gunung Abang. Tjok Gde poetically translated, "The Mountain of Gifts." Indeed, it was. This was my initiation to Bali, a rite of passage beyond my imagination. Be careful what you wish for.

RITES OF PASSAGE

A rite-of-passage is a special ceremony, ritual, or physical activity, used by traditional cultures for millennia to help individuals and small groups mobilize through a developmental transition to a new phase of life. Each rite is designed to help ripen or mature an individual, expose and integrate their limitations, challenge them to discover new strengths and innate qualities, embolden them to develop new skills, attitudes, and outlooks, prepare them to successfully navigate the next phase of their life, and make a positive contribution to their community and planet.

Common milestones for which a rite of passage are ceremoniously used in Indigenous cultures, demarcating a threshold crossing, can be grouped into five categories: birth rites welcome an infant into the world, rites for adulthood facilitate coming of age for youth, marriage rites demarcate the end of a solitary life and beginning of partnership, rites of eldership sanction adults to impart their wisdom to the tribe, and death rites open the doors to the beyond, beseeching spirit guides and ancestors to receive the soul during transmigration. From womb to world, child to adult, individual to couple, adult to elder, and elder to ancestor, an initiatory rite and ritual makes a deep imprint through the right brain, and deep down into the soul, to let go of one life and embrace the next stage of the cyclic journey.

We see the remnants of traditional religious rites in modern industrialized cultures—wedding ceremonies, baptisms for birth, confirmations and Bar and Bat Mitzvas, and funeral rites, but often they have been watered down and commercialized, losing potency and meaning, and therefore can fail to properly serve as a catalyst of psychological development.

Can you pull a frat boy out of a college hazing ritual and send them off for a weekend on a traditional vision quest with a First Nations community and expect similar results as their Indigenous members? Probably not. It's not just the ritual that matters. The worldview, sincere attitude, conducive lifestyle, sacred ritual imbued with meaning, methods for altering consciousness, and the post-ritual rewards and community are all necessary to make the process a bona fide catalyst.

Can you initiate an outsider, and expect it to work? Perhaps, if the culture or tradition is inclined to share its sacred wisdom and practices, and offers the full context, and the initiate exhibits the required prerequisites, it's possible for people from modern cultures that abandoned sacred worldviews to look to other wisdom cultures that have maintained unbroken lineages, and with humility and sincerity request their blessing. However, we must be mindful of spiritual colonialization; we can't assume our showing up is sufficient for cross-cultural exchanges and reciprocity. Even Jung questioned, as does the Dalai Lama, if it's not better to stay within our cultural matrix, reigniting the embers of our tradition's spiritual legacies.

MY INITIATION WITH JOE

Sometimes the initiation looks nothing like climbing a perilous sacred mountain or drinking a potent psychedelic brew. There are subtler variations, involving the age-old tradition of master-apprentice, and inevitably the passing on of an art, skill, knowledge, or craft. In artisan communities you can still find the institution of expert craftspeople, musicians, healers and the like, passing on not only their skill, but the mythology and cosmology that contains it, in an unbroken lineage, commonly from parent to child. I'm so fortunate in my lifetime to have received such an opportunity.

Of all the experiences I've had, perhaps the most rare, special, and influential was the nearly twenty-year apprenticeship and initiation I undertook with my mentor Joe Loizzo, a Buddhist psychiatrist, and first to offer a neuropsychological lens on the complete gradual path to enlightenment (*lam rim*) preserved in Tibet. His mentor is Robert Thurman, and *his* mentor is the Dalai Lama, so it's a sound lineage. I met Joe in 1999 when he welcomed me into his clinic when I was twenty years old, eager, having just returned from a four-month pilgrimage through Asia, seeking to establish a professional role that fused my love of Buddhism with a modern application in psychology.

I started by observing Joe work with his patients and his delivery of Tibetan-inspired interventions while tracking patient progress. Late into the night, I helped him compile teaching materials—tape recordings of guided meditations and hand-bound binders of esoteric knowledge Joe rendered elegantly into contemporary language. I took every course he offered, attended every symposium, read every book and paper he suggested, took copious notes, recorded and relistened to his advice until it was all internalized. I did menial tasks, such as cleaning his office and serving him tea, and tended to the day-to-day affairs of running a business that joined the spiritual with mundane. Eventually, Joe asked me to contribute to his teaching sessions, guiding meditations, leading discussions, sharing in the question-and-answer period. I was growing and being integrated into the fold, but there was no formal ritual, no dramatic ceremony. One could barely detect the progress, it was just living life.

By 2001, having completed my master's degree at NYU, under his guidance, Joe suggested I get a doctorate. He said it would open doors and, "give me more time to cook." Joe valued the slow *process* of gradual awakening. He knew it well, having himself been an apprentice for an extended period, late into his adulthood, completing his MD in psychiatry, then a PhD in Buddhist studies under Thurman. It was not until his forties that he started teaching and writing books. He saw the long game.

With trepidation I went to California for a doctorate in clinical psychology. It was five years of nearly unbearable struggle. I never fit in. I hated the dry, Western academic approach. The vibrancy of being on the cutting edge of something just emerging, a bridge between ancient and modern, science and spirit, which had set me ablaze, was replaced by something that made me feel uninspired. I missed being at Joe's clinic or the hospital, engaging clients, and was stuck in a classroom studying what I saw as meaningless statistical design, research methods, and testing protocols. In a moment of despair, I reached out to my mother and told her I couldn't bear another day. She encouraged me to give it up. "Why go through all the trouble and expense? Come home and we'll take care of you, we'll find something else to do—something a little easier." It was her best effort at comforting me, easing the pain, by bailing out when things got tough.

Whether it's external or internal, challenge arises. Why struggle? Why not quit and return to Eden? We will each need to answer this perennial question. Thankfully, I had long conversations with Joe about my doubt and depression, and he encouraged me instead to persevere, skillfully dangling enticing opportunities to work with him upon my return to New York, like a carrot in front of me to keep me moving forward.

I began focusing less on my struggle with academics, and more on what inspired me. In my clinical practicum working with clients, I could apply what I had learned from Joe, the contemplative psychotherapy method he created—it informed how I assessed a case, empathized with my clients's lived experience, and how I facilitated their healing, insight, and change. Behind closed doors with clients, I was drawing on an internalized spirit of Joe, play-acting as if I were him providing counsel. My imagination allowed Joe to live through me, to become me. The dullness of graduate school forced me to rely on the guru, as an inner spark of light. Later I developed in-service projects on Buddhist therapy for students and faculty and designed an eight-week meditation program for clients that would carry me through graduate school until I'd return to New York to work with Joe again.

The graduate school initiation ended in 2006. I had jumped through every hoop, all the doubts, boring courses, rigorous exams, numerous clinical hours, and the grueling dissertation. I was a doctor. I crossed the threshold. But the initiation was just beginning. First chance I got, I was back in New York with my mentor, working more closely and on bigger projects. Our relationship gained complexity; Joe wasn't just a mentor imparting knowledge, but now a supervisor guiding my cases, and by necessity, a de facto therapist watching my emotional blind spot—as well as a friend—although it wasn't always easy or smooth between us.

Apprenticeship often means delaying gratification, listening to the teacher, and biting your tongue, even—especially—when you disagree. Many times, I was redirected against my inclination, yet complied because of the enormous trust I had in Joe. Few people appreciate how difficult it can be to serve a mentor with body and mind for two decades. Once you take the initiation, you commit to fulfilling the

vision of your teacher no matter what you feel. You believe in the promise and vision they have of you, preceisly because you can't yet see it
clearly yourself. But the closer you are with someone, the more subtle
and hard to detect your projections, and the greater risk of mishaps. We
often had to process conflicts and misunderstandings. All the while,
Joe taught me about my mind, how to face difficulty, self-regulate,
communicate needs, and resolve traumas within the crucible of mutual
respect. *Solve et coagula.* In this way even the interpersonal challenges
were part of the path, likely the most instructive part of the initiation
and why top-down academia is so limited.

My initiation extended beyond the institutional. In 2004 Joe set
me up on a blind date with Emily and married us in 2008 in a private Buddhist ceremony in our home in Manhattan, with my father
present online as he battled cancer in Turkey. During that time, I
became Joe's Assistant Director, and Emily the Director of Programs
for the Nalanda Institute for Contemplative Science Joe founded, an
education nonprofit blending Buddhism and psychology. It was an
honor. The first time Joe invited me to speak, in front of an audience at Tibet House in 2008, I uttered barely three sentences. By 2012
I was solo teaching his four-year program, comprised of forty-eight
classes. None of this reflected the academic programs or institutions
I attended or the books I read. Instead, it was the outgrowth of our
mentoring relationship.

By 2017, my psychotherapy practice was thriving and I'd found
a comfortable niche as a Buddhist therapist working exclusively with
yogis and meditators to transform spiritual bypassing, depression, anxiety, trauma, and interpersonal conflicts into wisdom and compassion.
When I started my journey, I was a boy, in awe of my teachers; when
I concluded my initiation, I was a colleague—doctor, teacher, author,
husband, and father. After twenty years of hard work—successes and
failures, breakthroughs, and near breakups—in this meaningful and
challenging relationship, the most exhilarating and excruciating journey
of my life had born fruit.

TANTRIC INITIATION

My apprenticeship with Joe parallels the classical arc of the Tibetan Buddhist initiation. I want to reveal that progression briefly to give you a sense of the various components, stages, and their effects. For thousands of years, the unique way the Tibetans traverse the path towards enlightenment is for the student to take refuge in four jewels: Buddha as the historical figure who made it through delusion to enlightenment, becoming our guide; his teachings, the Dharma, our roadmap to navigate the journey; and Sangha, the travel companions who support us along the way. The diamond vehicle or tantric tradition of Buddhism preserved in Tibet made a unique innovation, drawing from its Indian forbearers by adding a fourth jewel, the mentor—guru in Sanskrit, lama in Tibetan. The mentor is seen as the three jewels combined, embodied, and revered as a living emissary of the historical Buddha. Rather than relying on scriptures and stories of past inspirational figures, we get to meet the Buddha live in the flesh.

Earlier in this book you'll note I call the mentor "the uplink." They're your direct connection to the awakened mind. In the guru, you not only receive the transmission through the lineage of all the disciples who similarly woke up in a legacy passed down from teacher to student, you get something more powerful, although often overlooked: a living presence and role-model for the embodiment of awakening. The way the teacher passes on the craft, the magic, goes beyond words, otherwise a book would suffice.

Finding a Mentor

How do you find a mentor? The first step is to understand the importance of a teacher no matter the craft, from music to sports, even the pursuit of enlightenment is enhanced by a guide who can show you the ropes. If you were a novice at the base of Mount Everest, could you make it to the summit alone? The primary criterion for spiritual progress is to find a qualified guide. The spiritual path is fraught with perils.

Someone who has traveled and reached the other side or at least gone further than you, will have something indispensable to impart.

The Causes for a Mentor

You must create the causes for meeting a teacher. Clarify your intention, collect good karma through virtuous acts, and dedicate the merits specifically to meet a teacher. Karma is the inner causes. Then, you'll want to go on an exhaustive external search, but timing and other conditions are beyond control, so focus on inner causes and be patient. Eventually, somebody will appear, or finding your teacher might be a synchronistic experience. Keep an open mind and trusting heart. Karma eventually ripens, we just don't know when.

Mentor Qualities

As a student, do your due diligence. Analyze the teacher to develop unshakable confidence in their embodiment of these essential qualities: ethics, mental quiescence, and insight into emptiness, or at least the profound understanding of emptiness. Further, teachers should possess a refined textual knowledge, artful delivery, infectious enthusiasm, wise profundity, perseverance, and patience. Mentors don't tire when their students need reinforcement, they don't get impatient. In a degenerate age when it's hard to find a mentor with such impeccable qualifications, they say to look for two in particular: 1) the mentor cares more about others than themselves, and 2) orients towards future lives more than just the present one.

In the Tibetan tradition, a mentee scrutinizes a potential guru for about twelve years before signing on. Take your time, be discerning, it's an important decision, perhaps the biggest in determining your evolution. Don't pounce and immediately prostrate to the first teacher you meet. Continuously check if their words and actions are congruent, and resolve your doubt so when the time is right, nothing holds you back.

Student's Responsibilities

There's a two-way contract, and students must also be ready to engage in genuine work with a teacher. Addressing the often-unconscious relational patterns of codependency and transference issues is necessary to working with a mentor. Be on the lookout to avoid replicating destructive childhood dynamics. At least have an awareness of your relational patterns so when conflict arises you can work with your own projections. Keep one eye on the mentor, the other on your shadow.

Seems obvious, but students need to be open-minded and receptive. If you know it all, then nothing new can be learned. Second, your intentions must be clear, why do you want to study the Dharma? What will you do with this sacred knowledge? A good student is always refining their bodhicitta, the aspiration to benefit and free all beings, including oneself. Finally, a student must be earnest and determined, pursuing the path as a matter of life and death.

Melding of Minds

If you're well-intended and the teacher has sound qualifications, something magical can happen: a melding of minds. This is one of the trademarks of tantra, called the Guru yoga practice. The Tibetans understood how relationships with caregivers shape young and impressionable minds of children, for better or worse. If the teacher is well self-actualized, in possession of numerous good qualities, then vicariously—through mirroring and relational imprinting—students can access and nurture their own good qualities and grow along the path. The method is unique and brilliant, it combines this proximity with a living master with a meditation-based virtual reality simulation designed to amplify resonance and expedite development. During visualization, one augments reality with imagined versions of their teacher fused with deity archetypes, enhancing their prowess, then merging the guru-deity into one's midstream in a process of internalization and integration. For this reason, be careful who you choose to mind meld with, because you'll become them!

PREREQUISITES FOR TANTRA

Before we can even discuss tantric meditation practice within the context of initiation, we need the foundations or prerequisites, called the
Three Principles of the Path to Awakening: *renunciation, bodhicitta,*
and *correct view.* In my estimation, the so called "power-tools" of any
spiritual tradition, including psychedelics, would be enhanced and the
pitfalls reduced, by adherence to these three. They are like wearing your
seatbelt in a highspeed racecar.

> *Renunciation* is the mindset or capability to disrupt your own cycles
> of stress and trauma—knowing how to circuit break unconscious
> patterns of self-imposed misery.
> *Bodhicitta* is the mindset or compassionate resolve to awaken for
> the benefit of others—being empathically sensitized to their pre-
> dicament, wishing to help them learn how to circuit-break *their*
> trauma cycles.
> *Correct view of emptiness* is the mindset or wisdom realizing the
> open, interconnected nature of reality—uprooting the reification
> habit at the root of trauma cycles.

All the Buddha's public or foundational teachings fit into these
three principles, which I've translated as self-care (for renunciation),
altruism (for bodhicitta), and quantum view (for correct view).

Six Ordinary Preliminaries
If the three principles guide one's spiritual life off the cushion between
meditative sessions, the six preliminaries guide one's visualization practice within the meditative session. You can refer to my book *Gradual
Awakening* for more details.

1. Create a sacred environment.
2. Set up an altar and make an offering.

3. Prepare the body and mind.
4. Evoke the mentor of the refuge field.
5. Follow the seven steps of the mentor-bonding process.
6. Offer the mandala (purified world) and dedicate merit.

On the Tibetan path we are constantly working between two worlds, actual and virtual, the real-life mentor and the imagined guru-deity, the three principles that guide life and the six prelims that structure meditation. Clearly the idea is to toggle back and forth until distinctions blur like in a waking dream, humanity and divinity unite. Let's continue.

Outer Preliminaries

To complement the ordinary preliminaries are four contemplations called the outer preliminaries: precious life, death, karma, and the sufferings of cyclic existence.* First, we recognize how our precious human rebirth, given the vast cosmology and rebirth possibilities, is the most fortunate and conducive circumstance for enlightenment. This reflection engenders appreciation for the life which we've karmically inherited; we've everything we need for liberation. Second, by contemplating how death is certain, yet the time uncertain, urgency is engendered to take spiritual advantage of our precious and fleeting opportunity. We then ponder karma, cause and effect, engendering a sense of agency and responsibility to orient us towards virtue and avoiding the evolutionary downgrading consequences of vice. Finally, we contemplate the suffering nature of compulsive or unconscious life, facing its misery, and engendering the determination to wake up, to be free.

Extraordinary Preliminaries

Progressing through our training, we now reach the extraordinary preliminaries. These are a form of purification practice that works on

---

*These are the first four steps, after guru and student, on the gradual stages of the path, lamrim, traced in my book *Gradual Awakening*.

deeper layers of consciousness, activating latent stores of unprocessed trauma, clearing blocks that bind subtle energy, and transmuting shadow emotions into virtues. There are different sets of preliminaries in various Tibetan lineages and here I introduce five: refuge with prostrations, bodhicitta accumulation, mandala offerings, Vajrasattva practice, and guru yoga.

Refuge and Prostrations

Done in conjunction with taking refuge in the three jewels—Buddha, Dharma, Sangha—are full-body prostrations. You're bowing, repeatedly to a greater source of wisdom, a more enlightened way of being. As you descend to earth, *solve*, you loosen your ego-fixation, and as you arise, *et coagula*, you seek to benefit of others. The physical prostration itself can be modified based on age, fragility, or injury, the most important thing to transmute is pride. These practices are meant to break your self-importance, your sense of being in control, and are done in sets of 100,000 repetitions—an incredible commitment, which can take years to complete. If you rush through them to check off the numbers, the teacher will spot this and send you, like the child's game of chutes and ladders, back to the beginning. Fittingly, the destination is less important than the journey.

Bodhicitta Accumulation

The second extraordinary preliminary is bodhicitta, the development of the altruistic resolve to awaken for others. It is initially combined with prostrations, then becomes the motivation underlying the other preliminaries, and eventually all spiritual practices. It is the mainstay practice. We bring body, speech, and mind into alignment, through actions—suffused with altruism. This set of 100,000 is designed to purify jealousy and the ways we feel competitive and envious of others who get the things we want or stand in our way. Bodhicitta is the natural consequence of our re-sensitizing to the plight, and taking universal responsibility, for others.

Mandala Offerings

Next comes the mandala offering, again 100,000 in number. A multi-dimensional practice, combining movement, mantra, and visualization. We use a plate to symbolize a sacred ground atop of which we construct the mythological Mount Meru with grains of rice—an axis mundi, Mount Olympus, the summit of enlightenment—simultaneously constructing it in our mind. Every aspect of construction has meaning, an imagined world filled with deities, objects, and flora. Since we grow so attached to the things we build in life—our work, body, identity—we practice giving it all away instead. Offering the mandala as soon as it's complete, wiping the slate clean to rebuild again 100,000 times as we transmute the poisons of attachment and clinging into the perfume of radical acceptance and generosity.

Vajrasattva Practice

Fourth is Vajrasattva practice. We visualize the luminous deity of purity, Diamond Hero, and recite his extensive hundred-syllable mantra designed to transmute aggression and the harm we've caused others based on misapprehension. The Vajrasattva practice doesn't involve a guilt trip, there is no mea culpa; instead it's based on wise understanding of how karma can be transmuted with self-compassion. We acknowledge the harm we've caused through anger, generate sincere regret, recite the mantra as an energetic antidote, and resolve to refrain from repeating the harm again. Very powerful soul sculpting.

Guru Yoga

The extraordinary preliminaries culminate in guru yoga, or mentor bonding—the prayers, visualization and supplication to one's teacher, and the melding of minds. Like water poured into water, the dissolution of fixed boundaries, and the merging of the guru into one's crown, past the throat, and into the heart chakra, transforms body, speech, and mind, displaces identity fixation, and the false conviction that we are separate from the world. Self and other are constructs in an unconscious hallucination;

the guru yoga practice orients you to the fluid nature of reality, letting you experience the world simultaneously from the vantage point of the mentor you admire. Appearances are merely mirages, and an underlying sensitivity to the malleability of reality is recognized with each repetition. In our daily life when things go wrong, accidents happen, losses and challenges befall us, the mental habit to collapse and react is replaced with more openness and creativity. When yoga is successful the external guru is installed in our own mind. Download complete. There is no separation.

Tests, Enemies, and Allies

At this point, I'd like to introduce another of Campbell's stages: tests, enemies, and allies. When you're in the secret world, you must face some challenges that you were knowingly or unknowingly avoiding in the ordinary world. You arrive a bit naive, untested, unprepared for the dark forces around and within you that rudely awaken, intimidate, bully, and take advantage of you. They remind you the world isn't a pleasure garden, it's hard, unjust, and terrifying. Evil is real. This is not a place for children or the innocent. You may want to retreat, but you can't, because the only way out now is through. Your eyes are open, that is the consequence of the departure, and now in the initiation you're heading into a good ass kicking, which is necessary to ripen your innate qualities, and draw out some latent skills necessary for the journey ahead. The enemies are within and without; the tests and allies are both internal qualities and external forces.

However, you're not alone. You have a mentor to guide you, and you'll find your tribe. Maybe each member has strength and weakness, like Dorothy's companions in *The Wizard of Oz*. Sometimes your allies are external—ancestors, like-minded companions, or spirit guides— sometimes they emerge as the voice of an inner guru, visions in broad daylight, or dreams—sometimes as inner qualities like generosity and perseverance beyond what you thought you possessed. Sometimes the mentor appears in human form, as a monk, spiritual elder, or a bodhisattva in disguise. At other times the mentor is a mountain, storm, or even a place of pilgrimage. It can be abstract, like an experience Emily had on her third marathon when an inner coach visited her—twenty miles in, six to go—she couldn't stop, couldn't turn back, but had nothing left, but was able to finish—a bit like me with the Wizard summiting the mountain when Green Tara's voice appeared.

Another way to understand tests, enemies, and allies, is to see them not as external entities, but as the inner practices, poisons, and medicines of transmutation in the extraordinary preliminaries. For examples, prostrations are the test, pride the enemy, and humility your ally. For the test of the 100,000 mandala offerings, greed is the enemy, generosity the ally, while for Vajrasattva practice, anger is the enemy, love the ally, etc. The mythos of the characters and challenges we encounter in the outer landscape are reflected in the inner soulscape.

Requesting Initiation

Once you've met your mentor and completed the ordinary and extraordinary preliminaries, if you have a pure intention to receive initiation into a deity practice you can make a sincere request of your teacher. They might not oblige, but if they do, they must themselves have all the prerequisites; they must have received the initiation from a qualified lineage source, and have completed the extensive deep retreats and mantra recitations of that deity. In other words, they must know that deity through and through, so their mind is suffused with the deity's mind, so that when you request the transmission from your mentor, you're asking to merge your mind directly with deity in an unbroken transmission. Lama Yeshe described the meaning of tantric initiation this way,

> What is initiation? It is the beginning of the experience of meditation and concentration, of penetration into the nature of the reality of all phenomena. Initiation leads us into the mandala of a deity and into the totality of the experience of that deity. It is an antidote to the dissatisfied, samsaric, fanatical, dualistic mind. During initiation we should completely let go of our preconceptions and fixed ideas of who

we are, of our limited self-image. Instead, we need to identify with the wisdom-mind of the deity, which is our own perfect potential.[1]

Thurman describes the pith result of initiation as:

The essential outcome of initiation is that, on both conscious and sub-conscious levels, you are imaginatively exalted in the actuality of your own potential enlightenment, physically, verbally, mentally, and intuitively. While you may still be far from full realization, your subsequent practice proceeds with that imaginative orientation. You meditate within the imaginative understanding that perfect enlightenment is fully immediate, and your practice is gradually removing impediments to your realization of that fact; you no longer assent to the idea that your enlightenment is somewhere beyond, "out there" in place or in time, to be reached later. Tantra is called the "resultant vehicle," because you practice from the position of having already achieved enlighten-ment, in contrast with exoteric methods, considered the causal vehicle because your practice accumulates the necessary wisdom and merit as you progress towards Buddhahood. Resultant-vehicle practice naturally involves tolerating cognitive dissonance. Your ordinary mind is falsely convinced that you're not enlightened, its stuck in the pride of ordinariness, so you momentarily suspend that disbelief to allow your nervous system to approximate or try on for size the enlightened state represented by your mentor. This antidote is called divine pride. Your visualization of bonding with the mentor-diety thus exerts a powerful counter force against your habitual perception of being unenlightened, while reifying attachment to both states, ordinary and extraordinary, are disrupted by the awareness of the voidness of both.[2]

Ironically, Geshe-la explained he doesn't grant tantric initiations often or easily, instead encouraging students to focus on lam rim, collecting merit, developing wisdom, and steadily enjoying the pre-liminaries. "They rush to receive the initiation," he said in one of our conversations, "but then nothing much happens, they're disappointed and soon abandon the practice." I said people rush, because tantra is sexy, while the preliminaries look like hard work. Geshe-la told me in that case initiation is just "hollow words." Another time Geshe-la told me, "True initiation is that you practice the three principles of the paths" (renunciation, bodhicitta and correct view). The final ceremony that grants access to the deity, following the four empowerments, Geshe-la says, these are like an "award ceremony" and all the hard work, years of preparation, intensive study and practice, is where the transformation comes from. "So don't be in such a rush with your preliminaries" he warned, "let the preliminaries be your main practice." I've know Geshe-la since 2006, nearly twenty years, and he is only now preparing us for initiation. Most would have considered this frustratingly slow or unnecessarily cautions, instead I see it as a sign of his great compassion. Sometimes a firm no, a thoughtful, consistent boundary, or a swift kick in the ass, is the hardest, but most skillful gift to give and receive.

JUNG'S INITIATION

After Jung's collision with Freud prompting his call to adventure, and his divergence from the materialistic paradigm, Jung's third departure is his break with his sanity, which I will reserve for a bit later when we go into the *ordeal* phase of the Hero's Journey.

Jung pushed back on Freud's reductionism, his soul yearning for a more expansive horizon to account for human health and healing. Jung's departure from Freud was a loss of trust in his authority, and a cultural criticism of scientific materialism. Jung turned to religion, myth, and archaeology and into occult disciplines from Gnosticism to alchemy to astrology. The parameters of exploration which Jung extended, what he called a *movement of therapy*, were perhaps ahead of its time. Jung didn't belong in the culture where he found himself. Jung would probably have been better suited for where we are in time now, engaged in energy medicine, the rise of the occult, embracing shamanism, and the psychedelic revolution.

Jung's original philosophy would be better received now. Unfortunately, when he first introduced his theories, Jung's psychology was considered too esoteric, too fringe. He danced the razor's edge of sanity.

Jung's Early Life

Jung was raised in the culture of the Swiss Reformed Church where his father was a pastor. Jung's mother was depressed. He was surrounded not only by immediate family members but by both his grandfathers, who were fascinating characters. One of his grandfathers was a physician, and would come to represent the extreme of science, while the other was a grand master of Freemasons, a secret society with historic ties to Rosicrucianism, and through it alchemy and esoteric teachings like hermeticism. The other grandfather was a theologian who had visions, conversed with the dead, and devoted his life to learning Hebrew (believing it was the language spoken by God and in heaven). These are some of Jung's ancestral imprints.

Jung mentioned two poignant reflections about his parents in his 1961 memoir *Memory, Dreams, and Reflections*.[3] "When Jung was just three years old, his mother had a nervous breakdown and spent several months in hospital. Of this event Jung wrote: "From then on I always felt mistrustful when the word 'love' was spoken. The feeling I associated with 'woman' was for a long time that of innate unreliability."[4] Jung's father was kind but weak-willed, and, in Jung's mind, too accepting of the religious dogma in which he had lost all faith."[4]

Once when he pushed his father for an explanation of the holy trinity upon which his entire faith was based, he received a tacit answer that left Jung unconvinced his father was fit for service as a priest, and by extension, for his paternal role. Though he has a family, Jung is effectively a young orphan.[5]

Jung's Primordial Fire

When he was seven years old, Jung recounts playing endlessly in the forests behind the house, and enjoyed building fires in caves. At this tender age he has his first vision, that he is tending to the *primordial fire*, a mythic motif of a wisdom keeper, an elder. And although a group of children also played in these caves, Jung wasn't interested in their games. He's curious and committed to the fire, drawn in by the sense that it is an eternal flame and he must be its custodian. Outside the cave, Jung sits upon a rocky outcrop and has an epiphany: "I'm sitting on the rock. But I'm also the rock being sat upon."[6] This early ability to split or expand the parameters of his psyche—identifying at once with his limited body but also beyond it with the rock—would foreshadow things to come.

Jung's Anxiety Totem

The insecure attachment style that strickened Jung as a result of his mother's depression and his father's spinelessness may have caused Jung to experience tremendous inadequacy growing up as a child. He couldn't do simple algebra, he was bullied and teased at school about his incompetence and idiosyncrasies. I assume this created a level of psychic pressure on Jung, which led to a kind of split personality. Early on, maybe around seven or eight, he writes that to console his anxiety, he takes a ruler from his pencil box and carves and paints a face on the top of it. He also paints a little stone and places them back in the case, which he hides in the attic of the family home. Every time he gets anxious, he excuses himself and secretly goes to the attic, where he speaks to his little ruler, and the mannequin somehow soothes him. Periodically he visits the mannequin, bringing scrolls inscribed in a secret language of his own making. Jung reports that many years later, he discovered that the carving of his figure on the wooden ruler that comforted him when he was a boy resembled the Aboriginal totems found in Australia.[7]

Jung's Split Personality

It's around this time young Jung experienced a predictable psychic split in his personality, foreshadowed by the description of his epiphany on the rock outside the cave. There were two forces within him: the young incompetent child who can't fit into his family or school life and the astute, confident elder interested in perennial and mythic themes. Jung calls these "personality one and personality two." As he wrote,

> Then to my intense confusion, I realized I was two different people. One of them was a schoolboy who could not grasp algebra and was far from sure of himself; the other was an important high authority, a man not to be trifled with. The other one was an old man who lived in the 18th century. He wore buckled shoes with a white wig and drove in a carriage with high rear wheels between a box suspended on springs. . . an ancient green carriage from a black forest drove past our house one day. It was truly antique, looking exactly as if it had come straight from the 18th century. When I saw it, I felt excitement.
>
> That's it. Sure enough. That comes from my time. It was as though I had recognized it because it was the same type I once had driven myself. Then came a curious sentiment. As though someone had stolen something for me. Or as though I had been cheated out of my beloved past. The carriage was a relic of those times. I cannot describe what was happening to me. What affected me so strongly? But it was nostalgia.[8]

Portal into the Netherworld

Jung's report of a series of odd experiences he had as a child indicate he had an extraordinary imagination, and the engagement of his fantasy life was probably self-protective, a way of maintaining psychic equilibrium. In another childhood story Jung recounts, when he was at school one day, he was pushed hard by another child to the ground, and it knocked him unconscious. Before passing out, he remembered his last thought: "Now I don't have to return to school."[9] It was his ticket out of social discomfort, a threshold crossing into dreamtime. He fainted whenever his mother got him ready for school or he had to do homework. The fainting grew so frequent his parents kept Jung home for six months, where he reports a sense of tremendous freedom. He needn't participate in the confines of the rigid structures of his family, school, and society. Instead, he's allowed to let his imagination run free; he plays in the river, goes into the woods, engages in more dialogue with his mannequin. He tends to the eternal fire, and rarely associates with others during long stretches of the day.[10]

We're witnessing the early genesis for what Jung called the process of *active imagination*, where he connects with his inner life, develops a relationship with potent images and archetypal symbols, and learns to create and live in nontemporal worlds that the Buddhist might call a mandala visualization. Not only was he not afraid of being alone on this journey through his interior landscape, but he felt more at home there than in his actual life. Some of these early childhood experiences primed Jung for later in life, like his departure from Freud's model and his inner journeys of near psychosis. For Jung, the unconscious was therapeutic, his imagination, the games he played, the worlds he created, protected him from the harsh blows and unwelcome encounters with everyday reality.

Furthermore, Jung was already touching transpersonal themes at such a tender age, the eternal fire, the sacred totem and mystical scripts, the illusory nature of the temporal self, and the elusive appearance of the transpersonal Self, and the transtemporal landscape where he could feel himself as an older and wiser soul, represent the early initiatory experiences that would later inform Jung's theory of the collective unconscious.

Jung Kills His Ideal

Now, flash forward. It's 1913, Jung has left Freud, he has also departed from the comfort, consistency, and predictability of his sanity. He is in the early throes of what he will later call his "confrontation with the unconscious." We're in the prelude to World War I, and tensions across Europe are mounting. We see how Jung, unlike many, entered his underworld willingly, the karmic seeds perhaps already sown. Jung reports having a dream wherein he encounters a "dark-faced savage"[11] in a rocky mountain landscape. In the distance he hears Siegfried's horn, from Wagner's famous opera, and is compelled to hide in wait for the musician, so that Jung and his companion might ambush and kill him. They dispose of the body, and a torrent of rain clears all trace of the murder. Jung feels like he got away with it but is later stricken with an unbearable guilt that he has killed something so beautiful. Jung awakens from the dream and is confused; he can't interpret its meaning. Jung's is assailed by an inner nagging that he must discover the meaning of the dream.[12]

Later Jung determined he murdered his heroic ideal, opening the possibility of new growth, embracing a new orientation, having crossed the threshold from Freud. He had found himself alone in uncharted territory. It's part of a series of inner explorations where Jung is willing to pursue his dreams and visions, despite unease, to mine them for the gold of the unconscious. His unconscious we can say, became his guide, and initiated him into the mysteries of the collective unconscious that became his core teaching.

He regularly plummets into the depth of his psyche, and on one occasion enters a cosmic abyss, what feels like the land of the dead.

> Near the steep slope of a rock I caught sight of two figures, an old man with a white beard and a beautiful young girl. I summoned up my courage and approached them as though they were real people, and listened attentively to what they told me. The old man explained that he was Elijah, and that gave me a shock. But the girl staggered me even more, for she called herself Salome! She was blind. What a strange couple: Salome and Elijah. But Elijah assured me that he and Salome had belonged together from all eternity, which completely astounded me. . . They had a black serpent living with them which displayed an unmistakable fondness for me. I stuck close to Elijah because he seemed to be the most reasonable of the three, and to have a clear intelligence. Of Salome I was distinctly suspicious.[13]

Much later Jung fully interpreted the couple as mythic and heroic archetypes—old wise man and young female muse—which transcend culture and epochs. Jung determined that Salome was his anima, his soul's latent feminine aspect, who can guide his reclamation of the lost feminine quality of himself. The inverse is the animus, the masculine counterpart of a woman, who can help her activate her latent masculine traits to become more integrated. Salome, Jung notes, is blind, she is being led by the wise old sage, the masculine form he is already well acquainted with since his early childhood escapades. Elijah is knowledge, Salome is love, personifications perhaps of the Greek Logos and Eros, or the Buddhist principles of wisdom and compassion. But there is a third character, the black snake, the symbol of transformation. You have Adam, Eve, and the serpent motif again, this time the unconscious is prompting Jung to resolve his family dysfunction.[14] Remember, Jung's mother was unreliable, he mistrusted women and love; Salome was blind, she needed to see again; and Jung mistrusted his weak father, and left Freud, so who can he admire and rely on as guides?

Philemon, Jung's Guru
Soon after this dream of the divine couple, Jung has another, in which the symbol of Elijah morphs into a new spirit guide, one that is distinctly more Egypto-Hellenistic in character. He writes of his first encounter with Philemon,

> There appeared from the right a winged being sailing across the sky. I saw that it was an old man with the horns of a bull. He held a bunch of four keys, one of which he clutched as if he were about to open a lock. He had the wings of the kingfisher with its characteristic colors. Since I did not understand this dream-image, I painted it in order to impress it upon my memory. During the days when I was occupied with the painting, I found in my garden, by the lake shore, a dead kingfisher! I was thunderstruck, for kingfishers are quite rare in the vicinity of Zurich and I have never since found a dead one. The body was recently dead—at the most, two or three days—and showed no external injuries.[15]

Jung develops a strong bond with Philemon through visions, dreams, and active imaginations that have the character of a Socratic dialogue, Jung the eager pupil, Philemon the learned teacher. One thing Jung noticed, was from his own unconscious representations, he was learning things he has never learned, thought, or understood before. He recognized the unconscious has a life of its own, almost like a separate entity, writing, "Psychologically, Philemon represented superior insight. He was a mysterious figure to me. At times he seemed to me quite real, as if he were a living personality. I went walking up and down the garden with him, and to me he was what the Indians call a guru."[16] "In Philemon, Jung had at long last found the father-figure that both Freud and his own father had failed to be. More than that, Philemon was a guru, and prefigured what Jung himself was later to become: the 'wise old man of Zürich.'"[17]

Fifteen years later, an Indian gentleman, a friend of Gandhi, visited Jung and they discussed the guru-disciple relationship. The gentleman disclosed he had his own guru, Shankaracharya, the great commentator of the Vedas who died centuries ago. Puzzled, Jung pressed him about his relationship with this teacher, and the gentleman confirmed the possibility for deep connections with beings long deceased who impart knowledge. Jung immediately thought of Philemon, and realized his experience wasn't unique, but a universal possibility. But for what purpose? None of this was rational or scientific, it wasn't making sense, whereupon a voice deep within him replied, "It is an art."[18] What Jung's initiation with Philemon revealed was secret access to the universal language of the collective unconscious, spoken directly from the gentle lips of his soul. This dialogue between Jung and his soul in the guise of Philemon, much like my reliance on an internalized version of Joe during graduate school, captures the essence and purpose of initiation.

BUDDHA'S INITIATION

Having renounced his kingdom and family to follow the path of a spiritual wanderer inspired by his fourth sighting, Siddhartha endured a six-year process of initiation. Soon after crossing the threshold, he met his mentors. Apprenticing to his gurus, embracing their methods, Siddhartha ardently practiced and exceled in achieving the highest states of meditative absorption. Showing the prowess of a virtuoso, and accomplishing the goal of his system, his first mentor said, "You are the same as I am now. There is no difference between us. Stay here and take my place and teach my students with me."[19] But Siddhartha was focused on resolving his existential dilemma of life and death, and while his yogic feats brought him to ecstatic states of rapture in which his awareness merged with limitless space, limitless consciousness, nothingness, and the peak of cyclic existence, they ultimately remained futile in his estimation. Though he could remain indefinitely in these states of absorptions, when he ceased his meditation Siddhartha returned to ordinary waking consciousness, where he found his existential dilemma unresolved. There was no lasting insight, no enduring liberation. He thought there must be another way.

After finding and following the method of his second mentor with equal devotion and determination and achieving similar states of absorption but equally dissatisfying results, Siddhartha resigned his apprenticeship, continuing his exploration solo. Not content to stay out of devotion, nor the desire to enjoy the fruits of high status as a meditation guru, just as he wasn't content to remain in the palace as a prince, Siddhartha pursued his quest for truth. Later, he found a small group of strident ascetics practicing austerities including fasting and sleep deprivation. Feeling a need to push beyond his limits of pain, fear, and starvation, he reached a point so emaciated his ribs protruded out of his back and he could barely stand. Close to death, a synchronistic memory arose: as a child in the palace orchard, he rested in the shade of a rose apple tree, with his father nearby. He had entered the first level of meditative absorption. Instead of collapsing his subjective-objective dichotomy into a state of oneness, he retained his capacity for reflection and discursive analysis. He wondered, "Could this be the path to awakening?"[20]

Flash forward years later with his five ascetics. Siddhartha had been pushing his body and mind to their extremes for six years, following methods that relied on full absorption, self-denial, and what we might now call *utter dissociation*—being disconnected from sensations in the body as a means of overcoming pain. He was trying to annihilate himself, thinking he would break on through to the other side, and be free. What was lost in those ecstatic and disconnected states was his reflective self-awareness, his ability to self-observe, and remain embodied. He decided to try again entering just the first state of absorption, while retaining awareness and observed the pleasures that arose as his mind became more concentrated. Rather than going deeper, disappearing over the crevasse of bliss or self-extinction, he analyzed, then realized that pleasure and pain needn't be perused or rejected, are neither inherently good, bad, nor real. It's the compulsive reactions toward them that spin the karma wheel. He continued through the ensuing states of absorption, higher levels of expanded consciousness—this time retaining awareness—and gained equally valuable insight. Pleasure and pain are part of the same continuum of human sensation, rather than pursuing pleasure only to become dissatisfied when it's gone, or avoiding inevitable pain, Siddhartha used his awareness to control his reactions, creating a stable equanimity that permitted all sensation to arises without his reactivity. He saw the merit in this approach, and realized he should eat something to sustain his body for further meditative experiments.

He accepted the offer of porridge from a village girl named Sujata, and three things happened. First, he incited the scorn and repudiation of his five companions who had sworn their allegiance to the dogma of extremism, so they ended up abandoning Siddhartha, considering his taking of food as a failure of commitment. Think about the flexibility of mind Siddhartha showed—he was heavily invested in this approach, and could have stayed wedded to seeing it through, but his commitment to truth meant he could shift direction and face the consequences of his pursuit of truth. The second takeaway from the story is the self-love he developed after years of self-denial. The symbol of taking food, the gesture of nourishing oneself, and of receiving help from others, exemplifies the fruit of dignity born from struggle. It's an act of self-love that differs qualitatively from the self-indulgence of his royal life. The third point, and most essential, is that Siddhartha discovered *a middle way that avoided extremes* of self-indulgence and self-denial: each of us can contemplate and mine this for gold.

Siddhartha spent the first twenty-nine years of his life chasing gratification and aggrandizement, and the last six years of his initiation perusing restriction and self-annihilation, neither of which had brought him the fruit of his grail quest; he was no closer to liberation. But he had stayed true to his intuition, his soul's whisper, and discovered a way to live in the world, and his body, in which he neither had to grasp nor reject pleasure or pain.

PLANETARY INITIATION

As a global community are we encountering an initiation, a series of crises, the malevolent forces of our collective shadow just as Siddhartha? Are we entering voluntarily, with eyes wide open, relinquishing resistance? Are we ready to take the red pill? Let's assume the astrological alignment—the Saturn-Jupiter-Pluto conjunction of January 12, 2020 foretold by astrologers like Maurice Fernandez that ushered in the Covid-19 pandemic—was our civilization's collective departure and planetary crossing of the threshold. There is a before-Covid, and after-Covid sensibility. In 2016, Fernandez predicted as much.

> The Saturn–Pluto cycle occurs roughly every 33 to 38 years, varying according to Pluto's highly elliptical orbit. This meeting of forces represents, among other things, the redistribution of power in the world or, in other words, which faction will make the decisions that affect the greater collective, whether this occurs in plain sight or behind the scenes. From a spiritual perspective, this cycle reflects a rite of passage determining who is most qualified to be the

custodian of resources, and thus regulates who will be in a position of influence. In its purest form, this cycle is one of the highest tests of integrity and morality for those in authority, along with a test of capacity and resilience. Beyond the management of power, this cycle is also about the skill to increase power and the value of resources.[21]

From astrology we transition to prophecy. The Seven Fires prophecy of the Anishinaabe tribe foretells the fate of the inhabitants of Turtle Island, a name given by the Indigenous peoples of the North American continent. Each of the seven fires offers the Anishinaabe a prediction, as well as a map and signs to follow during their migration to a new homeland, the challenges they will face, the test, enemies, and allies they will encounter, including betrayal, loss of their lands, and fracturing into splinter tribes. The Anishinaabe elders observe that six of the seven prophecies have already come to pass. They note that during the fourth prophesy they encounter "light-skinned" allies without weapons—the French colonialists—that help them prosper in mutual interest, and the armed light-skinned, the English, who sought to destroy them. Prophecies five and six foretold of the mass degeneration of their sacred views, causing their youth to disbelieve and abandoned the ancient ways, and heartbreakingly leaving the elders with no purpose for living. The Seventh Fire is only now being lit. The prophecy is about the times we're living right now, when those from modern secular cultures, who have abandoned spirit, and have grown sick from materialism, will return to the elders to request initiation into their sacred worldview.[22]

Ultimately, we are amidst a planetary initiation, a struggle between the forces of light and darkness, unclaimed projections of our collective unconscious. I'll let you determine for yourself what might constitute the immediate threat against humanity. Is it corrupt governments conspiring with Big Pharma and legacy media to distract, terrorize, and threaten our very sovereignty? Is it the looming specter of nuclear war between the last major superpowers? Or will it be a rogue state trying to usurp control over the global monopoly board? How about the environmental emergency fueled by multinational corporations and underpinned by an insatiable greed for infinite profit on a planet of finite resources? Or will it be the shadow side of the very technologies upon which we have become overly reliant, the backlash and unintended consequences of Artificial Intelligence, leading to the so-called singularity? Perhaps it will be the diabolical use of fifth generational warfare to wage a mnemonic crusade over our minds?

There is much agreement across sacred wisdom cultures, astrology, mythology, and prophecy that the world is at a crossroad, befouled by toxic relations characterized by disrespect, discord, and disconnection. Will we open our third eye to behold the truth of the darkness within us and around us? Will we bury our heads in the sand, blame others, or wait to be rescued? The Anishinaabe fathers say human beings will have two options to choose from, materialism or spirit. If they choose to open to spirituality, they will survive, but if they choose to live in denial and continue along the path of materialism, it will be the end of us. Eco-activist Vandana Shiva similarly asks us to consider, "We stand at a precipice of extinction. Will we allow our humanity as living, conscious, intelligent, autonomous beings to be extinguished by a greed machine that does not know limits and is unable to put a break on its colonization and destruction? Or will we stop the machine and defend our humanity, freedom, and autonomy to protect life on earth?"[23]

We must take the red pill, eat the forbidden fruit, confront fear, endure the loss of innocence, accept the pain and impermanence that inextricably characterize life, and most especially confront the darkness within our own psyche. The initiation requires the inner child to die, to be reborn an adult, a free-thinking agent of change prepared to face the ordeals ahead.

8
Ordeal
Taming the Dragon

MELUKAT—WATER PURIFICATION

The water is clear but frigid, rolling off my head and down my spine as my body trembles and contracts. I take another deep breath to self-regulate, silently reciting the Vajrasattva mantra as I brace for another dunk under the waterfall. It's a wonderfully potent symbol: baptism. Submerge, reemerge. *There and back again.* There are twin spouts where the sacred stream runs off, forming natural dual showers. The Wizard is beside me, under the other spigot. We're stripped down to our sarongs. We're in a stone-carved, open-aired, private enclosure designed for *melukat*, an ancient Balinese water purification ritual. We've been doing these rituals together over the last few weeks. One of Bali's most precious resources is its holy water, or *tirta* which is venerated along with the other four sacred elements, earth, air, and fire, and space as the *prima materia* from which the cosmos can be reduced, purged, and reconstituted anew in the universal pilgrimage of *solve et coagula*. Most temples that dot the island are built around natural springs and incorporate ornate purification baths.

Today is a special day. I've been invited by the Wizard's family to Ibah, his ancestral home for melukat. My buddy Phillip O'Leary, the

Wizard's sister Tjok Sri Maya, and the wizard's son Tjok Adi are with us as we process, dressed in ceremonial attire, from his house along a narrow path, through the jungle, down to a ravine. It's late afternoon, and the sun splinters fractals of golden light through the tree canopy. A sacred river runs through the valley, hugs the cliffside along the path, and its rush roars like thunder around the juncture. Close by, the Wizard tells me, are several caves, one of which his grandfather used for years as a solitary meditation retreat where he reached *moksha*, liberation, toward the end of his life.

The Wizard comes from a lineage of royal priests, warriors, and artisans originating from Java, a high born of the Buddhist-Hindu Majapahit kingdom that stretches as far back as the thirteenth century. They conquered the neighboring island of Bali and maintained on its stronghold an unbroken transmission of tantric Hinduism, while the entire Indonesian archipelago succumbed to Islamic rule. Just as Indian Buddhist tantra fused with the shamanic Bon religion in Tibet, Hindu tantra here is influenced by the preexisting traditions of animism held by the Indigenous peoples. This is a reason why the intense tantric energy of centuries of ceremony is palpable and perfumes the earth, water, fire, and wind in Bali.

The Kerthyasa family shrine is at the river's bend. Camouflaged like a reptile on the ravine face, it's open-aired, and merges seamlessly with the elements. It was designed and custom built according to visions by the Wizard's father, Tjokorda Raka, our enigmatic figure from the in-flight documentary that led me down the rabbit hole. I'm awestruck and pulled into the sanctum as if by gravitational force. Giant stone Buddhas and Ganeshas crop out of the foliage and are covered in layers of emerald moss as if they were remnants from some prehistoric age. There is no separation between spirituality and nature here. Shrines dot the landscape, and the trees are draped in ceremonial sarongs as if they're living priests. Mother Nature is the cathedral, the stones the altar, the music of the river her choir, and the host of spirits mild and fierce the congregation. Enchanted by this setting, I fall deep into active imagine.

Tjok Gde and Maya led us through prayers and ceremony as we intuitively distributed offerings of flowers and incense to the deities at little shrines, requesting blessings at each. Then, I caught a glance from Maya and savored one of her smiles as she gracefully reached into her basket of flowers. We didn't need words. Instead, she saw I was immersed in the magic she has grown up with. For the wisdom keepers, it must be gratifying that a foreigner would so love and venerate their land and relations with the spirits. My time in Bali has been an endless rain of blessings, and as I near the end of my stay, this visit to the Kerthyasa family shrine is yet another moment of ineffable wonder.

After the offerings, we transition to melukat. It's done in silence and is deeply personal, for there is no formal or correct way to cleanse the soul. I've plunged several times now under the icy water pouring from above. On a biochemical level, the cold has its way of activating the nervous system. But on a spiritual level, the purification is designed to splay you wide open, activate and release karmic blockages, and help energy run freely through the subtle body's channels. Halfway through the plunge I'm caught off guard by a wave of memories and emotions. I almost lose my footing. For a few minutes, I leave ordinary time and space and am cast back to the biggest ordeal of my life. While my guard is down, I start wailing and crying, inconsolably overcome. Seeing this, the Wizard and Phil flank me with their arms tightly wrapped around me for support. I collapse into a sea of tears and their strong embrace. I've no shame, these are my brothers, and I'm safe.

MY PUBLIC TRIAL

Three years earlier, I was enjoying the height of my career, a successful Buddhist psychotherapy practice in the heart of Manhattan, and a position as assistant director of the Nalanda Institute, the Buddhist non-profit Emily and I helped our mentor develop. Twenty years earlier, I met my mentor Joe Loizzo, who taught me everything I know. They say that when the student is ready, the teacher appears. I was, and he did.

But they rarely tell you what happens when the student is prepared to become a teacher.

Joe also mentored Emily, and we three built worlds together over two decades. There was tremendous love and admiration between us. We developed and delivered world-class training programs, co-edited a book, and mentored a growing number of professionals eager to integrate authentic Buddhist teachings and practices into their clinical work. Joe was my everything—teacher, father figure I never had and always needed, colleague, confidant, supervisor, and dearest friend. No person can ever fill all those roles, yet Joe did exceptionally well. The twenty years we spent together represented my life's most enriching and expansive chapter.

In the last couple of years in my relationship with Nalanda, I found myself parting ideological ways with the Institute and the politics they embraced, but predominately kept my views or concerns to myself and Emily. I had already begun to leave the fold of my mentor, departing the ordinary safe world of Nalanda, but ultimately there was an awful catalyst that irreversibly damaged my relationship with Joe and the community. I liken it to Jung's departure from Freud.

My ordeal occurred during one of our training sessions with a cohort of fifty therapists. I was teaching, and in a moment of vulnerability and mindlessness, I disclosed I was not taking female clients in my therapy practice as I feared the shadow backlash of the #metoo movement. It came from my mouth as a definitive statement of truth, with no further explanation. I didn't clarify that this was but a worry and not a declaration of fact. It landed in the wrong way.

This was during the height of #metoo—a critical watershed in history, a redistribution of power, a long-awaited reckoning of accountability for men's vile behavior, and the banding together of women in solidarity and collective strength. Like every movement, #metoo also possessed a cultural shadow. What my students didn't know was at the time of my lecture I was mired in a thorny net of psychodynamics with two female therapy clients with borderline personality disorder who were acting irrationally and hostile towards me, and who had made threats of bogus legal action or incendiary but false public accusations. I was being bullied, and I was terrified. Coumpounding this, I felt intimidated and powerless by the #metoo fervor; who would believe me—a straight white male in a position of authority—if these clients were to seize the opportunity to falsely accuse me of inappropriate or unethical behavior? I had fantasies of taking a break entirely from receiving any more female clients to protect myself from the stresses of those potentially career-ending encounters. These were escape fantasies, nothing more, in reality I continued to work with and receive new female clients, in fact they represented the preponderance of my practice.

The audience was primarily female and what they heard out of my mouth was disparaging. Given the times, it raised concerns and sparked outrage among some members of the group. Later that night, I received a phone call from Joe's wife Geri, saying I had offended and upset several women, I had caused them harm, and it would be best if we met as a group for a sincere conversation and apology. *Caused harm? What on earth did I say?* "Of course," I replied. I was prepared to take responsibility, clarify, and apologize, if necessary, so I agreed to the public meeting. If I heard the cohort's experience and expressed mine, naturally I felt we could reach a deeper, mutual understanding.

On the morning of the meeting, I received an email from Geri and another from Joe changing the plan. They insisted it would be counterproductive for me to explain the context of my comments. This request marked the division between Joe and me. Over the prior couple of years, Nalanda Institute had slowly become more politically active, evidenced by a strong bent towards social justice and Diversity, Equity, and Inclusion, and it became clear how profoundly this influenced the underlying power dynamics between the core directors. I was more centrist and moderate in my political views, sometimes provocatively animated in my demeanor, and preferred our Buddhist psychotherapy training not be infected by the insidious influence of politics of any kind, left or right. These made me a liability. Rather than asking if I'd be amenable, Joe and Geri recommended I allow the women to express their hurt and outrage without qualification or response from me. They insisted that any explanation might be misconstrued as "mansplaining," dodging accountability, and adding further insult to injury. It was implied that intent matters less than impact if at all, and recommended I engage in "mindful listening," empathizing with the hurt I caused and nothing more.

This struck me as lopsided and unproductive. Surely students— many of whom I'd known for years—would want to know why I said what I did. This cohort had been together for over a year, and we had formed a good rapport. I cared about them and was prepared to apologize for anything in my comment that may have indeed been inappropriate. But more importantly, I was ready to be transparent and vulnerable, disclosing my genuine fear and how it stirred my escape fantasies and doubt about which clients to receive. I thought it would be an excellent way to examine and humanize the unconscious of a teacher and therapist, and I was willing to explore my shadow with the group. This was true to my therapeutic approach, and felt more meaningful and instructive, especially within a group of clinicians in therapy training.

Ultimately, however, I acquiesced to the request; that was my biggest regret. Under the pressure of aligning with my mentor, I surrendered my conscience to appease him and the archetype of my narcissistic father he represented. This groupthink and relinquishment of power is pervasive in communities, secular and spiritual. We jettison our intuition, needs, and common sense if it means avoiding conflict or losing the safety and validation a group represents. In textbook codependency, I abandoned myself to maintain the love.

I sat under a bright light, alone on a slightly raised platform facing the group. The hour I spent there felt like public shaming and shunning. One by one, women voiced how they were hurt by my comment and expressed their anger and disappointment. I could feel the intensity of their rage not only for my thoughtless words, but as if I were a target for their unwitnessed and dismissed feelings. The institution's message was that this was a safe space for hurt and vulnerable people to lash out, and I was both catalyst and object. Even though the group shadow was on full display, I heard every word, I validated each experience of my triggering statement, and did not respond beyond, "Thank you." On the surface I was composed, but my inner child was in anguish. I had learned well under threat of abuse from my father, how to keep my mouth shut, submit like a coward, and dissociate from the overwhelming shame, fear, and powerlessness.

I felt each word viscerally, like a stone thrown. What was additionally alarming, I later discovered, was that those members of the group who weren't angry with me, who desired to hear my explanation, or who recognized the lopsided public trial and rush to justice as a concerning trend among leftist cancel culture, chose to remain silent. In other words, I wasn't the sole individual apprehensive about speaking up against the woke mob. After enduring an hour of this, Geri stood to align with the women who felt harmed and to share her disappointment: "Your comments made me feel icky." Nothing brutal, but it was the symbolism of her standing in solidarity with the others against me. We were co-leaders, team members, and more than that we were family. She could have remained neutral.

When it was over, I left the podium to sit in the front row like a child after a scolding. Joe took my place on the platform and continued with the class as if this was an ordinary evening. As we passed each other, there was a last, perfunctory, lifeless hug. I knew then, and there, it was over. After everything we shared, this was how it ended. He didn't look me in the eye, his posture was limp. The umbilical cord of our bond was severed. I felt I was a sacrificial lamb, deeply betrayed by someone I loved more than life itself. I could now empathize with Jung's realization that Freud could no longer be trusted.

The next day I received an email from Joe and Geri congratulating me on my courage and acknowledging how well it all went toward restoring community. There was no smiley face emoji, but there could have been. It was a final insult. The congratulations a kid might receive for taking his beating well.

Within weeks I resigned from Nalanda and never looked back. Emily took a different tact, one of more mature engagement and honest dialogue, trying to analyze what happened, process feelings, and navigate the shifting political tides of the organization. To no avail—three months later she also resigned. After twenty years of dedicated service her departure was squeezed between course announcements in a newsletter as if an afterthought. We were devastated. I walked through life disemboweled and in complete disbelief.

DEEPER INTO THE ORDEAL

Myths are maps for the soul; they provide narrative structures powerful enough to guide our development across vast time horizons. The gods of old weren't external agencies but personified archetypal energies, active in the collective unconscious, transcending time and culture, and expressing their conflicts towards resolution. Perhaps we can mythologize what we're living through now, encountering the universal motifs of death and rebirth, moral degradation and redemption, trial and treasure, collapse and renewal. The story is cyclic, which means we always have another chance to get it right. Individually the soul is born into this life to break an old contract, to complete unfinished business, and selects just the right conditions to get us to develop strength and rise to a challenge.

The Buddhists call this *advantageous suffering*, just the right mix of conditions, to create the friction necessary to start a redemptive fire. Collectively, the same seems possible. What we're enduring culturally right now on the planet, the authoritarian crack down, the exploitation for profit, the media deception, the degradation of morality, the culture wars, structural collapse of societies, and environmental crisis, perhaps are the adventitious circumstances we've unconsciously produced, or need, to help rouse us from our slumber of unconscious, hedonic, living.

To help us find the moral strength and courage to grow up, and take back our sovereignty and freedom, every heroine must face a rite of passage to reclaim what has been lost or forgotten. She must bring forth a lamp, a song, an elixir to transform darkness to light, bondage to freedom, separation to reconnection. We owe it to ourselves, and our souls, to delve into hero myths—the point is not to live complacently, but to die bravely, because conceding freedom is not living. Being obedient prevents free will; what we learn from the Garden of Eden, is that Eve's courage to disobey and fall from grace are spiritual virtues.

Without the promise of rebirth, death is stagnation in trauma. Likewise, without death, the nascent, prepubescent hero calcifies in an idealized paradise. Every hero who desires to ascend to heaven, must first descend into hell. If they manage to return as Queen or King, it's not long before they must be slain again, for anything allowed to endure at its apex becomes a new prison, resisting the cosmic rounds of infinite return. This is why we kill the Buddha when we meet him, because idealizing his journey prevents us from embarking on our own. Basking in the radiance of sun—fame, fortune, and success—must be unified with the luminance of moon—defeat, failure, and despair, reconciled in the cosmic mandala.

Jung writes in his *(The) Red Book*:

After death on the cross Christ went into the underworld and became Hell. So he took on the form of the Antichrist, the dragon. The image of the Antichrist, which has come down to us from the ancients, announces the new God, whose coming the ancients had foreseen. Gods are unavoidable. The more you flee from the God, the more surely you fall into his hand. The rain is the great stream of tears that will come over the peoples, the tearful flood of released tension after the constriction of death had encumbered the peoples with horrific force. It is the mourning of the dead in me, which precedes burial and rebirth. The rain is the fructifying of the earth, it begets the new wheat, the young, germinating God.[1]

Consider the motif Jung is raising, a poignant moment in the Christ story called the "Harrowing of Hell."

THE HARROWING OF CHRIST

Most of us are familiar with the term "Son of Man," a reference to Jesus, who was crucified on the cross, to redeem our sins. The same almighty and loving God that supposedly punished and cast out Adam and Eve from Eden, also sent his son to death, like a sheep to the slaughter. This being the mainstream Biblical version, creating fear of retribution and casting God as an authority to obey. In the esoteric version, Jesus is the archetype of the hero we must each become, the Christ consciousness we strive to emulate, called the *Imitatio Christi*. God hasn't turned his son into a gatekeeper for the fear-based faithful to express their blind allegiance to and earn redemption, a long-internalized archetypal model the current globalist elites have intelligently managed to co-op and exploit in a modern secular iteration of mass mind control.

Instead, Christ is a metaphor of the sacrifice we each must make, and the spiritual death of the ego we must endure, freeing us of a restrictive identity, shallow urges, and narrow bandwidth of consciousness, so that we can find and align again with our own truth and taste the deathless state. It's the quintessential story of Jung's process of individuation. What is less known about the story is not Christ's brutal death on the cross, having necessarily been betrayed with a kiss and cast out by his disciple Judas, but what follows his death. Three days after the crucifixion is an episode called the Harrowing of Hell, which precedes Christ's resurrection.

It's the Christian tradition's version (see plate 7) of the Tibetan tri-phased cycle of death, bardo, and rebirth. During the harrowing, Christ descends into hell, where he knocks three times on the gates of Hades, and to the surprise of those tormented there, he bursts through the doors. In this dramatic gesture, one that mirrors the earth-touching pose and proclamation of the Siddhartha just before becoming Buddha, awake, Christ proclaims his willingness not only to die, but to face the most horrific shadow of our collective psyche.

While the crucifixion demonstrates surrender, and the resurrection's full transcendence, it is at the bardo gates of hell, where fear is alchemized into love. Christ's attempts to rescue and emancipate the outcasts and hostages of the underworld are a poignant metaphor for the voluntary encounter with all the unavoidable consequences of negative actions.

Who does Jesus find in the darkness of hell once its doors have been broken through? All the sinners. All those who have been cast out—Eve and Adam, but also Satan, the anti-Christ and keeper of shadow, who has been suspended there for eternity. Again, we must look at this not through the exoteric, but the mythopoetic lens, wearing Campbellian and Jungian bifocals. Hell is the unconscious, a repository where all the unacceptable and ugly bits not tolerated by the ego and society are repressed. They're never destroyed, only held in suspended animation, their calls and influence bubbling up when we least expect it, met with an increasing counter-force of repression. Christ consciousness dies to the ordinary world through a great trial, an unimaginable betrayal, a Judas kiss, or a Joe's lifeless hug, and a descent into hell—the belly of the whale, a forbidden place, charnel ground, where no one, save the initiated, venture. This is the depths of the shadow, where we find the lost fragments of our past, of ancestry, like pottery and two skulls broken under the pressure of trauma, cast out into the darkness by authority, guilt, shame, and fear, branded as sinners, unworthy, unlovable, incapable. No amount of compensatory acrobatics at the surface level of consciousness performed by the ego—seeking validation, fame, success—can silence the lambs of our missteps, or rescue the castaways. Nothing can fill the void. What is required is not an over-compensation, a spiritual bypass, bio-hack to a summit of greatness, but a harrowing descent into the valley of darkness. A cycling backward, a re-membering—literally reassembling fragmented pieces, shards of the broken mirror of the soul, a making whole again—in the inclusive embrace of loving Christ consciousness. We must go there, to the tragic depths, and come back again.

If Eve and Adam represent the esoteric feminine and masculine energies in the side channels of the subtle body, their descent from the Garden, and a voluntary departure having been initiated by the trickster serpent of divine wisdom, then hell is the alchemical crucible, where the toxic emotions of aggression and lust are purified, distilled, under the forces of the inferno. Masculine energy purified of insecurity so that it can be deployed as confidence, courage, wrathful compassion, and creativity. The feminine energy purified of subservience, so it can be deployed as divine intuition, regenerative wisdom, and noble leadership. Christ consciousness comes to rescue, re-member, and make whole again. To integrate trauma so the force of fragmentation and dissociation is transmuted into potent insight. What nearly destroys us becomes our strength. Like Jonah in the belly of the whale, there can be moments of grace, forgiveness, and redemption, even after we have failed ourselves, as I did in a moment of cowardice, having forsaken myself, abandoned my diamond queen of intuition. If it takes a betrayal and crucifixion to provoke redemption, then so be it, we shall not die in vain, but be reborn wiser for it.

Unlike the Buddha, Christ has a relatively short teaching career, and so after his resurrection, he initiates twelve apostles (Judus replaced by Matthias) as his emissaries. His ascension to heaven symbolizes our possibility for rebirth—Christ consciousness, through these twelve avatars, from the One into the multiplicity of the world. The One becomes the many, the ocean contains each drop, the drop contains the ocean, heaven and earth are re-envisioned as non-dual.

JUNG'S CONFRONTATION WITH THE UNCONSCIOUS

It's Christmas, 1912. Jung is still a year away from his unceremonious split from Freud, but the fracture between them is deepening as they head in divergent philosophical directions. Jung has a dream, and writes:

In the dream I found myself in a magnificent Italian loggia with pillars, a marble floor, and a marble balustrade. I was sitting on a gold Renaissance chair; in front of me was a table of rare beauty. It was made of green stone, like emerald. There I sat, looking out into the distance, for the loggia was set high up on the tower of a castle. My children were sitting at the table too. Suddenly a white bird descended, a small seagull or a dove. Gracefully, it came to rest on the table, and I signed to the children to be still so that they would not frighten away the pretty white bird. Immediately, the dove was transformed into a little girl, about eight years of age, with golden blond hair. She ran off with the children and played with them among the colonnades of the castle. I remained lost in thought, musing about what I had just experienced. The little girl returned and tenderly placed her arms around my neck. Then she suddenly vanished; the dove was back and spoke slowly in a human voice. "Only in the first hours of the night can I transform myself into a human being; while the male dove is busy with the twelve dead." Then she flew off into the blue air, and I awoke.[2]

Jung reports in his memories that he is stirred by this dream, later he uses the words, "activated by the archetypal process in the unconscious."[3] Remember this, as it's the telltale sign of the soul calling us to adventure. He connects some of the dots, the emerald table with the emerald tablets of Hermes Trismegistus, the twelve dead with the twelve apostles and the twelve signs of the zodiac, and the dove, a reference to the holy spirit, but the full picture, and the meaning of the dream evade him. Though he examines with his rational intellect, to no avail, he admits he has no further explanation and resigns to continue to pay attention to his fantasies. One of the threads he follows is the notion that though something appears dead, yet it remains alive.[4]

The theme reemerges in another dream. This takes place in a large Roman necropolis in Arles, France, in which he is walking down a street lined with sarcophagi dating to the Merovingian times. On top of the tombs are corpses, uniformly supine with their hands neatly clasped in front of them. One dead body is from the eighteen-thirties, the next from the eighteenth century, and the last from the twelfth century, a crusader in chain mail. As he gets close to each, to his surprise and disease, his attention seems to revive them. The theme of death and life continues. Jung agreed with Freud that the vestiges of our past remain in the unconscious, but remarks that "dreams like this, and my actual experiences of the unconscious, taught me that such contents are not dead, outmoded forms, but belong to our living being.

Jung is following an unknown path; he's turning himself over to the unconscious, unsure where it's taking him, and rather than getting clarity and answers, things are only becoming murkier, and leaving him with more questions. As a good psychologist would, Jung makes a thorough investigation into his childhood, just as Siddhartha did, searching his history for answers, but Jung finds no resolution in his remembered past to his dilemma about the meaning of these dreams and fantasies. His memoirs capture the moment when he surrendered to the mystery of the unconscious.

> The dreams, however, could not help me over my feeling of disorientation. On the contrary, I lived as if under constant inner pressure. At times this became so strong that I suspected there was some psychic disturbance in myself. Therefore I twice went over all the details of my entire life, with particular attention to childhood memories; for I thought there might be something in my past which I could not see and which might possibly be the cause of the disturbance. But this retrospection led to nothing but a fresh acknowledgment of my own ignorance. Thereupon I said to myself, "Since I know nothing at all, I shall simply do whatever occurs to me."

Thereupon surrendering to his unconscious, releasing defenses, relinquishing control from the left mode, and allowing himself to be consumed by the whale, Jung experiences a memory when he was a boy of eleven or twelve, again like Siddhartha had a childhood memory under an apple tree while his father was nearby in the field. Jung recalls playing with his toys, and building castles with stones and mud. He was lost in the expanse of imaginary play back then, before the world grew incredibly calcified and real as a burgeoning adult. It strikes Jung as he writes:

> "There is still life in these things. The small boy is still around, and possesses a creative life which I lack. But how can I make my way to it?" For as a grown man it seemed impossible to me that I should be able to bridge the distance from the present back to my eleventh year. Yet if I wanted to re-establish contact with that period, I had no choice but to return to it and take up once more that child's life with his childish games. This moment was a turning point in my fate, but I gave in only after endless resistances and with a sense of resignation.[5]

Jung is beginning to recognize that there is no final death, no moment of expiration, that our past is not just static vestiges like old cloths in a musty closet, rather there is a vibrant energy that animates us from the unconscious, a hidden dimension where parts of our child-hood, ancestry, and beyond, live on, and every so often tries to make contact, like aliens from another planet, with us. This powerful idea inspires his writing of the book *Flying Saucers: A Modern Myth*, Jung's attempt to understand and convey the role of the unconscious and its mechanism of projection of powerful archetypal themes, accounting for the phenomenon of extraterrestrial visitations, which he perceived were a transformation of archaic visitations of angles and spirits now replaced by UFOs (or UAP) in a modern context. Something is alive in us on a collective level, and trying to communicate an ancient story, but in a contemporary way. Most of us dismiss the signs outright, others become fixated or paranoid with the signs but misperceive them as externali-ties, few look to their unconscious for the "understory" being told, or retold, to decipher their coded meaning. Jung is in freefall now with his own unconscious, like Alice down the rabbit hole to Wonderland, the unconscious is his mentor, he continues to dream, observe his fantasies, and begins to have vivid, even prophetic, visions. Of these he wrote, "if someone has a vision it doesn't mean that he is necessarily insane. Perfectly normal people have visions in certain moments." In October 1913, Jung wrote:

> While I was alone on a journey, I was suddenly seized by an over-powering vision: I saw a monstrous flood covering all the northern and low-lying lands between the North Sea and the Alps. When it came up to Switzerland I saw that the mountains grew higher and higher to protect our country. I realized that a frightful catastrophe was in progress. I saw the mighty yellow waves, the floating rubble of civilization, and the drowned bodies of uncounted thousands. Then the whole sea turned to blood. This vision lasted about one hour. I was perplexed and nauseated, and ashamed of my weakness. Two weeks passed; then the vision recurred, under the same conditions, even more vividly than before, and the blood was emphasized. An inner voice spoke. "Look at it well; it is wholly real and it will be so. You cannot doubt it."[6]

Jung is taken aback by these visions of revolution, and concludes he's going mad. By the spring and early summer of 1914, he experiences a thrice-repeated dream of an arctic storm that blankets the entire region under a thick layer of ice. The canals and forests are completely frozen over, and everything is dead as a result. The third and final repetition of the dream ends differently. Jung says, "there stood a leaf-bearing tree, but without fruit (my tree of life, I thought), whose leaves had been transformed by the effects of the frost into sweet grapes full of healing juices. I plucked the grapes and gave them to a large, waiting crowd" . . . a month later, he continues, "on August 1 the world war broke out. Now my task was clear: I had to try to understand what had happened and to what extent my own experience coincided with that of mankind in general."[7] Jung's year-long journey into Hades, the underworld, led him to realize the unconscious was a vibrant and living dimension of reality, communicating with consciousness through universal symbols. He also saw it possessed a predictive intuition or genius, what the Buddhists would call a third eye of wisdom. Nevertheless, for Jung the experience of opening to such a potent force was bewildering and destabilizing. But Jung was resolute, unwavering like Siddhartha in his conviction, as he risked going deeper to make sense of these messages from his unconscious.

Jung was frequently so activated, that he used the yoga he learned in India for self-regulation, calming himself down just enough, so that he could continue to explore the labyrinth of his mind. Siddhartha's innovative technique fused concentrative calm with penetrative insight. I've found no account in Jung's writing to suggest he was aware of the details of this Buddhist technique, so I can only assume he naturally came about something similar. He wasn't trying to escape the powerful upsurge of imagery, vision, and dream, rather he sought to make himself receptive to them without being drowned by them. He discovered that emotions are powerful currents that can take one off course, so rather than cutting oneself off entirely to the emotions, Jung felt it was more important to identify the image or symbol within the emotion; that the image was the ship carrying a bounty of information, while the emotion was the sea. He dove into the right brain during active imagination, memories, fantasy, dreams, or visions, to collect images like oysters, and to tolerate the swoon of the unconscious long enough for pearls to reveal themselves, allowing him to return to the surface of waking life and to left brain for integration. These back-and-forth sojourns between states of consciousness and brain regions created considerable cognitive dissonance, and Jung began to fear that he might split apart, like a diver getting the bends due to the water pressure on ascent. Jung recounts:

It was during Advent of the year 1913—December 12, to be exact— that I resolved upon the decisive step. I was sitting at my desk once more, thinking over my fears. Then I let myself drop. Suddenly it was as though the ground literally gave way at my feet, and I plunged down into dark depths. I could not fend off a feeling of panic. But then, abruptly, at not too great a depth, I landed on my feet in a soft, sticky mass. I felt great relief, although I was apparently in complete darkness. After a while my eyes grew accustomed to the gloom, which was rather like a deep twilight. Before me was the entrance to a dark cave, in which stood a dwarf with a leathery skin, as if he were mummified. I squeezed past him through the narrow entrance and waded knee deep through icy water to the other end in the cave where, on a projecting rock, I saw a glowing red crystal. I grasped the stone, lifted it, and discovered a hollow underneath. At first I could make out nothing, but then I saw that there was running water. In it a corpse floated by, a youth with blond hair and a wound in the head. He was followed by a gigantic black scarab and then by a red, newborn sun, rising up out of the depths of the water. Dazzled by the light, I wanted to replace the stone upon the opening, but then a fluid welled out. It was blood. A thick jet of it leaped up, and I felt nauseated. It seemed to me that the blood continued to spurt for an unendurably long time. At last it ceased, and the vision came to an end. I was stunned by this vision. I realized, of course, that it was a hero and solar myth, a drama of death and renewal, the rebirth symbolized by the Egyptian scarab. At the end, the dawn of the new day should have followed, but instead came that intolerable outpouring of blood—an altogether abnormal phenomenon, so it seemed to me. But then I recalled the vision of blood that I had had in the autumn of that same year, and I abandoned all further attempt to understand.[8]

THE RED BOOK

Jung was an astute archeologist of the mind, what Thurman calls a psychonaut. During his long years of confrontation with the unconsciousness, starting with his rupture from Freud in 1913 and lasting until 1917 (about the duration of a classic Tibetan tantric retreat), he took extensive notes, reflections, posing questions, making connections, decoding symbols, and drawing images as if in a field guide. He did so in what are now called The Black Books, a voluminous collection of six personal diaries not intended to be read by others, and not released to the public until 2009. They were personal, raw, and unedited.

Jung would use these diaries as his first pass on sensemaking the inner frontier. But after the outbreak of World War I in August 1914, Jung was struck by the cultural implications of his prophetic visions. They had transpersonal and global implications, and were more significant than a record of his personal experience. He coalesced his most significant findings and creative material in another book, more prized than his journals, the mothership of Jung's underworld sojourn, he called *Libre Novis*—New Book—later popularized as *The Red Book*, a red-leatherbound folio containing the results of his self-inflicted experiments with truth, observations from his intrapsychic voyages, written in calligraphy, containing exquisite paintings by Jung (see plate 4) and documenting his process of individuation between 1913 and 1916, including his ordeal and pseudo psychosis—a veritable descent into madness. When I completed the lecture series "Return with Elixir" in December, 2019, one of my students, an avid astronomer named Matthias, gifted me the hardbound version of *The Red Book*. Dramatic, oversized, and heavy, it looks like a cross between Merlin's book of spells and an alchemist's medieval illuminated manuscript of remedies. Jung's imagination is splayed open and naked for all to see, and it's bewildering and exquisite. When I received this gift, it was my confirmation that despite my initial hesitation, and despite losing many students when I elected to follow a path less traveled into mythological and Jungian territory, I had become receptive to my unconscious, its mysteries, and synchronicities. Despite having never formally studied Jung, I opened myself up to his spirit for initiation, through his memoirs, inviting his presence and allowing him to teach the universal process of individuation through me. It was a symbolic gift of lifetimes, confirming what Jung discovered: the past is available in the present; the dead never die.

JUNG EATS A CHILD'S LIVER

During the years in which Jung was fully committed to his work on *Liber Novus*, he was burning the candle at both ends, oddly without seeming functional impairment. By night he was turning himself over to dreams, playing with the edge of sanity, and detailing his accounts in his epic tome, while during the daytime he maintained his psychotherapy practice, seeing a full caseload of patients. He lectured, wrote extensively, and even served as an active-duty officer in the Swiss army between 1914 and 1918 during World War I. Tracing the hundred-year odyssey of Jung's (*The*) *Red Book* from its private inception into controversial publication in 2009,* journalist Sara Corbett's New York Times article titled "The Holy Grail of the Unconscious," synthesizes the masterwork as a

> phantasmagoric morality play, driven by Jung's own wish not just
> to chart a course out of the mangrove swamp of his inner world but
> also to take some of its riches with him. It was this last part—the
> idea that a person might move beneficially between the poles of the

---

The Red Book was controversial for a number of reasons, firstly it wasn't clear Jung himself ever intended it to be made public, so as a personal diary on display it may represent a violation of his privacy. One that his family eventually conceded to after his death weighing the personal violation against its potential contribution to society. More broadly, the material contained within *The Red Book* are reflections of the unconscious, often shocking, jarring, and easily misunderstood aspects of Jung's mind. How might these elicit images and themes shape public opinion of Jung and his legacy if poorly or superficially interpreted? There is also a sub segment of detractors against Jung's work in general, for example those who claim he was antisemitic, or misogynistic. Given such allegations why should his work receive so much attention? Perhaps worth restating is that Jung in general, and *The Red Book* in particular, open doors to the soul, a subject not well tolerated in our overly skeptical, paradigm of scientific reductionism. *The Red Book* violates the conventions of our time, and leave some of us feeling uneasy.

rational and irrational, the light and the dark, the conscious and the unconscious—that provided the germ for his later work and for what analytical psychology would become. . . . The book tells the story of Jung trying to face down his own demons as they emerged from the shadows. The results are humiliating, sometimes unsavory. In it, Jung travels the land of the dead, falls in love with a woman he later realizes is his sister, gets squeezed by a giant serpent and, in one terrifying moment, eats the liver of a little child. ("I swallow with desperate efforts—it is impossible—once again and once again—I almost faint—it is done.") At one point, even the devil criticizes Jung as hateful.[9]

The gruesome scene Corbett refers to when Jung eats a child's liver comes in the context of one of his pseudo-psychotic visions. Jung came across the mutilated corpse of a young girl and was filled with grief and rage. A veiled woman appeared insisting Jung atone for a crime committed by another man by eating the child's liver. Atoning for a crime rekindles the story of Jonah in the belly of the whale. Mortified and disgusted, Jung resists but eventually concedes. He writes, "I kneel down on the stone, cut off a piece of the liver and put it in my mouth. My gorge rises—tears burst from my eyes—cold sweat covers my brow—dull sweet taste of blood—I swallow with desperate efforts—it is impossible—once again and once again—I almost faint—it is done. The horror has been accomplished." The woman who demanded this cannibalism throws back her veil, revealing a gentle face, and tells Jung, "I am your soul."[10] What are we to make of this ordeal? Remember Jung is encouraging us to look past the bedrock of emotions, and mine for symbols. Here, the obvious one is consuming the liver of a mutilated child, it creates revulsion, absolute disgust, but what might it mean?

I can think of two possible interpretations, the first involves the cannibalism, a ubiquitous metaphor in esoteric literature and rites, not a literal act, of consuming flesh to merge with the deceased, to take on its power, or to maintain its vitality in a continuity. In tantric visualizations one's own body may be decimated and boiled in a skull cup to purify it (*solve*), then its remaining elixir consumed (*coagula*) to confer everlasting life. The same is true in the Christian context of the Eucharist, as Christ's body is ceremonially consumed as bread, and his blood as wine, to allow the holy spirit to inhabit in us. Elders of the First Nations similarly consume the organs of a fresh kill in their sacred buffalo hunt, so the spirit of the animal lives on.

The second possibility is a reference to the myth of Prometheus, who like Jonah disobeys Zeus, God, steals his fire and sacred knowledge, and bestows its magic upon humans. As a punishment for his offense, Prometheus is sentenced to eternal torment. He is chained to a rock, and each day visited by an eagle, a symbol of Zeus, who consumes his liver. The organ regenerates during the night and the visitation and torture continue in an endless cycle. In Greek culture, the liver was seen as the seat of human emotions. In Chinese medicine the liver governs energy and is responsible for circulation, digestion, and emotional regulation. In Western allopathic medicine the liver is the only organ capable of regenerating itself. We now have multiple vectors of interpretation, cannibalism is a ritualized symbol for rebirth, and specifically the liver confirms this. But the myth of Prometheus is a teaching that for our gifts (of fire, knowledge, magic, or genius), we must pay an unavoidable and unbearable price (of emotional torment, sacrifice, pain, and near-death). Jung's soul is conferring upon him the perennial wisdom that without trial, there is no treasure. No redemption, without sin. No break-through, without break-down. An unimaginable, seemingly impossible, sacrifice must be made to achieve eternal life. If you want to ascend to heaven, you must not only be betrayed and crucified, but endure the consuming fires of hell.

Jung's confrontation with the unconscious, his willing loss of sanity, his epic discoveries of the frontiers of the collective realm, and his embodiment of the pilgrimage of *solve et coagula* which he named "the process of individuation," qualified him to write the introduction for an ancient text translated by Dr. Y. W. Evan Wentz: *The Tibetan Book of the Dead*. It was 1927 when it was released, and the world was still reeling and trying to make sense of the magnitude of the death and devastation resulting from World War I. Jung had seen human darkness firsthand, through prophecy, war, and within his visions, and he knew these ancient books of esoteric wisdom were confirmation of his conclusions: if you desire liberation, you must pay the ultimate price.

TANTRIC ORDEAL

The *Bardo Thodol*, literally "The Great Liberation through Understanding in the Between," was intended to be a manual for the dying person, to aid them in the transition through intermediary states of consciousness into liberation, not unlike a guidebook for global travelers. The *Bardo Thodol* is the ultimate pilgrimage guide to rebirth, and Thurman's translation, in which he provides a remarkable synthesis of the Tibetan science underpinning it and an intelligently compiled collection of auxiliary prayers for broader context, is in my estimation the most complete and authoritative book on the subject. It's supposed to be read as a meditation manual, memorized, and contemplated by those in preparation for death, comprised of a complete set of prayers and practices, visualizations, and mantras, to calm the nerves and transform one's fear into heightened lucidity. Often, laypeople are unable to make this rigorous commitment to spiritual practice, and thus the book, or passages from it, are read to them by the mentor and loved ones during the death process. They believe the soul can hear the guidance even while the stages of dissolution are unfolding, helping them recognize the signs of dissolution, and relate to deities as alleys to follow, not enemies to avert. If one doesn't achieve liberation in life through dream yoga and meditation, one has as a last resort the chance to awaken in the dissolution process at the time of death, and awaken to reclaim the soul.

If one misses the opportunity at any of these junctures, one heads into a period, not exceeding forty-nine human days, representing an odyssey of the soul through liminality in which one is visited first by gentle angels who softly try to coax you to recognize your true nature. And if that fails, one crosses another threshold where one is visited by more fierce deities who use wrathful compassion to accomplish the aim (see plate 1). If one is bereft of the collections of merit and wisdom to create the necessary causes for the deities to have their remarkable influence, provoking liberation, sadly one will enter into the great trial, a judgment similar in archetypal imagery to descriptions in classic literature like *The Egyptian Book of the Dead* and Dante's *Inferno* as the soul faces the consequences of our negative actions in life.

The *Bardo Thodol* concerns itself with six between states, three encountered in the lifespan, and three within the deathspan. No matter the type of bardo, initiation and preparation offer the traveler the opportunity to awaken within the gaps, and gain conscious freedom from the karmic momentum of samsara (or trauma) recreation, driven by delusion, afflictions, and reactive actions. The three bardos within the lifespan are:

1. Bardo of rebirth, between past life and taking on a new body
2. Bardo of dream, between waking consciousness and deep sleep
3. Bardo of meditation, between ordinary consciousness and meditative absorption

The three bardos within the deathspan are:

1. Bardo of dying, between initial sign of dissolution and post physical death liminality
2. Bardo of reality, between post physical death and realization of pure consciousness
3. Bardo of becoming, between pure consciousness and physical manifestation at rebirth

Consciousness researcher Ralph Metzner succinctly describes the intervals and meta process:

The teachings of the Bardo Thödol, in outline, are that immediately at death, in the bardo of the moment of dying, highly proficient meditators who can maintain one-pointed concentration will be able to attain liberation. Most people are not able to concentrate, however, get caught up in fear and confusion and enter into the second phase, called the bardo of the experiencing of reality, in which there are visions of "peaceful and wrathful deities." The deceased is reminded not to be overwhelmed by either the heavenly or the hellish visions, but to remember that they are all projections of one's own mind. Due to lack of training and/or preparation on the part of most ordinary people, the bardo traveler, after repeatedly lapsing into unconsciousness, then finds himself in the third phase, the bardo of seeking rebirth, in which he wanders about seeking to orient himself again to ordinary existence.[11]

LORD OF DEATH

If we pass through the stages of the odyssey of death and rebirth unable to break free with discriminating wisdom, we encounter the Lord of Death. Researcher Sam Woolf has noted, and I agree, the content of one's hallucinations, projections and visitations may be largely individual and culturally specific, just as one might expect from a psychedelic journey, although, this not always the case.[12] You may project your guilt and shame, anger and longing, in personal ways, appearing in familiar guise of culture-bound archetypes. Deities of the Hindu and Buddhist pantheon described in the text, may not be relevant for those outside those cultural matrices, but the process of undergoing an archetypal judgment is universal. A passage from the *Bardo Thodol*, succinctly captures this moment within Campbell's stage of the ordeal.

Hey, noble one! You named So-and-so, listen to me! This suffering of yours comes from your own evolutionary acts; there is no one else to blame. It is your own evolution, so pray strongly to the

Three Jewels. They can protect you. If you don't pray to them, don't know how to meditate on the Great Seal, and don't meditate on an Archetype Deity, then your native angel will count out a white stone for each virtue you accumulated, and your native demon will count out a black stone for every sin. Then you will be very worried, angry, and terrified. Trembling, you will lie, saying, "I committed no sins!" But then Yama, the Judge of the Dead, will say, "I will look into the mirror of evolution!" When he looks into the mirror of evolution, all your sins and virtues will clearly and distinctly appear therein. Your lies will not help. Yama will tie a rope around your neck and lead you away. He will cut off your head, rip out your heart, pull out your guts, lick your brains, drink your blood, eat your flesh, and gnaw your bones. But since you cannot die, even though your body is cut to pieces, you revive again. Being cut up again and again, you will suffer immense pain. When the white stones are being counted, don't be afraid, don't panic, do not lie! Don't fear Yama! Your body is mental, so even if it is killed and cut up, you cannot die. In fact, your form is the void itself, so you have nothing to fear. The Yama-deities are your own hallucinations and themselves are forms of the void. Your own instinctual mental body is void. Voidness cannot harm voidness. Signlessness cannot harm signlessness. You should recognize that there is nothing other than your own hallucination. There is no external, substantially existent Yama, angel, demon, or bull-headed ogre, and so on. You must recognize all this as the between![13]

There are two critical points to note about this passage, and implications on how we practice, live, and die. The first is: ethics are paramount; living a moral life, sensitized to the consequences of our actions of body, speech, and mind, is protection against the so-called judgment. This is true in any tradition. The commandments and the ethical prescriptions that underlie all esoteric traditions, are nearly all the same, and share the common understanding that how we see, speak, and relate to other creates our reality for better and for worse, so discipline your impulses, and cultivate your empathy or you'll reap in the bardos what you sowed in life. The second point is more subtle, and perhaps less articulated in other traditions. This *liberation in the between* is only possible because the nature of awareness is empty and pure. In its ordinary, samsaric condition consciousness is contaminated like a river sullied by false convictions rendering us sick, but the nature of water is fundamentally clear. Mind is fundamentally luminous, blissful, and knowing. Rather than living in fundamental sin, our original Buddha nature is, has always been, will always be, pure.

This subtle level of awareness, the Buddha nature, is in fact the soul, says Thurman.[14] In his glossary he defines the clear-light more explicitly, "It is a light like glass, like diamond, like the predawn twilight, different from the lights of sun, moon, and . . . darkness. It is an inconceivable light, beyond the duality of bright and dark, a light of the self-luminosity of all things.[15] Hence 'transparency' is a good rendering, as is 'clear light,' as long as 'clear' is understood as 'transparent' and not as 'bright.'[16] Here it's fitting to decipher the phrases "voidness cannot harm voidness," which is to say only unreality, that is delusion, can harm us. If we understand the ultimate nature of things, how things are mind constructions, hallucinations, then the angels mild and fierce, the demons and lords of death, our past actions, and their day of judgement, and even the soul itself, experienced as fixed, independent, and real, is more like theater, like a dream. This gives us reassurance and refuge; that because all things are illusory-like, no stain can eternally blemish the soul.

For the Tibetans, *discriminating awareness or wisdom is itself liberation.* Whether it's in this life, or in the death process, in waking, sleep, dream state, or meditative equipoise, whether one is conscious or unconscious along the spectrum, our ordinary mode of perceptual experience is one of a subtle hallucination cross contaminated by karma and trauma, firing automatically, projecting a mosaic of as yet unprocessed content onto the blank screen, the open nature, of reality, compelling us to react to the reflections like funhouse mirrors in a circus. At each interval between states of consciousness, and at each of the six bardos, there is a gap, a moment of optimal vulnerability for a stroke of insight, a moment of redemption within the belly of the whale, for the light of Christ consciousness to break through the gates of Hades.

BUDDHA'S ORDEAL

Having taken the rice porridge to bolster his strength, and committing to avoid the extremes of self-indulgence and self-denial, Siddhartha wanders on from his disappointed companions who cast him out of their dogmatic ascetic cult, into the wilderness alone. He finds a grove outside a village and a banyan tree under which he sits and determines after following the paths of many teachers without success, to resolve to find his own way, to sit until his aim is accomplished. It's a remarkable symbol of the utmost commitment to one's unique process of individuation, a commitment, to discover for oneself the ultimate nature of things.

Siddhartha wants to return to the method of meditation that seemed promising and that led him to the milestone of the middle way, keeping his awareness serviceable for introspection and insight whilst yoking it with a concentrated flow state. He starts looking into his mind for the elusive answer of liberation, a resolution to the existential plight of the human condition, which has propelled his entire six-year pilgrimage since leaving family and home. What emerges is not the truth he seeks, but the demon that guards the treasure, the archetype of the devil lurking in the recesses of his unconscious. It's a key moment—the assault of fear and guilt from childhood and ancestry, the evasive need for comfort and acceptance, compelling us to seek for worldly refuge through countless lives. The demon Mara approaches first in the guises of Namuchi, with seductive and demure daughters, each soft spoken and kind. Sound familiar? You may remember her as one of the "peaceful deities" described in the *Bardo Thodol*. In Siddhartha's striving,

Namuchi tries to lure him away from the innermost cave, reminding him in a tender voice—as my mother did with me when I was despairing in my doctoral studies—that there is no point to the struggle, he can relinquish his torment at any time and simply enjoy a good life. "O you are thin and you are pale, and you are in death's presence too; A thousand parts are pledged to death, but life still holds one part of you. Live, Sir! Life is the better way; you can gain merit if you live, come, live the Holy Life and pour libations on the holy fires, and thus a world of merit gain. What can you do by struggling now? The path of struggling too is rough and difficult and hard to bear."

Here Siddhartha gathers up energy bound by his own psychological hindrances of grasping and aversion, and sees them for what they were—projections of the mindscape—and transmutes these enemies into a single ally of determination. Then comes a moment of bravery—not fleeing death, not hiding from our fear, but facing it consciously, to expose its unreality. Siddhartha says, "None but the brave will conquer them [these minions], to gain bliss by the victory. Better I die in battle now, than choose to live on in defeat . . . I sally forth to fight, that I may not be driven forth from my post."[17] Siddhartha holds his ground.

Death is certain and imminent, but what matters more is how we die, willingly with the heart of courage. At this moment Mara, manifest more wrathfully, accompanied by ferocious hoards, attempting to unseat the prince, demanding Siddhartha produce a witness that can attest to his worthiness, his right to claim victory. Mara approaches Siddhartha and asks: "Are you worthy of supreme enlightenment?" In a single act, Siddhartha doesn't look up towards the heavens as Christ on the cross might have done, but downwards, touching the Earth, asking Her to bear witness. Having witnessed all his previous lives, the momentum of his virtue has led to this moment, Mother Earth replies, "He is worthy! There is not a spot on the Earth where he has not already offered himself to the attainment of Enlightenment and the welfare of all beings!" With this proclamation, Mara, his army, and daughters disappear. As he sees through the projections, they vanish.

Siddhartha's temptation by Mara mirrors the temptation of Christ in the desert. It's the same archetypal motif; the devil tells Christ, why suffer purification, you can be a king and all the world your kingdom. It's the same epic moment, the ego suggesting you don't need a heroic journey. Once you're willing to die, resistance stops, there's nothing to coerce or threaten you with. When we face our fear it loses its power, the energy is drawn up like a sword from a paralyzed stone where it was once bound, and the irony is the moment when the demon of death is faced, we experience the birth of renewed vitality, releasing everlasting life. *Fear is not conquered by brute force; it's tamed by the wisdom eye that recognizes its unreality.* Emptiness can not destroy emptiness. If you die to your fear, accept death while staying resolute to truth, fear is transmuted into courage. Truth prevails. Wisdom is the most potent weapon against the devil and its minions, this is what Jonah came to understand in the belly of a whale, the act of grace comes when night is darkest, and every resistance has failed. You must surrender and allow death to swallow you whole, knowing it's not terminal. Recognizing ego as unreality, frees you from the bondage of self-grasping.

REFLECTIONS ON ORDEAL

By the force of karma, we will all face the consequences of our actions, or inactions, and we will all die. In life, and in death, there is no escaping the trial, so we have two choices: try and outrun our fate, as Jonah did, only to be swallowed by a terrible creature of our own making, or consciously approach the cave, that which we fear most, and willingly descend into hell, to voluntarily be obliterated by the darkness. I resisted and buckled, as Jonah did, on the dais in front of my mentor and peers. I lacked the courage and conviction to stand up straight, and speak my truth, the betrayal I encountered and the death that ensued were brutal. But none more brutal than the regret of betraying myself. In the darkness of my reflections the tragedy haunted me for an entire year, like Jonah's regret for three long days and nights, until we encounter with the lord of death Yama in the bardo, and our merits are weighted against our sins, as we plead for redemption.

Grace is available if we're willing to learn from our mistakes, willing to explore the darkness, to be overcome by madness, to look for the symbols carried in the torrent of emotions, and ultimately to listen to our soul's guidance. God is omnipresent but appears in many forms, a snake, tree, veiled maiden calling us to consume a bloody organ, to process and digest that which we detest, to be crucified, so that others might eat of our sacrifices and gain eternal life.

Ultimately there is no single life, no terminal death. There is only the soul's continuity, the precession of the equinoxes, the eternal return. Because voidness cannot destroy voidness, there is nothing substantive to fear. Our nature is pure, unblemished, everlasting, it's only our hallucinations, fabrications, projections of unresolved traumas from childhood and ancestry, that appear to descend upon us like demons. These hordes of Mara can be seen through with the wisdom eye, but only if we dare to draw close enough to face them, accepting the worst possible fate with honor and courage. What can we learn from mythology, Tibet's thanatology, from what Jung called the "mythopoetic imagination?"[18] While the world runs toward the light that unceasingly evades them, the hero descends into the darkness, for that is where the treasure lies.

PART III

Fruition

Fruition is the Embodied Application in the World

Just as the master altruist arrives at the hard-won summit of enlightenment savoring the vast vista of cosmic oneness, wisdom simultaneously recognizes the journey is not complete without an equally arduous return journey back down to the marketplace to offer the nectar of universal compassion to awaken living beings still ensnared in the nightmare net of their collective hallucination. So too does the hero who pulls sword from stone rest not in the afterglow of personal triumph, but makes an about-face for a return journey home to deliver their boon, overcoming reverse trials and tribulations that help metabolize their elixir boon, emboldening their message, which can only come to full and final completion when imbibed and celebrated by the communal tribe.

9
Treasure
Claiming the Sword

BELULANG—MEDICINAL GARDEN

It's my second visit to the Wizard's medicinal grove at Belulang, in the pristine countryside an hour north of Ubud. He's cultivated his garden to spec, with delight and attention to detail. It's his little oasis, and Tjok Gde becomes more ethereal here—like a fairy in flight—as he procures his plants for his tinctures and remedies. We're surrounded by wildflowers and herbs, sitting under a thatched roof hut with a blazing hearth at its center. Woodsmoke mixed with the scent of lemongrass perfumes the air. The Wizard's hut is nestled in the shadow of a hill above us.

On top of this hill sits a thousand-year-old Shiva temple. They say its origins stretch back beyond the arrival of the Hindu diaspora from Java, well before the twenty-three generation's old linage of the Majapahit of which the Wizard is the living heir. Originally perhaps, beneath the black lava megalithic stones of the Shiva temple was a sacred site for the Indigenous islanders, the Bali Mula, meaning root or original people, who practiced an unadulterated animism in communion with the land and its spirits. They believe that Bali is a living entity recycling healing energy, comprised of three mandalas, the top of sacred mountains form the crown mandala, the Kerthyasa family spring at Ibah and other temples inland around Ubud represent the middle, and the temples dotting the coastline along the sea represent the outer mandala. Energy flows up from the Indian ocean, condenses water into precipitation, carried by the winds, and then rains upon the mountains inland, flowing down though the rivers and springs, heated by volcanic and geothermal land features along the way, the energy descends again through all the elements: earth, fire, water, wind, recycled back into ether and diffused across the oceans again. It's a dance of disintegration and reintegration, the pilgrimage of *solve et coagula*, a process of purification and regeneration as Bali herself inhales and exhales.

Like the subtle-body maps of alchemic traditions, East and West, with its complex of channels, chakra hubs, energetic winds, and nectar drops within the human body, the Bali Mula knew how to follow the arterial lines along the body mandala of the island, locating the nexus points where the energy was potent and available at sacred springs, and there constructed temples and shrines to serve as portals for healing and expansion of consciousness. When you practice meditation and participate in ceremony at these sites, you're refining your attention like an antenna to align with the frequency of energy admitted at these places of power. The sacred geography of the island with its temple network act like an intermediary between the cosmos and the psyche; *as above, so below*. To drink and to submerge in its holy waters, to summit its mythical mountains, to eat heritage rice from its spirit guarded terraces, to brew natural tea with its wildflowers over woodfire, is to commune with the divine mother that is Bali. Before the development of Balinese Hinduism, the Indigenous religion was known as *Agama Tirta*, Sacred Water. No one knows how old or how holy this Shivite temple is, the hillside we're spending our last days together planning our future is shrouded in mystery.

Five minutes down a dirt trail, flows a narrow river, with a stone outcrop under which is a *tirta*—natural holy spring. This is a site in the middle section of the body mandala of Bali. We've just performed melukat, the water purification ceremony (described earlier in chapter eight), and *canang sari*, flower offering, down there not but an hour ago and are now resting for a refreshing citrus laced beverage that tantalizes my taste buds and puckers my lips. As the Wizard and I dream aloud, what we're doing is going back in time, to orient our movement forward. Just as mythologist Campbell and his heir Phil Cousineau taught, the heroes of all times have all made the epic journey not by rushing forward blindly, but by revolving backward through mythic time, to claim a treasure and bestow a boon for humanity.

During the ceremony near the spring, I was seated right next to Tjok Gde, along with a few other villagers. He didn't lead the ceremony this time. Instead, and in my honor, he invited the local priest of Belulang to perform the rite. It's getting close to my return home, and we're squeezing in one last day together, like the last drop of citrus in my tea. We sit close to each other. I can hear the prayers under his breath, they're growing more familiar with each repetition, while I shadow his every move. We offer the five beautiful traditional Balinese prayers and flower offerings.

First we wash our face and hands, sit comfortably on the grass in front of a moss covered boulder altar flanked by an emerald and crimson swirl of flora. We each have a parcel of assorted multicolored flowers, called a chanang. When these are assembled by the village women they are envisioned as a mandala, and right before we offer them, they are rinsed in wafts of incense.

The first prayer with empty hands in is to your own soul, the Atma, and the air element represented by your breath, may it be illuminated on its journey from bondage to liberation.

The second, with a single white frangipani, is to Surya, the sun god, the fire element, may it continue to bring light, dispelling the darkness, sustaining life for all.

The third, holding multicolored flowers, is to the Trimurti, the confluence of the three supreme gods, Braham, the creator, Vishnu, the sustainer, and Shiva, the destroyer, coalescing air, fire, and water elements, so that the complete cycle of birth, life, and death is seen not as a singular terminal tragedy, but as a sacred, eternal continuity.

The fourth prayer, again with multicolored flowers, is to Ida Sanghyang Widhi Wasa, the supreme Trimurti manifest as the specific deity or spirit of the particular place you perform the ritual. It is the universal manifest as the specific protector of the land under your seat, and thus represents the earth element. Here one can invite one's personal mentors and ancestors, so that the entire field of beings is honored as sacred. The Wizard adds a moment of veneration of mother earth here.

The fifth, returns to open hands, a prayer of gratitude for the good that nourishes and heals as well as the hardship that fosters growth and appreciation. All the elements have been alchemized through intention, prayer, and offering, and thus all experiences in life can be seen as a blessing, so rejoice.

At the conclusion the priest sprinkles holy water over us. The right hand is cupped in the left, and is then held up and filled with holy water three times for drinking, and then three times to wash our head and face. It is a baptism. A final handful is filled with grains of rice which are pressed into the forehead, the temples and the throat, with the final few eaten and sprinkled onto the head. The rice is symbolic of rebirth and prosperity. The whole ritual can be done in 15 minutes, but it represents a timeless process of remembering you are not an ordinary being in a disenchanted world, but a divine being in an enchanted one. Very close in character to the Tibetan tantric practices of divine pride and pure view, in which you see yourself and all others as the deity, the environment and its contents as mandala, hear all sounds as mantra, and taste all experiences as nectar.

Each time we go through this ceremonial sequence, it becomes more familiar, more effortless, allowing my rational mind to get out of the way and my diamond queen of intuition to come forward spontaneously in the flow. The ceremony is the theater of intuition, ritual, divine dance, prayer, and song. Combining these, we give ourselves over to the right brain, descend into the shadow, and beyond into collective unconscious, the great mystery, finally gaining access to the soul, and then bring her forth from the frontiers of transpersonal consciousness back into the body and everyday world. The setting for this ceremony is stunningly beautiful, set amid the jungle surrounded by rice terraces, situated adjacent to the stream and sacred spring, with natural rocks and trees as the shrine. The sweet smell of freshly blooming flowers is carried on the breeze. Nothing but grass and fertile earth underneath us. All breathtakingly natural, simple, and unadorned. Just after the priest sprinkles holy water over us, a drizzle fell from a clear sky. The Wizard says, "Very auspicious, rain without clouds." My heart is wide open from the initiations, prayers, and ceremonies, and tears fall from my eyes. Not tears purging despair, but ones of joy. Magic exists.

I sip the Wizard's brew, and it's as soothing as one might expect of any elixir. The sleepy village of Belulang is known for its natural hot springs, where people come from all corners of the island to naturally treat various ailments, aware that the island is a living entity with magical powers. The first time the Wizard brought me here was only three weeks ago, but it now feels like lifetimes according to the mythic dimension we've been inhabiting. The last time here, within the first hour of our walking through lush rice terraces overlooking many centuries-old temple complexes at the center of a village, I knew. The diamond queen had found her home. This was the place I had been looking for, where I wanted my family to start a post-Nalanda, post-pandemic life.

To say Bali is special seems trite. The land here is exquisite, lush like the Garden of Eden, largely untouched beyond the hubs of commercial activity wreaking havoc. In the distance along the eastern horizon, you can see the peaks of three sacred mountains, like a holy trinity of sisters, Batur with its active volcano and caldera, Bautkaru the second holiest peak, and Agung, the holy epicenter of the island's mandala, a mythical Mount Olympus, towering over the lesser-known Abang, which initiated me. But it's more than the sacred geography. More than the ancient temple complexes, the hot healing springs, the beautiful ceremonies, abundant tropical fruits, fragrant flowers, and the simple village life in the outskirts that have been unchanged for a century. It's being with the wisdom-keepers that speaks most to my soul, as we immerse in the sacred ways of the past to construct a vision of our future together just as the world collapses. Without the wisdom keeper, we're lost, orphaned in a chaotic world. For what good is the natural beauty of paradise if you have no soul? Eve and Adam sacrificed everything to teach us this. I was looking for healing and regeneration in my personal life, but the world is also going through the death process yearning to be reborn. We've reached the end of an aion, sick and spiritually malnourished after a four-centuries long chapter fixated exclusively on the material realm.

Bali represents one of the few remaining cultures on the planet where the old ways are still alive and can help us return to our senses so we can again live in harmony with others, the natural world, and the spirit world, as the philosophy of Tri Hita Karana recommends. It's just days away from my return to New York, I miss my family terribly, but I'm relishing the treasure I've been so fortunate to earn here. Kinship in sacred view. Everything my astrologer Lynn Bell predicted has come true. Every note has been so perfectly sung. I've fallen in love. If we're willing to cross the threshold and depart the ordinary world to follow the magic, so too does the reward await us after our confrontation with the ordeal. There is no treasure without trial, no rebirth without death, no genius without madness.

THE PEARL IN THE OYSTER

The pearl contained within the oyster is a natural byproduct of a self-preserving response to a foreign irritant or invasion. No invader, no pearl. In the months after I departed from Nalanda following the heart-breaking fallout with Joe, I wandered aimlessly as a disembodied ghost. Utterly lifeless and dissociated. Every day was a struggle to get up, to bathe and eat, to move past the gut-wrenching disbelief, despair, and anger of the betrayal, and to perform my functions even remotely as a husband, father, and therapist. At times, to be perfectly honest, life had lost its meaning.

A lesson that emerged from my post-ordeal reflection was how unprepared I was for change and death. When the mandala is not adequately dissolved with the same intention as it was constructed, it's liable to be swept away by a torrent when we least expect it. Joe and I never discussed when or how our relationship dynamic would evolve or end. We carried on as if it would be ideal forever. Nothing lasts forever. Every relationship has its purpose and must be fluid and dynamic to adapt. Stagnation creates rigidity that makes life brittle. And brittle things eventually break. Inevitably there would be a changing of the guard. What should we expect from a mentor-student relationship done right? Naively neither of us anticipated an abrupt ending. It was a mistake, one that anyone currently enjoying a mutually enriching relationship of any kind would do well to consider.

It seems obvious in retrospect, but if everything ends, why don't we plan for it? We could have communicated with respect our differing values and political ideologies and prepared to adapt our roles that could work for both. The Tibetans say your last thought or deed before death determines your next rebirth. It's called *throwing karma* because it thrusts you into one of the six realms of existence. If we use it as an analogy, how we end relationships determines how future ones begin. If you don't have merits, no recognition or redemption, your soul follows the principle of familiarity, and seeks out similar experiences, even painful ones, until it learns its lesson, until it finishes the business of this life. If one life ends badly, tainted by hurt, anger, and broken trust, perhaps the next is followed by more idealization and grasping, or suspicion and defense. Round we go in a downward devolution. If, however, endings are prepared for mindfully, celebrating for what was achieved, and surrendered with dignity, as is advised in the *Bardo Thodol*, perhaps one rides the residue of separation into the bardo between with more clarity and energy for optimal reconstruction on the other side.

Eventually, I wanted to learn from the betrayal. I didn't want to bring the hurt, defensiveness, and distrust into my next life iteration. Perhaps my most profound realization post ordeal, was to come to terms with how *my experience of betrayal was primarily based on my projections.* No doubt by now, you would have noticed that I experienced my public trial, the precursor to my exit from Nalanda, as a public execution, as a punishment and shaming. It would be easy for me to leave it there and play the victim role, transforming my beloved mentor conveniently into a villain, and to write him off. Most of us do this. Victim and villan are two interdependent sides of the same coin. The mind enjoys the simplicity of black and white thinking. Crafting crude binaries that allow us to avoid the struggle with complexity; and more importantly to avoid accountability for our own involvement or complicity in the ordeal. Vax, no vax, mask, no mask, liberal or conservative. These are simple binaries. Neat little categories. You can fall into one, and point fingers at the other. It's easy, like child's play. Both sides thinking they own the truth, while the other is a threat. It's more challenging to remain in the rough currents of nuance, tolerating ambiguity and uncertainty posed by the shades of grey. Real people are shades of gray. Our lives are more complex than any of these binaries, labels, groups, or political ideologies.

My work with Jung and Tibetan Buddhism asks me to take responsibility for my mind, past karma, and shadow that gets projected on the blank canvas of the world. Buddhism and Jung are for the mature, not children playing the victim. How I feel and react is not caused by externalities. Externalities can be catalysts for sure—but the causes are our own unprocessed traumas. Obviously, there is an interdependence between internal cause and external condition, Joe and Geri contributed to our mutual collision and rupture, but I'm responsible for my side. That is key. We can only control things from our side of the street. And more so, we must examine the disgust and aggression we've projected and take responsibility for the darkness within us. Increasingly in our cancel culture, fermenting on victimhood and outrage, personal responsibility seems something few are ready or able to take.

I had to come to terms with the terrifying reality that I was complicit in the betrayal I experienced with Joe. I was as capable of healing someone and saving lives as I was of destroying and ruining them. Both realities are extremes on the continuum within us. We're all mirrors of and for each other. The admiration and love we see and have for others reflects our goodness, the virtuous karma we've cultivated in the past. What we despise and reject in others, reflects past divisive karma, the unintegrated parts within our shadow, which have not yet been "redeemed" and having nowhere to reside must be cast off and out into the world as "other." This is not to suggest solipsism, it's not all a projection, others and their actions do exist. It's a matter of taking the higher road as personal accountability always allows us to learn and grow, even from injustices. Knowing that I'm capable of betraying my students, my beloved boys, even myself in the same devastating way that I experienced betrayal with Joe and my father when I was a child, keeps me more aligned with truth and integrity.

The Buddhist teachings on karma suggest we've done everything possible in the past, virtue and vice, and the seeds and residue of negativity karma are just lying in wait, like active landmines in the Cambodian killing fields, ready for the unsuspecting conditions to come together to be tread upon. There are angels and demons within us alike. It's easier to see them outside of us, elevate them, and equally demonize them as others or "exiles." But we can all be Jeffrey Epstein and even Jeffrey Dahmer, just as we can all become the Dalai Lama. You can't fully accept there is a Buddha within you unless you're prepared to face Mara and her hordes of minions. To pull the sword from the stone, to command its power, is to accept the terrifying responsibility of wielding it. This is why the bodhisattva or altruistic resolve to awaken for the benefit of others is such a radical mission—because it accepts that of all the possible motivations a person can adopt, the one driven by compassion is the most powerful. It gives you the greatest sense of purpose, but isn't meaningful unless you have also tasted the possibility of being a slave to your own dark triad of psychopathy, narcissism, and Machiavellianism.

All the stories I've shared to this point portray the heroine and hero facing the ordeal of the dark night of the soul, because that is the only path to the light, the only way to draw sword from stone. The stone in a dark mass, hardened and immobile. It represents the trauma and dissociation in our unconscious paralyzing us, sapping our energy, and rendering us inert. The hero quest to the underworld is to face our fear, the terrifying dragon that guards the treasure must be tamed through direct confrontation. The years we spent in denial, and on the run, only gave more power to our foe. Only when you die—completely surrender—is your fear of death transformed into an elixir. *If you die before you die, then you'll never die when you die.*[1] The sword—the elixir—is immortality, it is confidence, power, love. It's the gold that you seek to create through your dissolution. When you pull sword from stone, raising it from the unconscious, overhead, and aligning it to your true north, so that all your energies in your subtle body are again unbounded from dark forces, purified, liberated, and aligned with truth, then you can knight yourself, receive coronation as King or Queen, as a sovereign of your body, mind, and world. The pearl abides in the oyster, the soul in the shadow, buddha nature in the unconscious, and no other place.

POST ORDEAL CORONATION

Five months post ordeal, I was making progress and beginning to heal. Emily and I processed the loss nearly every day, sometimes for hours after the kids had gone to bed. We took turns being a support while the other fell apart. Surviving the ordeal together brought us closer. People often blame themselves for trauma, or they blame others and never go through a proper accounting and consideration of all sides. Staying with our death process, we managed to go through the stages of grief organically. It took time, but it worked. Accepting our misfortune, raging, grieving, soul-searching, ultimately generating compassion for ourselves and then Joe, released the energy bound-up in blame. The love on the other side of betrayal is matured through trial and has a different character than its naive predecessor. It's imbued with wisdom instead of idealism, ironically more conditional and self-respecting than unconditional and self-deprecating. It's easier for people, including myself, to stay angry rather than drown in the well of despair, but I let myself sink, be swept away on the currents, washing up on the shores of Bali two year later, with the Wizard there to receive me. Perhaps my overwhelming moment in the water purification at the Kerthyasa family spring helped me access and embody the last remnants of loss and sadness lingering in the shadows. I'm grateful for that now, for all of it.

By October 2018, I was about to lead a pilgrimage to Nepal with another of my teachers, Geshe Tenzin Zopa. I had nurtured a relationship with him for the last twelve years parallel to the one with Joe, and in a stroke of synchronicity, I had asked Geshe-la, not Joe, to write the foreword to my last book *Gradual Awakening*, even before the fallout. One thing I learned from the betrayal in the weeks of self-analysis with Emily was it severed a primitive and long-standing co-dependence, stemming from my childhood experience of being subservient to my narcissistic and alcoholic father. I was Joe's assistant and his spiritual son. I could have hung on to that deferential position forever. Nothing in the world could have severed my tie with him so instantly, so completely, other than such a dramatic and unsuspecting betrayal. What a blessing in disguise. It forced me to leave the nest and discover the strength and wisdom within me I only thought was present in those I admired. That's the pearl in the oyster of trauma. It can awaken you, albeit rudely, and serve as a catalyst for discovering inner resources you never realized you had. But you must take the beating first. You must lose everything. You must die to be reborn. *Solve et coagula*. You must be broken apart, for the energies to be released from the old edifice to be recast anew. The severing I experienced wasn't just the outer relationship with my dear mentor and the community I left, but also the legacy of my childhood insecurity, which fed my fear and naive dependency on others. I didn't believe in myself without Joe. I didn't have a separate identity without him.

To individuate and become what we're meant to be, we must first separate from the childhood dynamics that keep us small and stuck in the shire of safe but self-limiting possibilities. What I lost in innocence, I gained in confidence. Though I lost my mentor, I found myself. Dispelling the youthful idealization opened the door to a more mature perspective where I could see that we're all just human, each with our flaws and genius, each capable of loving-kindness and devastating destruction. Discernment is a higher order virtue born of surviving the trials of life. That's why I say mature love is ironically conditional, or wrathful, it demands respect and reciprocity, and is not ill placed where it can be taken for granted or misconstrued as weakness. I don't blame Joe now. The rupture needed to happen, and without the public trial, the boy in me would have never died to be reconstituted as the man and teacher I've become. I no longer need to idealize someone or hang on their coattails, any more than I need an enemy to blame for my misfortune. Having properly processed the disbelief, bargaining, anger, and grief at the loss of Joe, I could emerge a more mature adult, wiser for my ordeal, and see Joe in a new light, as just another human being, his virtues replete with vices. Instead of fixating on how things ended, now I can appreciate the incredible job he did teaching me everything I needed to know, including how to die well, over the course of our twenty years together. I love Joe, and thank him with all my heart. I forgive us both for the tragic collision of our reciprocal ricocheting projections that all too sadly characterize the insufferable shadowlands of samsara.

Eventually, every safe-haven becomes a prison, unless you keep risk-taking to update and reboot. We're each forced to recognize when our needs are met, and our time together has served its purpose. One clear example that my childhood dependency needs were being integrated is that I didn't transfer those infantile yearnings from Joe onto Geshe Zopa. Although Geshe-la acts in the guru role as Joe once did, I've the ego flexibility to be deferential, his superior, or his equal, whatever the situation might require. I love learning from Geshe-la, he's genuinely a realized being, I place my head at his feet in ceremony, but I work independently too. The tight calcification of roles and needs has been replaced by intuitive and fluid roles, supported by freedom, joy, and immediacy of the moment. The diamond queen of my intuition, known in the Tibetan tradition as the inner guru, has become the focus of the devotion I once outsourced to others.

EMBODYING THE TREASURE

What happens between the pilgrimage to Nepal in October 2018 and February 2021 sipping tea with the Wizard in Belulang could best be described as embodying the treasure and returning with an elixir. On the heels of a most magical journey through the Kathmandu Valley and inspired by Geshe-la's impeccable teachings and my newfound confidence, I returned to New York to rebuild my life, including a new mandala, a school of my own where I could teach my brand of trauma-informed Buddhism, free of identity politics. I called it the Contemplative Studies Program (CSP), and now the Gradual Path. Along with my partner Alison Graham, we designed and implemented a comprehensive curriculum consisting of intensive teachings, pilgrimages, community forums, and service projects.

Little did we know when we launched the CSP that the pandemic would soon strike. Fortunately for us, we found refuge in the cloud with a new online Dharma community. In the nearly four years that ensued the CSP kept us focused on our spiritual development and supporting one another through thick and thin. We invited world-renowned guest speakers, traveled on group pilgrimage to Sri Lanka in November 2019, raised donations for nunneries abroad, created a brave space for stimulating debate free of subservience to any political ideologies, graduated dozens of committed students, and formed bonds that will last lifetimes. We created so much to be proud of and grateful for.

Like a racehorse behind the starter gates, there was a massive build up of creative energy inside me post ordeal. The stone in which the sword is embedded is calcified, inert energy, bound by constricting forces of fear and shame. Once the wisdom eye is open, calcification dissolves, the once bound energy releases the soul in the service of regeneration. While on pilgrimage in Nepal, I launched my book *Gradual Awakening* at Kopan Nunnery. It was a symbolic convocation, bookending my death and rebirth process, once seated on a dais in front of Joe being stoned by my peers, now I sat side-by-side with Geshe-la on a dais in a shrine hall amidst the chanting swirl of 700 nuns. Following our return from pilgrimage I emerged from metamorphosis, leading the CSP, teaching over seventy classes and recording over 200 hours of new material, fusing Tibetan Buddhism with contemporary subjects including psychology and trauma research. The third course of that program was called Return with Elixir, which now forms the basis of the pages you're reading. It is my boon for you, having recovered my soul.

Synchronistical, just after course three, the pandemic of 2020 hit, and the world was instantly cast into darkness, so we converted the CSP into an online dharma center and lifeboat in the cloud during the lockdown. On the heels of my personal and now worldwide ordeal, I found my confidence, authentic voice, vision, and purpose, and led over 200 students through our generation's most significant global crisis. When the hour was darkest for the collective, I had already died and was reborn, I possessed immense energy and conviction, stepped up and into the fray, having already faced my shadow and claimed the sword, I could rally my community through pandemic contractions into our collective dark night and beyond.

THE BOROBUDUR MANDALA

As I take another sip of tea, the Wizard and I dream aloud about the future. Our bare feet hang over the hut floor, slightly raised on teak platform stilts, and our toes wiggle in the wet grass below after a midday shower. We've been engrossed in the natural fusion of our mutual interests, a synergy of inner and outer alchemy, Tjok Gde's passions for Balinese Tantra, physical alchemy, and natural medicine, with my blend of Buddhist Tantra, trauma-informed psychotherapy, and Jungian shadow-work. *As within, so without.* But I also disclose to the Wizard a vision I've had for another pilgrimage—to the island of Java and on to Bali. I envisioned summiting the Borobudur, largest mandala and Buddhist megalithic structure in the world, bringing together, after centuries of separation, the twin tantric traditions of Vajrayana Buddhism and Tantric Shivism in a ceremony of reunion (plate 9).

The Borobudur mandala was built in central Java in the ninth century by the Vajrayana Buddhist kings of the Sailendra Dynasty and is positioned in an elevated area between twin active volcanoes—Mount Sumbing and Mount Merapi—and two rivers—Progo and Elo. Like mount Kailash for the Tibetans, the ancient Sailendra culture believed that the Merapi volcano was the physical manifestation of the mythological mount Meru, the axial center of the cosmos. Later in the twelfth century King Kertanegara of the Singhasari Kingdom is often credited with fusing the lineages of tantric Shivism and Vajrayana Buddhism into a unique syncretic form of religion known as Shiva-Buddha agama. This persisted in Java for two more centuries, during which time the Majapahit Empire arose and maintained the syncretic religion before the Islamic invasions forced their royal court to exodus to Bali. For political reasons over the years, the fusion of Shiva-Buddha split, Buddhism taking a lesser role until it faded, while tantric Hinduism merged with animistic traditions became prominent in Bali. Yet at one time the Wizard's ancestors may have made pilgrimage to Borobudur to conduct Shiva-Buddha ceremonies venerating both deities as different manifestations of the same essence. Something in me wants to "go backward to go forward," to reclaim this lost union, but I'm unsure why.

The enormous structure of Borobudur (see figure 9.1) is a three-dimensional mandala, the largest of its kind in the world, symbolically a deity's celestial palace, 118 meters on its four sides, consisting of nine platforms, neatly stacked like a pyramid—six square and three circular—topped by a central dome or stupa, which uncoincidentally as we shall see is missing its chatra or crown at the very top. The glorious monument is adorned with 2,672 relief panels brilliantly displaying the life of the Buddha and the legacy of his teachings in pictorial form. Images being easier to learn and digest, the monument is a living library of Buddhist wisdom. In fact, the Borobudur is an ancient film or movie, but rather than light being projected through silicon images as they rapidly rotate frame by frame across a projector screen, the pilgrim is the one who circumambulates past the reliefs on the gallery walls. Within the mandala are 504 Buddha statues, and around the dome at the summit, precisely placed, are 72 Buddha statues, each seated facing outwards in a ring around the central stupa at the top. The monument invites the pilgrim on a physical journey that represents the gradual path to enlightenment. One must circumambulate the periphery, the unconscious, then ascend the passageways, where the bas relief teachings guide you toward wisdom. One ascends through the three dimensions of reality, the material world of sense craving, the higher form realm of the deities and the formless realms of most subtle and sublime consciousness, before arriving at the summit, and the symbolic achievement of liberation. The monument provides a catalyst for a rite of passage, the human procession through these realms as consciousness is refined and purified, just as the Buddha's own mind was under the Bodhi tree, until freedom is achieved. It's psychodrama at its best, priming the pilgrim's mind through ritual reenactment, so that the physical experience and mental map of the spiritual journey can later be transposed on the actual journey of one's life, allowing one's inner intuition to lead, based on visceral memory.

These details at Borobudur—the location, the precise structural alignments and dimensions, and the number relief panels—and number of Buddha statues don't strike me as random or arbitrary. For example, the 72 Buddha statues, to my novice eyes appears to be significant number in astrology. The number 72 is a primary number linked to the earth's axial precession, which causes the apparent alteration in the position of the constellations over the Great Year period of 25,920 years,

Fig. 9.1. Borobudur Mandala, Magelang, Central Java, Indonesia.
Photo by Zaenulihsan91.

or one degree every seventy-two years.* In addition to initiatory rites, I speculate the monument is likely also an ancient time machine calibrated to the equinoxes. Further corroboration comes from renowned expert on the Borobudur John Miksic who suggests the architectural layout and orientation of the monument coincide with the sunrise on Vesak in May, symbolically linking its design with the sacred timing of Buddha's enlightenment and birth.[2] This is consistent with the astrologically-informed design of the Angkor Wat in Cambodia, aligned precisely with the sunrise on Spring Equinox, as well as Stonehenge, England (winter solstice), and at Chichen Itza, Mexico, where a serpent-shaped shadow appears to slither down the steep steps of the pyramid exactly on the spring and autumn equinoxes. The ancients were too brilliant to leave such things to chance. I sense the details at Borobudur

---

*In some instances I have rounded the number, 24,000 to match the Yuga cycle, or here rounded to 25,800, but the technical number tied to precession is 25,920. 25,920 years of precession ÷ 360 degrees of a complete cycle − 72 years per degree.

all have astrological meaning, and serve a specific purpose, but research on the astronomical alignments of the temple are, as yet, scarce.[3]

JUNG'S TREASURE OF INDIVIDUATION

Borobudur in Java, like Angkor in Cambodia, the Pyramids in Egypt, and the Asklepion in Greece, were theaters for active imagination, which helped initiates and pious pilgrims alike heal and enact the purpose of life: metaphorically dying to reach immortality. Now all that remains of these places are the monolithic stones baking in the heat. Gone are the rituals and the sacred knowledge that knew how these structures were aligned with greater cycles in the stars, and how to use them to manipulate the subtle energies in our bodies, so that initiates might become angels of light, transpersonal, transtemporal beings aligned with divine purpose.

We know that Jung turned to esoteric sources like these to help him make sense of his inner experience, temporarily abandoning science and rationality because they were ill-equipped, then relinquishing Gnosticism because it was too archaic, later going East to Chinese alchemy which pierced his heart, then Indian yoga and Tibetan tantra, all proving effective signposts on the path, so that Jung could return home to Western alchemy, which became his template in mapping the human development of the personality.

The principle of individuation was neither new nor coined by Jung. The Greeks, including Aristotle, had explored it, as well as his contemporaries Schopenhauer and Nietzsche. Jung describes "principum individuationis [as] individual differentiation, whose isolated character removes it from the realm of general biological phenomena."[4] The human being is more than matter, the soul inhabits the body, but seeks to differentiate itself from the body and all other persons. If the individual doesn't successfully differentiate, if it drowns in the family or society, becoming indistinguishable from the collective, Jung felt this would be equated with meaninglessness and death. Jung describes the individuation process as, "the process by which individual beings are formed and differentiated; in particular, it is the development of the psychological individual as a being from the general, collective psychology."[5] He continues, "individuation is practically the same as development of consciousness out of the sphere or original identity. It is thus an extension of the sphere of consciousness and enriching of conscious psychological life."[6] Individuation is an innate impulse to become separate from others yet whole, integrating our conflicting parts, thus unique. Expressing one's authenticity is different from expressing one's individuality; the latter is a mode of the ego, the former sourced in Self.

METHODS OF INDIVIDUATION

The Swiss psychologist Jolande Jacobi describes individuation as "a maturation process of the soul and aims at the fulfilment of the personality through the greatest possible extension of the field of consciousness."[7] According to Jacobi there are two methods by which the process of individuation can proceed, one is natural, the other, conscious. The natural process is akin to a biological drive, occurring largely unconsciously, as if the development of the personality is a byproduct of circumstances in which one has lived passively as a bystander or victim. Here the joys and sorrows, the successes and tragedies that characterize life, leave their imprint. Those that blindly chase success and attempt to avoid failures, just as biology primes us to seek pleasure and avoid pain, have their personhood shaped largely by externalities and circumstance. This mode of individuating is the more common, and characteristically driven by overcompensation for developmental trauma.

For these people it can be said that the construction of their personality has been formed based on an unconscious chain reaction, originating with trauma, producing pain, requiring defenses, and habituating over-compensatory reactions, resulting in a rigid identity formation, maintained through interpersonal reinforcement contingencies. This is my interpretive observation of clinical cases combining lenses from Buddhist-dependent origination theory, attachment theory, and trauma-informed psychotherapy. In one of my clients, Henry, it looked something like this: his personality was forged in the crucible of the rejection by his father and the incessant criticism of his mother, indoctrinating him to the mythology of his incompetence, because as his mother repeatedly shamed him that he "lacked backbone." This origin story left Henry impotent and depressed, later criticized by his own wife as "weak," and rejected by his children for being perceived as "aloof and uncaring." Out of necessity, Henry's unconscious created a defensive structure, including emotional dissociation, hyper intellectualization, passivity, and conflict avoidance which ironically reinforced his family's scorn. I suggest that these early defenses begin as state-specific best attempts to adapt, but grow over time and repetition into personality traits. In other words, self-protective mechanisms over generalize and become intractable, self-replicating modes of being. In effect, our personalities or personas are byproducts of natural accommodation and protective adaptations to inner pain, shame, and the social environment.

My clinical work with Henry was to go back in order to go forward. We needed to leave the safety and stasis of his rigid ego and maladaptive defenses, delve into the unknown underworld of his shadow, where we faced his own childhood trauma, and even uncovered the ancestral legacy of his father, who was the victim of childhood molestation, and who could never effectively mirror Henry as a result. From within the oyster, we discovered the pearl of his vitality from the grip on fear and shame. We fused his personal mythology of having no "backbone," with the Arthurian myth, to help him pull sword from stone, align with courage, and rise to confront his fears. Henry eventually learned how to feel his full range of emotions, meeting his shame with love and acceptance in a way his mother could not, processing the transgenerational trauma his father could not, and bringing his right-brain, embodied presence and vitality, back online to forge more loving bonds with his family.

As in Henry's therapy, the second process of individuation is conscious, one in which the individual takes a more active role in their development by descending into hell to rewrite the soul-script that has—up until now—been on auto-play. If the genesis of the chain reaction begins with trauma, activates pain, initiates defense and overcompensation, results in the calcification of identity, and maintains itself through interpersonal reinforcement, then the job of the conscious or contemplative individual is to willingly trace the chain reaction to its origin, identify the weakest link, and break the chain. According to the Buddhist model of dependent origination the gap of optimal vulnerability lies between pain (sensation) and over-compensation (reaction). We must realize there's no avoiding pain; you can run but you can't hide. Our best attempts to avoid it become our prisons, but if we face and feel pain head on, it ripens us. Incredibly, the trauma event occurring earlier in the firing sequence can also be revised, as Jung knew from his visitations with the dead, everything in the unconscious lives on, and so all the events we've ever experienced can be re-experienced in new ways. Current neuroscience of trauma and memory concurs; the conditions of safety, acceptance, and love defining healthy attachment can serve in the present to revise the encoding of the past as we re-experience traumatic memories in therapy. Nothing is static, nor ever lost.

Conscious individuation goes into the shadow and meets the trauma head on, like the demons in the bardo. The relational bond with therapist or guide and one's awareness create the necessary conditions of safety, stability, and introspection, that, like Siddhartha's dual method of equanimity and investigation, allow the energy once invested in resistance to no longer reinforce defense and compensation, but release into experiences of feeling and knowing. Pain allowed to be felt naturally dissipates like an electric charge finding completion, there is no need to resist or redirect energy in an adverse reaction or repetitious narrative. Pain can then increase tolerance, shame can be transmuted into self-acceptance, fear can be used to develop courage, and rage fashioned into assertiveness. Once the emotions have been transmuted through this alchemy, they can be deployed in the service of regenerative self-construction.

The exiled parts of us, fragmented and cast out, like the multitudes trapped behind the gates of hell, are calling out to be remembered and reclaimed by Christ consciousness. By paying attention to the shadow, to the less developed, or exiled aspects of the psyche, we bring them back online, into the greater mandala of wholeness. Jung suggested we spend the first half of life building an ego, and the second half connecting with soul while recognizing ego's fluidity. This contrasts with Buddhist psychologist Jack Engler's misleading statement that unfortunately put ego in more binary extremes expressing, "You have to be somebody before you can be nobody."[8] The point is we need ego to function in the world, and we also need soul to experience meaning, it's the denial or reification of either that leads to dis-ease, bondage, or spiritual bypass. Healthy identity or ego is forever being formed, but in adulthood it needs to be soul-directed, more inclusive, ever-expanding, dynamic, exhibiting creativity and adaptability to the environment. This transpersonal movement in the second half of life is usually facilitated by spiritual traditions and methods. For the secularist it's more challenging, though perhaps now the methods of psychedelics and pilgrimage can make an important contribution. In Jung's case he experienced direct encounters and ongoing relations with his spirit guides, and insists one meets the anima (the inner feminine side of a man), or the animus archetype (the inner masculine side of a woman), appearing as intermediaries between the ego and the Self to help us integrate our exiled "contra-sexual" opposites. Eventually, one meets the mana personality, the closest representation of the Self, commonly appearing as the wise old sage archetype, in Jung's case as Philemon, in tantra the deity, in shamanism a spirit animal.

The archetypes lead you closer toward your soul, the mana personality is but an external projection of mind, ultimately, it is the soul itself we've longed for (nostos) and can now recognize directly. Just as the *Bardo Thodol* calls us to awaken within the various between-states to recognize appearances themselves as the clear light nature of mind. The soul cannot be discovered with the left brain, with ordinary, rational consciousness, nor in the ordinary world through language, the soul is reclaimed by the right brain, refined awareness, beyond the recesses of the personal unconscious, in the vast and limitless collective unconscious. It speaks in the language of symbols, dreams, imagination, metaphors, myths, and meditation. It's eternal, yet always present. I call this later, conscious process of individuation *soul sculpting*; it makes the pilgrimage from the periphery to the center, to the Self, and then returns, working inside-out (soul to world), bottom-up (soma to intelligence), and right-to-left mode (intuition to reason), in the service of integration. There, and back again.

ARCHETYPE OF THE SELF

Jung's notion of the Self evolved through his thinking and writing. He felt that the first half of one's life span was dedicated to developing the ego, his "personality one" strengthening identity in the world, while the second half involved working with the shadow to discover the soul, his "personality number two," achieving a relationship or marriage between the two aspects, resulting in a sense of wholeness and meaning. Whereas the ego is the center point of consciousness, the Self is the totality of the psyche. The Self includes the ego, conscious, unconscious, shadow, and collective unconscious. It's the center and the infinite periphery, containing all. Amanda Butler of the Jung Society of Utah writes:

> Jung defined the Self as "the totality of a person's being," and the word is capitalized to denote its centrality and sacredness. Jung believed that the Self is the "central force guiding our development: he saw this energy expressed in our ability to change form and evolve, while maintaining our personal identity," and as "the blueprint of our potential unfolding and the path to greater unity of the conscious and unconscious in us. Jung saw it perpetually reorienting us toward balance and guiding us into greater wholeness." In this way, the Self may be seen as an inner companion that can provide guidance and support, even in difficult times.[9]

In the second half of life a relationship is made with the Self that does not obliterate the ego, nor persona, but instead now sees them as practical aspects and uses them wisely as modes of authentic self-expression in the world. Thus, the claiming of the treasure for Jung, the pulling sword from stone, is to realize oneself as this transcendent Self, while simultaneously embodying a functional ego that can work toward the manifestation of the Self's aspirations in the world. The ego must be fluid to accommodate the Self, dynamic and ever changing, it remains in constant communication henceforth; the ego at the end of the journey cannot be the same limiting, rigid, and brittle ego prior to developmental stages in the process of individuation. Ironically, the Self is not only the culmination, but the process of individuation itself, and even the origin. The Self is the alpha and omega. The Buddha nature is present at ground, path, and fruition. For me, this is when the notion of Self begins to sound like God, guiding Adam and Eve as the trickster serpent toward free will, guiding Jonah in the belly of the whale to voluntary redemption, there all along for Jung as his childhood ruler mannequin, through his dream and visions, and eventually as Philemon. In fact, Jung said as much, that the Self "might equally well be called 'the God within us,'" careful to not confuse this with the external God of the masses that rules through authoritarian fear. [10]

Perhaps I'll take it one step further and equate Jung's notion of Self with the Buddhist notion of voidness, ultimate reality, which is not a static or absolute thing, independent from the world of experiences, but is an absence, a negation of intrinsic reality, which allows all phenomenon of the conventional world to arise, abide, and cease like a waking dream. Emptiness, they say, is like a womb, from it reality is birthed, made manifest as a temporal illusion. It has no beginning or end, cannot be created or destroyed, and upon analysis cannot even be found. It defies any word or label, is inconceivable with ordinary consciousness, is not a nothingness, or an abyss, rather emptiness means relativity. Emptiness is interdependence, relationality. What if the Self Jung described was more akin to the ultimate nature of things described in

Buddhism, the emptiness that is the womb of possibilities? Jung's notion of Self doesn't strike me as a thing or static essence, but as the source in which all dimensions of human and divine, personal and transpersonal, are made manifest. Although I find no direct account in his writing of Jung making this connection between the Self and emptiness, what is apparent is that he did equate the Self with a powerful symbol, the mandala, which is literally an empty palace for an empty deity to be visualized so we may remold our empty-relative self.

JUNG'S MANDALA

Jung was captivated by two archetypal symbols that expressed the essence of the Self: Christ and the mandala. Christ is the union of opposites—divinity and humanity, heaven and earth—bearing the weight of all sin yet offering salvation. He is in the world, but not of it. Christ upon the cross embodies the alchemical formation of the four quadrants with a center point, like the Mount Meru mandala represents the axial mountain surrounded by four continents, also represented by the five flowers in the Balinese offerings. This sacred number five represents the transmutation of the five elements, earth, fire, water, wind, and space, the first four represent the body, while the fifth, spirit, is at the center. The crucifixion is a reenactment of *solve et coagula*; Jesus shows the way to confront evil in us is to take on the burden of sin and seek redemption, to purge the contaminated aggregates of body and mind, to willingly accept the death of ego and flesh, and descend into the underworld. We liberate the captives of the collective unconscious, to *re-member*, collecting the fragments of psyche, the opposing forces Adam and Eve, and having united them we ascend, returning the many back into one, from darkness into light, the whole being reborn and renewed with spirit. This is the claiming of treasure in Christianity, the path of assuming Christ-consciousness at the center of the mandala.

Jung's personal experience with mandalas began toward the end of World War I when he was already experiencing distressing visions and the onset of his split, both with Freud and with consensus reality. He writes, "I sketched every morning in a notebook a small circular drawing, a mandala, which seemed to correspond to my inner situation at the time. With the help of these drawings I could observe my psychic transformations from day to day. . . . My mandalas were cryptograms . . . in which I saw the self—that is, my whole being—actively at work."[11]

Jung used the daily practice of mandala drawing to track his unconscious, it was a self-observational tool and a mode of Self-expression. In his clinical practice he encouraged his patients to paint and draw, using their imaginations to give voice to their unconscious, and like the priests of the Greek Asklepion, Jung would interpret their drawings in session, to generate a Socratic dialogue, not only between he and his patient, but to mirror a relationship between the patient and their psyche. Sometimes his patients produced a mandala spontaneously, other times they were assigned. Sometimes there was just one mandala, other times it was a series where archetypal themes would unveil a process occurring that could be track along an evolution.

In my clinical practice, I worked with a young man who, through his process of individuation, divorced his wife and quit his job at the height of his career. I helped him fall in and through a cavern of despair, a voluntary psychic unraveling, that by his report felt more like a controlled demolition. At almost every session, he produced a mandala, which we explored and interpreted together, giving a voice to his unconscious. In the drawings we saw coarse aspects, like his mood, perhaps impacted by the events of the week, but what was more revealing was the evolution we assessed over time. We saw the pivotal stages and milestones of our work, the mandalas like a feedback system, enabling us to track and confirm progress or course correct, while he traveled deeper into his inner landscape. Over the course of three years we could visually determine when he was coming undone, the turning point, and when he reached the stage of integration. Similarly, Jung found merit in his clinical use of mandalas, leading him to conclude the mandala is ". . . the exponent of all paths. It is the path to the center, to individuation."[12]

The cosmograms, sacred geometric designs organizing the cosmos and psyche, were pivotal during and after Jung's dark night of the soul and his claiming the treasure, as is revealed in his *(The) Red Book*, which includes exquisitely detailed mandalas drawn in his own hand (see plate 4). Toward the end of his career, when he was coalescing his theory of personality, in his last book *Mandala Symbolism*, Jung concluded, "a mandala is the psychological expression of the totality of the self."[13]

The two-fold movement of the individuation process is the analytic movement and the synthetic movement. The former refers to the task of breaking down unconscious material through analysis. Jung describes it as "analytic separation" which includes "dismembering both identities one has forged with figures and content that have primary basis in reality outside of the psyche, and those that are grounded first and foremost in the psyche itself" (Stein, 2013, loc. 169). The latter movement which he calls "synthetic" happens simultaneously and requires the individual to pay careful attention to the archetypal images and figures which appear in dreams and fantasies. He describes, "this movement involves taking up this new material into the patterns of conscious functioning and everyday life."[14]

THE BOLLINGEN TOWER

Not only was Jung an expert painter, incorporating alchemical versions of the mandala in paint on paper recorded in *The Red Book*, but his genius inspired him to construct a three-dimensional mandala as his home. In 1923, a year after his mother's death, Jung constructed a stone tower, again with his own hands, outside the village of Bollingen on the banks of Lake Geneva. As Jung wrote, "In Bollingen, silence surrounds me almost audibly, and I live in modest harmony with nature. Thoughts rise to the surface which reach back into the centuries, and accordingly anticipate a remote future. Here, the torment of creation is lessened; creativity and play are close together."[14]

His original conception was to build in the style of a round African hut, where a hearth would burn at the center and the extended family would gather round, representing the wholeness that is still palpable in Indigenous societies. Over the course of twelve years, in four stages, the single tower grew to look more like a small medieval castle. Jung noted a quaternity had arisen with four separate though unified dwellings. Jung was aware through the construction of the mythic dimension of the Tower, and of its intended use—like megalithic structures of old around the world built for the purpose of ritual rebirth—not only did he acknowledge there should be a room for retreat, to practice yoga as he witnessed in dwellings during his travels through India, but later concluded,

> From the beginning I felt the Tower as in some way a place of maturation a maternal womb or a maternal figure in which I could become what I was, what I am and will be. It gave me a feeling as if I were being reborn in stone. It is thus a concretization of the individuation process. During the building work, of course, I never considered these matters. I built the house in sections, always following the concrete needs of the moment. Only afterward did I see how the parts fit together and a meaningful form had resulted: a symbol of psychic wholeness.

To say that the Tower at Bollingen reflected Jung's soul, the culmination of his journey—claiming treasure and returning with elixir—is no understatement. As he wrote,

> At Bollingen I am in the midst of my true life, I am most deeply myself. Here I am, as it were, the "age-old son of the mother." That is how alchemy puts it, very wisely, for the "old man" the "ancient," whom I had already experienced as a child, is personality No. 2, who has always been and always will be. He exists outside time and is the son of the maternal unconscious. In my fantasies he took the form of Philemon, and he comes to life again at Bollingen.[15]

In 1950 Jung desired to express how much the Tower meant to him, and used a synchronicity to his advantage. He had ordered specific blocks for his cornerstone, but when the delivery arrived the stone mason had gotten the measurements wrong, leaving Jung with an oversize square shaped block. The mason offered to remove it, but Jung's intuition felt drawn to the stone, and he said he had to have it. He placed it in his courtyard by the lake and began to chisel inscriptions in its sides. Much like the inscriptions in the towers at the temple of Apollo at Delphi, Jung's inscriptions reveal the quintessence of his journey home.

On one side Jung carved an inscription in Latin taken from The Rosary of Philosophers, a sixteenth-century alchemical treatise, which translates as, "Here stands the mean, uncomely stone, Tis very cheap in price. The more it is despised by fools, the more loved by the wise." The verse refers to the alchemical lapis, which is despised and rejected by the uninitiated, just as most repress the shadow, only the wise know where the elixir is hidden. On a second side of the stone, Jung carved a depiction of a Telesphorus figure, a homunculus bearing a lantern and wearing a hooded cape. It's surrounded by a Greek inscription that reads, "Time is a child—playing like a child playing a board game— the kingdom of the child. This is Telesphoros, who roams through the dark regions of this cosmos and glows like a star out of the depths. He points the way to the gates of the sun and to the land of dreams." Jung fabricated this quote drawing on Heraclitus and Homer's *Odyssey*. The second side also contains a four-part mandala of alchemical significance, the top quarter of the mandala is dedicated to Saturn, the bottom quarter to Mars, the left quarter to Sol-Jupiter [male], and the right quarter to Luna-Venus [female]. On the third side of the stone, the side facing Lake Geneva, Jung said he let the stone speak for itself, and inscribed in Latin alchemical sayings, "I am an orphan, alone; nevertheless I am found everywhere. I am one, but opposed to myself. I am youth and old man at one and the same time. I have known neither father nor mother, because I have had to be fetched out of the deep like a fish, or fell like a white stone from heaven. In woods and mountains I roam, but I am hidden in the innermost soul of man. I am mortal for everyone, yet I am not touched by the cycle of aeons."[16] On the fourth side, Jung wanted to inscribe the "cry of the Merlin" the magician of legend who was misunderstood and exiled, and whose voice echoed in the forest, yet no one could understand it. Jung saw his depth psychology as a continuation of Merlin's legacy, which he thought few would comprehend. Jung left the fourth side empty. The Tower at Bollingen still stands, the mandala of Jung's soul lives on in stone.

BUDDHA'S TRIUMPH

Siddhartha departed the palace, was initiated, but left his gurus, discovered the middle way on his own, and overcame an ordeal, then, like Jung, claimed his treasure—*enlightenment*. Siddhartha had just vanquished Mara as if waking from a dream, there was no need to run or fight; what he did instead was draw on consciousness, a higher order of protection from fear, to see right through his projections. Remember, Siddhartha consciously positioned himself beneath a banyan tree, his back against its trunk, his body cooled in its shade, its roots surrounding him as if in embrace, as he faced the rising sun. Again, the classic mandala motif. Like Christ on the cross, his body at the center of four quadrants, Siddhartha is seated in perfect alignment, his channels opening to the arterial system of the tree, connecting heaven and underworld—as above, so below— with the prince as the center point (see figure 9.2 on page 268).

Siddhartha's quest has taken him here and there on a six-year long journey, but now he knows where he must look for the answer: *within*. This is telling for those of us travel weary, having chased sense pleasures around the world, or even wisdom teachings from this book or that teacher. Ultimately, they're not the source. One cannot transcend through the grace of another, no one can bestow illumination, it must be realized by oneself alone. Following the dissipation of Mara, Siddhartha continues under the banyan tree for seven days, refining his

Fig. 9.2. Buddha Shakyamuni and Scenes From His Life. Tibet, 19th century,
pigments on cloth. Collection: Rubin Museum of Art.
Gift of Shelley and Donald Rubin, C2006.66.222 (HAR 275).

introspection, proceeding through the levels of jnana, or concentrative equipoise, whilst retaining his wisdom eye of critical analysis. Through his novel method it's said he gained three profound realizations across the *three watches of the night*.

In the first watch of the night, Siddhartha sees with his wisdom eye all his countless past lives. He sees his births and his deaths, what he looked like, what clan he came from, even what he ate, how he died each time, and how he was reborn, with the same level of specificity and detail. Not unlike a life review by those who report a near death experience, except what flashes through his mind is every single life form and every relation he has embodied since beginningless time. Inconceivable. What gets disrupted in this vision is fixation, the holding on to any sense of permeance or substantiality to his being. Siddhartha experiences his soul migrating through rebirth across time not as a static, unrelated entity, in the way some traditions like the Greeks or Hindus posit an unchanging atman but as an ever-evolving continuity.

In the second watch of the night, Siddhartha with the wisdom eye sees the transmigration of all other sentient beings. He sees their births, lives, deaths, and rebirths. Not only this, but what is also revealed is the mechanism of karma which compels each iteration of life for each being. He sees souls caught up in vice and struggle deteriorate, and transition into unfavorable, or lower, realms of existence where they must reap the consequences of their actions. Likewise, he sees beings committed to virtue, die and transition, reborn in more favorable, higher realms, where they taste the sweet fruit of their past actions. Nothing is random, nor is there an external agent in control, beings are driven from one life to the next by their activities, and create their destiny. Having seen how an individual's fate is unknowingly predetermined by their delusion, Siddhartha is struck with compassion for migratory beings.

In the third watch, Siddhartha sees with his wisdom eye the multifold manifestations of suffering that entangle living beings. Understanding and abandoning their causes, he realizes their cessation, and finds the path to liberation. This four-fold framework became

Buddha's Four Noble Truths—noble because they require the wisdom eye to discern. More specifically, Siddhartha recognized the truth of *dependent origination*, the causal mechanism underlying the creation of suffering, a twelve-fold cycle (chain) in which one factor influences another automatically resulting in misery.

The twelve links proceed from ignorance or *misperception* of the nature of reality, *traumatic imprints* are then conditioned, then consciousness is distorted, then *mind and body* are cross-contaminated, then the *six sense faculties* are adversely primed to the inner and outer environment. Next, *contact* with sense objects produces addictive sensations and serves as a catalyst for karmic ripening of the past, then an *emotional urge* is elicited to either grasp or repel accordingly. On the basis of this urge, *karmic reactions* of body, speech, and mind are habituated, (which are the seeds instantaneously sowed for the future). The culmination of these habits then creates one's *identity* in this life, which then compels a self-iteration in the future, or a *mindless birth* in a new life, which inevitably results in *mindless death*. The cycle repeating itself unendingly.

This twelve-fold cycle is the origin story for compulsive life, or traumatic existence know as samsara. Once life is seen as conditioned by causes, Siddhartha saw that the chain link could be disrupted. As I mentioned previously when discussing Jung's framework for the process of individuation, the softest target lies between sensation and urge, since the former (sensation) represent the ripening of the past karma which cannot be undone, and the latter (urge, literally thirst, *tanha*) is the planting of a new karmic seed, the gap between them represents the field of quantum possibility, and thus the opportunity for freedom. If conscious awareness and agency can intervene in the automated cycle, misery-making can be averted, and one can consciously soul-shape destiny in a more enlightened trajectory. Having searched tirelessly for a solution to the existential predicament of compulsive life and death, Prince Siddhartha achieves his aim. He realizes reality as it is, how mind constructs reality through karma based on the open nature of the soul.

Plate 1. Peaceful and Wrathful Deities of the Bardo.
Tibet, between 1700–1799 CE, mineral pigment on cotton.

Plate 2 (top). Sol (Sun god) within Zodiac. Mosaic, Hammath Tiberias Synagogue, Israel, 286–337 CE. Photo by Fabrizio Comolli.

Plate 3 (left). Baptism of Jesus by Saint John the Baptist with procession of the Apostles. Ceiling mosaic, Arian Baptistry, Ravenna, Italy, 5th–6th century CE. Photo by Petar Milošević.

Plate 4. Carl Jung's "The Solar Voyage and the Sea Monster."
From *The Red Book* by C. G. Jung, edited by Sonu Shamdasani,
copyright © 2009 by the Foundation of the Works of C. G. Jung,
used by permission of W. W. Norton & Company, Inc.

Plate 5. Vajrayogini, standing in a blaze of fire, imbibing blood transformed into amrita from a skull cup (kapala). Kham Province, Eastern Tibet, late 19th century, pigments on cloth. Collection: Rubin Museum of Art.
Gift of the Shelley and Donald Rubin Foundation, F1997.19.2 (HAR 290).

Plate 6. Epiphany of Dionysus, rising triumphant from the sea, bearing the drinking horn (rhyton) of wine transformed into ambrosia. Mosaic, from the Villa of Dionysus, 2nd century CE, Dion, Greece. Collection: Archeological Museum of Dion.

Plate 7. Stories of the Life of Christ, including crucifixion, harrowing, and resurrection by Giovanni da Rimini, 1305 CE, tempera on panel. Collection: Palazzo Barberini and Palazzo Corsini, Rome, Italy.

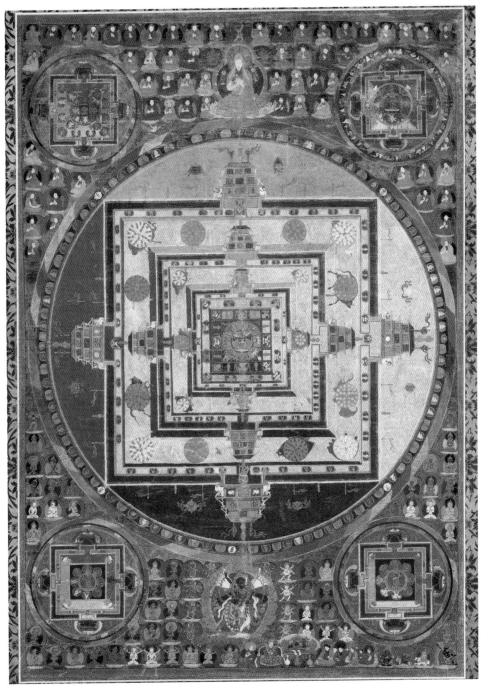

Plate 8. Mandala of Kalachakra (The Time Machine), aligning cosmos with psyche, and integrating masculine with feminine principles.
Central Tibet, 16th–17th century, distemper on cotton.
Photograph copyright © 2025 Museum of Fine Arts, Boston,
Frederick L. Jack Fund, 58.691.

Plate 9. Borobudur Mandala, Magelang, Central Java, Indonesia.
Photo courtesy of Alea Film. Published January 22, 2024, via Unspalsh.

Now awake, now Buddha, he declares, "Delivered am I; the rounds of rebirth is ended; fulfilled is the Holy Life; done is what needed to be done. There is no more of this state again." Having seen the separate self as an apparition and exhausted the fuel of compulsion, he proclaims:

> Through the round of many births I roamed without reward, without rest, seeking the house-builder. Painful is birth again & again. House-builder, you're seen! You will not build a house again. All your rafters broken, the ridge pole destroyed, gone to the Unformed, the mind has come to the end of craving.[17]

THE MANDALA WOMB

We left the Tibetan three-phase map following death and dissolution, in the bardo before rebirth, highlighting the confrontation with Yama, Lord of Death, and other deities mild and fierce encountered in the between dreamscape, which must be recognized as mere projections of the mind based on our past karma. Upon this recognition, grasping and aversion cease, no further karmic impetus is injected into nightmare-making, and as the Doors song goes, we "break on through to other side" to what Thurman unabashedly calls the clear-light the soul. More often it's called the dharmakaya, body of truth, Buddha nature, the natural state of awareness, or the realization of emptiness. It's pure, uncreated, indestructible, undefiled, beyond time and space. It underlies all things, all phenomena and experiences. It has been here since beginningless time, and will be forever.

Creating and incubating a new enlightened identity and world is the focus of the second phase we're now in, based on dissolving our ordinary and reified identity, melting down and purifying its constituent elements, into the prima materia of clear-light, then reverse engineering oneself into a tantric deity or angel. I call this a coronation because during the tantric initiation process when you are granted the four initiations you are empowered by your teacher to see yourself as you are, divine. Now you must rehearse that divinity until you become convinced of it. In other words: "Fake it 'til you make it."

At the most advanced tantric practice—called the completion stage—this is achieved ostensibly by transforming one's actual mind, brain, chemistry, and physical body through manipulation of the energy in the subtle body. In provisional tantric practice—called the generation stage—this is achieved by way of visualization and approximation only. I liken this to a flight simulator which cultivates wisdom and compassion simultaneously through pure view and divine pride. Pure view or ultimate bodhicitta recognizes everything as empty—the mandala, deity form, objective world and its contents, all experience, consciousness, even emptiness itself—all lack intrinsic reality and appear like a dream. With this pure view, one can construct a new reality, a new mandala of self, world, and experiences to benefit oneself and others, to hasten enlightenment, just as a magician conjures an illusion to delight their audience.

The other aspect, divine pride, is the motivation behind the reconstruction of the self in the aspect of a deity, and the world in the aspect of the mandala. Whereas the ordinary world was constructed in the basis of delusion, narcissism, hubris, fear, and grasping, the enlightened world is birthed to existence based on relative bodhicitta, love and compassion. The pure view of the deity is complemented by royal dignity that enjoys the bliss of taking responsibility for the welfare of all beings, like an ethical sovereign cares for their kingdom. We must have three aspects to avoid the pitfall of imagining oneself as a deity; without a foundation in *renunciation*, *altruistic resolve*, and *insight into emptiness*, we can reify our deity identity like we did our ordinary identity, confused that it possesses inherent existence. We can similarly grasp at our reality construction of the mandala world, and be driven by base instincts to use this powerful magic for selfish gain, malice, or some other unworthy, egocentric motivation.

So how do we proceed with our divine flight simulation from the clear-light stage? In effect we've already died, lost our ordinary body by dissolving its five elements, and purified consciousness by going through the three further stages of dissolution, and now we've arrived at spacious, free floating clear-light consciousness. So first, we re-arise in a dream body or hologram body made of pure, luminous energy. You imagine your soul takes on an energetic form. Next, we need a space to inhabit, the diamond seat under the banyan (Bodhi tree) upon which Siddhartha becomes a Buddha, an alchemical crucible to create gold, or a womb to re-enact the psychodrama of enlightened gestation. Enter the mandala. Liedy and Thurman explain "in Buddhist usage, a mandala is a matrix or model of a perfected universe, the nurturing environment of the perfected self in ecstatic interconnection with perfected others. It is a blueprint for Buddhahood conceived as attainment not only of an individual's ultimate liberation, but also as the attainment of such release and bliss by an individual fully integrated with his or her environment and field of associates. . . . Within the vision of tantra as a world-creating process, mandalas are models used for creating Buddha-worlds."[18] We're redesigning our minds using the blueprint of divine architecture.

Next, the space must be infused with the right energy and vibration. Enter the mantra. *In the beginning there was the word, and the word was God.* The Greeks called it logos. Our ordinary neurotic life, at its most fundamental level, is vibration, which produces thought, which is shared through speech, from which our consensus reality is co-constructed. Energy and words are so powerful, they create our reality, without refining them, no imaginational process can translate into a full manifestation of an enlightened alterative. Our unwavering conviction is the single-most important variable in determining the outcome and success of our actions in the world. In the traditional tantric imagery, within the center of the mandala, a lotus emerges to serve as a throne (representing renunciation) atop of which follow sun and moon disk cushions, representing the altruistic resolve and the wisdom of emptiness respectively. These are the three foundations, the three principles paths. Emerging from the disks is the mantra, often depicted in its most essentialized form as a single seed syllable. Each deity is represented by its own harmonic resonance, its enlightened affirmation, or mantric phrase coalesced as a seed symbol. Joe taught me to consider a bespoke affirmation that best represents one's own ideal, growth, or evolutionary destiny, and to imagine it as a brilliant exclamation point made of diamond light, occupying the center point.

From the mantra comes the body of the deity, referencing the birth of form from vibration, and the vibration itself from wisdom realizing emptiness conjoining with compassion and renunciation. The form of each deity is unique, each archetype represents a distinct vibratory energy in the human psyche, lower tantric deities like Manjushri represent wisdom, Green Tara enlightened activity, and Medicine Buddha natural healing. The more advanced archetypes such as Yamataka, the Foe Destroyer, is the wrathful manifestation of Manjustri, the wisdom that fearlessly stares down death itself. Whereas Vajrayogini (see plate 5), the diamond queen, is Tara, the divine mother goddess, in her wrathful manifestation, naked and erotic, nipples erect, she stands in a ring of fire, imbibing nectar from a skull cup, alchemically transforming the potency of sexual desire into great bliss, birthing enlightenment from orgasmic ecstasy. These deity archetypes are fused with the living spirit or presence of one's mentor, allowing one's devotion to amplify the experience as the as the mentor bonding process ensues. Thurman and Joe likewise encourage students at the entry level to use whatever archetypal imagery they choose, from whatever tradition, expanding the parameters of the practice beyond the Buddhist pantheon, whilst still adhering to the psychological mechanism and principles active underneath the theatric display.

TANTRIC TREASURE

We've now constructed the mandala, and activated the mantra that has transformed into the deity. We can review the next four steps in the sequence of mentor-bonding (guru yoga, described in chapter seven) that comprise the second or liminal phase for reverse engineering the soul in the bardo: *admiration, offering, disclosure/purification*, and *rejoicing*.

The treasure is discovered within relationship; the nectar is love. Not the child's naive love characterized by stasis in idealization, co-dependence, and deference, but wise love matured through trial and heartbreak, and allowed to emerge on the otherside with greater dignity and self-respect. We begin the guru-yoga with the first step of *admiration*, evoking a sense of awe and wonder of the mentor that opens the mind and heart to be reoriented toward them as a new pro-parent, which we've consciously selected as adults (rather than inherited as children) to refashion and role-model our enlightened identity around. Admiration is our north star, hero-worship and idealization are necessary initial conditions to establish safety in adolescence. Think of Jung who neither felt close to his mother, nor respected his father, his unconscious dismissing them as suboptimal models to avoid. Without suitable mirrors, for Jung this necessary stage of idealization in development was arrested and later played in adulthood with Freud.

Next comes *offering*, presenting gifts to the mentor, actual and imagined, including your own body and mind. Lay these before the deity's feet, surrender everything in a spirit of gratitude, and let karma do the rest. Think of Siddhartha and Jung apprenticing themselves to reputed masters, serving them with all they had. The karma of generosity results in the sense of abundance. Through acts of devotion, we receive the master's blessing. With the bond forged, proximity leads to deeper intimacy, secure attachment, and reciprocity, blazing the neural circuitry of communion between mentor and student.

The third step is *disclosure*; search your heart, mind and past, identify your shortcomings, fears and doubts, missteps, and compulsions. Look at history, ancestry, and collective legacy for the karmic imprints of vice, and confess them, take accountability for them so you can be, like Jonah, redeemed. Do a thorough and honest inventory on how you have betrayed or abandoned your own authenticity, and vow "never again." The Buddhist practice of *purification* is inserted at this step because it recognizes how disruptive the imprints of our past negative actions can be, influencing our future in repeated cycles of misfortune. Go back and clean up your mind stream, so you can move forward with your life. Face the bardo deities mild and fierce, and heed their efforts at mirroring the projections of your shortcomings. Seek forgiveness and redemption. The process of disclosure is not based on guilt and shame, useless wastes of energy; purification is not a punishment, it's a liberation through seeing, based on healthy regret, knowing how cause and effect works, a willingness to take responsibility, to make amends with oneself and others. These are foundational social skills needed if we hope to maintain close working relations and bonds.

The disclosure step includes a short purification exercise through what are called *the four opponent powers* (refuge, regret, remedy, and resolve), the powers of refuge (in the mentor) and honest regret were discussed above, while the power of the remedy to counter imprints of past negative actions is achieved through the harmonic resonance of the Vajrasttava mantra recitation. Finally, through the power of resolve, one vows going forward to self-observe and restrain from misaligned impulses. You can see the theme repeating of going back in order to go forward. In this way, the practice of purification prevents repression, accumulation, and repetition of karmic tendencies; it's a proactive method of soul sculpting. Jung was ready to be vulnerable and to disclose his fears, unfortunately Freud was not. His mentor's insistence on maintaining authority at all costs masked Frued's insecurity creating resistance and obstacles in the bond. Mature love doesn't defend, it holds the tender heart of insecurity in its embrace.

Step four, *rejoicing*, having focused on where we need improvement, now we counterbalance the brain's negativity bias by focusing our mind on all our positive gains. Having come through an honest, sometimes painful self-assessment of our shortcomings without Freud-like defensiveness, we can now accept our own gifts. The good qualities we admired externally in the mentor, have been internalized as are our own reflections. This stage generates healthy pride for all the virtues we and others embody and enact; leveling the hierarchy in the relational dyad between mentor and student. There is no greater positive reinforcement than joy, so keep yourself developing towards fully internalizing your ideal by celebrating your victories. Even while Jung struggled in his confrontations with the unconscious, he acknowledged the beauty in the darkness, and expressed gratitude for the discoveries he made there. While he was not able to achieve this step with Freud, Jung found in Philemon a worthy idealized projection from his unconscious to pass through the stages of development and to arrive at a greater self-acceptance.

These four steps, admire, offer, disclose, and rejoice, rely on our natural mammalian attachment circuits and instincts to bond with healthy parental figures, so we can proceed through the classic psychological stages of child development from idealization to identification. As we'll see later, steps five through seven of the bonding process will carry us through the remaining developmental horizons of internalization and integration, culminating with our sense of having become what we once admired externally. Of course, that which we seek, the treasure, can only be found in the terrifying cave of intimacy, first appearing as a discrete and distant quality projected externally in the mentor. To taste the nectar, we must brave betrayal, because the pearl is the oyster, it is only within the mutual vulnerability of the alchemical mentor-bond where our own elusive divinity is discovered. Having alchemized fear into love, let's set our sights on the journey home.

10
Return
Bestowing the Boon

SACRED ISLAND-HOPPING

The early morning sun steadily creeps like a centipede over the rolling hills in the East, sending us a kiss of tangerine light while the South Sea breeze keeps us refreshingly cool. Perched on a high bluff looking North, we're greeted by the glorious expanse of Afales Bay, with its surrounding mountains stretching like two giant arms in either direction, circling round to form a generous embrace, covered in a blanket of dense pine that descends right down to the waterline. Beyond the bay is the island of Lefkada and the mix of turquoise and midnight blue that distinguishes shallows from the depths of the Ionian Sea. This is not Bali, but another mystical island, Ithaca in Greece. My second home. Emily and I have hiked up here on our morning walk to one of my favorite places. My mother's house, situated on a nearby cliff facing Afales and surrounded by an orchard of three-hundred-year-old olive trees, is not more than a twenty-minute walk from here along an ancient cobblestone path built by the Venetians over five centuries ago. We've come up here on a micro-pilgrimage to the archeological site of *Agios Athanasios* or Homer's School for a special ritual. This was where, synchronistically, years earlier, I listened to my soul, and changed the direction on a dime to live a mythological life.

The ruins of a Hellenistic church serve as our ceremonial inner sanctum and stand like a sentinel keeping watch over the centuries, poised halfway between the mountaintop village of Exogi and the Ionian Sea. Exogi, by the way, translates as "beyond the world," and that's what it feels like up there at my brother's house, where you can touch the clouds. The roof of the church where Emily and I sit is gone, but the small hand-hewn stones that form its walls have stood the test of time, and you can catch a glimpse of the bay below through one of its remaining portals facing north. A perfect photograph in this window frame captures a timeless view of a thousand lost words of awe.

There's also an altar in this roofless chamber. Perhaps it was used to make offerings to Demeter, goddess of the grain before the second hand of the Great Year made an incremental shift causing the world to transition from the Hellenistic to the early Christian period. At some point, like the sea's changing tide, the Virgin Mary replaced the goddess, but no less venerated. Today, we've set up a statue of the Indo-Tibetan Green Tara in her place, arranged offerings of harvested olive branches from my mother's house, and wild prickly mint and fragrant local lavender collected along the way. We've set out the traditional seven water bowls in the Tibetan style and made three prostrations, our bellies and foreheads meeting the smooth stone below us, with its Ancient Greek inscriptions that, to our mind, remain undeciphered. It's the same divine mother appearing in different guises over the aions, the universal archetype of maternal, unconditional love manifesting in various cultural forms throughout the epic motion of the stars. To the ordinary eye, they're blasphemously different icons, but to the esoteric, they're all one. Emily and I have much to celebrate and more blessings to request of the mother.

The church, like a chapter, is only one part of the story. Its small brick wall is held up by a base of megalithic stones, more perfectly cut and placed, and from the even older Mycenaean period than their more minor, roughly cut cousins above. They say these monoliths are the remnants of the Palace of Odysseus, the hero of Homer's epic tale. Emily and I have been on our own odyssey these past years, and the island of Ithaca makes a fitting mythological weigh station on our journey between distant lands.

There is debate whether Homer walked these hills, started a wisdom school here that now lay among the ruins, and wrote his masterwork with the majestic Afales Bay offering a haven to the sea vessels of antiquity, all serving as his literary inspiration. What is not in debate is that there was an actual palace here, its legacy hidden under the church, safeguarding its ancient secrets. The treasure is never found in plain sight. It's buried deep within us, obscured in the secret world, awaiting those willing to make the sacrifice to claim it. Just as the journey is both private and shared, the treasure is both a personal victory, and a gift for humanity.

The treasure is a metaphor for the inner qualities we seek in the depths of the shadow that can help us evolve in the individuation process. And more than these qualities, it's the soul herself, a pearl in the oyster, the acorn containing a vast potential to become a giant Oak tree. In my case, the treasure was my confidence, threatened into paralysis by my narcissistic father when I was a boy, the sword could only be claimed years later upon my facing my dependency fears with Joe. For others, the treasure is self-love or compassion after years of being bound up in denial and self-preservation from abuse. It may be the rays of wisdom dawning from a dark night of confusion, finding your voice after a trans-generational legacy of trauma and being silenced. For the Wizard Tjok Gde, it was wielding the wand of his alchemical prowess after leaving his own metaphoric palace comforts and confines. For Siddhartha it was enlightenment, complete liberation from the cage of delusion since beginningless time. For Jung, it was the Self, the spontaneity and creativity of his nature, and his inspiration to weave together psychology and mysticism after his confrontation with the unconscious. In all these cases, the discovery of treasure is not the end of the journey; what good would any of these gifts be if we had no one to share them with? The hero quest is profoundly personal and social, uniquely individual, but ultimately collective. The treasure makes no sense when kept for oneself in solitude. Instead, only when we return home triumphant to bestow the boon to others, which is no small task. The return can be as treacherous, if not more so, than the departure.

Homer tells us that King Odysseus of Ithaca reluctantly chose to depart his beloved wife Penelope and son Telemachus to fight in the Trojan War. He might have never left if he knew what an enduring succession of complex challenges would await him. For nearly ten years, his route twisted and turned through a surprising array of horrific trials of unimaginable hardship, each forcing him to confront the demons of crippling fear, castrating self-doubt, and merciless longing to be reunited with his beloved wife and son. While Odysseus ventured from island to island, battling mythical creatures and facing the wrath of the gods, he also wandered blindly in the depth of his shadow, lamenting if he would ever return home to his family and walk the shores of Ithaca again.

No one wants to suffer the trial of ten years of despair and aimless wandering. The difference between common folk and the hero is that such hardship ensures a more evolved being with greater capacities than she ever knew possible before she left, will return to take her seat on the throne. Though the nascent qualities, skills, and vision that define the hero are hard won through trial, their value is only fully actualized during the home-bound stages of the return. These qualities must be integrated into one's being, supplanting one's former modus operandi, and further, the hero herself must be integrated into the web of relationality with the wider community. For the cycle to complete itself, her presence and boon must be accepted and appreciated by the web of relations she left. This is not always the case. While we admire and celebrate the victors of the hero's quest, how many of us are willing to follow the thread into the dark labyrinth or set sail for Troy without the promise of return? And if that weren't enough, while you might embark, tame a dragon, and claim a treasure, the return journey can be as or more treacherous than the departure. Remember, more climbers die descending the summit than on the ascent. Reintegrating into ordinary life post-breakthrough, whether brought on by psychedelics, meditation, alchemy, psychotherapy, near-death experience, or pilgrimage, is significant, but garners scarce attention.[1] It can take years to integrate a flash of insight, not everyone makes it home, and if they do—unless it's a Disney production—there is no guarantee of a hero's welcome.

NOSTOS

A word in Greek used in Homer's tale—*nostos*—is bittersweet for Emily and me as we feel the late morning breeze brush our sun-kissed faces. As we know, nostos means longing to come home and is the sentiment that serves as the single thread running through all the complex plot twists and character changes of the Odyssey, which mirror our lives. The longing for home, or nostalgia to return home, is the underlying thrust of every conscious being. Please take that in. Is there anything more universal in the human saga? We're each a wandering soul yearning to return home, to our source in the *mysterium tremendum et fascinans* (terrifying and fascinating mystery), that both attracts and repels us.

Emily and I have completed our ceremony and sit together on a perch near the church, relishing the bay view, silently metabolizing the long miles of terrain covered behind us like a ship's wake while the path before us remains untouched. The now healed wounds we sustained through the ordeal with Joe and the subsequent departure from Nalanda were later followed by another blow—the devastating loss of a new business MindStream, a contemplative co-working and teaching space in the heart of Manhattan. Eight months after opening, the pandemic lockdowns brought us, like so many others, to the brink of bankruptcy, and we lost our financial nest egg along with our dream, a place of our own to call home. More than the money was the stress and uncertainty we lived with, taking its toll on our nervous systems. Daunted but undeterred, Emily and I decided to move from a commuter town outside Manhattan to the countryside to wait out the pandemic.

We bought a new house, and Emily set out to build our mandala again. But it never clicked for us there; it ticked all the conventional boxes, but was bereft of magic.

When I returned from my pilgrimage to Bali and my saga with the Wizard, I asked Emily if she would consider relocating to Indonesia. We consulted Lynn Bell for the astrology and discovered the move would be good for us, especially the boys who would be immersed in magic, and allow for their imaginations to run wild, but Lynn cautioned us not to decide for at least a month.

Time passed slowly as we deliberated. What was at stake was pulling the kids out of school for a second time, a second move within the pandemic, and leaving the network of friends, family, and colleagues we had established over twenty-five years. Losing a familiar culture, language, and way of life. We were still in the throes of another pandemic wave, compounded by war in Ukraine, an energy and food crisis, and rising inflation. The US was falling apart during its Pluto return. Why further destabilize our lives?

A move didn't make rational sense. "I want to follow the magic," I told Emily. "I know the math on the move will never add up." The leap of faith is not supposed to make rational sense, faith is conviction in the unknown. There is no safety net save your intuition. That's why most people remain in their ordinary world, even if it's miserable, and refuse the call. The devil you know is safer, and from an evolutionary perspective, safety seems a more compelling drive to ensure survival, that our programing seems to make us sacrifice joy and wonder by default. That is, unless we override our instincts and consciously become willing to die, to see what's on the other side. If you follow the magic, your risk-taking is the price for the reward.

There were a few sleepless nights, a few arguments, and even tears, but a month after I returned from Bali, on cue with Lynn's astrological prediction, Emily and I decided to take the leap and move to Bali with the kids. We listed our house for sale, sold or gave away our possessions, and bought one new suitcase each to pack the most precious contents of our lives. It took only a month for us to sweep away the sands of another mandala that took more than two decades to build. *Bardo Thodol* is a manual for dying, so that you can fully live, and this is what it can look like to voluntarily let go and lose everything, for the chance to gain another life. The day we dropped off Oscar, our dog, who sadly couldn't join us for the journey, at our friend's house, we were all crying.

We moved to Bali to start a new life and rebuild a mandala inspired by the wisdom keepers like Tjok Gde, the philosophy of Tri Hita Karana, and the prospect of reuniting Shiva-Buddha on the sacred island of the Gods on the other side of the world. But first we had to make a stop to visit my mom on the sacred island of Ithaca. From birth to death, bardo to rebirth, round and round, the empty mandala is constructed, consecrated, and destroyed in an unending cycle of living theater, it's driven by Apollonian reason and Dionysian madness, two inseparable sides of the same coin.

BUDDHA'S RETURN

After Siddhartha's enlightenment under the Bodhi tree, his claiming the treasure to become the Awakened One, it's said he spent seven weeks meditating in silence and solitude upon and around the Diamond Throne. While the final breakthrough occurred during the three watches of the night, and delusion was overcome at dawn, I look at these seven weeks in the biographical accounts as a period of metabolization. The Buddha was installing his insight into the nature of reality into every fiber of his being. As anyone who has been on a pilgrimage or a psychedelic experience can attest, it's difficult to articulate the transformation. Doubt arises as the Buddha thinks:

> This Dhamma that I have attained is deep and intense, hard to see, hard to realize, peaceful, refined, beyond the scope of conjecture, thoroughly investigated, subtle, to be experienced by the wise. But this generation delights in attachment, is excited by attachment,

craves for attachment, and enjoys attachment. For a generation delighting in attachment, excited by attachment, craving for attachment, enjoying attachment, this/that conditionality and dependent co-arising are hard to see. This state, too, is hard to see: the resolution of all fabrications, the relinquishment of all acquisitions, the ending of craving; dispassion; cessation; unbinding. And if I were to teach the Dhamma and if others would not understand me, that would be tiresome for me, troublesome for me.[2]

Here we have the beginning of what Campbell called the final three stages of the Hero's Journey: the road home, resurrection, and the return with elixir. The road home from the special world is not an easy one; it can be as challenging if not more challenging than the original departure. Just as there was a refusal to answer the call to adventure, when the nascent hero doubts they can embark, there can come another moment of hesitation on the flip side of the cycle, where one has to let go of the special world and face the cognitive dissonance of the marketplace. This is the Buddha's perplexing hesitation, he has discovered ultimate freedom, the resolution of human existential angsts, but he is unsure whether anyone can comprehend the magnitude of his revelation given their addictions to the material world. Underlying his hesitation is that his revelation must be experienced directly, by each and every soul, it cannot be transmitted by the laying on of healing hands in a ceremony, or through faith by believing in the master's words, or through ritual offerings in the fire, nor incantations of sacred mantras. It must be earned through purification, merit making, and through experiential insight by one's own efforts alone.

Just as the Buddha was inclined to remain silent, dwelling in the bliss of liberation, staying quiet as a hermit in the forest, and keeping the secrets of his revelation to himself, because no one would understand, there is an account in the Majhima Nikaya describing what changed his mind.[3] Brahma—the creator god, and highest lord of the Vedic tradition, like Zeus—approaches the Buddha and implores him to teach, saying, "Let the Exalted One preach the Dhamma! There are beings with little dust in their eyes; they are wasting from not hearing the Dhamma. There will be those who will understand the Dhamma."[4] The Buddha searches with his wisdom eye across the vast horizons of time and space and sees living beings at different stages of evolution, some with little dust in their eyes, and some deep in ignorance, some have keen faculties, others still dull, some possess good qualities, while others remain mired in evil. The Buddha has a vision of a pond containing multi-colored lotuses. Most of the flowers he observes remain under the water's surface, a few have risen to rest at the level of the surface, and one has risen to breach the surface and stands tall, petals unfurled above the waterline. The Buddha thus recognizes that if even one single soul might be ripe, to receive his teaching, so that she might develop full awakening, then it would be worth his efforts to teach, his words would not be in vain. And so, it's from compassion for even one soul, that the Buddha is moved from the Diamond Throne, to teach the dharma, saying to Brahma who implored him, "Open for them are the doors to the Deathless, Let those with ears now show their faith. Thinking it would be troublesome, O Brahmā, I did not speak the Dhamma* subtle and sublime."[5] With this the Lord Brahma is pleased and disappears.

The Buddha is motivated to share his wisdom, thinking of these beings with "little dust in their eyes" who are prepared and so immediately remembers his first gurus Āḷāra Kālāma and Uddaka Rāmaputta who had already achieved great concentrative powers through meditation. Through divine means, the Buddha learns that both teachers have died, Āḷāra seven days before, and Uddaka the previous night. These deaths are no coincidence. The Buddha already needed imploring from the highest Vedic God to teach, he has just managed to galvanize his compassion knowing a few select beings may comprehend his revelation, and now he discovers they have passed. These are the

---

*Dharma is Sanskrit, Dhamma is Pali.

tests of one's resolve that occur on the road home. Nothing is easy, given, or straightforward. Soon after, the Buddha thinks about his five former companions who practiced severe austerities with and who abandoned him when he took food. They possessed incredible determination, perhaps they're ripe for the teaching of liberation, so the Buddha heads from Uruvella (Bodhgaya) to Isipatana (Sarnath) where he saw them last.

On the way the Buddha is stopped by a wandering ascetic named Upaka, who notices something extraordinary in him. Upaka acknowledging his faculties are clear, his complection is pure and bright, asks him who this guru is, what spiritual method he follows, whose teachings does he profess? The Buddha replies:

> *"I am one who has transcended all, a knower of all,*
> *Unsullied among all things, renouncing all,*
> *By craving's ceasing freed. Having known this all*
> *For myself, to whom should I point as teacher?*
>
> *I have no teacher, and one like me*
> *Exists nowhere in all the world*
> *With all its gods, because I have*
> *No person for my counterpart.*
>
> *I am the Accomplished One in the world,*
> *I am the Teacher Supreme.*
> *I alone am a Fully Enlightened One*
> *Whose fires are quenched and extinguished.*
>
> *I go now to the city of Kāsi*
> *To set in motion the Wheel of Dhamma.*
> *In a world that has become blind*
> *I go to beat the drum of the Deathless."*

> *"By your claims, friend, you ought to be the Universal*
>   *Victor."*
> *"The victors are those like me*
> *Who have won to destruction of taints.*
> *I have vanquished all evil states,*
> *Therefore, Upaka, I am a victor."*[6]

It's said that upon hearing this mouthful of a proclamation, Upaka basically says "good for you, pal" and keeps on trekking down the road, leaving the Buddha in his wake. He turns his back on the Buddha, a symbol we should each remember and anticipate. These lesser aspects of the story are seldom recounted or remembered, because they pale in comparison to the grand victory over Mara, but they're the shadow aspect of claiming the sword. There are people who won't see you as you are, most especially once you're transformed. Your breakthrough and victory are invisible, or lost on them. You can spend ten years earning your doctorate, you can summit Everest, you can heal your trauma, but no matter what victory, insight, or expertise you might attain, remember few people will recognize, validate, or even care. On this path there can be no more yearning for the rewards of the material world, fame, validation, wealth. Instead there can be only pure motivation to live your authentic truth regardless of outcome or result. The Buddha was driven by compassion to teach, and if he freed only one person from suffering, it was worth it.

The Buddha continues his journey to Varanasi, and from there to the outskirts of the deer park now called Sarnath. As he approaches his former crew of five strivers, he senses they're conspiring to reject him. The Buddha thinks they will not offer signs of respect, but will address him commonly. As he arrives, they do offer him respect, yet they address him commonly. The Buddha explains he has reached the deathless state and he has come to teach them so that they might also cross over to the other shore from homelife into homelessness, a metaphoric description of liberation. The five remain skeptical and ask the Buddha a series of questions, doubting someone like Siddhartha has achieved the highest aim. They do this three times, challenging and denying his realization, just as Peter disowned Jesus three times before the rooster crowed.

Finally, the Buddha delivers his first sermon, known as the Four Noble Truths (the medical model of freedom (discussed in chapter two): suffering is to be understood, (symptoms) its causes abandoned (diagnosis), liberation attained (prognosis), and the path pursued (treatment). Over the course of weeks, the five absorb it all, and just as the Buddha promised, each is liberated. Thus starts the enlightenment revolution. Whereas the Diamond Throne at Bodhgaya is symbolic for the possibility that each can gain enlightenment, the first teaching to his former crew of five seekers at Sarnath represents the dispensation of the art and science, and the beginning of the Buddha's nearly forty-year teaching career.

Remembering the vision of the lotus pond, "If it benefits even one, I shall teach," he focused on changing one mind, opening one heart at a time—nothing else. Not building a platform, or a religion, gaining fame or followers, just meeting people where they were and trying to help. This is why it's said the Buddha taught ten thousand types of teaching, one for each unique encounter.

It's worth mentioning the Buddha eventually returned to his home kingdom, like Odysseus to Ithaca, where he reunited with his wife and child, whose love and ultimate wellbeing motivated his initial exodus from the palace. They became his students, internalized their nectar, and achieved the immortal life.

COMING DOWN FROM THE MOUNTAIN

It's difficult to depart the ordinary world, harder still to defeat or tame the dragon, but once the treasure is claimed, as I have described above, the return home with elixir is no cake walk. Campbell himself admitted, "bringing the boon back can be even more difficult than going down into your own depths in the first place."[7] The Disney version of the McMonomyth easily misleads, and would have us believe that after claiming victory against an inner or outer adversary, the world inevitably receives us with open arms in a grand hero's welcome. Not necessarily true.

As with each step of the ever-winding and unpredictable journey, the last phase of the return—its completion—is mired in potential pitfalls, and capable of breaking even the most battle-tested hero or awakened altruist on her final leg. The attention paid to the front end of the hero's quest is disproportionate, as if life after claiming the sacred chalice overflowing with elixir is an afterthought. Perhaps this disproportion reflects a blind spot in our collective psyche; we're more focused on the victory, libidinal cathexis, emotional catharsis, or a mind-blowing orgasm, than on the entirely unspectacular, often confusing, personal process of descending to basecamp stumbling and fumbling along the way. I'd like to amend that now.

PREPARATION AND INTEGRATION

Front-end preparation that precedes the treasure must be complemented by back-end integration, so that the tasting of nectar transforms self and world. When I lead Buddhist pilgrimages throughout Asia, I begin with an orientation session. Authentic shamans who conduct plant medicine ceremonies offer something similar during their initiation, which helps to create a conducive (mind) set and setting, and primes the initiates for the inner landscape and experiences ahead, normalizing the challenges of leaving one's familiar world (of waking consciousness) and entering an unknown territory of the dreamtime. As we have seen, the departure can be just as disorienting, terrifying, lonely, and exhausting as it is exhilarating and filled with hope and wonder. Just prior to, or soon after, our return home from pilgrimage, I also offer a reorientation session—this one is significant, as it supports the integration of insights freshly earned by the initiate, and their re-integration into society. It's complemented with ongoing community support, like in the Twelve-Step Program for those in recovery, or *sangha* for spiritual seekers, we integrate better with the presence of at least three factors: other like-minded people to engage with, practices, rituals, or projects that keep the flame of learning stoked, and long-time horizons, for as the biographies of Campbell, Jung, and Buddha that I've recounted, the integration phase can sometimes last for years.

THE SLOW COOK OF INTEGRATION

The post treasure process of integration is both external and internal, it involves re-assimilating back into the social tapestry of family, friendships, community, and society we originally left, while offering one's newfound gifts in a way that is meaningful to others. For this to occur, an internal process of embodying the gold discovered must also take place, it can't remain a flash of brilliant insight achieved during a meditative breakthrough for example, or the residual afterglow of a mindblowing three days of plant medicine ceremonies, but requires what I call a "slow cook" or a gradual period of metabolization that allows for the reconstituting of a new identity, motivation, and lifestyle. Once one's gift is realized, one also must learn how to embody and share it in a way that benefits others. It's not just pulling sword from stone, but learning how and when to wield it. Embodying the treasure and sharing it are not the same thing. From the Jungian perspective integration involves the realizing of one's soul—the transpersonal Self—but then undergoing a slow cook of developing a new functional and relational ego, one more adaptive and reflective of its totality that can tolerate the union of its opposites.

THE BUDDHIST FIVE PATHS
OF INTEGRATION

The Buddhist tradition also acknowledges what I consider a developmental map of psychological preparation and integration in which the primary breakthrough—insight into emptiness—is (contrary to popular belief) not the culmination of the journey.

Called the five paths of the bodhisattva, the first two paths of *accumulation* and *preparation* are provisional to the development of insight, they build up the necessary karmic force or merit, ethical discipline, altruistic motivation, conceptual understanding of emptiness, and meditative skills for the third path, that of *seeing*, in which one experiences emptiness directly.

This third path is the summit of the mountain, the taming of the dragon of the delusion of separateness, the claiming of the treasure of non-dual insight and altruism, in which one's previous efforts over countless lifetimes bears fruit, one accomplishes gnosis, subject and object dualism collapses, and one achieves union with the ultimate nature of reality. Importantly, this third stage "of seeing" marks only the halfway point of the journey of full enlightenment, as one must still integrate this nondual view, as yet unstable, into one's being. From the summit, one descends the mountain.

The fourth path of *meditation* acknowledges that in descending the mountain, having seen the limitless vista of the nature of things, one can no longer create any further negative karma (and thus suffering) based on distorted perception and afflictive reactions, however, one is still prone to the karmic residues of the past (before direct seeing). I liken this to a steam engine in which no further coal is added to the furnace, yet due to the build-up of momentum over countless lives, the locomotive continues to progress along the tracks, until it comes to a standstill. In Jungian terms, despite having faced our shadow, broken through the event horizon of the collective unconscious, and gained a profound, life altering encounter with the soul, or Self, we still must "come home" to a new ego that will functionally relate to and improve the world.

The final Buddhist path, in contrast with the Jungian notion of being in perpetual process of integration with the shadow, suggests there is a definitive line one crosses when one becomes fully enlightened, fully integrated. From the Buddhist perspective, life doesn't end there beyond the line of no return, but one's way of being is so thoroughly and irreversibly transformed that there is no falling back into delusion, and no further reservoir of negative karma to activate. One is totally liberated and free to "play" in the dance of appearances for the benefit of others. One abandons even the teachings, and just plays jazz with life. This final path justifiably is called *no more learning*, and is what Siddhartha realized in silence during the weeks after awakening.

In sum, on the road home there are no exemptions; we must work through all the blind spots and backlog of our conditioned habits and their consequences. The only way out of samsara is through it. Whether it's a meditative realization, a psychedelic vision, a psychotherapeutic stroke of insight, a near-death experience, or some other profound break-through, the journey down from the summit continues to involve surrender and release as our old way of being dies, creating space and giving rise to new one, in a voluntary, conscious metamorphosis.

CAUTION ON UNEARNED WISDOM

This gradual process of assimilation or lack thereof is why scandals involving adept meditation masters and gurus can still occur, despite their having high and valid realizations, like the Zen Kensho, a spontaneous, but momentary and experiential insight into selflessness or emptiness poetically described as a flash of lightening, for we can still be prone to the karmic propensities and results of past misguided thoughts and actions. Further, this is why, the Zen poets write, "after the ecstasy, the laundry," to remind us not to get stuck on the mountain top, but to come down to the marketplace, not to confuse the exotic taste of oneness, with the everyday nectar of nonduality. The deceptively nonchalant approach to profound insights characterized by Zen Buddhism help keep ego inflation and hubris in check, restores a baseline humility after the grandiosity of climax, and reminds the self-assured and smug that the job of enlightenment is not complete until you return to the ordinary world, walk the dog, and do the laundry as you did before you left. First you see the mountain, then you don't see the mountain, then you see it again (through clear eyes). First, you're someone (overly fixed and identified), then you're no one (having seen your ultimately open and selflessness nature), then you're someone again (integrating selflessness back into unique and authentic personhood).

To caution further, Jung warned us to be aware of "unearned wisdom," precisely because if you catch a helicopter to Everest's peak, while you might bask in the radiance of your summit selfie, you never gain the rich experiences and skills that can only come by suffering the entire climb. Without the prerequisites, or the tantric preliminaries, it's possible "the high-res view" of reality born of psychedelics will only overwhelm, confuse, destabilize, or inflate you. Beware of unearned wisdom. Same might be true with our having developed new, incredibly powerful AI technologies that might give us access to an unfathomable amount of knowledge, and with it a false sense of entitlement and competence, but, like an apprentice too quickly taking her master's blade, we're ultimately ill-prepared to wield. Without the necessary preliminaries, the provisional psychic infrastructure that emerges during the trials of initiation (think about those sets of 100,000 Buddhist Ngondro repetitions I mentioned in chapter seven) the structure and soil of one's psyche is not functionally cleared and made serviceable to receive the seed of insight. This is why I'm cautious about the explosion in interest in plant medicine, with modern, secular folks with little traditional understanding or consistent self-work rushing into ever accessible psychedelic ceremony during weekend retreats the world over.

I've the same concern for backend integration as I do for the lack of frontend preparation. Without the ongoing communal container, expert guidance, and continued ritual practices that are part and parcel of traditional cultural contexts, initiates can struggle to consolidate what they have learned, and translate that learning from superficial bursts of knowledge, into personal, deep, enduring, embodied, and socially impactful wisdom. Ironically, psychological maturity is therefore needed to experience a breakthrough on the front end, and is required to be deep-ened to prevent mishaps like ego inflation, narcissism, or psychic disinte-gration on its flip side. As I've said before, venturing to find the soul and return with the elixir is everyone's birthright and mandate for mean-ing, but not everyone is a hero, even if you take psychedelics or go on pilgrimage. As with the cultural appropriation of mindfulness medita-tion and yoga, and diluting, secularizing, and mass-marketing psyche-delic ceremony, I expect we'll see more cases of it going wrong—relapses, re-traumatization, psychotic breaks, grandiosity, and re-emergence of clinical depression—because of side-stepping the active ingredients main-tained in traditional contexts that ensure the careful, gradual prepara-tion and integration necessary for bona fide psychological development.

EXTERNAL ASSIMILATION

While the return is considered essential in closing the loop of the Hero's Journey, Susan Ross's research on Campbell's monomyth reveals a sur-prising dearth in practical advice on exactly how integration occurs. Ross writes:

> When Campbell explained that the journey must "bring out again that which you went to *recover, the unrealized, unutilized poten-tial in yourself* [emphasis added] (2004, p. 119), he discerned that the boon is at essence, the initiate's unutilized potential to become established, substantiated, and realized. Although he refers to the boon with qualifiers such as wisdom, knowledge, or gold, in this and other remarks, he indicates that psychospiritually, the treasure and the self/hero are one and the same. Campbell clarified, the "whole point [of the journey] . . . is the *reintroduction of this potential* [the realized self] into the world . . . you living in the world" (p. 119). The words "living in the world" connote a functioning participant in society, and I argue, a person who possesses a state of being in which her strengths are actualized and used. In other words, she

"must *integrate* it [the boon/self] in a rational life" (2004, p. 119) and live in the world as that integrated self, in *possession of her potential* such that the self is reified. If these statements have veracity then the monomyth, as it has been rendered, may be unfinished.

Later, Ross identifies three potential outcomes for external assimilation with the world at the conclusion of a heroic journey. The first involves a rejection also known as the "refusal to return," a mirror reflection of the initial "refusal of the call," when either the world rejects the hero or vice versa. Ross says, "The first path of integration transpires if the initiate rejects society and returns into the bliss because 'no one cares about this great treasure you have brought . . . there is no reception at all, you go back into your own newly unified whole and let the world go stink' (Campbell, 2004, p. 120)."[8]

This was my experience when I returned to the US after my first pilgrimage to India at age twenty, brimming with inspiration after five life-transforming months in a Buddhist monastery, meeting my first teacher Godwin, meditating daily, taking refuge under the Bodhi tree, and healing my soul for the first time. The first six months back on the Wheaton College campus in rural Massachusetts were brutal for me, a total mind fuck. Nothing had changed there since my departure, it was the same people, the same parties, drugs, sex, and debauchery filled nights. With my interest narrowed or specialized, I had trouble fitting in before I left, but could never have imagined feeling more alienated on the flipside of pilgrimage. If anyone dared asked how my trip was, I soon learned it was obligatory, and so cribbed an equally banal one-line response to appease the awkward interaction. The more I thought on it during my long nights alone in my room, the music blaring next door, as I prayed in front of my Tibetan painting of White Tara, how could any of them understand what I had been through, what words could I use to describe something so powerful yet so unfamiliar to them? Ultimately there were no words, and so I remained silent. In isolation, my meditation practice slipped without support. The brilliance of the supernova I had experienced was overcome by the humdrum of ordinary life. Sure, I started a meditation group on campus, and co-directed the first Students for a Free Tibet chapter, but even those endeavors were mere approximations to my monastic immersion in Bodhgaya. But the worst of it was to accept the hard truth that my peers didn't care about me or what I had been through, they were more interested in getting high, laid, or hopefully both. The result is I walked the campus for the last three semesters of college divided, having returned only in body, while my spirit remained in a bardo of longing to return. My only consolation was the self-discipline I applied to my honors thesis combining Buddhism and psychotherapy, which helped me sublimate some of my disappointment and yearning, and advanced my career. Despite having research to focus my attention, I longed each day for that feeling of being alive again, the sense you get on the adventure where risk and reward straddle you on either side of the tightrope as you make your way between the Twin Towers. Not surprisingly, a month after graduation I jumped on the first chance I got to return to Asia and be with Godwin, having largely held my breath, a stranger in a strange land, for nearly eighteen months. What gets integrated in this version of the return is that the boon is "for your eyes only" and the blind, uninterested, world can pretty much go to hell.

THE CONFORMIST RETURN

The second version of integration is what I characterize as a conformist approach: the world needs a specific boon from you, and to reintegrate back into society the hero is compelled to hide or swap their treasure, for the one the world expects. "Campbell explains that the individual attempts to give society what it desires as opposed to giving the gift that she truly received, and thus the treasure is destroyed."[9] An example of this is a pilgrim named Erin, a teacher from the Midwest, mother of three, with a controlling husband. Most of her predeparture hesitation to answer the call to adventure resulted from her compliant personality, and the pressure she felt to be dutiful, responsible, and available to her children and family's needs. In the weeks of painful deliberations over email before we left, I could see her being torn apart—half of her desperate to follow her soul's longing to transform a mid-life crisis into adventure, the stronger half terrified to abandon her brood, overcome by feelings of guilt and shame, and underneath it all the fear that if she cracked that window, even slightly, the edifice of her imbalanced family structure would crumble. Who would she be when she returned transformed?

So often the treasure that caregivers like Erin discover on pilgrimage is that their inner child, never mind soul, has been neglected, their personal needs have gone unmet, they're starved for attention, exhausted by conflicting demands, and putting on a brave face to lift those around them. It's a painful realization to discover our compassion and resourcefulness can be codependency in disguise, leaving others overly reliant, and the caregiver emotionally anorexic and deprived.

The dragon of Erin's justified-yet-suppressed rage at rendering herself invisible needed to be confronted, processed, and expressed to reveal the buried treasure of self-worth, dignity, and her deserving of love. As rude an awakening as it was for Erin and others like her on a journey to a sacred land halfway across the world, it could only happen because of the brave steps she took to separate from the family system, fleeing the unconsciously self-made prison as it were, venturing into the wilderness of possibility, paying the price of vulnerability. Better a two-week pilgrimage than an extra-marital affair. Having pulled sword from stone, Erin's insight into her emotional deprivation and need to nourish herself compelled her into an action stage, where she resolved to set clearer boundaries, negotiate for mutual respect and reciprocity, and validate and nourish her dreams. During the last days of pilgrimage, she and I stoked this fire of aspiration, as she committed to be more forthright, strident, self-affirming, and uncompromising. "Things are going to change" was her mantra. She returned home a powerful new heroine. Or did she?

Sadly, what can happen upon return is the old mold of the family or societal dynamic can pull us back into familiar patterns, like an addict newly sober who can't yet resist temptation. Because Erin's husband and kids endured her three-week absence, there was a greater burden and expectation placed on her when she returned. Like a rubber band pulled taught, snapping. Thus, Erin's boon of self-assertion and self-care was short-lived, and easily lost. The precious gains she made on the adventure, her precious elixir hard won, was swiftly conceded in the blink of an eye. She did not have the time needed to incubate and integrate her new insight, nor to restructure her family dynamic to make it more conducive for flourishing. Yes, the world demands a boon, but if the heroine has not fully transformed, she might ruin her treasure.

The consequence of not being spiritually mature or psychologically fit upon return is not only the loss of what treasure was gained, but the damage and toll of a relapse, which can further erode confidence to even greater levels than before departure. In psychotherapy, the risk of re-traumatization must be diligently assessed, before, during, and after exposure therapy. You don't want to over stack the weights in your cross-fit program or you risk injury. The same is true in recovery, as the more relapses one sustains, the deeper the groove of addiction, and the more hopeless one becomes. The dance between risk and reward takes place on a razors edge. Remember, not everyone who embarks, or even claims treasure, returns a victor. Only after several years of working with me in contemplative psychotherapy along with a second pilgrimage to punctuate her transformation, did Erin move into a more enduring transformation, that not only changed her fundamental pattern of codependency—and within this her impoverished self-view—but corrected the external imbalances of the dysfunctional family system that had maintained her inertia. Eventually, Erin did separate from her husband, who was a narcissist, emboldened, to start life anew. And while her kids were impacted, Erin was finally willing to eat liver to taste newfound freedom.

THE ALCHEMIZED RETURN

The third option of the return is one that involves, unsurprisingly, a *gradual transmutation*. Following my book *Gradual Awakening*, perhaps that is what I could have called this one. It avoids the two former examples as extremes, not to return at all on the one hand, and to return with a compromised boon on the other. This approach to integrating involves "trying to find a means or a vocabulary or something that will enable you to deliver" the boon in a way that society is able to receive . . . "some little portion of what you have to give"[10] The key here is not to contort the wisdom to suit others or yourself—rather, to deliver the essence of part of the message intact.[11]

Think of this like a business strategy, on one hand you can make a killing selling what people want, but not feed your soul. On the other, if you only follow your heart—what Campbell called "follow your bliss"—maybe no one cares what you're selling, and soon your business fails. What's the right balance? While discovering what makes your heart sing, where there is alignment, is the first step, it is insufficient. One further step is necessary, to see how this insight or skill can be conveyed in a manner that makes it more accessible to others. There is an art to delivery, and this is where successful entrepreneurs distinguish themselves from the pack of regular sale folk. The entrepreneur doesn't care only about the money or success, because they're living their passion, but monetary and social rewards come anyway because they have been thoughtful about how to meet their consumers on their terms. The Buddhist call this *upaya*, or skillful means. You're driven by the bodhisattva vow, but recognize it's not a one size fits all situation. To be truly effective, the heart of service must be accompanied by an understanding of the individual needs and dispositions of the recipient, like a hook that perfectly matches its latch.

INTERNAL ASSIMILATION

From a psychological perspective we can get more granular about this last leg of assimilation, which few discuss. Ross's research found that the journey home included nine substages that I'd characterize ironically as requiring a second departure and a second death. She therefore adds a second cycle to Campbell's monomyth, proposing a hybrid depicted in a figure eight or infinity motif, comprised of a masculine, outward journey of departure (preparation, ordeal, and treasure-claiming) representing the *solve* side of the continuum, combined with a feminine, inward journey of integration and return representing the *coagula* side. The former phase qualitatively more masculine—outward, active, expansive, and conquering; the latter more feminine—inward, receptive, consolidating, and regenerative.[12]

JUNG RETURNS A MYSTIC

The last few chapters of Jung's memoirs collected under the name *Memories, Dreams, and Reflections* contains a stunning but succinct account of visionary experience, which appropriately symbolizes his return with elixir.[13] Jung and a friend are in Ravenna, Italy, visiting a sacred site, the tomb of Galla Placidia, which he had visited twenty years earlier, and recounts on both occasions how "deeply stirred" he was by the mood of its interior, and the mild blue light that fills the room.

On his second visit, Jung is a little shocked to find that where there were originally windows, were now beautiful and detailed mosaics. On the south side, a depiction of the baptism of Christ in the river Jordan. On the north side, a depiction of the Exodus, the parting of the Red Sea, through which Moses led the Children of Israel. The third mosaic on the East depicted the biblical story of Naaman being healed of leprosy having been told by Elisha to submerge seven times in the Jordan River. The fourth mosaic on the West side of the baptistry, Jung notes was the most impressive of all, and that he and his companion stopped for twenty minutes to discuss the role baptism rituals played in antiquity. The mosaic depicts Christ saving Peter from sinking beneath the waves. [14]

Jung noted these rituals were more than symbolic reenactments of death and rebirth; they may have involved literal submersions, a real threat of death to ensure that the initiate experienced renewed life. Jung could remember specific details about the mosaic, including Latin inscriptions he tried to decipher. Their visit to the tomb was a short one, and the couple wanted to buy a few postcards of the scenes at a nearby shop for a keepsake. No such photos were available, so they decided to find them when they returned to Zurich. It turns out after several attempts, Jung and his friend were unable to find images of these mosaics. They had never existed. Jung writes, "As we know, it is very difficult to determine whether, and to what extent, two persons simultaneously see the same thing. In this case, however, I was able to ascertain that at least the main features of what we both saw had been the same. This experience in Ravenna is among the most curious events in my life. It can scarcely be explained."[15]

What was the significance of these visions? In 405 CE Queen Galla Placidia made a stormy winter crossing from Byzantium to Ravenna. In honor of her harrowing adventure and survival she built the basilica of San Giovanni in Ravenna to symbolize the perils of the sea. Jung wrote that he felt a deep connection with Galla Placidia, thought she was another version of his animus, his soul, trying to teach him something through these mysterious encounters. But what? Looking closely at the four mosaics projected from Jung's mind on the walls of her tomb, one finds two common motifs: water, a symbol of the unconscious, and the healing or rescue each scene depicts. Peter is saved from drowning by Christ, the Israelites by Moses. Naaman is cured of leprosy, and in the last mosaic Christ himself is baptized by John, rebirth by water. I take this to mean Jung's soul was revealing the triumph his unconscious played in saving and transforming his life. By the end of his career Jung had accomplished something altogether unique, rather than vilifying the unconscious as his mentor Freud had done, Jung had turned himself over to it so faithfully, as to be guided by it. Ultimately the baptism Jung experienced wasn't one in the river Jordan, or the Red Sea, but in the murky, often perilous, and symbolic waters of his unconscious. It wasn't a rescue mission outsourced to an external god or guide, but undertaken directly by his soul. Judson remarks about this reversal stating:

> The aim . . . is to affect a reversal of the relationship between ego-consciousness and the unconscious, and to represent the unconscious as the generator of the empirical personality. This reversal suggests that in the opinion of the "other side," our unconscious existence is the real one and our conscious world a kind of illusion, an apparent reality constructed for a specific purpose, like a dream that seems a reality as long as we are in it. It is clear that this state of affairs resembles very closely the Oriental conception of Maya.[16]

Whereas in Tibetan Buddhism the aim is to stabilize and refine consciousness to make it serviceable for a descent into the unconscious, where it can uproot the *mulaklesha*, the primal instinct of self-grasping, ending the cyclic spin of self-construction and misery. For Jung, there is more of a relational dance between worlds, an ongoing process of mutually enriching descents and ascents, plummeting into dark depths, bringing the gold to the surface to bask in the light. Jung showed over the course of his life the ability to willingly submerge into uncharted waters, into mysteries, encounter the symbolic language of the soul, integrate its messages, and return to the world a more self-actualized human. Consequently, his boon is a profoundly unique blend of psychology and mysticism.

By the end of his exquisitely lived mythological life, as evidenced by his visionary experience at Ravenna, Jung was fully literate in the language of the psyche, he spoke in symbols, and navigated its dreamscape. For him the ordinary and special worlds had blended, becoming nondual, expressing the integration of his most beloved symbol, the mandala. Jung was born a misfit, renounced the kingdom of science and the crown as heir apparent to Freud, labored through the dark night of the soul, and returned a mystic. Jung's voluminous written legacy remains largely obscure to the mainstream psychology community, and like the Buddhist tantras, much misunderstood save for the few initiated, scholars and practitioners of a tight but humble community of adherents, the Jungians. The world of psychology went the way of materialism, even Freud was buried soon thereafter, psychoanalysis replaced by behaviorism, then the cognitive revolution, and now cognitive neuroscience reigns supreme.

But we've hit our tipping point, and the zenith of materialism means the influx of a new frontier in healing that Jung would likely have enjoyed. The trauma revolution brought in yoga and the East, with its emphasis on healing bottom up from the body, and from there new developments in energy work, sound therapy, and psychedelics means the portals to the realms of the numinous have reopened.

Inevitably, people will find Jung's work of interest, his commitment to shadow work, to alchemy, to astrology, to intuition, and to the arts, to myth, dreams, and esoteric knowledge making him such a rich and dynamic synthesizer of human experience and culture, that I anticipate his ideas will experience a renaissance in the years ahead, amid the turning of The Ages when we need his guidance most. Because nothing is ever lost, and nobody ever dies—Jung taught us that—he will be there for us to guide our pilgrimage.

TANTRIC REBIRTH

Our second or bardo phase of the twelve-fold sequence of our Tibetan visualization involved the mentor-bond steps of admiring, offering, disclosing and rejoicing. Now we enter the third phase—rebirth—involving the last four steps of: requesting blessing, presence, dedication, and rebirth.

Stage five, requesting the blessing, marks a "turning point" of internalizing the vibration of the deity, a mantra or affirmation, their altruistic motivation, and divine quality, like wisdom, compassion, or healing. It's ironic, humorous even, that human beings must project their qualities at an external archetype, only to accept them later as part of their soul all along. As Jung wrote, "Today I am directly conscious of the anima's ideas because I have learned to accept the contents of the unconscious and to understand them. I know how I must behave toward the inner images. I can read their meaning directly from my dreams, and therefore no longer need a mediator to communicate them."[17] In the spirit of my mentors Thurman and Joe, most often, we reserve the stage of requesting guidance for receiving the bodhisattva vow, the altruistic resolve to awaken for the benefit of others. If you consider the energy or motivation that compels an unenlightened life to be predominated by self-interest—resulting in misery for all—then if we're going to do a full reboot, we need to generate the vibration of altruism, which results in joy and benefit for all.

Imagining one's sincere request is met with delight, the mentor deity sends a wave of nectar lights from their heart that hovers above your crown. Depending on your level of experience and initiation this part of the sequence could incorporate your subtle body channels and hubs being purified. The nectar drop kisses your crown chakra at the center of its 32-petal lotus, purifies your body of karmic imprints, and transforms your relationship with any future moment of terrifying death and dissolution into the truth body, reminding you that the dharmakaya of clear-light is ever available even when the hour is darkest. The nectar drop descends again from crown to the throat chakra, pierces the center of the 16-petal lotus, purifying your speech of unskillful elaborations, and converts all your future experiences of confusing liminality, any bardo between, into the blissful body. Finally, the drop descends to the heart chakra, the center of an eight petals lotus, purifying mind of subtle karmic obscurations to omniscience, and converting any future experiences of mindless rebirth into the supreme emanation body of the Buddha. We imagine there in the heart chakra, the seed of bodhicitta is impregnated into your subtle mind, your soul. The deity's vibration, that which animates it, becomes yours, your soul activates and aligns with the vibration of altruistic resolve. You are suffused with wise compassion, though the world is an empty illusion, out of empathy, love, and compassion you forever seek to rouse sentient beings from their nightmare construction, until all are awake and take delight in the mandala. Now we've formally begun to reboot, beginning with the triumph of tasting the nectar of bodhicitta. As Geshe-la likes to proclaim after conferring the bodhisattva vow at a sacred site in the real-world, "Now your life is meaningful!"

If you're new to this process it can feel idealistic, *and it is*! You can't use reason to reprogram yourself at this level of being, it's prelingual, symbolic, mythopoetic. That is why the ancients used myth, ritual, art, song, and sometimes psychotropic substances. We're working with potent images, and affirmations, like conjuring a spell or living in the dreamscape, as we override and revise the subtlest code determining who we are, what we can be, countless years of karma and evolutionary habit, how we see the world, and how we orient ourselves and act within it.

The next stage involves a second request, that of presence, asking the deity to be reborn in one's own mental continuum, taking up residence in the center of one's own heart chakra. We're asking not just to receive a blessing from the deity, but to *become* the deity. The deity begins by absorbing into itself, the entire merit field of tutelary beings, all the lineages of wisdom and compassion of the tradition, and the spirit or refuge tree itself. Then the deity dissolves from toe to crown, inwards toward the heart, so that all that remains is a single nectar drop, the essence of the Buddha's pure body, speech, and mind, which then hovers above your crown. Like the Eucharist, when you symbolically ingest Christ's flesh and blood, becoming one with Christ, atonement, at this stage we symbolically receive the nectar drop, first kissing the crown chakra and transforming our hologram body* into the physical body of the deity. As you

---

*The hologram body is the body made of energy that consciousness assumes following the stages of dissolution when the course physical elements die.

breathe, try to perceive your soul inhabiting the luminous angel body of the mentor-deity. Then the nectar drop descends the central channel, into the throat complex, where you attain the perfect eloquence and skillful speech of the deity. Now imagine your words bringing others delight and liberation. Then the drop descends again and enters the heart chakra, where you actualize the deity's holy mind, the dharmakaya, realization of emptiness. You now see the luminous interdependence called emptiness-appearance of all things with confidence and are without fear. You now have been alchemically transformed into a tantric deity, seated on a throne, ruling justly over the dominion of one's own mandala. While this description is how Thurman and Joe taught me to make the symbolic rebirth process accessible to lay, non-tantric professionals, depending on the tantric deity and text, there are variations, nuances, and complexities.

I want to paint a broad picture that captures your imagination with the sublime mythopoetics of the Tibetans, while the actual technical details, explanations, and encoded meaning I leave to the lamas that will confer specific initiations to those who qualify. In the more advanced perfection or completion stage practice when one is working with the energies in the subtle body, one requests the presence as before, but when the nectar drop hits the crown it descends down the side channels instead of to the throat, drawing down impure energy, the grasping instinct in the white, left channel, and aggressive instinct in the red, right channel, which pour into an imagined crucible or scull cup four fingers below the naval. Then the toxic energy of the reification habit that calcifies and distorts the reality of self and world is drawn down the central, blue channel, and mixed in the cauldron below, like an alchemical brew. In certain texts like the sadhana of Vajrayogini, graphic imagery of decimating the ordinary delusory body and mind into parts is visualized, to likewise be thrown into the burning skull cup in a ritualized ego-sacrifice. The contents of the cup are heated over fires and purified, as in an alchemical alembic.

As one begins to draw up the purified substance—the elixir—from the skull cup, it appears as a red drop (symbolic ovum) and travels on the yogic or secret pilgrimage up the center channel to the navel, reaching the heart chakra. Simultaneously, as the red drop ascends, a white drop (symbolic sperm) is released from the crown chakra and descends on pilgrimage to the throat, then heart chakra. As breathwork, visualization, and manipulation of energy converge, the two—above and below—are joined in symbolic fertilization, with a third, the Buddha nature, one's own soul, gestating new life. This choreography is mapped by the yogi onto the stages of dissolution or natural death process described in the *Bardo Thodol* so that after the experience of white luminance and red radiance, the merging of the two drops with the Buddha embryo, one enters a liminal space just as the sign of midnight (imminence) arises, and consciousness is temporarily lost. The three entities, the holy trinity, become one. In the midnight womb, the red egg and white sperm produce the sacred deity body of your next life, while the Buddha nature, the soul, imbued with all its good qualities accrued over countless lives, serves as the subtle consciousness, the deity mind of the next life. From within the sheer darkness, consciousness reboots and breaks through the event horizon of separation and dualistic thinking, recognizing its enlightened nature, realizing the inner sign of clear-light (transparence). The enlightened embryo is now impregnated and gestates in the mandala womb of the central channel of the heart chakra, and will be reborn as a deity being driven by the bodhisattva vision and vow. A tantric rebirth combining subtle body anatomy, mythopoetics, and visualization. A secret pilgrimage as wondrous as the external pilgrimage to Eleusis to drink a psychedelic brew, revealing the greater mysteries.

When I train students in this simulation, they also rehearse a task they anticipate performing in real life, something that might be anxiety provoking, or represent a stretch in their capacity. Rather than imagining, as we typically do, a poor outcome, rejection, or failure, they rehearse from the enlightened point of view, starting at the result or goal of being a deity or master altruist, allowing mind, speech, and body to recalibrate from the experience of competence and success.

The stages following request for presence are dedication and rebirth, the former usually involves extensive prayers for guidance and gratitude toward the heavenly host of angel archetypes, that they may continue to remain available to support your full embodied actualization. I ask students to pray in whatever way is meaningful, perhaps Jung prayed to his unconscious, his soul, to continually guide him. Students must remember that these kinds of visualization practices, while still in the realm of simulation and imagination, accrue large amounts of positive karmic momentum or spiritual force. In the dedication we earmark and channel this force solely toward the manifestation of our highest ideal.

In the final stage, rebirth, we see ourselves as the deity, descending like an avatar into our ordinary body that's meditating below us. We fully inhabit it, like adorning familiar clothes. In the post-meditation session, students adhere to vows to retain pure view that all beings and experiences are empty and fluid, and to retain divine pride, that our mission in the magical performance of life is to help others awaken from their nightmare-making. No matter what we do, where we are, or what happens to us, our practice to retain pure view and divine pride in the world not only ensures the continuation of the collection of wisdom and merit, but makes life purposeful and meaningful.

I've found some students report more vivid and visceral experiences of transformation when they combine this visualization script with the vibration and harmonics of a sound bowl, human song, or intensive breathwork, and when appropriate psychedelics, all means to alter consciousness. We speculate sound and entheogens were pivotal in healing sessions at the Asklepion in ancient Greece and at Dendera in Egypt and in many other traditional medical systems. The sound journey, intensive breathwork, and judicious use of plant medicine can facilitate brain facilitate brain integration, elevate consciousness, and accelerate learning, while the mythopoetics, imagery, and mantra help soul-sculpt at the deepest level of mind and brain.

THE RETURN OF KING & QUEEN

Modern versions of the hero's myth that continue to captivate our imaginations today include the three-act sequence articulated by Campbell, with the final act reserved for a glorious rebirth. The Matrix trilogy concludes with *Revolutions*, the Lord of the Rings trilogy concludes with *The Return of the King*, and the original Star Wars trilogy concludes with *The Return of the Jedi*.

As I was curating my group pilgrimage to Java and Bali in 2023, coinciding with the writing of the conclusion of this book, the *return of the king* quietly emerged as an archetype of significance. Following the bread crumb trail of the unconscious that first led me to Bali, then to prince Tjok Gde Kerthyasa, living heir of the Mahapajit legacy, then to the vision of a group pilgrimage to the iconic Borobudur mandala in Java, and from there to the peculiar urge to reunite Shiva and Buddha in a joint ceremony at its sacred summit. I didn't know where I was heading or why, but after extensive spelunking on the internet I found a Belgian anthropologist based in Java, by the name of Patrick Vanhoebrouck, who helped shed light on the bigger mosaic that was being constructed. Patrick is an expert in Javanese tantrism and shamanism. Like me he offers pilgrimages to the megalithic sites in Indonesia, and like me he is usually accompanied by a traditional lineage holder from the land.

Patrick has no website, he prefers to remain incognito, but when I obtained his WhatsApp number and contacted him, he responded quickly. Patrick was kind enough to indulge what I thought was going to be a few simple questions about Borobudur, but our initial conversation lasted over an hour and included multiple synchronicities, including how Patrick and I both studied at Kopan Monestery in Kathmandu in November, 2006, exactly when I first met Geshe Tenzin Zopa, although Patrick and I never met amongst that group of 200 students. It was as if we had crossed paths on our spiritual journey, stepping into one another's footprints along the way, but had only caught up with each other now.

Vanhoebrouck guided me through a Buddhist-Hindu history of the island of Java leading to the Majapahit exodus, including the pre-history of the lost civilization of Lumera which, along with Atlantis, might have been the stronghold and propagator of an older, high civilization that preserved the legacy of building monolithic structures and the sophisticated science for achieving enlightenment, generously bequeathed to the cultures like Egypt, and Greece, as well as to the cultures in the archipelago of what is now modern Indonesia. Patrick described how the architecture and position of the Borobudur mandala in particular were perfectly aligned within the landscape to correspond with the heavens above as an earthly replica of the mythological Mount Meru. From Vanhoebrouck's Shivite overlay, the Borobudur complex is positioned within a larger sacred geographic mandala comprised of nine sacred mountains, he collectively called the Dewata Nawa Sanga, forming a nine-pointed compass or wheel, eight spokes and one hub, comprised of power places for healing and magic, eight of them in the eight cardinal directions, with Gunung Sumeru at the center, its name derived from the mythological Mount Meru. [18] The Borobudur mandala complex is believed to be the macrocosm reflected in the microcosm, and Patrick—who was eager to cut to the chase, told me, "when you visit the mandala with your students, explain to them that they're staring into a mirror of their own inevitable Buddhahood." Vanhoebrouck insists the structure is an intermediary between the energetic alignments of the stars, and those within one's body and mind, based on the principle of correspondences as above, so below, as with in, so without. Borobudur is an ancient machine once used for transmitting the frequency of peace and harmony. This alternative explanation for an ancient monument's purpose is echoed in the research of Christopher Dunn in "The Giza Power Plant" where he presents a provocative theory suggesting that the Great Pyramid of Giza was not a tomb as is conventionally thought but an advanced technology for generating and transmitting energy.[19]

Then I shared with Patrick that I had had a vision to set a stage at the top of the Borobudur mandala where my teacher Geshe-la would offer the bodhisattva vows alongside a local wisdom keeper, in a symbolic reunion of Shaivism and Buddhism. While I didn't know why it was so important, or what it meant, I asked for his thoughts.

To my bewilderment, Patrick said, "I had the same vision." For the past fifteen years Patrick had been living in Java working intimately with the local wisdom keepers, including his guru Mangku Jitho, a Shiva-tantra master from Lawu. Influenced by his time spent studying Tibetan Buddhism at the Kopan monastery, Patrick had always wanted to do a joint ceremony with a Tibetan lama and his Javanese teacher at Borobudur, but never had the opportunity. *Until now.* Like brothers from another life, Patrick and I seized the synchronicity to combine our visions, each of us bringing our spiritual mentors from disparate traditions into contact, the Borobudur mandala serving as a sacred nexus point, a symbolic crucible for the fulfilment of a joint vision of the future. When I asked about the serendipity and the timing, Patrick didn't hesitate; he said it must be related to the *Sabdapalon prophesy*! A vaguely remembered reference from my first meeting with the Wizard, now I was fully intrigued. "Better you look online," he said, "It's not something I feel comfortable discussing in a first meeting." Now he had my full attention! I was drawn in and captivated, perhaps the way Adam and Eve were tantalized by the forbidden fruit. That night, while Emily and the kids slept, I tore through the internet and discovered why my unconscious had me hooked like a fish on the line.

The Sabdapalon prophecy is based on the visionary prediction of Sabdapalon, a Hindu-Buddhist high priest and the spiritual advisor of King Brawijaya V, the last ruler of the Majapahit dynasty in Java, during their influence throughout the Indonesian islands and eventual conquest of Bali.[20] The Majapahit Empire stretched through the Indonesian and Philippine archipelagos, including Singapore and Malaysia, to Thailand, where it traded and with another Hindu-Buddhist Empire, the Khemer, builders of Angkor Wat, another famous mandala also based on the mythological Mount Meru and is considered "the largest religious structure ever built."[21] When King Brawijaya bent the knee in 1478 converting to Islam during the Muslim invasion of the region, Sabdapalon is said to have cursed the king, and—during a period where the Majapahit were migrating East to Bali in the late fifteenth century—righteously proclaimed he would return in the future, some five centuries later, at a time of widespread political turmoil, civil unrest, and natural disasters, to reclaim the island from the invaders and restore the exquisite Buddhist-Hindu synthesis that characterized his earlier civilization, called Shiva-Buddha agama.[22] This specific merger of Tantric Shaivism and Vajrayana Buddhism was once a syncretic religion unique to Indonesia that lasted centuries before the demise of the Majapahit. A last remaining remnant of its elegant philosophy persists in the motto, "Unity in Diversity" broadcast by the government of modern Indonesia. Sabdapalon said, "When Mount Merapi erupts and its lava and ashes fall to the South-West with a terrible smell, that is the signal that I will be coming soon."[23] In this prophecy perhaps Patrick and I had found a context for our peculiar interest in the reunion of Shiva-Buddha, heralded by the return of a mystic who will vanquish the invaders from the Island of Java and restore its former sovereignty and glory. Had our vision somehow found its place within a larger metaphysical context? Was the collective unconscious active in each of our personal imaginations?

If further confirmation was needed, another wisdom keeper and guest on my pilgrimage, Made Griyawan, a master painter in a thousand-year-old lineage from the artisan region of Batuan in Bali, also shared a vision he had during the pandemic. In a reoccurring dream Made saw a life-size Buddha statute half buried in earth to the waist. When he asked his local priest what the symbolism might mean, instead of providing an interpretation the priest led Made down a path in a remote part of his village to the ruins of a temple. Although born and raised in this village, Made had never seen it before. When they entered, there in the courtyard he saw the Buddha statue from his vision, emerging waist-up from the ground, as if unearthing itself like the trunk of a tree. At his art studio in Sukhavati, I told Made about the visions Patrick and I both had. After hearing this, he smiled with his glorious white teeth and boyish innocence and said in his broken English "Siwa-buda agama, Siwa means liberation, Buda means love, we need both, they come together again." But the synchronicity didn't stop there.

The Sabdapalon prophecy bore a striking resemblance to another prophecy I was more familiar with, the return of a king to vanquish the Islamic hegemony and user in a golden age. Although there seems to be no historical evidence for any connection between these prophecies, they seem uncannily similar.[23]

THE SHAMBHALA PROPHESY

The Shambhala prophesy is discussed within two disparate traditions, in Hinduism it appears in the Kalkin Purana, and in Vajrayana Buddhism appears in the Kalachakra tantra.* The Kalkin Purana is a Hindu text from roughly the 1500s that describes the lineage of the ten incarnations or avatars of the god Vishnu over the vast cosmic Yuga cycle. It may be based on the earlier Vishnu Purana from the fourth century CE, which discusses eight of the god's incarnations. The myth begins with Braham beseeching Vishnu for protection from the onslaught of evil during the dark age of the Kalu yuga. Responding to his plea, Vishnu vows to be reborn as Kalki in a hidden land known as Shambhala, galvanizing a brave army to fight off an invasion, even if it takes him lifetimes. The seventh, eighth, and ninth reincarnations of Vishnu were Rama, Krishna, and the Buddha respectively, the Hindus claiming and venerating the enlightened prince Siddhartha as a manifestation of Vishnu. The tenth and final avatar of Vishnu is yet to come,

---

*I was told in an email correspondence with Tibetan scholar John Newman of New Collage of Florida, an expert and well published researcher of Kalachakra, that "there is no evidence to indicate that the Kālacakra was known/existed in that part of the world [Sumatra, Java, Indonesia] prior to the modern period. Thus, it may be doubtful that there exists a literal or historical link between the Shambala and the Sabdapalon prophecies. But that doesn't negate a more mythopoetic connection as a universal archetype emerging in different cultures, just as pyramid building arose at around the same time in disparate geographical locations from the Mayalands to the Nile delta in Egypt.

but the devout expect Kalki to return, destroying evil, reclaiming his throne in Shambhala, and ushering in the golden age, the Satya Yuga.

Interesting parallels exist within the Sabdapalon and the Shambhala prophecy based on the Buddhist Kalachakra tantra. But first a note, that Jung would have absolutely loved the Kalachakra. Although I can find no evidence that he encountered the literature, I'm left with this impression of a smile on his face when I read some of it. The Kalachakra tantra, translates as the "Wheel of Time," though I prefer Thurman's more imaginative "Time Machine" and is represented by perhaps the most intricate and exquisite mandalas (see plate 8) in all the Tibetan tradition. Mythologically, the tantra was requested by the first king of Shambhala, King Suchandra, and delivered in Dharanikota (now Amarvati), India, by the Buddha himself, who was bilocating, simultaneously delivering the transmission of the wisdom of emptiness on Vulture Peak in Rajgir, India. In Dharankota, the Buddha transformed into the blissful and fierce, four-faced, 24-hands, deity Kalachakra with his consort Visvamata (Kalachakri) and delivered the transmission of the tantra to a royal assembly of nearly a hundred kings and emissaries hailing from the magical kingdom of Shambhala, who then returned home to practice and safeguard the teaching for centuries, later condensing them into the short form known as the Sri Kalachakra we know today. This actual text is dated most likely to the tenth century CE and belongs to the highest class of tantra, the unexcelled yoga, it's the most integrative text in Vajrayana Buddhism, containing a perfect and purposeful synthesis of cosmology, psychology, sociology, myth, prophesy, ritual, and subtle-body visualization.

The Kalachakra contains five chapters, the first deals with cosmology including the vast Yuga cycle and its aeons based on Indian astrology, including the twelve zodiacal periods that comprise death and rebirth of the universe, even noting the elemental building blocks of matter, something akin to atoms, and finally describing the Shambhala prophecy. The second chapter deals with the microcosm of the human mind and body, including gestation and birth, the subtle body with its energetic channels, winds, and drops, and how these can be manipulated through contemplative practice to alter states of consciousness from waking, dream, sleep, and bliss. Between the first two chapters we see how the Kalachakra decisively coordinates a mirroring or reciprocal relationship between the cosmos above, and the psych below, correlating the external flow of civilizational descent and ascent in the long cosmic cycles of space and time, with the internal flow of energies and micro cycles of the breath within the mandala of the subtle body.

The third chapter deals with the initiation, the fourth with the suite of contemplative practices and techniques, including the generation and perfection stages visualization of the mandala and deities along with embodied manipulation of energy through the channels to access drops of bliss, and the fifth chapter deals with the resulting experience of enlightenment, human perfection as the deity itself. Perhaps this is why Jung would be so keen, for it's in the Kalachakra that one sees the most explicit version of Tibetan Buddhist alchemy, which felt like a homecoming for Jung when he discovered the Western counterpart in the later stages of his career. But the Kalachakra is more than a psycho-spiritual tool for the individual to master themselves, it's also a socio-cultural power-tool presenting a utopic vision for social harmony leading to an enlightened society. This is where the Shambhala prophesy is most relevant within the broader Kalachakra tantra.

According to Tibetan scholar Alex Berzin the Shambhala prophesy tells of king Suchundra who comes from the mythical land of Shambhala to request of Buddha the Kalachakra tantra which he brings to his kingdom where it's disseminated among the people and safeguarded. The king and his successive heirs unify the stratified caste system and take the title of the Kalki, chieftains, based on the mythology of the Vishnu avatar lineage. Several centuries later there will be an invading army of barbarian hoards that threaten to destroy the people, their kingdom and their spiritual way of life. After a succession of twenty-four Kalkin, the twenty-fifth (Rudra Kalki), will rise to defeat the enemy, restore order, and usher in a golden age.[24] Elsewhere, Berzin dates the predictions of the prophecy more specifically to between 2424 or 2425 CE (in the 5,104th year after the death of Buddha)."[25]

Like the Sabdapalon prophecy, the enemy of the future is described in the Shambhala prophecy as "barbarian forces" with high technology and as invaders called "mleccha," which most scholars consider a Muslim incursion of North India, part of an anticipated broader Islamic domination of the known world at that time. [26] Berzin speculates the vision of the future was naturally influenced by the geopolitical context of the Himalayan region during the tenth century in which it emerged, in and around modern-day Kashmir including the Swat Valley. He states, "that fear would have been further heightened when eastern Afghanistan came under the rule of the Sunni Ghaznavid allies of the Abbasids in 976 CE"[27] and perhaps this fear was projected into the future as a possible dark age that include the conquest of Shambhala itself. A poignant socio-political insight grows from the Shambhala vision that is important for us to keep in mind. This period of anticipated Islamic invasion involves turmoil and chaos, so the Shambhala prophecy describes the Kalachakra tantra employed as a tactical defensive weapon, a force for good, wielded by the twenty-fifth and final king of Shambhala, Rudra Kalki, as a nonsectarian political device for unifying diverse peoples. Rudra Kalki will make the tantric initiation open to all, Buddhist and Hindu alike, Jains, and even Muslims, diverse groups holding moderate rather than extreme or dogmatic views, all brought together under one umbrella, and unified in a spirit of mutual respect in the face of a common enemy: extremism.

The initiation is not used for religious conversion, rather it's designed to eliminate the caste system, unifying members into a single diamond or vajra caste of brothers and sisters, dismantle the ridged socio-economic structures that polarize and sustain division and inequity, and restore a sense of harmony between diverse members of society without forcing them to bend the knee to a single political authority or ideology, or abandon their respective faiths. *The Kalachakra magically creates unity while respecting diversity.* The same message of tolerance is captured in the Shiva-Buddha motto "Unity in Diversity." Remarkably, the same signature of the incoming aion balances individual sovereignty (Leo) with collective unity (Aquarius).

Is Shambhala an external kingdom, or an inner metaphor? Western explorers of Tibetan Buddhism who encountered the Shambhala prophecy in the early 1800's became enchanted and tried to seek out the kingdom as a physical place, the so-called Shangri-La, somewhere in Tibet, near sacred Mount Kailash or perhaps in the Gobi Desert of Mongolia. But all their efforts and external seeking went in vain.[28]

This led some to conclude that Shambhala was more of a metaphysical concept, not to be found in space and time at all, but rather a transformed state of consciousness, or a nonlocal pure land arrived at by way of spiritual practice. I prefer the third Panchen Lama's middle way, when he says, "A person who travels the world looking for Shambhala cannot find it. But that does not mean it cannot be found."[29] This is a feeling I know well as a pilgrimage guide, leading me to conclude that it's not the destination that changes us, it's the journey. But we still need an orientation, a north star for our compass as we travel a physical terrain toward a sacred source. Ultimately, perhaps Shambhala is both an optimal state of mind, and a place for those with eyes to see. Where the prophecies of Sabdapalon and Shambhala are aligned is that we're living in a time of fragmentation and chaos; a battle is raging between the forces of good and evil, and when the hour of our demise seems upon us, a just king and queen will return to restore order, reconcile opposites, and foster unity without dispelling diversity. By now, you should know who those monarchs of good will are. If you're still waiting for a courageous hero to protect you from tyranny, or the arrival of a just king to lead your land, you've missed the universal message and call to adventure of every myth and prophesy ever told. The sword to claim is yours alone, atop your head the rightful place to rest a crown.

11
Therapeia
Pilgrimage & Psychedelics

JOURNEY TO DIVINITY

The old woman's face is weathered, her wrinkles tell a story of centuries of hardship that she and her kin have endured as nomads exposed to the extreme elements of the high Himalayas, yet she smiles. Her hands clasp in prayer above her crown, and effortlessly as breath, she utters the sacred mantra: *Om Mani Padme Hum.* Her hands touch her throat and heart as she lowers herself to the ground in full prostration onto the ancient rocks beneath her. Her eyes are unblinking in the cloud of dust; her internal gaze is likewise unflinching, transfixed on Chenrezig, the deity of compassion with a thousand arms.

The woman rises, carefully takes three steps forward, and repeats the prostration. She will continue like this—step by step, bow by bow, mantra by mantra—for days, perhaps weeks, or even months. She is bound for Mount Kailash to circumambulate the sacred mountain, as her forebears have done for generations before her. For Buddhist and Hindu pilgrims, Kailash is more than a physical mountain peak in the autonomous Tibetan region of China, it's also a mythopoetic archetype, a sacred summit of the gods, and the sublime nexus point of the mandala of the universe. This celestial axis unites heaven and earth at the center of the cosmos, what Jung called the axis mundi. For the Buddhist it's the abode of Chakrasamvara, the tantric manifestation of bliss that realizes reality beyond the distorted veils of perception. For the Hindu it's the abode of Shiva, destroyer of delusion and revealer of liberation. More significant than the destination, is how we journey on pilgrimage that is transformative. Each prostration itself is the embodiment of *solve et coagula*, a descent to the ground where the poisons which contaminate the soul are purified, followed by our rising up again motivated by the bodhisattva vision and resolve. The prostration is a Tibetan form of baptism, similar to the melukat ceremony described in chapter eight without the water which follows the same archetypal motif, submerging for purification, and reemerging for rebirth. Done repeatedly over weeks and months, the mythopoetic art starts to have a visceral impact on mind and body. By the time one arrives at the destination, they've become what they seek: the deity in the mandala.

As we've made our way through a vast landscape on a timeless journey, I now want to discuss how to apply what we've learned. I can't think of two more relevant methodologies to directly encounter, or participate in *solve et coagula* than pilgrimage and psychedelics. We are familiar with the modern word psychotherapy, which comes from the Greek *psyche*, meaning soul, and *therapeia*, meaning attending to, or healing, so I'm going back to go forward, suggesting pilgrimage and psychedelics are psychotherapies in the original sense. Perhaps you have an activity that facilitates *solve et coagula* that you consider a *psyche therapeia*?

PILGRIMAGE TO A SACRED SITE

Pilgrimage condenses the journey for spiritual liberation that can take an entire human lifetime or more into a few short weeks on the road. Many possible motivations compel one to venture to a sacred destination, but perhaps none is more profound than devotion. In general, devotion is a universal quality of intense yearning and commitment— we can be obsessed with our favorite sports team, wedded to our job, or madly in love with our partner, but for the pilgrim, devotion is to the transcendent ideal, by whatever name; God, enlightenment, or the ground of all being. A pilgrim is motivated to abandon what ordinary people covet, face what most run from, and endure what many cannot bear to serve, surrender, receive, or achieve what is considered the treasured aim of their spiritual practice.

While most of us conditioned by the modern materialistic way of life can't reasonably expect to understand, let alone embody the nurtured devotion exhibited by our pilgrims prostrating their way to mount Kailash, we can nevertheless spark and fan the nascent flames of devotion within us. It may start when we answer the faint call of interest in a photograph, song, or story that points toward adventure in a distant land. Devotion may be further refined through an initiation, like when a Buddhist pilgrim takes formal refuge in the Buddha, Dharma, Sangha, and bodhisattva vow thus consecrating their commitment to a new orientation for evolution. Or it may go well beyond, where one's entire way of being—outlook, attitude, and lifestyle—are so thoroughly subsumed that an utter rebirth of the individual can occur. To understand this profound motivation deeper, we can look at the pilgrimage's origins as embodied devotion.

BUDDHA PRESCRIBES PILGRIMAGE

Buddhist pilgrimage dates to the Buddha himself. To ease the anxiety of his disciples, who feared the impending loss of inspiration as the time of his death grew close, the Buddha prescribed visits to physical sites linked historically with the significant milestones of his biography. Often depicted in paintings (see figure 9.2 on page 268), these sites include his miraculous birth in Lumbini, where the young prince renounced his kingdom, his middle way discovery at the Dungeshwari caves outside of Gaya, his enlightenment on the Diamond Throne under the Bodhi tree in Bodhgaya, his first teachings to his five former friends in the deer park at Sarnath on the outskirts of the holy city of Varanasi, his first transmission of emptiness on Vulture Peak in Rajgir, his teaching of the Kalachakra tantra in Amaravati, and finally his passing into parinirvana in Kushinigar after a nearly forty-year teaching career. Through the power of association, these sites would not only become reliquaries of his remains for commemoration but virtual representations of the Buddha where his living presence could be accessed. More so, places of veneration came to signify the potential to awaken anyone who visits them with the heart of devotion. Consequently, the ethos of pilgrimage was born, and for centuries, Buddhists from all around Asia venture to auspicious places connected with the Buddha and all the subsequent spiritual masters to perform karmic acts of generous offering, purification, textual recitation, and meditation to activate their latent potential for enlightenment.

The significance of pilgrimage may be lost on those living a secular life, but all religious and spiritual cultures have their form of sacred journey. As my interest in offering pilgrimages stems back to my first trip to India when I was 20 years old, I've had time to develop a rationale for its importance that my students and clients can appreciate. One in-road to discovering this relevance comes from the Old English word *hale*, which is the root for holy, whole, and heal. These words are a reminder that the endeavor to reach a holy site is a catalyst for reclaiming wholeness, which is the most profound form of healing mind, body, and spirit.

PURPOSE OF PILGRIMAGE

The most obvious value of pilgrimage comes from its transformational aspect as a mythological rite of passage. A pilgrimage is neither a vacation nor a sightseeing tour. However, for cultures that still engage in this practice, it serves as a rite of passage bearing three critical phases: departure, initiation, and return. Leaving home, pilgrims metaphorically die to their attachments to family, career, comfort, and most importantly to their limiting beliefs and worldviews. Something essential to one's identity must be sacrificed or surrendered to create space for something new. Then one passes through a liminal phase in which sacred land, sites, and wisdom keepers bestow knowledge and usher pilgrims through trials that help mature their latent qualities. Initiation intelligently uses hardship to empower the neophyte in the process of creative self-redesign, just as fire is used alchemically to transform base metals into gold. Not content to hide away in some mountaintop hermitage savoring realization for themselves, the pilgrim is motivated to re-enter society to share a life-affirming message—the elixir—with their communities.

It's possible to enter a mythological journey without physically leaving home, just as it's possible to learn French from a book while living in Chicago. But who will argue against the profound depth of learning afforded by living amongst the Parisians in cultural immersion, expeditiously transforming body, speech, and mind by walking for weeks in their shoes? This suggests that there is an actual value to the physical sites and destinations that cannot be replicated at home. The sacred qualities are not just projections of mind alone, as these holy places are unique portals imbued with the energetic charge of devotion from an endless stream of pilgrims dating back to the Buddha himself. The energy and association invested at the Bodhi tree in Bodhgaya by pious pilgrims differs significantly from that of the Eiffel Tower by admiring tourists. Thus, interdependence between the devoted mind and the accumulated energy invested makes sacred sites unique. That one must travel to these sacred, often remote, destinations inevitably raises challenges. A pilgrimage, done correctly, will also crush you, activate your remaining fears and doubts, and force you to confront your shadow in the most vulnerable place and inopportune time. These difficulties have been essential in the rite of passage since the pilgrimage's inception. Each trial is precisely the friction needed to spark the alchemical fire, shake loose old habits, purify karmic seeds, and clear the deck for regeneration.

For example, the cost of pilgrimage might well marginalize people. However, consider that devout Muslims save for years to make their *haj* to Mecca, pious Christians on the Camino de Santiago, and some Tibetans sleep by the roadside on their way to Mount Kailash. The greatest gathering of human beings on the planet, the Kumbha Mela on the banks of the sacred Ganges, attracts rich and poor Hindus alike to fulfill their aspiration. It's important to consider in our modern, secular culture that while pilgrimage seems financially unfeasible for many, too far from home, too long a time commitment away from work, which may in part be because we don't yet prioritize spiritual activities like we prioritize forms of enjoyment, vacation, secular education, and retirement, I've found that those who sacrifice the most to go on pilgrimage often have the most meaningful and transformative experiences.

PILGRIMAGE AS PARADIGM THERAPY

In my twenty years of observing our modern culture through the trials of my psychotherapy clients, meditation students, and myself, a picture of our current problems has emerged. Depression, anxiety, stress-induced physical syndromes, pervasive meaninglessness, and the apathy that have grown to epidemic proportions do not just have a biomedical origin. They also arise from psychological and cultural causes and conditions. Despite our technological advancement, modern materialistic culture is misguided in other crucial domains of life, and we now exhibit the widespread symptoms of what I call a "sickness of paradigm." Jung asked himself where all the gods went when they left Mount Olympus, and concluded that they disappeared into the unconscious of modern man, their neglect manifesting as sociopathy and neurosis.[1]

I view western, secular societies as the result of a four-centuries-old transgenerational trauma characterized by a pervasive disconnection from spirit. Spirit encompasses the invisible but vitalizing source of all life. As a result of throwing the baby of spirituality out with the bathwater of organized religion during Europe's Age of Reason, we also became unmoored from spirit and certain profound orienting principles like interconnectivity and virtue. We're now cast adrift. Once God was proclaimed dead, we no longer maintained a coherent worldview that included meaning and morality. We lost a connection to and respect for our bodies, rituals, consciousness, mythologies, nature, ancestors, cycles of time, the cosmos, or the divine. Orphaned through this pervasive separation, our modern culture has predominately forgotten who we are and why we're here.

This spiritually deprived, materialistic worldview our culture has recently adopted now confuses consciousness with brain activity and our sense of human purpose with material gain. Despite the technical precision of our modern drugs, surgeries, and therapies (in large part emerging from the Cartesian split of mind from body and both from spirit), materialist and scientific worldviews have not yet presented a sufficient remedy for the deeper, more causal roots of our fragmentation.

For years, I've been synthesizing sacred wisdom from Tibetan Buddhism with modern neuroscience and psychotherapy to offer a more coherent map of reality and comprehensive guidelines for how to live well. I endeavored to integrate these streams in my last book *Gradual Awakening*. Within all these offerings, I contend that a profound cultural renaissance based on a synthesis of cross-cultural disciplines is not only necessary for us to recover optimal wellness as individuals but essential for our survival as a species on the verge of self-imposed mass extinction. In my online courses I introduce students to an authentic spiritual worldview, prayers, meditations, rituals, an ethical lifestyle, a group service project, and pilgrimage to sacred sites, each explained and justified through the lens of current trauma research and neuropsychology. What is needed most is a holistic paradigm therapy that addresses our impoverished worldview and a hedonic lifestyle, which offers a reconnection to *hale*—our healthy, holy, and whole self beyond just the physical dimension, and a *therapeia* of the psyche.

I first discovered the healing power of sacred sites when I was twenty years old while on my first pilgrimage to India. I was suffering the symptoms of root-trauma-induced depression and disillusionment with modern consumerist society. My exposure to Buddhist culture amplified at the holy places over those five months changed the entire trajectory of my life. Consequently, I went on pilgrimage another five times before I started designing and leading journeys myself. In 2016, twenty years after I first was in India, I led a group to the sites of Buddha's awakening. I invited Geshe-la to lead our group in traditional teachings and rituals at sacred sites, including refuge and the bodhisattva vows under the Bodhi tree, ground zero of the world's awakening revolution. These ceremonies, like powerful mind-altering substances, though not as radical, reorient human vision nevertheless, galvanizing meaning and purpose. What can be discovered through this inner vision is that human beings are more than bodies driven by a genetic imperative to survive a single lifetime, as our current scientific dogma would have us believe. Evolving in parallel with genes on a material realm, we're also infinite consciousness driven by a moral imperative across countless lifetimes, here to learn profound lessons and ultimately to awaken to our interdependence with all of life. Since the dawn of humankind, every major culture has concurred in some form with this spiritual outlook; the only exception is the new kid on the block—our current industrialized culture.

A poignant memory that best captures the therapeutic power of pilgrimage occurred in 2018 when Geshe-la and I co-led another group to the power places of the Kathmandu Valley in Nepal. This was my death and rebirth rite of passage after leaving Joe and Nalanda. At the end of the tour, dressed in traditional white, we gathered at the ancient Boudhanath Stupa, with its iconic Buddha eyes gazing with compassion in all four directions, and received the bodhisattva vow, which is the altruistic resolve to orient one's entire evolution toward awakening for the benefit of others. At the culmination of the ceremony, after we'd each made the pledge, Geshe-la's refrain was, *"Now your life is made meaningful. . . now your life is finally meaningful."* At that moment, we connected with the timeless, transcendent, ineffable. It left us speechless and in tears of joy. I knew then that this was medicine for the soul we had been searching for, the elixir. Experiences like these will leave eternal imprints in our collective memory—and while we will undoubtedly continue to struggle with the vicissitudes of life, none of us are confused any longer about who we are and why we're here. That is what I mean by paradigm therapy, a reconnection to the lost and secret human dimensions of life beyond the physical that only a sacred wisdom culture and practice can provide. This is the medicine missing from our current allopathic and biomedical treatments, the dogmas of scientism, and our over-dependence on the rational mind. Through pilgrimage, it dawned on me how profoundly healing an immersion into sacred wisdom culture can be not only on an individual but also on social and cultural levels. Geshe-la concurred with my observation on another pilgrimage we co-led from Nepal to India in 2022. At its conclusion, he grabbed my hand and squeezed tightly, thanking me for organizing the tour and saying, "more learning and transformation took place in these two weeks on the road than years of committed study and practice at home." That is the power of fully embodied immersion, living with your master and fellowship, deep in practice amid the sacred sites. There is just nothing that can compare, and perhaps this is why the asklepia were so effective at healing and endured throughout the millennia.

Having taken the bodhisattva vow with Geshe-la at the Boudhanath Stupa, I pledged in 2018 to lead one pilgrimage with him annually, "sharing the elixir" in small doses with our students and doing my part to help heal our struggling culture and restore balance. Inspired by the Buddha's encouragement that we embark on sacred journey to connect with his experience as our own, I've led tours to Nepal, India, Sri Lanka, Java, Bali, and Japan.

Having discovered the one key—*solve et coagula*—that unlocks all esoteric doors no matter the culture, it's possible to venture beyond Buddhism and Asia to activate sacred ceremonial sites like the Temple of Hathor at Dendera and the Great Pyramid of Giza in Egypt, the Telesterion at Eleusis, the Asklepion at Epidaurus, the Temple of Apollo at Delphi in Greece, Stonehenge in England, or the Temple of the Jaguar at Tikal in Guatemala. I can now envision Geshe-la teaching from *The Tibetan Book of the Dead*, along with its Egyptian counterpart, within an ancient necropolis in the Middle East. Once we understand the universal archetype, we're free to go anywhere and rekindle the flame that has died out within most megalithic sites, and as the aion transitions and more people start waking up, we will bring these sites back online to scale the revolution. We can appreciate each as a gateway or energetic portal into the underworld, through which the timeless rite of passage of separation, initiation, and return can be undergone, and the psychodrama of death, bardo, and rebirth re-enacted. In so doing, each pilgrim will encounter both the trial and treasure of venturing to a holy land to encounter a series of sacred sites that mediate the circumambulation of cosmos above within their psyche below.

MY PSYCHEDELIC THERAPY

It's late 2020 when I find a lump on my right testicle. I'm ashamed to discuss it with anyone and terrified because it's getting bigger. The size of the mass is somewhere between a golf and tennis ball. It's more than disrupting normal functioning. Every time I handle my business down there, I'm filled with dread. Emily is the only other person that knows. Sex is out of the question. After her desperate attempts to get me to see a urologist, I reluctantly agree.

I'm in the waiting room at the doctor's office of a hospital in Westchester, New York. It's full of people looking at their phones, anxiously awaiting their fate. It's like a clinical purgatory. Will it be cancer? Will I need surgery? Will I survive? My name is called. But it's the nurse asking me to pee in a plastic cup. "Give me a sample," she says through the glass window, barely making eye contact. "Toilet's down the hall to the left." More waiting. It's a sterile waiting room, with plastic decor unchanged since the eighties—a drop ceiling and incandescent lights. Finally, I'm called to see the doctor. He's an older guy wearing the classic white lab coat that's supposed to instill deference.

"How you doing," he says. It's a statement, not a question, which opens our awkward exchange. Before I answer, he asks me to strip down and lay on the table, pulling a disposable sheet of thin paper for me to lay on while forgetting to ask my name or introduce himself. Time is money around here, I guess. I'm meat on the conveyor belt. Two minutes of squeezing and prodding down there, he speaks in one run-on sentence: "Yup, you have a hydrocele, a collection of fluid, do you have children, or more to the point, do you want any more?" Before I answer, he says, "if not, we should operate. It's not cancerous or life-threatening, but it's sizable. It's a procedure lasting less than an hour." He snaps off his rubber gloves, pops the trash can open, and disposes of them in a well-rehearsed routine. "It takes about ten days to recover. No sex or physical activity during that period and we'll keep you nice and comfortable on drugs for the week." I can tell he's already thinking about the next poor guy in line, waiting outside the door in purgatory. It's routine, nothing much to worry about.

I'm still digesting all this shit. *Cut open my scrotum?* I've barely answered the question about more children, and he's already invited the nurse to schedule me for the procedure. My drawers are still around my ankles.

"Hold on, what causes this?"

"No idea," he says matter of fact.

"Well, how do we know it won't come back?"

"There's a small chance it will."

"Small?"

"We don't know."

"You're going to cut me open without a guarantee it will fix anything because you don't know the underlying origin of the problem?" I'm still in delayed processing mode, but the irritation has set in.

"That's right, buddy, sorry to say, it's your call, wait and let it get bigger, or schedule the surgery." Now he's curter.

It's a total shit show, industrialized medicine, devoid of dignity and human connection. Modern materialistic culture has empowered doctors to act like mechanics and treat us like machines. There is no soul here, not even a trace. If we could return to the holistic worldview that characterized the Asklepion, we could integrate powerful surgeries and medicines when necessary, restoring the fundamental dignity that the body can heal itself through attitude and lifestyle change.

In the weeks that follow, I endure a rapid-onset episode of depression. I'm emotionally blindsided, like a train wreck. The thought of going under anesthesia and being cut terrifies me, especially in that region. I make the grave mistake of Googling the procedure, find a YouTube video of the surgery, and nearly pass out. It looks like butchery. In the days that follow, given no alternative, I start decompensating. First, I have nightmares involving drowning, an inability to breathe, and suffocating—utter powerlessness. In a several-day sleeplessness haze, I actively imagine that death is imminent. I couldn't explain it. It wasn't rational. I was dying. At forty-six my life was over. Although I'd been told the mass was benign, I may as well have had cancer. As Emily and I processed the procedure, I was often in tears, consumed by images of the anesthetist, the operating theater, and the scalpels.

One morning, as I walked my son Bodhi to the school bus and waved goodbye, I was overcome by the sense that it was the last time I'd see him. I drifted home, found my way to the walk-in closet, and fell on the floor wailing. It felt like I'd never see my kids grow up. What was wrong with me? It made no sense.

One night I woke up from another nightmare choking and gasping for air. Emily got me some water and a Xanax. My panic grew worse. But in reviewing the dream, I made a meaningful connection. I was drowning in water. *Fluid. Choking. Death.* Yes, my father died nearly ten years earlier. He had survived sixteen months with pancreatic cancer, a heroic effort. They cut him like a sow in an abattoir. They slashed him, pumped him full of drugs, and in less than a year I watched him fade from a strapping 240-pound man to a ninety-pound raisin with bones sticking through his skin bag. And he was one of the lucky ones; the average life expectancy of stage-four pancreatic cancer is less than four months. The day he died, his lungs filled with fluid. Effectively he drowned to death in my arms.

In the weeks after my diagnosis, something was arising around death, and I needed to connect the dots. I was terrified to go under anesthesia. My astrologer equated this with an utter loss of control. The dreams and my father's experiences involved fluid, my drowning, there was fluid in my testicle, and fluid in my dad's lungs. And surgery, both of us getting cut, in an undignified way. But the real heart of the agony was the thought of me losing consciousness, akin to my father losing his life. I made the connection that I was experiencing a post-traumatic reaction with delayed onset. My medical condition had triggered implicit, unprocessed memories, and although my situation was benign in real-time, the unconscious was reexperiencing the loss of control and the fate of agonizing death. My ordeal put me out of touch with reality for a good month. Like Jung, I was adrift in the tumultuous sea of my unconsciousness, where reality and rationality are distant echoes off on the horizon as you tread water and look for shore.

Despite bringing to light the unconscious association between my lump and my dad's death, I still had to deal with the reality of my condition. I took a two-pronged approach, the first was finding a specialist who could deal with the mass in a noninvasive way, and the second was dealing with the psychological trauma. After a few days of scouring the internet, I found a doctor in Chicago who performed a nonsurgical procedure for draining the collection without my having to go under. There were only two in the country that I could find; the other was in LA. Doctors are trained now to avoid draining and opt immediately for surgery because the fluid often returns. I called up Dr. Levine, and we had a chat. I like him immediately. He was charming and kind, and he listened. I describe him as a man with a high emotional IQ. I told him about the trauma associated with my father and why I couldn't go under anesthesia. He understood me right away and said, "I'll take care of you."

The following week, Emily and I flew to Chicago and went to see Levine at his office that day. He shook my hand and greeted me with dignity and respect; he explained the procedure and invited Emily to stay in the room. He was everything the other doctor was not— genuine, warm, empathic. Before I was lanced, Levine gave me a slight numbing agent on the gurney, but I retained consciousness. While it was taking effect, I asked them both to leave the room. That's when I had a little chat with my dad. Laying there on the bed, I told him I missed him, I was sorry for how much misery he endured. I told him he would love to watch my boys grow up. I asked him if he was proud of me. I could feel him there as tears rolled down my face. And although I didn't hear him reply, I felt comforted and safe. I was allowed to be a kid again; "Daddy's scared little boy." Some part of me needed to connect with Dad as that scared little boy lost and frozen in time, because when my Dad was dying he needed me to be the put-together adult for him. The terrified inner child had, by necessity, been exiled, and could now be reclaimed, like in the harrowing of Christ, reassembled. The procedure went well. I walked within an hour and was on the plane home the next day. Though there is no complete cure, one dimension of my condition on the physical realm had been temporarily resolved. I'll never forget Dr. Levine's generosity of spirit. He, like Dr. Tunjai in my father's case, remind us all how empathy is the real medicine, both without and within.

The second approach I needed to take was psychological. I needed to deal with the post-traumatic residue activated by the pseudo-near-death experience. It had been on my mind for some time, and now psychedelics felt like a pertinent option.

I spent nearly a month in preparation for my medicine journey. I chose to use psilocybin mushrooms and to go with Emily and another friend experienced with hallucinogens, to a nature reserve.

I treated the process as any Tibetan ritual, taking refuge and generating an altruistic resolve. I clarified my intention for taking the medicine, wanting to face my fear of dying and death. I sipped the mushroom tea while we walked on a trail immersed in brilliant fall foliage, a mesmerizing blur of red, yellow, and orange leaves. It was a sunny cloudless morning. The roar of the river echoed through the valley. As the medicine kicked in, and I could feel my senses altering, somewhere between departure and initiation, I could read the tell-tale signs of crossing the threshold. Something happens to our ordinary sense of the time-space continuum. It collapses, like entering a separate but parallel universe, where reality is more fluid and malleable. While there was some fear, there was also the safety net of confidence born of preparation to protect me. I spent weeks studying the marks and signs of the psychedelic journey, speaking with experienced psychonauts about dosage and process, securing a natural setting and time of day conducive to my temperament, and refining my intention. I even consulted Lynn Bell on the correct astrological alignment for a successful soul journey into the underworld.

From the corner of my eye, while walking on the trail, I noticed something around fifty meters away, down a slight slope, that caught my attention and pulled me toward it. I left the trodden path, made my way down the rocky embankment, and the girls graciously let me follow my intuition. A grove of trees had formed a half circle like an amphitheater around a single felled tree, weather-beaten and stripped of its bark. Its smooth, white underbelly seemed to light up against the cascading panorama of foliage that served as a backdrop. What I sensed was this was a ceremonial site with magnetic energy. The confirmation came as I drew closer and discovered a buffalo or cow skull, propped up and facing me, like a gateway guardian, with its two broken horns, deep recessed eyes sockets, and long protruding snout. The bull, buffalo, or cow head skull, called the bucranium, is a ubiquitous symbol of death and rebirth across cultures and dates back to the Neolithic period. It's often depicted in stone relief on Greek and Roman temples, where initiates of the mystery schools enjoyed sips of *kykeon*, a psychedelic brew, at the culmination of nine-day initiatory ceremonies where they were overcome by Dionysian passion and granted divine revelations of the deathless state. The bull skull is found across the planet wherever ritual magic exists, known by many names from the tribes of Java to the elders of the First Nations of North America. The bull head is also associated with the central archetype deity in Tibetan tantra called Yamantaka, translated by Thurman as *the death destroyer,* he who terrifies the root afflictions of cyclic existence, thus granting the boon of immortality. I made an offering to the bull head, it granted me access into the amphitheater, and I entered. Unlike the horrors of my earlier trials, this death was sought and accepted voluntarily, without resistance. As I removed my jacket and lay down on the smooth surface of the single fallen tree, it felt fated.

Initiation gives way to the ordeal. I had enough consciousness to know the setting was a perfect answer to my aspiration, and this is where I'd undergo a death rehearsal to face my fear. I spread my arms apart, forming the intersection of the cross, fingers touching the earth, the rest of my body suspended in animation a foot above the ground, propped up by the sacred tree. There is always a sacred tree in mythological time, connecting the heavens with the underworld, a highway for descending and ascending the unseen realms of spirit, acquiring nectar like the water bearer Aquarius to deliver to the thirsty masses. As I looked up above me, a webbed network of tree branches became a swirl of living tendrils, an incredible kaleidoscope of geometric patterns pulsating in rhythm with my heartbeat. I began to sink into the tree; my torso became its trunk, my arms its branches until there was no separation. I was the tree, the earth below, and the sky above. I was neither here nor there; I was the birds, the faint roar of the river, and the wind in all directions, yet none of them.

There was no localized sight from a narrow vantage point of my eyes, no hearing from my fleshy ears; there was just seeing and just hearing. No boundary between where "I" began and ended. Then a voice emerged, not in vocal syllables or sound but presence; I recognized it instantly. My father encouraged me, as I did him, "to let go." I whispered it in his ear while he was dying, reassuring him I'd take care of Mum and his worldly affairs. Now it was his turn to comfort me. Somewhere deep in my being, below the surface of rational intelligence, emerged the diamond intuition that I'd not die alone. Just as his parents were there to receive him during his transition beyond, just like I'm there for my boys when I pick them up after school, my dad will be there for me. And someone will be there for you, a rebirth on the other side of the gateway between lives. None will be alone. No one is ever alone. I felt that with every fiber of my being, and for a moment, the residue of fear that had gripped me for months was gone, dissipated like an echo through a cavern. The energy of fear that had consolidated around the story of death and calcified when I watched my father's passing was relinquished, allowed to dissipate, to be creatively repurposed. Alchemical transmutation.

When there is heavy turbulence on an airplane, we brace for impact, our muscles constrict, and we instinctively, though irrationally, grasp the armrests as if they would help. Similarly, energy was being recruited in defense against my perceived demise, an ego and physical death, and was thus recruited for self-protection and self-preservation. The mushrooms helped me surrender those defenses, to let go or dissolve the tight grip, and allowed me to pass through the death threshold, entering an ocean of luminous, undifferentiated light. Forms collapsed, as did sounds and sensations. Time and space were irrelevant, revealed to be utter fabrications of the mind. My identity was similarly irrelevant, and what became apparent was how much energy I wasted on the longings and fears of my life story, the drama, desperations, the regrets, and the joys which reinforce more grasping, all are taken to be so real. They all became superfluous, like a child growing too old for her stories of Santa Claus. All that was left was raw conscious awareness with nothing to push away or pull toward. The underlying energy of awareness was freed from compulsion because it had been seen through the multifaceted projection normally assumed to be so utterly real. There was only rest now, profound and peaceful rest. I desperately needed this after living in hypervigilance and traumatic arousal for those past months. I had entered the realm of the soul, what I now call the soul-scape, timeless, faceless, nameless, the ever-expanding periphery and eternal center—all things contained within, yet no findable thing unto itself.

As I write this, the mental fabrication of my chattering ordinary mind fumbles clumsily to compose something, but absolutely no words can capture these ineffable mystical experiences. The numinous defies description and laughs as poets, artists, and philosophers all attempt to capture it nonetheless. The mystical experience is as effervescent and as ungraspable as the wind in a dream. I don't know how long I laid there, suspended in time immersed in pure unadulterated consciousness, in the bardo between worlds, but it might as well have been an eternity. The Tibetan yogis call this state of luminosity, rigpa, and once they become well acquainted with resting in it during meditative equipoise, they attempt to retain this quiescence, or non reactivity, in post meditation when the world of appearances and thought forms return. There, and back again.

As mysteriously as I entered the numinous heartland, she, my diamond queen of intuition, gently gestured me out, ushering me from formlessness back into form, from undifferentiation, back into separation. Before crossing the threshold from the secret world back to the ordinary world, she reminded me to impress on my consciousness all I had seen and learned, to bank the insight born of direct experience. And so, I prayed to remember and dedicate that this potent and affirming message I had received would be retained in consciousness like a sacrament, a treasure trove, or a secret mantra. As the medicine waned, the world was beckoning me back into low-frequency vibration, fear and longing, and the drama of adorning and protecting my identity. "Please, remember to remember, we never die alone; death is a doorway," I chanted. "There is nothing to fear."

After returning to my body and rising from the cross, I made my way past the bull skull guarding the ceremonial amphitheater and found it was the broken tangled roots of an upturned tree stump. I could faintly make out the eye sockets, snout, and horns, but the magical world of the dreamtime faded as afternoon turned to dusk. I processed the experience with Emily and my friend while we walked along the trail. "What a powerful medicine this is." I reiterated: "If treated with respect, used intentionally and sparingly, and under the right conditions." It can certainly break down barriers and give access to subtle states, profound insights, and novel dimensions. It was as if several weeks of trauma therapy could be collapsed into a single plant ceremony, just as the Tibetans believe lifetimes of haphazard evolutionary experience born of trial and error can be collapsed into a three-year tantric retreat comprised of four sessions of yoga per day. Each session, plant or yogic, an opportunity to die and be reborn, until the immortal soul is reclaimed, and the delusion of false dichotomy between life and death intuitively resolved.

THE SHADOW OF PSYCHEDELICS

While I respect the power of plant medicine, I'm skeptical about the explosion of interest in psychedelics we're currently undergoing, even while there are credible success stories and a growing number of validated studies to support profound mental health benefits.[2] There is a shadow to everything, and as Jung reminds us poignantly, we should beware of unearned wisdom. That is, breakthrough experiences derived from potent psychotropic remedies have potential for revelation, but are only half the equation, our mind and its condition of receptivity and maturity, is an equal and necessary partner in the alchemical relationship. It's worth reiterating that tasting the elixir is only half the journey, one must also return home, slowcooking newfound wisdom and translating its impact into a boon appropriate for others. The return from the psychadelic high must be done without substances, one must rely on ordinary consciousness to complete the cycle. I've seen folks stumble at this juncture, not integrating properly compels them straight back to more ceremony in the same way I returned to Asia at the earliest opportunity for the "high" of more pilgrimage. My young mind was simply not capable of marrying the special with the ordinary world.

If we lack the internal psychic structure developed during the traditional initiatory rites of passage, be they contemplative, shamanic, or therapeutic, I'm not convinced the benefits of these plants and substances outweigh the risks.[3] We should be wary of handing out psychotropics like candy, to vulnerable clients desperate to overcome their suffering from long-standing traumas. Some clients, looking for quick fixes, might lack the necessary preparation, such as failure to create a conducive mental set or find a suitable environmental setting. They also may not have yet cultivated consciousness to the degree that will allow profound insight to make its new home in their being, and might not receive the absolutely crucial follow up post-ceremony care and attention that would ensure their wellbeing and insights are maintained and shared within their community. There is also the danger posed by institutions profiting from churning out psychedelic assisted therapists and guides to meet the new demand of interested clients. How well trained can we expect these guides to be after completing just a nine-month certificate program? We may see the same potential limits on competency as we do with the ubiquitous 200-hour teacher training models within the context of the yoga boom and mcmindfulness fad. The difference now compared with two decades ago when these trainings and trends emerged is that we live in a much more politically polarized environment, where, as my own experience with the Nalanda Institute can attest, the shadow of political agendas can creep into any training program leaving therapist and client alike unduly influenced. Time to cook, appropriate challenges, and ongoing supportive in supervision and communities free of dogmas are all needed for both therapists and clients to integrate and mature. What qualifies a spiritual guide is not worldly credentials, but how many times they have consciously died and been reborn, how deep into the darkness have they ventured, and how embodied is their wisdom and compassion upon return.

The Greek mystery schools didn't use psychedelics in the recreational way many of us do now; the height of their multi-day rituals capped by intoxication with a psychedelic brew provided them direct encounter with their inner god Dionysus, god of wine, ecstasy, fertility, and madness, also known as the liberator from inhibitions, fear, and self-censorship. In my favorite image, the epiphany of Dionysus (see plate 6), he emerges in a triumphant rebirth from the chaotic sea of the unconscious, in his between-world chariot drawn by panthers, wearing a crown of ivy, holding the wand (thyrsus) and the wine horn (rython) containing the elixir of immortality.

The myth of mother-daughter dyad of Demeter and Persephone, female counterparts of Dionysus, and a Greek corollary to the Tibetan Vajrayogini, similarly reveals a story about altered states of consciousness with a sacred elixir granting immortality. Still, as I shall describe in the section entitled "Eleusinian Mysteries," it would have been in the context of being initiated for months or years in a lifelong practice, with a cogent philosophy, coherent cosmology, and consistent community, where that revelation would have been incorporated back into their ordinary consciousness and daily life through ongoing ritual bound by secrecy. What happens on the tail end of the ceremony for initiates, would have been continued practices to draw the insight of immortality—the elixir—into their new experience of everyday life. This would not have been guaranteed by the medicine itself, but by the guidance of hierophants, their teachings, practices, and rituals.[4] To this day, I still have a bit of a lump in my nether regions to remind me of inevitable change, that I'm a work in progress, and there is no greater teacher than death. I now wear my lump like an amulet, reminding me of my inevitable demise, yet orienting me to achieve the deathless. We don't get over countless generations and lifetimes of fear built into our DNA with a mega dose of mushrooms, but we can reframe our attitude toward life and death, seeing human mortality as an invitation to forge a new relationship with being both human and divine, being part of the impermeant dance of the material world while also a soul beyond it.

PSYCHEDELICS AND SUBTLE-BODY YOGA

Whether it's a physical pilgrimage, a psychedelic journey, or subtle body yoga to activate kundalini, there are some uncanny similarities to underscore. For example, on pilgrimage, we reach the Mahabodhi Stupa at Bodhgaya in India. On this site, the Buddha attained awakening; the temple proper is situated within a mandala with four gates in each cardinal direction, and three concentric pathways leading into the inner sanctum. I've discussed this as a vision in the introduction, which I incorporated into a meditation practice for my students. The circumambulation allows for the purification of ego, the *solve* to occur as one makes the journey from the periphery to the center to fulfill Jung's symbolic notion of wholeness and union of opposites. At the center is a womb for rebirth, *et coagula takes place*, one assumes the role of Buddha by sitting on or near the Diamond Throne under the Bodhi tree and adopting a new outlook, attitude, and lifestyle. It's a bit of psychodrama easily digested by the right brain alchemically potentized with devotion, allowing one to relish the reenactment of Siddhartha's enlightenment as one's own destiny.

Within the context of psychedelics, some version of purification with diet, smoke, water and incense, intention gathering and ceremony is then complemented by physical purging, as is the case with Ayahuasca, which represents the *solve* phase. Then when the medicine takes over, the energies ordinarily bound up by egocentric identification and protection are freed to be subsumed by Ayu, the mother, or divinity herself, who leads you on a spirit quest through alternative dimensions, bestowing the gift of insight or horror, as the case may be, as you reconceive the world and yourself *et coagula*.

In subtle-body yoga, the mandala is not a physical location but a visualized internal environment. The central stupa and spirit tree are overlaid around the heart, protecting the Diamond Throne, a chemical drop of mind-expanding bliss. As mentioned, one makes a virtual procession, called the secret pilgrimage, to imbibe this nectar. The inner circumambulation draws down contaminated energies from the side channels and fuses them in the sacred chalice, igniting the inner heat (tummo) to burn, purify, and dissolve these energies from grasping, aversion, and misunderstanding, then directing pure energy back up the central channel to the Diamond Throne at the heart, where one is rebirthed a Buddha.

ELEUSINIAN MYSTERIES

The *therapeia* of pilgrimage and psychedelics needn't be mutually exclusive or separate endeavors. At least one ancient Greek mystery school used both in tandem. At Eleusis, a town not but thirty minutes outside of modern Athens, is the sanctuary where perhaps the most famous mystery school of the ancient world drew thousands of participants each year for an extensive pilgrimage and initiation involving sacred substances. For nearly two thousand years, from roughly 1450 BCE–392 CE, the cult of Demeter assembled initiates to make a ten-day pilgrimage along the Sacred Way from Athens to Eleusis, re-enacting rites and rituals representing the myth of Demeter, goddess of the Grain, and her daughter Persephone (Kore) as recounted in the Homeric Hymns.

The myth occurs in three acts we're now familiar with, the trinity motif of separation, initiation, and return. Act One involves the abduction and rape of the innocent maiden Persephone blindsided while frolicking in the flower fields by the lord of the underworld Hades, prompting the end of innocence and a descent into hell. Act Two involves Persephone's initiation as queen of the underworld, where she learns the art of discernment to pass moral judgment over souls, while her despairing mother Demeter, failing to find her beloved daughter in the overworld, loses her vitality and fails to produce the annual harvest. Act Three involves Demeter reclaiming her power to restore the harvest and feed the hungry, which she cunningly uses as a bargaining tool with the gods to temporarily release her daughter Persephone from the underworld for six months each year, after which she must return. The myth is an account of rebirth naturally tied to the seasons, and to the harvest that sustain life. Demeter, an archetype of fertility residing in the overworld, creates and renews life, while her daughter Persephone, archetype of judgement and death, resides in the underworld. Mother and daughter, separated and longing for one another, reunite for a brief triumphant period in the spring of each year. Not only representing a union of opposites, left and right brains, order and chaos, life and death, loss and bounty, but highlighting their nonduality, a single cyclic continuity of the soul's eternal demise and resurrection, that must be embraced in its totality, and celebrated in ancient agrarian societies of the Near East.

The archetype of the fertility goddess and of the death-rebirth motif possibly evolved from earlier civilizations like the Sumerian goddess Ishtar or Inanna, and later the Egyptian goddess Isis, who used her magical powers to revive her husband Osiris, bringing him back from the dead. In the Eleusinian mysteries, the rebirth myth not only involves the divine mother and daughter, but a third party to form a trinity; Demeter's segregate son Triptolemus, to whom she bequeaths the sacred wisdom of the grain, and who flies around in a mythological chariot drawn by dragons delivering to Greece the life bestowing art of agriculture.

In *The Immortality Key,* Brian Muraresku argues that the rising power of Christianity may have absorbed the matriarchal myths of the ancient Near East, in what is known as the pagan continuity hypothesis, an idea discussed in chapter three.[5]

The Christian patriarchy produces its own version of the holy trinity of father, son, and holy spirit, and Demeter's rebirth motif may have been subsumed in the three acts of Christ's crucifixion, harrowing of hell, and resurrection. Perhaps at one time Muraresku argues, even the Eucharist, the ritual eating of bread and drinking of wine representing the internalization of Christ's body and blood, may have involved the psychedelic potions used in the Greek mysteries, which would have taken the symbolic reenactment of resurrection into the realm of experiential gnosis. This became too threatening to the political and religious establishment of Christianity; to safeguard the church's power, the psychedelic substance was replaced with inert substances of flour wafer and grape juice.

As for the pilgrimage itself, thousands of initiates would have gathered each year in September on the Spring Equinox at the base of the famed Acropolis in Athens as the priests transported sacred objects from Eleusis to bless the rituals and sacrifices of the opening ceremony. They would have been preparing themselves for this day for at least half a year following the initiations of the so-called lesser mysteries, which prescribed daily preparatory spiritual practices just like tantric preliminaries. Then there would have been a mass purification with crowds of initiates walking together in droves to the coast to bathe in the sea, not unlike scenes we see today of the naga babas, the naked sages, covered in cremation ash, bathing in the Ganges during the Kumba Mela in India, the largest sacred gathering of humanity in world history. As the Eleusinian pilgrimage continued, there was a festival dedicated to Asclepius, god of healing, who entered my visions as described at the beginning of this book, and whose presence likely would have been beseeched by pilgrims through dreams and visions and during their long 21 kilometer (13 miles) walk from Athens to Eleusis.

Considering that the prior few days were focused on purification, we can assume fasting and sleep deprivation, combined with the strenuous walk in the sun, would have contributed to many experiencing hallucinations and alterations in consciousness. But as if that weren't enough, imagine, upon arrival at Eleusis, being met by the awe-inspiring sight of the Telesterion, the great hall that could house 3,000 people. Inside, gathered in the dark, initiates would have had a multisensory experience—touching sacred objects passed around by the hierophants, listening to initiatory sermons and instructions, then, as speculated by some, imbibing a sacred brew of wine spiked with psychoactive ergot procured from nearby wheat fields.[6] Symbolically consuming Demeter herself, each became the mother goddess, falling into psychedelic intoxication and participating in reenactments of the death-rebirth myth of Demeter and Persephone, including the climactic moment at the mouth of the Plutonium, a cave representing the gates of hell, where mother and daughter were symbolically reunited in a triumph over separation. At the climax of this collective transformation of consciousness, each initiate would have experienced their soul and the deep gnosis of immortality. The impact of the ten days would dramatically influence how they lived the rest of their lives, guided by virtue, meaning, and purpose, and how they possibly died without fear. Initiates of the Eleusinian mysteries vowed secrecy by penalty of death about these sacred rites, and it is likely because of these vows that much of this narrative remains speculative. However, the state did sanction and support these initiations, and they were maintained for centuries, so you might ask: how is so little known? Some conclude that the psychedelic experience was so powerful and compelling, so life affirming and altering, that initiates felt a strong allegiance to their beloved mysteries, and thereby complied honorably with their vow of silence, helping preserve the initiations for future generations.[7] Just imagine as the world turns if we could revive the mystery schools, with life-long courses in mythology, cosmology, ritual, and meditation, punctuated by the *psyche therapeia* of annual pilgrimage and psychedelic ceremony to facilitate each citizen's awakening!

As you may remember, from the Buddha's biography we see the final attainment of the deathless under the Bodhi tree, and are told through the Jataka tales that it took his soul countless lives of merit collecting to reach this lofty goal. And then there is Jung, whose willingness to die, (to surrender) to his unconscious in order to be saved by it, and who had a visionary experience of the scenes of baptism on the walls of the tomb of Galla Placidia, leaving the impression that he also experienced a metaphoric rebirth that he relished in.

Through temple rites in Egyptian and Greek mystery schools, and other traditions, we can speculate that initiates would have undergone a profound mind-altering experience, perhaps facilitated by psychoactive substances or sound meditation that gave them access to a deep visceral experience of resurrection. This motif is built into our Tibetan visualization, with the last four stages, the reenactment of resurrection, rehearsed each day, or four times a day while on retreat, so the experience displaces our habitual sense of being ordinary with the pure view and divine pride of the deity at the center of a mandala. And finally, the journey of pilgrimage or psychedelics ensures those who embark shall never return the same. These *therapeia* are revelatory; sickness is dispelled by attending to the soul. With the third eye open, one beholds the world in silent awe.

MANY GATES, ONE KEY

These threads of pilgrimage and psychedelics, show how the loom of *solve et coagula* can be overlaid on almost any process if we adopt the mythological lens and use it to our advantage. We can *mythologize* our life, making it a powerful story of transformation, instead of a tragic story of powerlessness in the face of life's inevitable misfortune.

Like the medieval alchemists turning metal into gold, you now possess the one key that opens all esoteric gateways, turning adversity to advantage, and transmuting the mundane into magic. Once you've adopted this mythos, I hope my reflections have offered you the space and time to process your understanding of the cyclic stages and milestones mapped out by Campbell, Jung, and Tibetan alchemy, cosmology and whatever other timeless exoteric traditions you value. The point is to allow us to gain the facility, language, vision, and confidence to circumnavigate outer, inner, and secret terrains and return to the beginning all the wiser, having ventured there and back again. By transforming our experience of tragic life into a heroic journey, we can reexperience unavoidable hardship and unrelenting trials as a catalyst for growth, delivering the boon of meaning and purpose to our societies that need it desperately. By transforming our trauma-induced arrests in psychological development into a successful individuation process of authenticity, we can restore wholeness from fragmentation, integrating the split-off aspects of our personal and collective unconscious into the totality of the Self, then bring that totality to bear on a more adaptable ego in the world. And by transforming the terrifying cycle of traumatic birth, mindless life, and terminal death into voluntary *dissolution*, sublime *liminality*, and altruistic *resurrection*, we can savor the nectar drop of immortality—the elixir—that is our fundamental nature and aspire to share it with others. Because *solve et coagula* is a universal archetype, there are limitless paths up the sacred mountain, and entrances into the supreme mandala. This single esoteric key opens every spiritual gate. What mysteries lie ahead are now yours to discover, savor, and share.

12
Reunion
End of Separation

ABOUT-FACING OUR FUTURE

As we reach the culmination of Elixir, each of us locating ourselves at various stages in our personal journeys, let's also relocate ourselves collectively on the cusp of the turning of The Ages. From the vast vantage of the Great Year, our cosmic clock, we're awash somewhere in the sea change between the Piscean to Aquarian Age. The archetypal signature of, individual sovereignty and decentralized unity overhead points to our future, while the cultural and systemic institutional collapse we experience now are an inevitable part of a larger cyclic process of societal death and renewal. As the tide shifts, above and below, toward the next Platonic month, we can ask: Where are we heading? What stand must we make? What steps will we take to influence future generations? Rather than be swept away by the currents of habit and fear, we can do an about-face and forge a new trajectory. Astrology, mythology, and prophecy can help us galvanize our collective energy and forge forward with clarity of vision, courage of heart, and purpose in action.

SHADOW AT THE DAWN OF AQUARIUS

In one of his last books, *Aion*,[1] Jung was most concerned with the inner source of the external struggle for power he anticipated between collective movements of ordinary people and their authoritarian governments, systems that come to occupy the role of God, long since abandoned in the last age. The internal struggle within everyone is a moral battle between the forces of virtue and vice. The symbol of Christ of the waning Piscean Age, one that long served the function of mediator between these inner forces, has given way over the past four centuries to the archetypal anti-Christ of materialism, leaving us in moral free fall. Now with the waxing of the new aion, we welcome the archetypal water bearer of the Aquarian Age, with the downflow of vertical power delivered horizontally to the masses, each of us now having more agency but also more responsibility for the consequences of our individual actions. Since symbolically there is no longer a god in heaven nor guru on the throne, no externally projected authority or parent ideal to guide and protect us from our base instincts and each other, to regulate our passions and redeem our flaws, both Jung and Nietzsche predicted one of two things, we would outsource the organizing structure left by religion to government and nationalism, or we would succumb to no structure at all, and suffer the ensuing chaos, despair, and apathy of nihilism.[2]

Jung saw an alternative to these two catastrophic results: we must all reclaim our soul, become God-like, Christ-like, a mature parent, a responsible agent for ourselves and others, knowing the difference between good and evil, and making the wiser choice. We must accept how reckless and destructive we can be, like Adam and Eve, to awaken and adhere to a virtuous alignment. Evil is a real and present threat, Jung warns, which is why *Aion* has a more ominous reputation than his other works. Jung wrote:

> The approach of the next Platonic month, namely Aquarius, will constellate the problem of the union of opposites. It will then no

longer be possible to write off evil as the mere privation of good; its real existence will have to be recognized. This problem can be solved neither by philosophy, nor by economics, nor by politics, but only by the individual human being, via his experience of the living spirit.[3]

As Jungian astrologer Liz Green further emphasizes, "Jung stated the shift into the *aion* of Aquarius 'means that man will be essentially God and God, man. The signs pointing in this direction consist in the fact that the cosmic power of self-destruction is given into the hands of man.'"[4]

Jung's reflections in *Aion* leave us with a foreboding and ominous feeling about humanity on the cusp of a new epoch. As we experience the convergence of crisis around us, I think most of us experience a sinking feeling that our civilization is on the brink of collapse and that human blindness and greed are too pervasive and too powerful to amend. We can all feel helpless and immobilized at the sheer magnitude of the tsunami approaching. That moment of existential doubt is precisely when we need to remember the hard-earned lessons from our pilgrimage of the soul. Like my moment of paralysis in class in front of my angry peers, and later in the birth canal on Mount Abang with the Wizard of Bali, we can embrace the challenge of our collective dark night filled with terror, a planetary initiation that could eventually aid our evolution, if we just *put one foot in front of the other*.

THE REUNION OF SHIVA AND BUDDHA

Emily and I are at the highest temple on Bali, Puncak Penulisan, situated on a peak on the Agung Batur caldera, 1,745m above sea level. It's Bali's oldest temple, thought to be built in 300 CE, during Bali's bronze age, well before the Majapahit arrived in the 13–14th century. We've come "to register our soul here," as advised by the wisdom keeper Pak Sedana, the Wizard's trusted ally, who suggested we do a ceremony here to ask Bali for "permission." We're dressed in traditional sarong, we've come with a large quantity of offerings, with sincerity in our hearts, and on behalf of our boys, to ask Mother Bali and all her deities to receive us.

Sedana tells us the Puncak Penulisan Temple contains the meaning of the summit where "sacred records are writen." This is where you register your soul, perhaps as immigrants do when they first arrive in any country. "Once you register, you're granted the blessings for all your spiritual and mundane affairs on the island," he says. This is where your destiny is written, where your soul's sacred purpose is kept in the library of records for eternity. Sedana asked the high priestess of the temple to join us for ceremony, but she couldn't come, so he begins with the offerings and our five short prayers at the base of the temple, requesting our admission before we ascend. We then climb a series of well-worn steps, flanked on both sides by lush jungle. The design of the temple complex is unique, forming a pyramid of seven terraces with 300-stairs covering seven junctures to the top. The seven terraces are symbolic of *sapta loka*, the upper realms of existence in Hindu and Buddhist cosmology. Yes, it's a stairway to heaven, to register our soul's intention in an ethereal hall of records. Once we arrive at the summit, standing between the large iconic split gates that guard the temples of Bali and Java, called *chandi bentar*, the priestess awaits us.

Sedana is a little breathless from the climb up and looks surprised to see her there. He turns to me with a sheepish grin saying, "you have good karma, she wasn't supposed to be here, but she's managed to appear just as we reach the top." He introduces us. Her name is Jero Ning, she's clad in all white and looks young, maybe in her thirties, but most Balinese have a youthful radiance that obscures their age. Her English is good, her smile infectious, as she greets us. She takes us through the gates into the temple's open aired courtyard, surrounded by four gateways in the cardinal directions, perched atop the mountainside peering off onto a sea of clouds with the Indian Ocean beyond. There are old stone-carved statues here, in neat rows, a cacophony of deities, in groups of seven or eight, lifted off the ground by teak wood altars, protected with bamboo thatched roofs. It's simple compared to the ornate, newer Hindu temples. This one is raw and natural, with origins tied to the Bali Mula, the original islanders. We're the only ones here. It's like a dream.

Jero Ning tells me few tourists come here, they mostly head for the mother temple Baisakhi at Mount Agung. In fact, she tells me, even those who do climb the stairways, often don't see the temple when they arrive, they only see the surrounding forest, and return to the road below. I ask if she means they literally can't see the temple. She replies with a wide smile, "Yes, some can't see the temple, for them it remains hidden." It's not a point I take lightly, there is no single monolithic world, there are different worlds for each of us, conditioned by our own perception. Indeed, emptiness, the lack of intrinsic reality, forms the basis for our visualization practice. It's not that we're overlaying a more real and concrete perception atop an already reified world, rather we're cleansing our perception and infusing the actual open, luminous, and fluid nature of reality with a conscious dream so it can reflect back to us a harmonious world. Fortunately for us we were able to experience the temple, receiving from our own unconscious an important initiation, just as Jung's visions on the naked walls of the Baptistry in Ravenna helped him heed and celebrate the life-saving message of his soul.

As we walk barefoot around the shrines along the periphery of the temple courtyard paying respects to the deities, I can feel the smooth mosaic floor beneath my feet. At the center of the courtyard is a flower mandala made of white stones that pop out in contrast to the black lava ones. As we walk to the main shrine at the Eastern gate, the priestess inquires as to why we've come. I tell her we've moved to Bali to start a new life, to raise our family, and be in ceremony with the wisdom keepers. "We've come to Penulisan for blessings," I say, "and to request permission for my pilgrimage to Indonesia, which I've been planning for over a year."

"A pilgrimage?" she asks.

"Yes, I'm bringing my Tibetan lama Geshe Tenzin Zopa and thirty pilgrims to Java and Bali."

Jero's eyes get wide. "When I was a girl I fell into a deep trance,"

Jero Ning tells me. "I started inscribing sacred letters in a book, but no one could understand the language. Eventually I came to this temple, my duty now is to perform the ceremonies here." I found out later that this trance and Jero's ensuing visions were a sign of her spiritual genius and gift to the community, and she was elevated to custodian of the temple. "Many years after my vision," she went on, "some of the visitors of the temple looked closely at the inscription I wrote and thought it might be Tibetan."

I asked if she'd ever received a Tibetan lama here, and she said no. I told her when I bring the group here, I'll ask Geshe-la if he can read the script from her childhood visions. I'm getting an intuition that something fated is unfolding, the mark of the numinous pervades. I ask if she's heard of the Sabdapalon prophecy.

"Yes. When I was a girl, my father told me about it." I urge her to continue. "It's about the time we're living in now," she says, "a time when things are most difficult, many wars, people are confused and act badly."

I ask about Shiva-Buddha agama, what does it mean? She looks at me with tenderness and says, "this temple is Shiva-Buddha, this is the home of Shiva-Buddha, both deities are here." "All these statues around the temple, all these different statues. . . " she gestures elegantly in a circle with her palm facing up, lifting my gaze.

Then suddenly my eyes were open and I notice what I hadn't before, Shiva statues standing side by side with Buddha statues, blending into a harmonious assembly of deities, even Shiva lingams dotting the space along with Buddhist stupas. A perfect reflection of diversity within unity. "No wonder I felt so at home," I thought to myself.

Jero Ning says the Sabdapalon prophesy is about a 500-year period of darkness and separation that is followed by a reuniting of Shiva and Buddha like twins separated at birth. Uniting her hands to prayer position in front of her heart, she said, "It's time for things to come back together again." With each repetition I feel the symbolism deepening past my conceptual mind and whispering to my soul.

"What do you mean?" I pry further.

"Shiva and Buddha were once one, then we got lost in a dark time, and now we must make the two into one again," she says.

"Like merging streams?" I ask, an image of Aquarian Ganymede pouring ether into water flashing across my mind.

"Yes," she says.

"Why is it so important?"

"Because we've lost our way, there will be danger and destruction, we need to bring the mind and the heart back together. We need to purify the soul, otherwise there is too much darkness, too much destruction." She looks at Emily and me with compassion, points to her head and says: "All you Westerners have too much thinking, not enough feeling. I've been praying for Bali and the world for a long time, praying from my heart, in Bali we use our heart, it keeps the volcano, Gunung Agung, silent." She repeats, "The world must feel more with the heart. We need to be still and silent, we need to connect from the heart. . . . This is what Sabdapalone means, it's time to reconnect."

Along our journey we've come across many symbolic couples, separated and longing to reunite. There's the king of reason, the brain's left mode, and the diamond queen of intuition, the right mode, who last reigned together during the Renaissance, which ended around 1600 CE ushering in a period of imbalance that roughly coincides with the five dark centuries prophesized by Sabdapalone and Shambhala. There's King Odysseus lost at sea, separated from his beloved wife Penelope, longing to return home to Ithaca, to source, to the soul. And of course, the mother and daughter of the Eleusinian mysteries, with Demeter and Persephone's emblematic reunion after their terrible hardship of loss and separation. Now we add Shiva and Buddha, symbolically reminding us to unite love (in the world) and liberation (from it) just as a prophesied cataclysm ushers in a new dawn. All these metaphors point to the reconciliation of opposites, the reunion of lost fragments, at the center of the mandala.

Jero places a chanang, a small basket of flowers, at the feet of eight deities against the Eastern wall. As incense envelops us, I think of how they have been watching over the hall of records, the ancient inscriptions, and our soul contracts since beginningless time. Now is the time for reunification, just as the Aquarian age dawns, as the night of dissociation, fragmentation, and destruction is thick upon us. My presence in Bali, finding the Wizard, the magic I've been following, the trail towards the Borobudur mandala, the reemergence of Shiva-Buddha, the Sabdapalone prophesy, uncanny synchronicities with the wisdom keepers, are evidence my unconscious has been guided by universal archetypes active in the collective field.

The three of us walk to the center of the temple courtyard. Sedana sits on a platform under a small thatch roof preparing for ceremony. He has our woven baskets of beautifully arranged flowers and incense ready for us. Jero asks me when my pilgrimage group will arrive in Bali. I say we'll be here the last week in September. She giggles but says nothing. I ask her why.

"Your pilgrimage is during the holiest week of the year for our temple, it's when we celebrate the full moon on September twenty-sixth. You'll be here with the lama and your students, for the holiest time of year, please come," she says. Sedana overhears her invitation, he takes out his phone, looks at the calendar and the dates when I've booked him to help lead our group, then he looks up at me through his thick glasses shrugging his shoulders, and says, "I can't control any of this, this is the divine flow of Bali."

The priestess takes some holy water from a silver vessel off the altar and sprinkles it over us in preparation. We clean our mouth and wash our face. She sits in front of us facing East. At our own pace, silently, as I myself had done with the Wizard repeatedly on my previous trip to Bali, we make the five prayers and flower offerings. This is the first time I'm not looking to someone else for guidance, it's part of me now, the meaning well internalized coming effortlessly through the ritual as it's meant to, rather than clumsily complicated by it.

The priestess begins to chant, and the world slips away. At first, it's a beautiful, soft chant, a faint melodic mantra, and I lean forward to listen. But gradually, and between periods of deep, exaggerated, almost socially inappropriate, sighs, Jero's voice begins to deepen, into another, more robust, almost masculine voice entirely, and the vibration and tone of her chanting shifts into more of a Tibetan style throat singing. She is going into trance, beginning to channel the divine energy. Feeling weightless, I surrender for the ride.

A vision comes to me. It's a varja, the tantric double pronged scepter representing the diamond intuition of emptiness, personified by the female Buddha Prajnaparamita. Years ago I had passed along a similar object, a golden vajra dagger or phurba, to its rightful owner the magician Damien Echols, and now my unconscious was gifting one to me. I see it clearly spinning rapidly on its horizontal axis like a helicopter blade, counterclockwise, surrounded by flames, the way a space shuttle returning to earth at such a speed might catch sparks of fire. The vajra shrinks down to the size of a grain of rice, still rotating, and descends my central channel from the crown, past the throat, and slips into my heart chakra. The moment it merges there I feel incredible waves of sensations, first a release from grasping that feels like the cooling of moonlight luminance described in the stages of dissolution, then an upsurge of reassurance that feels more warming, like the early sun rays of twilight radiance. I intuit that everything is coming together, has a divine purpose, the culmination of my journey, all the trials and tribulations, mysteries and revelations, starts and ends with a single affirmation: *change the vibration*, from constricting fear to quantum openness, from disembodied intellect to intuitive embodiment. I savor and breath as the vajra energy expands beyond my heart engulfing my entire body, creating a voluminous sense of openness as vast as midnight imminence. The world is created *out of* emptiness *through* vibration. It seems difficult to comprehend that statement, but when you're in the divine flow with a master you can easily recognize how sublime subtle energy coursing through your body, generates a blissfully open state no matter the external circumstance. Nothing is more fundamental in determining our experience of the world than these two vibrational settings—fear and openness—they are the difference between living in hell or heaven. On the next breath, within this space of openness, arises a sense of confidence, an unshakable knowing, which feels ever so close to the descriptions of the clear-light transparence of gnosis. Just like in my psychedelic journey, these unadulterated insights are as visceral as they are vivid, but paradoxically as ephemeral and fleeting as a lucid dream. They last only a few flickering moments, but their residual impressions are enduring. There is no objective world out there, only the one we conjure from our vibrational setting or allow malevolent external forces to manipulate to hijack us. That is what all the prophecies about this time are suggesting, from the Seven Fires of the Anishinaabe, the Kalki and Vishnu Purana, Shambhala prophecy, Sabdapalone prophecy, Jung's vision of the dawn of Aquarius, Sri Yutekshwar's commentary of the Dwapara Yuga,[5] and even Graham Hancock's poetic reading of the Lament of Hermes. They're all forecasting something similar. We've descended into a dark age caused by our separation from spirit and have been overcome by hedonism and destruction, we're in a spiritual war between the forces of good and evil, between egocentric blindness and altruistic vision. But we are now entering a bardo, a transition to a new aion, on the upswing of the Great Ages. There is hope rising in the East on the new dawn of a new day. We are it. If only we assume the throne and wear the crown.

Remember, the bardo is a between, a place of liminality pregnant with possibility, a pivotal turning point, for an about-face, for a new future trajectory of civilization. Collapse and creation coming together. Those that can tap the right energetic frequency at the core of our being, loving openness over fearful scarcity, widen their third eye of wisdom, awaken from the nightmare with lucidity, recognize the wrathful onslaught of Mara, the bardo beings mild and fierce, as primarily projections of mind, and turn toward the light of authenticity within unity, will recognize themselves as magicians and conjure a better dream.

Campbell said, "The dark night of the soul comes just before revelation. When everything is lost, and all seems darkness, then comes the new life and all that is needed."[6] The terror of an encroaching cabal, ruthless elites, totalitarianism, AI takeover, ecological and economic collapse . . . these are all projections of our own unintegrated shadow, our own fear-based hallucinations. As long as we remain unwilling or unable to alchemically transmute the poisons of our greed, hatred, prejudice, fear, and ignorance, into the elixirs of confidence, courage, clarity, and divinity, they will be unconsciously projected into the world, ricochet back, and destroy us. But we cannot work top down, we cannot sort through the deluge of information and misinformation with the left mode of intellect alone, we cannot solely use our heads. As Jero suggested, we must "see" or "know" with our hearts, we must drop into the body, plunge below surface appearances into the vast quantum ocean to align with source, embody left-right integration, assume ourselves as angels, and rise aligned together to recreate the world. The fragmented world is but the macrocosmic reflection of our inner fragmentation. The archetype of Aquarius-Leo in its most exalted expression points to each of us claiming our individual authenticity and sovereignty within a sense of communal unity and harmony. If you remember but one thing from the *Bardo Thodol*, let it be that *voidness cannot destroy voidness*, recognition is liberation. Ultimately there is nothing to fear.

Now is the time for Shiva-Buddha, for love and liberation, for us to reunite reason and intuition, mind and heart, heaven and earth, spirit and matter, and return to the world a battle-tested elder ruling over the darker sides of our human nature. The Dwapara Yuga and the Aquarian Age are both characterized as periods of advanced technologies. Concomitant with the rise of AI potentially leading to transhumanism as we risk becoming ever more robotic and digital, is the inverse of this shadow, the rediscovery of organic power tools that can make us ever more exceptional human beings, such as tantra, high magick, plant medicine, esoteric wisdom, each designed to turn us into angels, turn our body into pure vibration, conduits of divine energy and information flow. After years of aimless wandering, we are awakening to realize we're not separate from, and conquerors of, nature but are its most self-conscious expression within the quantum field, the *unus mundus.*

No matter how dark the forces waging war within and against us might be, nothing can harm us if we embody pure view and divine pride. Dharma, meaning reality as it is prior to our projections and hallucinations, is the ultimate refuge, the ultimate protection. Both trauma and peace are vibrational settings within us, and interdependent with the external circumstances. *As within, so without.* The complex task we all face can be focused. Don't allow yourself to be distracted or paralyzed by the magnitude of the external crisis or volume of bad actors around you; make sincere efforts to change your frequency and your perspective on reality will shift. If you're anything like me, *changing the vibration* is neither easy nor lasting, have patience and self-compassion, it's not like there's an on-off switch. When we tip into fear or anger, remember the *Bardo Thodol* teaches us the multifaceted kaleidoscope of external angels and demons and our overblown reactions to them are merely distorted projections, let each of these encounters remind us to do an about-face and turn within. Pause, elongate the out breath, let the karmic storm of paralysis or outrage pass, and then mobilize by focusing on just the next step ahead.

At the conclusion of the ceremony Sedana spoke to Jero in Balinese. He turned to Emily and me and said, "She says there is a lot of goodness in each of you, but you're still not fully ready."

"Not ready for what?" I asked.

"For the direct transmission," he replied. "Jero says by September, in time for your pilgrimage, more will be revealed to you, you must be patient."

I thought to myself: my vision in ceremony is about becoming a suitable conduit for vibration, a human antenna for divine flow. Jero confirms there is more fine tuning to do, perhaps directly with her, with my teacher Geshe-la, or with Bali Herself. The priestess says more will be revealed, and I trust her. Our destiny has been written upon the mystical mountain at Puncak Penulisan. Emily and I leave in awe and reverence.

It's said by the onset of the Dwapara Yuga, the Vedic Bronze Age version of the Great Year, human beings have unimaginably powerful technologies and high degree of intelligence, but relatively scant ethics and wisdom. Eventually and inevitably, we'll recognize how powerful we are, and match our technical prowess with human sensitivity and genius. Many more will be aligned directly with source to let its divine energy flow through us, societal solutions will be developed as a result, and planetary regeneration hastened. At this stage in the cosmic pilgrimage, it's only a relatively few wisdom keepers like the Dalai Lama, Geshe-la, the shamans of the Amazon, first nations elders, and mystics of Bali like Jero Ning who reflect to us what we're all capable of when we tap the source. We're all gods, but we must start acting like them.

THE CHATRA IS NEVER BROKEN

Flash forward several months after my vision of the spinning vajra proclaiming *change the vibration* within Jero Ning's trance atop Puncak Penulisan. Its late September 2023 and we're about to summit another iconic temple structure, the magnificent Borobudur mandala in Java, with my pilgrimage group. After a year of preparation hatching plans with the Wizard, and following the breadcrumb trail of signs I could scarcely comprehend, the time has finally come, but first, we need to introduce the two masters that will set the stage of our historic joint Shiva-Buddha ceremony.

The Belgian anthropologist Patrick Vanhoebrouck receives us at the ashram of his guru, Shiva-tantra master Mangku Jitho, situated in the isolated hills on sacred mount Lawu in Central Java. I've arrived days in advance of the main pilgrimage group with three companions, along with our master Geshe Tenzin Zopa who represents the Buddhist tantra side of the equation. After several days of warming up together, feeling each other out, during joint ceremonies at various holy sites, comingling their Sanskrit and Tibetan mantras with the vibration from their respective tantric bells, the two masters quickly become very fond bedfellows.

Though they share no common spoken language, what they exhibit in their embodiment is something all future world leaders would do well to learn, humility, mutual respect, curiosity, kindness, and above all open-mindedness. Anyone who thinks the time of the guru is dead, or seeks to dismantle the patriarchy, hasn't met the right guru. Both these men have their masculine and feminine energies dialed into perfect alignment, and seem to gel effortless together like jazz sensations Miles Davis and John Coltrane, despite only just meeting.

On the third night, in the ashram's low lit shrine room, the two silhouetted masters both make stunning revelations in the context of determining the nature of the ceremony they will co-lead with my group at the top of the mandala. Mangku Jitho discloses that during the pandemic he had been approached by a committee overseeing the Borobudur with questions about its chatra, the crown above the center most stupa, prompting him to consult the spirits of the land around the monument as an intermediary. Several nights before we arrived Jitho had a dream that a Buddhist entourage of five visited him at his ashram for an important mission, among them was His Holiness the Dalia Lama. The dream was an omen for our group's arrival days later serendipitously coinciding with *tilam*, the astrologically significant "dark moon," when it appears missing in the night sky, just before a new lunar cycle. Like stones slowly inlaid in a mosaic, Jitho eventually grasped the bigger picture concluding that now was time for the chatra of the Borobudur to be regenerated. You see, while the entire complex of the largest mandala structure in the world is very well preserved, the central spire, or crown, that usually sits atop the stupa at the summit's center is mysteriously missing. Given how magnificent and ornate the monument is, this missing piece is barely noticeable to the ordinary eye. The fact remains, the chatra is broken, the symbol of world unity is incomplete.

Mangku Jitho predicts that a joint Shiva-Buddha ceremony, a confluence of twin tantric traditions, as may have been performed at Borobudur centuries ago by the Singhasari kings, and later Majapahit priests, could now, once again, be enacted between he, Geshe Tenzin Zopa and our group to complete the chatra, and make whole a symbol of peace during a time of great chaos. Seen in this light, the Borobudur mandala may be more than a ritual site, perhaps it's an ancient technology, situated in just the right geographic location, built with unimaginably precise cosmological alignments, and designed to widely broadcast a vital message (recall figure 9.1 on p. 254). By reactivating the chatra, we'll turn the dormant mandala back on.

Geshe Zopa concurred enthusiastically, disclosing that he too had been pushing for years for the chatra to be restored, even presenting a petition to the Indonesian government following an inter-faith conference at the monument, and emphatically advocating the importance of completing the symbol of peace and harmony. Like seeds scattered to the wind, the petition seemingly never took hold. But very palpable creative sparks were now flying between the two masters—we all felt what Jung meant by the unconscious being activated—as the synergy and synchronicity of our long-awaited meeting built towards a crescendo in the darkness of the shrine room. In Mangku Jitho's reflection, Geshe Zopa had met an equally adept and committed partner to the cosmic cause.

The only problem was where the hell is the chatra? Do we find it buried somewhere and unearth it like the Antikythera mechanism off the coast of Greece or the lost Gobecli Tepi complex in Southern Turkey? Do we rebuild it? If so, who rebuilds it, out of what materials, according to what design, and who gets to install it? My thoughts raced, but were proven to be overly rational and reductionist. Mangku Jitho's poignant solution, like any qualified spiritual master, was so far outside the box of my limited thinking, as Vanhoebrouck translated, "the chatra is not restored physically, but energetically." Geshe-la quietly nodded his head with a cheeky smile that suggested he had been in uncanny coherence with Jitho all along, from the moment they met, right up to the plan they would execute.

As we have seen, the tantras, the so-called *resultant vehicle* of both Shaivism and Buddhism, begin their meditative practices with the end, like the snake eating its tail, assuming the destination first, envisioning oneself dissolving then arising as an enlightened deity at the center of the mandala, and then circumambulating backwards to manifest awakening in the ordinary world. Counter intuitive to conventional thinking or exoteric practice, esoteric traditions work backwards by "remembering" that divinity is our natural state, rather than gradually progressing forwards from an ordinary state of imperfection towards an exalted goal. First you change the inner vision and vibration to peace, then you rebuild the outer world to match that signature. "Wow. Of course!" I recollected the vajra vision I had atop Pencak Penulisan, "to change the vibration," and Jero Ning's mysterious prediction that "more would be revealed" by the time my pilgrimage rolled around, and low and behold here we are, not only about to reunite Shiva and Buddha, but energetically recrown the Borobudur, bringing it back to life.

I reflected on the implications of our newly hatched ceremony for the future, on our restoring civilization, on rebuilding anything for that matter, your body after injury, your relations after betrayal, from the bardo before rebirth, begin first by channeling the right energy, frequency, and vibration within. Recall in our visualization practice following the stages of dissolution, out of emptiness, emerges the seed syllable or mantra vibration, then the appearance of the deity dawns. This casts a different light on the often-cited Biblical verse from John 1:1 "In the beginning was the Word, and the Word was with God, and the Word was God." The Word, from the Greek *logos*, is the divine force that creates the manifest world, the first principle of order that shapes chaos, and comes to represent Jesus, God's heavenly love incarnate on earth. We're talking about the virtuously aligned energy within us being the most powerful force of creation, and possibly as an extension, how ancient monolithic structures may have harnessed and amplified that energy like a modern day nuclear reactor.

Imagine with me now, in the context of civilizational collapse and regeneration, that we replicate the ceremony at Borobudur elsewhere, reactivating ancient monolithic structures across the planet from the nearby enigmatic pyramid Gunung Padang in West Java dated inconceivably to 20,000 years old, to Angkor Wat in Cambodia, largest religious monument in the world, and beyond, each ingeniously designed by our ancestors to be energy conduits, resurrecting them like Lazarus from the dead to perform their originally intended purpose, to widely broadcast much needed signals of healing, peace, and harmony through the world. Imagine not one but hundreds of these structures forming a vast network of spiritual cell towers are "switched on." Perhaps I've lost you, the idea seems so far-fetched, bordering on sci-fi fantasy or worse New Age psychobabble.

I draw upon biologist Rupert Sheldrake's theories, which propose that corresponding human thought patterns or energetic signatures can influence each other across time and space in what he calls *morphic resonance* through nonphysical networks shaping physical reality and behavior he calls *morphic fields.* Our morphic resonance across these fields Sheldrake contends is what underlies, for example, the documented efficacy of intercessory prayer explaining how our intentions and thoughts can have a profound healing impact on others whom we feel connected with or concerned about, even at a distance and without them knowing. It's not such a unique or modern concept admits Sheldrake, "Even Einstein's space-time field of gravitation is a universal, cosmic field holding everything together and linking the entire universe, in fact, making it a uni-verse. It does the same thing as the World Soul or Anima Mundi of neo-Platonic philosophy. It embraces the whole cosmos. There are levels upon levels of morphic fields within fields, within which we are embedded. Human life is embedded in vastly larger fields of organization."[7]

It's fascinating to speculate about the possible roles of precisely designed monolithic structures as conduits for human energy and intention. Unexplainably, there are sets of three pyramids within a single complex whose dimensions may correlate with the three stars in the belt of the constellation of Orion, found wide distances apart at Teotihuacan, Mexico City, Giza, Egypt, and Xi'an, China. Their similar design may have a common underlying wisdom long forgotten in history, and their purpose as energy conduits or antenna may have relied on an interconnected web known only recently in science as morphic fields. Scholar of sacred geometry Robert Gilbert suggests this "invisible energy matrix, which is the source of all physical manifestation" was well known and manipulated millennia ago by the so-called *Masters of the Net* of ancient Egypt.[8] The speculative notion that various ancient civilizations may have cultivated an inner or esoteric science, possibly with a much older common origin, and then used these massive structures to harness and emit subtle energy during initiation, has gained popularity through the works of Hancock, Bauval, West, Silva, Wilcock, and others but is dismissed by mainstream archeologists.[9] As the paradigm pendulum swings from scientific reductionism back towards the center, as we remember more of who we are awakening from the slumber of amnesia, perhaps we'll see more public receptivity and a deeper unearthing by scholars substantiating these more mystically inclined theories about monolithic structures.

If talk of using high technology to broadcast human energy and intentions remains too obscure a notion, then leave that aside for a moment and focus on the more important premise. Ancient civilizations the world over understood a well-initiated human mind itself to be the most powerful technology on the planet. From Egypt to Greece, India to Tibet, cultures developed soul science and inner tech to advance human evolution towards metaphoric golden ages. The advance technology these physical megalithic structures represent, while important, pales in comparison to what the ancients knew about our god-like capacity for destruction and creation. This couldn't be more relevant to what we survived during the pandemic. It wasn't a virus that killed us as much as the widespread contagion of fear. The subtle energetic signature of terror within each human mind was, intentionally or not, hijacked and amplified across all countries by the interrelated network of government, media, and technology, leading to, for the first time in human history, an utter global lockdown with incalculable devastation. If such a dramatic consequence is possible, what might the inverse look like, if modern cultures reclaimed their ancient soul sciences, understood humankind's innate divinity, harnessed virtuous intentions, and spread a contagion of love and openness across interconnected fields? Shambhala is not found in any specific location but is realized anywhere on earth when we embody the right energy together.

ENTER THE MANDALA, LIVE THE MYTH

As the two masters uncovered a plan for ceremony, Vanhoebrouck remarked to me, "this is very powerful, what we are about to do together hasn't happened here in five centuries, and it will have massive ripple effects on the future of the planet." And though he didn't mention it, we caught a glimpse in each other's eyes, and I knew we were both thinking about the Sabdapalon prophesy. The time for the return of the king is now. There is no way to rationally explain how independent of each other Patrick and I, two strangers, both had the same, very specific vision of our masters from disparate traditions in a joint ceremony belonging to a religion long since passed, atop the largest mandala in the world. Likewise, there is no rational explanation for how, independent of each other, both those masters, Jitho and Zopa, had recognized the importance of restoring the chatra, making the mandala whole again, "switching it on," inconceivably through vision and vibration alone. And there is no rational explanation for how the four of us all came together on sacred Mount Lawu, combining diverse prophesies, visions, dreams, and synchronicities, into a single unified tapestry, so that pilgrims from around the world could commune in ceremony to reactivate a monument from slumber after five centuries, at the time when darkness is descending upon our civilization. All this defies logic but remains true.

Campbell, Jung, the tantras, and Sheldrake, however, might all concur very comfortably, that there is indeed an esoteric explanation outside the limited box of the current paradigm, knowing well that there is morphic resonance through morphic fields, as well as the timeless alchemical principle of correspondences, revealing complementary forces in cyclic motion beyond what our five senses can perceive, which help us to align the signatures of the stars in the cosmos above, with the universal archetypes in the collective unconscious in the psyche below, synchronizing them, so that their encoded symbolic meaning is deciphered, and a potent opportunity for transformation seized, by those who have been made ready by initiation.

Hopefully by now you're enticed to join us for our epic pilgrimage through the Borobudur, to not only enter its three nested physical structures—the mandala, stupa at its center, and chatra at its top—but also delve into their symbolism, living out the mythology revealed by the interplay of cosmos and psyche. To the skeptic, these three edifices may seem mere remnants of a forgotten era, a pile of neatly arranged rocks left behind by a primitive, superstitious civilization to bake in the sun, devoid of significance in a disenchanted world. Yet, having traversed the winding paths of our shared Elixir odyssey, may you now tread in our footsteps across the megalithic stones of the Javanese landscape, guided by the whispers of intuition and heeding the mythic signs of the soulscape, with your third eye aglow.

Our intrepid band of pilgrims, led by twin masters embodying the dual traditions of Shiva and Buddha, converges at the mandala's base for ritual ablution—water purification—preparing us to cross the threshold between worlds. Mangku Jitho, garbed in pristine white, reminiscent of the father drop that descends from the crown in the subtle body pilgrimage, while Geshe Zopa, draped in crimson robes, resembling the mother drop that ascends from the navel, each begin to draw closer together towards the heart nexus after centuries of separation. The mandala, the first symbol, an enigmatic womb of rebirth, becomes our crucible for alchemy, where masculine and feminine, light and shadow, reconcile their differences to find union. The monolithic structure beckons us to transcend the mundane, circumambulating its periphery, traversing its labyrinthine corridors past its 2500 empowering reliefs, ascending consciousness through levels and stairways, guiding us to shed the snake's skin, transmuting human poisons into healing elixirs.

Reaching the mandala's summit, we next encounter the stupa, the second symbol, the vessel of emptiness, Dharmakaya, the boundless openness permitting the utter transformability of all manifest phenomena. Voidness can never destroy voidness. Therefore, there's nothing to fear. Here, after three prostrations, Geshe-la kindly confers upon us the Bodhisattva vows, each of us resolving to use every single moment, over every single lifetime, for as long as space endures and for as long as beings exist, to awaken and dispel the misery in the world. Out of the vast horizon of infinite possibilities, a singular resonance, one specific vibration, love, the logos, is called forth from the womb to reconstruct ourselves and the world.

Following the vows, the group surround the stupa on the uppermost platform, ourselves encircled by a ring of 72 Buddhas, the complete celestial dial of the precession of the equinoxes, all looking skyward where the third symbol, the physical chatra, remains a missing piece, rendering the entire mandala inert. An outer reflection mirroring our inner fractures and wounds, echoing across fragmented societies and a world on the brink. Amidst the tumult of five centuries past—an odyssey through volcanic eruptions, political upheavals, paradigm shifts, and the global pandemic portal of 2020, Mangku Jitho, the father drop, and Geshe Zopa, the mother drop, finally reach the center point of the womb, to activate the spiritual gene with crystal clear visualization and high frequency vibration. The buddha nature embryo, known as the indestructible drop, finally merges with mother-father drops, the trinity gestating a new Bodhisattva being, just as the long-awaited reunion of Shiva and Buddha heralds a return to primordial unity, where individual consciousness dissolves into the cosmic ocean, coalescing in a timeless embrace with the eternal.

In the hush of revelation, the diamond queen whispers, "change the vibration, from fear to love." In the beginning was the word, and the word was God. Every sacred journey asks us to die to be reborn, to go through the dark night to find the new dawn, to be so thoroughly consumed by the scorching self-immolating fire of our worst-case fears, that nothing remains but our authentic voice, the sublime song of our soul. Can you hear it? Eventually, remerging from unity, returning to separation, there and back again, to our senses, I recalled how surreal life is, like a waking dream, and savored the last few fleeting moments in the illusion-like aftermath, awash in peace and harmony.

It's not often one gets a chance to partake in such a historic occasion, perhaps once in a lifetime if we're lucky. Of course, we never wanted that feeling to end, we wanted to remain there in the ineffable equipoise of awe at the summit of the Borobudur, but every heroine who finally claims her crown, must make her way back down to the villages below, to rouse others from slumber, restore order, redeem missteps, and rebuild anew.

Less than a year later, April 2024, a committee sanctioned by the Indonesian government announced plans to restore the physical chatra, the seed of Zopa's petition once scattered to the wind finally finding fertile ground.[10] The unfolding events of our group pilgrimage to Borobudur, the historic Shiva-Buddha ceremony led by Geshe Zopa and Mangku Jitho, and the mythopoetic implications of these archetypal symbols for our global civilization at this time of transition, are all captured in a stunning documentary mini-series by filmmaker Matthew Freidell called the Missing Peace and hosted for free on Youtube. The series playlist can be accessed with this QR code.

THE LAST STAND

As I proposed at the outset, we're amid a convergence of crisis, with every sector of society in need of a reboot. Just as the tide is shifting between aions, people's movements are emerging across the globe to push back on authoritarian, top-down control—the old guard giving way to the new—but not without a final struggle. Just as the prophecies have foretold, and just as our cyclic diagrams have illustrated in this book, we're circumambulating counterclockwise, heading into a period best described as *going back to move forward*; a revolution, revival, reunion, reclaiming, restoring, and even a return of king and queen.

Perhaps it will be another pandemic, banking and economic collapse, or energy crisis. Some argue that the ecological crisis is primed to be exploited as a terror tactic forcing us into unnecessarily austerity measures with little tangible environmental benefits.[11] A central bank digital currency combined with a social merit system could be surreptitiously introduced for "our safety and convenience," but if we look at how Chinese dissidents were tracked and restricted from their own monies for expressing views counter to the state, or how the truckers' protesting in Canada had their bank accounts frozen for disagreeing with the government's position, we see how it can easily be used as a method of totalitarian social control.

Like the pandemic and the post 9/11 "war on terror" before it, fear of an invisible threat is being weaponized for population control to further the interests of a few at the expense of most of the world. That is, unless we the people have the presence of mind, the counter force of virtuous energy, and the courage to reunite and resist.

I'm reminded when I was a schoolchild in Hong Kong of the iconic image of "Tank Man" the sole objector to the brutal military crackdown of the peaceful student protest during the 1989 Tiananmen Square massacre in China. His bravery standing defenseless in defiance in front of a tank is forever seared in our collective memory. It was a David versus Goliath moment, but the celestial tides have turned. No longer do we await rescue from a solitary, extraordinary hero, the incoming archetype is that of an army of ordinary people, you and I, expressing unique differences, but united in a common cause. Gandhi called it a truth-act (satyagraha), the masses finding alignment in truth and quantum open-mindedness and standing up straight with conviction, having pulled sword from stone, to participate in a nonviolent revolution (of The Ages) against mass deception and authoritarian thought control, the likes of which George Orwell and Aldous Huxley predicted. [12] It's not the 1% who hold the power, it's the rest of us, if we can unite. Although wisdom dispels fear, our greatest enemy, we still need compassion, our greatest ally, to act in the world. Yet another example of nonduality, the merging of twin streams, wisdom and compassion, a union that dispels the delusion of separateness.

For the Buddhist, compassion is galvanized through the bodhisattva resolve which will underlie the intelligent redesign of social systems and ethical alternatives to the diabolical conditions of materialism we've been collectively complicit in over the last hundred years. This is a stand of another kind; it creatively redirects our efforts so we can manifest a new world born of a clearer vision and purer motivation. The inner stand, a lunar journey, stops the compulsive revolution of fear, greed, and hatred that fuels our collective self-harm, while the other, the outer stand, a solar journey, moves backward to move forward, from the ashes of societal collapse, reviving lost ancestral wisdom, regenerating sustainable solutions, and reuniting fragmented society just as the Shambhala civilization mythopoetically describes the Kalachakra tantra. Shambhala exists wherever those aligned in pure energy build together a mandala in their external reality.

This book has focused on our inner revolution, the lunar quest. Meanwhile the seeds for outer revolution, the solar quest, are already planted and even sprouting. *As within, so without.* Just look carefully. In the energy sector we are disrupting Big Oil with renewables such as solar, hydro, wind, geo-thermal, and ethically guided nuclear power. Of course we'll need to be vigilant that renewables themselves don't become a new Trojan horse used by power hungry elites to mislead us, leveraging increased social controls, and catalyzing a massive wealth transfer with no tangible net impact on the environment. Banking cartels and fiat currency are being displaced by crypto currency, not the central bank variety but the decentralized version on the block chain, with greater transparency, in peer-to-peer networks with no middleman, allowing us to reclaim the true spirt of free market capitalism underpinned by an ethical heart. We are calling out Big Ag—monoculture industrial farming and Frankenstein food production—for depleting the topsoil and making our populations sick for profit, while returning (like Tjok Gde in Bali) to the heritage methods of our ancestors who cultivated local, seasonal, fresh, and nutrient rich food grown with naturally regenerative farming methods. Massive multinational corporations that have genetically altered and reengineered our food beyond recognition, spiking it with so much addictive salt, sugar, and fat—essentially turning the population into junkies—show a complete lack of consideration for ethics and our wellbeing. The masses may soon rally to divest, voting to spend their money elsewhere, showing where true power lies.

In Bali, a hundred years ago, they had no need for waste management systems because everything produced and consumed was naturally biodegradable and flowed in a natural circle economy. Now single use plastic underpinned by a disposable mentality of convenience chokes the rivers that carry sacred *tirta*, like plaque clogs the arteries of the human heart. Once again, we are beginning to overcome these challenges by looking back at our ancestral ways for answers, most especially the underlying holistic worldview of interconnectivity, reverence, and reciprocity that can make life on this planet sustainable.

Next, the medical industrial complex, with its reliance on Big Pharma, high tech surgeries few can afford, and soulless, overly rational doctors, are experiencing a mounting backlash, as we turn to the past for natural, holistic, and preventative remedies, soul-centered healers, psychedelic therapies, and traditional forms of healing that are land-based, communal, and cost-effective at their roots.

As for the corrupt governments and politics that have swung to ideological extremes, fascist style nationalism and single-group supremacy on one side versus neo-Marxist style communism and "wokism" on the other, these will eventually burn themselves out, and the remaining preponderance of moderate minded, tolerant people who respect real diversity of viewpoint will wake up and see through the fifth-generation warfare tactics that seek to pit us against one another, dividing and conquering over partisan lines. If we want to instill hope in our future, we must re-infuse spirit into governance embodying some version of the Shiva-Buddha creed of "unity in diversity."

What I've observed in Bali is that while the economy and politics ostensibly default to the *banjar*, the local community governance of each village, to maintain law and order, the entire island remains unified under the Tri Hita Karana philosophy of harmony, which, as you may remember, optimizes a three-fold relationship between other human beings, mother nature, and the spirit realm. As individuals move to reconnect with spirit, the governments of largely secular societies that comprise our post-industrial world must accept they have lost the trust and confidence of the people and failed to unify them with a common vision and set of values while respecting their individual differences. The Dalia Lama's secular ethics for a new millennium, not a Trojan horse for Buddhist conversion, but inspired by the Kalachakra tantra and Shambhala vision, offers intelligent recommendations for secular societies to re-infuse humanist principles of ethics, mindfulness, compassion, eco-sensitivity, and sustainability that have been lost through modernization. [13] As we reclaim the individual soul, we'll likewise reclaim society's collective soul, lest its shadow emerges as another in-group's hegemony.

PLANETARY RITE OF PASSAGE: A SECOND SHOCK

As I hypothesized at the outset, each crisis converging around us today is underpinned by our fragmentation from soul, our disenchantment from the natural world, our being overrun by shortsighted and self-centered drives of greed, hatred, and prejudice. I'm cautiously optimistic that the tell-tale signs of societal decline and degeneration are potentially self-generated opportunities for alchemical transmutation. The collective unconscious may be hastening a global death process so we can be reborn; we're coming undone at the seams, precisely so we can be reassembled around a more awakened ethos. The wisdom of the Elixir journey is to never avoid or waste a good crisis, but to bravely seize it as a doorway to regeneration.

After years of stability and growth, like all natural cycles, we've hit our collective tipping point, and face civilizational decline, precisely because the time is ripe, above and below, for composing the next chapter of our collective evolution. It's not a conscious, suicidal death wish, but perhaps an impulse from the soul to rouse ourselves from slumber, a rude awakening. This is a planetary rite of passage to end our collective innocence and obedience, a developmental next step towards maturity, allowing each of our inner gurus to take responsibility for our destiny. It's time to eat the apple, leave the garden, and each become what we were meant to be.

The author, futurist, and psychedelic researcher Daniel Pinchbeck seems to think so. He suggested in his epic lecture "Planetary Initiation" in 2016, that due to our blindness in jettisoning tractional rites of passage, Western culture may have unconsciously created the causes and conditions for a self-imposed "shock" to our system, a metaphoric Zen caning, to help us awaken. Pinchbeck's poignant remarks touch on themes similar to the ones I have drawn on in this book, weaving together traditional wisdom and neuroscience with psychedelics and cultural critique, to suggest that the collective unconscious may be guiding us, not tripping us up. Pinchbeck writes:

> An idea that the thinker Joseph Chilton Pearce developed in his book, *The Biology of Transcendence* is that although the prefrontal cortex develops through adolescence, it actually requires a second kind of artificial shock to reach its full functioning. And that's why all these Indigenous and traditional cultures around the world have initiation ceremonies that are often very difficult. They could involve the psychedelic experience through ayahuasca or peyote. Or they might involve in Australian Aboriginal culture the walkabout, where people have to fast and go on vision quests in the wilderness and so on.

Modern civilization was the first one that did away with these types of initiation events, and therefore people develop without that second shock which potentially leads them to shift from a purely egoic sense of identity to a more kind of transpersonal state of consciousness. Which even if you only have that experience a few times can act as a kind of permanent reference point, where you're aware that on some level there's a unity of consciousness underlying your separate identity.

Western modern civilization ended up kind of caught in a trap locked in its egoic structure, and based our whole trip on kind of hyperindividualism, accumulation of resources, and so on. And we've now reached a point where we can't go further than that. And in a sense we could look at the idea that we've subconsciously, unconsciously, somehow self-willed this ecological crisis to bring about our own transformation, our own transcendence.[14]

A FINAL PLEDGE

It's been a multi-year odyssey, one that began with panic attacks on the bustling island of Manhattan, followed by a vision on the sacred island of Ithaka in Greece, that carried me through the collective dark night of the pandemic, landed my family and I on the other side on the tantric island of Bali, and culminated with our group pilgrimage and Shiva-Buddha ceremony atop the magnificent Borobudur mandala. Along the way, I followed the hero threads of cosmology, mythology, pilgrimage, prophecy, psychedelic medicine, Tibetan alchemy, and Jungian psychology into the labyrinth, where I encountered dark forces of personal despair and mass deception, but where too the light of my soul and the confidence to speak my truth were revealed. A single theme underlies the world's esoteric literature: *solve et coagula*. To die to be reborn. Likewise, a single image repeats itself over the centuries, the mandala, the womb of integration, from the Hermetics of Egypt and Greeks, to the Shiva and Buddhist tantras of India and Tibet, to the medieval alchemists to Jung.

My search for the elixir—and my return, still unfolding—has changed me. I'm no longer the same person. I live a mythological life now, guided by the stars above and the diamond queen within. I sold my house and all my possessions. I no longer practice therapy in the same way, gone is the cinder block Manhattan office, and the collared shirt. Now I am equally adept in the shadows, while most seek solely the light. I have fewer clients, and I don't mind. My marketing strategy is not based on sensationalized messaging or Instagram followers but on aligning with the right vibration and good, old fashion word of mouth. My method is madness, a Dionysian descent into chaos, while most seek order. My *therapeia* are pilgrimage and psychedelics, inner and outer journeys through the underworld. My colleagues are wisdom keepers not psychiatrists. My goal is not transcendence from the world, but wise embodiment within it.

My two boys are no longer captive in a concrete jungle, spoon-fed right-left extreme ideologies, trained to sit long hours memorizing data, placed on a cocktail of potent medications to control the symptoms of their souls screaming out how unnatural their world has become. Rather they're being raised without walls, in sacred ceremony, surrounded by spirit trees, the diamond queen of their imaginations inhabiting their young active bodies rightfully encouraged to play and run wild.

As for me, I'm still slow cooking on my journey home, riding the rite-of-passage-induced aftershocks necessary for rebirth. Although Emily and I made it to the other side of the planet having followed the magic, and trice island-hopped, we're still not yet integrated into Balinese society, and can't claim this as our final stop. It's a reminder that wherever we arrive in life, be it a place, with a person, or an accomplishment, is only a milestone in the journey, better seen as a new jumping off point. The chapters of the eternal saga never end. What's more important than the destination, is granting the soul permission to lead us on a ride. *That has been the main point of this entire book.*

Make your pledge, affirm your sacred bodhisattva vows: *Sentient beings are numberless; I vow to save them all. Traumatic afflictions are inexhaustible; I vow to alchemize them. The supreme truth of emptiness is incomprehensible; I vow to actualize it completely. The great awakening is unattainable; I vow to embody it eternally for the benefit of others.* Now, hear the cries of your loved ones, strangers, and adversaries, even Mother Nature herself, drowning in the deluge of samsara's delusions and afflictions, set off from the Diamond Throne under the Bodhi tree connecting heaven, earth, and hell, on your onerous return journey, the slow cook of integration back into ego, from the brink of the void, from the formless event horizon, back into form, from the special realm of the numinous and the eternal, back into the limitations of space, time, and matter, as an avatar of wise altruism, compelled by the bodhisattva vision and resolve.

In your left hand you bear the holy grail of Christ, the upturned skull cup of Vajrayogini, the kykeon chalice of Demeter, the wine horn of Dionysus, containing the elixir of immortality, while in the right hand you hold the sword of discriminating wisdom, the wand, the staff, the vajra, the ceremonial pipe, high above your crown. Whomever is ready to receive this ambrosia, this amrita, this nectar, and through it gain, as you have, eternal life, let them drink, but temper your compassion with discernment, for this secret, this sacrament, this boon, this *elixir*, is only for those who are ready, lest they become dangerously drunk, mad, or self-consumed. What you give with the left hand, you guard with the right, you must know the difference between the two, and who is ripe to benefit in their own time.

We've come full circle, the alpha is the omega, the ouroboros snake eats its tail, through departure, initiation to return, through ego, shadow, to Self and back, from death, through bardo, to rebirth again, it is accomplished. The mandala is constructed, consecrated, destroyed, and recreated. The turning of The Ages in the firmament above is calling for a regeneration of the planet, just as the collective psyche below calls for a reunion from separation. We have already done it. The chatra is complete. All of us feel now our purpose is fulfilled. It's a big dream, but one that has been transmitted to those with eyes to see and ears to hear throughout all epochs, in the pilgrimage of the cosmos without beginning, through all twelve signs of the zodiac and each archetypal civilization, across vastly discrete esoteric cultures from Greece to Tibet, without interruption since time immemorial. Let your king of reason unite with the diamond queen of intuition, taking up chalice and sword, to rule with wisdom and compassion, uncompromisingly in the dual revolutionary stands, inner and outer, lunar and solar, for personal authenticity and civil freedom, for love and liberation, for self and other, for this life and the next. Knowing our planet's destiny—a treacherous dragon guarding a marvelous treasure—none of us can afford to think small.

Nostos:
The Return of Longing

Phil Cousineau

And so as long as you haven't experienced this: to die so as
*   to grow,*
You will remain a troubled guest on this dark earth.

FROM THE HOLY LONGING,
JOHANN WOLFGANG VON GOETHE, 1814

In 1984, I co-led an art, literary, and mythology tour around Ireland with the poet Robert Bly and the storyteller Gioia Timpanelli, in search of the Celtic Mysteries. One night, in front of the flickering peat fireplace at the legendary Shelbourne Hotel in Dublin, I gathered our group to listen to Bly recite a few of his own poems and then several of his notable translations, including Goethe's famous verses. The choice was uncanny in the way it evoked the mythic yearning at the heart of our quest. The moment Bly intoned the plangent last lines, I heard an echo of the great Irish writers who had frequented the famous hotel, such as W. B. Yeats, James Joyce, Edna O'Brien, and

Seamus Heaney, often capturing in their work the deep Irish reverence for the soulful life.

To die so as to grow is not only a marvelous poetic phrase, it is the metaphysical realization that spiritually-minded people throughout the ages have experienced whenever they ventured deep into the underworld to confront the dark forces of their nature and emerged from the great pilgrimage grasping what Dr. Miles Neale calls here, in *Return with Elixir*, the elusive boon of regeneration treasure.

By *elixir*, the author is referring to one of the most numinous words in the language, dating as it does back to the Arabic word *al-iksir*, and beyond that to the Greek *xerion*, a powder for drying wounds. In Miles's usage, an *elixir* is a potent solution (in every sense of the word) that helps seekers recover from their wounds. The damage might come from the searing knowledge of one's own mortality, the injury could be psychological or physical, or the pain the result of encounters with our modern political and environmental catastrophes. Despite the wide range of wounds, there are a variety of cures to deal with them, and there is often beauty in the scars we bear. This word "wound" too, has deep roots, as evidenced in our use of *bless*, from the French *blesseur*, "to wound," which suggests that often our true blessing can be found in our wounds. If we learn, as Miles Neale strives to prove here, how to truly deal with them.

For Miles, this implies returning to our most trustworthy elixirs in three main ways: mythically, psychologically, and alchemically. This requires a movement to the timeless source, the ground of all being, if we are to find what he terms "the path of regeneration," and discover or rediscover the secret of immortal life. For this reader, the road resembles not the usual one-time circular journey but a spiral one, which turns tighter and tighter in on itself until it reaches the center of the labyrinth of our own inner world. Turn again and again, as Yeats suggested in his poem about the ever-widening gyre, or as the historian of religion Mircea Eliade revealed in his evocation of the "eternal return" to the sacred origins of existence, or the depth psychologist James Hillman who advocated a "revisioning of the soul."

And then there is the numinous notion of T. S. Eliot, expressed in his melodic *Four Quartets*, "We shall not cease from exploration. And the end of our exploring will be to arrive where we started and know the place for the first time."

In this ambrosial book, Miles evokes several rhapsodies on this theme of conscious dying in the service of conscientious living. His mythopoetics reveals an urge to develop a series of practices to aid our psychological well-being and take the necessary pilgrimage to "reclaim the soul." If the reader has detected here a certain repetition of "re" words, that is no accident. Years ago, in 2004, during a panel at the Mythic Journeys Conference in Atlanta, James Hillman told me that when in doubt about the vitality of one's inner life, we might consider placing exactly that prefix in front of our verbs. "The use of *re* signals a turning back to the depths," he reflected, "so we might 'reintegrate,' 'revivify,' 'rejuvenate,' or even 'reorient' ourselves."

I remember feeling refreshed by the idea.

Still, I need to express a graceful caveat. The guidelines for an effective return to the healing elixirs that have been developed over the centuries do not necessarily point us "forward and upward," which happens to be the trajectory of the *spirit*, but "back and down," the movement that follows the true direction of the *soul*.

The psychologist and literary critic Edwin Edinger writes in his study *Moby-Dick: An American Nekyia*, a reference to the underworld journey in the Greek myths, is back in time and down into inner space. The descent feels more like agony than ecstasy because it hurts to grow, painful to expand our consciousness. The psychodynamic instruction for youth may be to "Grow up!" into the spiritual realms—but the recommendation for later life reverses the direction so we might "Grow down," down into the soul. The danger for psychological health is that the relentless move up, up, and away into the future is invariably the service of the ego, whereas the move down into the depths uncovers the rich loamy soil of the underworld.

The wisdom of knowing the difference is vertiginously expressed by the Danish philosopher Soren Kierkegaard, "Life must be lived forwards but understood backwards."

Regarding the return journey, I think now of the great innovation made by my own mentor, the mythologist Joseph Campbell, when he taught early iterations of the hero's quest to his students at Sarah Lawrence College. When I interviewed him at his home in Honolulu, in 1985, the doughty scholar became animated and drew a circle in the air with his forefinger and then exclaimed in a high-pitched voice that he used to inform his classes, "This is your soul!" Then he drew a wavy line through the middle of the imaginary circle to delineate between the upper and lower worlds, waking and dream, and finally added a flourish of arrows to express the direction of the journey—which wasn't *clockwise* but *counterclockwise*. To underscore his pedagogical point, Campbell insisted that ordinary waking life takes place in *chronological* time, but the *extraordinary* life occurs in Kairos or sacred time. This is an invaluable distinction because he helps explain why dreams, stories, art, and all manners of soul work create the uncanny feeling of *stopping time*.

Many years later, I found my notes of our interview in an old spiral notebook, reminding me how he added, "Besides, eternity isn't measured in the length of time but in its intensity."

As he does throughout his book, Miles reminds us that returning to the elixir, the true essence of our existence, the treasure of immortal life, requires courage as well as a certain cartography. Fortunately, he provides us with thorough maps of the inner realms to help the reader navigate the labyrinthine paths of the soul, which he has culled from his lifelong studies in mythology, depth psychology, Tibetan alchemy, Jung's individuation, archetypal movies, and the reports of his many patients and students. While we often think of the marvelous mythologem of the gold thread as the main source of help for the hero who negotiates the labyrinth, there is another one, more troublesome, but just as useful, which Campbell called "the *dark* thread."

I first heard-tell of the trickster scholar's description of this mythic image at his home in the heart of Greenwich Village, in the spring of

1987, when he insisted that the telltale sign of true art was a certain black thread that ran through a piece of music, a painting, a song, a poem, or an epic. When I asked him what it signified, he said without hesitation, "The black thread is an indication of our mortality, the ever-present reminder of death." I never for a moment thought the image was morbid but remember feeling grateful that he added that the inclusion of the metaphorical thread reflected a robust consciousness, one that helps us glean meaning out of our lives, especially in times of crisis, as we are experiencing.

Since that coruscating conversation I've come to admire the remarkable "Havana Lectures," from 1937, delivered by the Spanish poet and playwright Federico Garcia Lorca. There, Lorca describes what many experience but few can name, the role of *duende*, "the spirit of the earth," the alternating light and dark current of the soul, what Lorca's translators have called "the blood surge," a pulsing image of the presence of death lurking over our shoulder. Lorca quotes a master-guitarist as telling him, "The duende isn't in the throat but in the soles of the feet," in contact with the ground of all being. Elsewhere, the poet says, "In every country death has finality. . . . It arrives and the blinds are drawn. Not in Spain. . . . A dead person in Spain is more alive when dead than is the case anywhere else." In a surprising coda, he cited Saint Teresa of Avila, who said, "I die because I do not die."

While reading Neale's *Return with Elixir*, I was struck by his reference to Jung's injunction, in *The Red Book*, "It is wise to nourish the soul, otherwise you will breed devils and dragons in your heart." For myriad reasons, the evocation of a return to the soulful life is a sign of the *cri de coeur* commonly heard in modern times. I think now of John Steinbeck, a close friend of Campbell's in the 1930s, who expressed the urge in the figure of Tom Casey, in *The Grapes of Wrath*, who says, "A fella ain't got a soul of his own, but on'y a piece of one great soul." Who cannot help be moved by the way Ray Charles moans, "Whoa, I believe to my soul right now." Or feel a gasp reading the poet and essayist Mary Oliver's poignant reminder of the need to pay attention to the sanctity of our lives, "Ten times a day something happens to me like this—some strengthening throb of amazement—some good sweet empathic ping and swell. This is the first, the wildest and the wisest thing I know: that the soul exists and is built entirely out of attentiveness."

Regarded in this light, the holy longing that moves like a wave through the mind is heroic in the deepest sense of the word, a true call to adventure, the selfsame one signaled by Campbell in his myth of the hero. Mind you, the author is not enshrining the ego-driven narcissists of popular culture but the Transcendentalist view described by Emerson, "The hero is one who is immovably centered." And the version defended by the poet May Sarton, "One has to think like a hero to merely behave like a human being."

This book is positioned by the author as a manual for meditators, yogis, psychonauts, and psychedelic wayfarers who have committed to embarking upon perhaps the greatest pilgrimage of all, which the world's wisdom literature has taught us for millennia requires us to leave our ordinary consciousness for an extraordinary one, which resembles the movement of a ship through a series of locks in a canal. The mythically oriented reader will hear yet another echo of the hero journey, which Joseph Campbell told me in the interviews I had with him for our documentary of the same name (1987) wasn't his idea alone. Instead, he was proud to give credit to the French anthropologist Arnold van Gennep, in his 1909 study, *Les Rites des Passage*, for the template. There, Gennep demarcated the tripartite model of the rituals common to many primal cultures into Separation, Transition, and Return, the three main stages of human initiation ceremonies, which were necessary to mark the major transitions of our lives.

I feel this is an important point to delineate because it amplifies the beautiful notion of soul work that lies at the heart of Miles Neale's book as being remarkably interactive. His lapidary approach invites readers to engage in a series of self-analysis practices that include recording their dreams, synchronicities, epiphanies, struggles, visions, mandalas, poetry, shadow material, and visionary experiences.

The genius of this approach is that it evokes a certain, often sensual, feeling of familiarity, as if he were asking us to come home again to our deepest sense of self. Advisedly, he considers this a form of *gnosis*, esoteric knowledge, inspired by Homer's epic poem, *The Odyssey*, in which the hero's ten-year voyage from Troy to Ithaka is described as a *gnostos*, the desire to return home. This ancient and elegant notion was originally based on the tradition of the *nostoi*, travelers' tales told by sailors and soldiers that described the inevitable ordeals that occurred on the long sea journey back to home and hearth.

While this is an elegant parallel to the practices advocated here, the author adds another layer of meaning, the evocation of the Bodhisattva vow, which reminds us of the noble and selfless virtue in Mahayana Buddhism of achieving spiritual perfection by returning to the world in service of others, thereby helping free them from the veil of illusion, the world of constant pain and sorrow.

In other words, in mythic terms, we dare not come home *alone*, unconcerned about our fellow human beings, unmoved by the sanctity of the world around us.

Instead, as the scholar Joe Meeker has pointed out in his analysis of the *Odyssey*, the true meaning of the adventure is to return home with the elixir of wisdom not for selfish purposes, but to help *restore our family and revive the land around us.*

The coruscating brilliance of Miles Neale's approach to the mythologem of the elixir is that it provides the reader with a primer for the Greek ideal of the well-lived, thoroughly examined life, and the Buddhist ideal of an altruistically oriented life, which is to say the soulful existence, and to help us along he offers a wide array of mythopoetic, archetypal, and alchemical guidelines that help us turn creation into re-creation, disenchantment into re-enchantment, framing into reframing, so that we experience our current crisis as a pilgrimage through death and rebirth to reclaim our very souls.

PHIL COUSINEAU, MYTHOLOGIST,
WRITER, AND FILMMAKER

Notes

CHAPTER 1. VISIONS

1. Campbell, *The Hero with a Thousand Faces*, 2.
2. Dillard, *The Writing Life*, 32.
3. Mark Vonnegut, *The Eden Express* (New York, NY.: Seven Stories Press, 1975), 208.
4. Hancock, "The Lament of Hermes, read by Graham Hancock."
5. James (Sákéj) Youngblood Henderson, *"Ayukpachi*: Empowering Aboriginal Thought" in *Reclaiming Indigenous Voice and Vision*, ed. Marie Battitse, 260.
6. Benson, *Timeless Healing*, 20.
7. Carod-Artal, "Psychoactive Plants in Ancient Greece," 29–30.
8. James Hilman, *The Dream and the Underworld*, (Manhattan, NY.: Harper & Row, 1979), 12.
9. Direct quote from a personal email correspondence with Phillip Cousineau. Nov 7, 2022.
10. Fernandez, "The Saturn—Pluto Conjunction And the transits for the year 2020."
11. Jung, *The Collected Works of C.G. Jung Volume 18: The Symbolic Life*, trans. R.F.C. Hull, para. 1660.
12. Cain, "John Vervaeke on Wisdom and the Meaning Crisis."
13. Vervaeke, Mastropietro, and Miscevic, *Zombies in Western Culture*, 43.

CHAPTER 2. PANORAMA

1. Tarnas, *The Passion of the Western Mind*, 443; and Cain, "John Vervaeke on Wisdom and the Meaning Crisis."
2. Intergovernmental Panel on Climate Change (IPCC) "IPCC, 2021."
3. Matthews, "Are 26 Billionaires Worth More Than Half the Planet?"

4. Evelyn, "Amazon CEO Jeff Bezos Grows Fortune by $24bn Amid Coronavirus Pandemic."

5. Abbott, *The Handbook of Fifth-Generation Warfare*, 125.

6. Nochaiwong, et al., "Global Prevalence of Mental Health Issues Among the General Population During the Coronavirus Disease-2019 Pandemic."

7. World Health Organization (WHO), "Suicide."

8. Suitt, "High Suicide Rates Among United States Service Members and Veterans Of The Post-9/11 Wars."

9. Siegel, *The Developing Mind*, 78; and van der Kolk, *The Body Keeps the Score*, 265; and Maté, *In the Realm of Hungry Ghosts*, 51–54.

10. Vervaeke, "Awakening from the Meaning Crisis."

11. Vervaeke, "Awakening from the Meaning Crisis."

12. Vervaeke, "Awakening from the Meaning Crisis."

13. McGilchrist, *The Divided Brain and the Search for Meaning*, 15.

14. McGilchrist, *The Divided Brain and the Search for Meaning*, 8–11.

15. McGilchrist, *The Divided Brain and the Search for Meaning*, 8.

16. Siegel, *The Developing Mind*, 311.

17. McGilchrist, *The Divided Brain and the Search for Meaning*, 445.

18. Jung, *Aion: Researches into the Phenomenology of the Self (Collected Works of C.G. Jung Vol.9 Part 2),* trans. R.F.C. Hull, 105.

19. Grasse, *Signs of the Times: Unlocking the Symbolic Language of World Events*, 113–127; and Fitzgerald, *Signs of the Times: The End of the World and the Coming Golden Age.*

20. Fitzgerald, *Signs of the Times: The End of the World and the Coming Golden Age.*

21. Fitzgerald, *Signs of the Times: The End of the World and the Coming Golden Age.*

22. Fitzgerald, *Signs of the Times: The End of the World and the Coming Golden Age.*

23. Grasse, "Ray Grasse: Uncovering the Lost Tomb of Osiris."

24. Grasse, "Ray Grasse: Uncovering the Lost Tomb of Osiris."

25. Fitzgerald, "Signs of the Times: The End of the World and the Coming Golden Age."

26. Hegedus, *Early Christianity and Ancient Astrology*, 6.

27. Taylor, *Metaphysics of the Gods*, 182–84.

28. de Beer, *The Renaissance Battle for Rome*, ch. 1.

29. *Encyclopedia Britannica Online*, s.v. "Studia humanitatis Philosophy of Education," accessed May 16, 2023.

30. Sister Miriam Joseph, *The Trivium*, 3.

31. Keynes, "The Personality of Isaac Newton," 1.

32. Freud, *A General Introduction to Psychoanalysis*, 171.

33. Nietzsche, *The Gay Science*, 181.

34. Nietzsche, *The Will to Power*, trans. Walter Kaufmann and R.J. Hollingdale, 9.

35. Pratt, "Nihilism."

36. Firestone, "Nietzsche's Best Life," 377.

37. Kaufmann, *Nietzsche*, 307.

38. Pinchbeck, *How Soon is Now*, 215–16.

39. Fitzgerald, *Signs of the Times: The End of the World and the Coming Golden Age.*

40. Grasse, *Signs of the Times*, 224–25.

41. Siegel, *The Developing Mind*, 2–10.

42. Grasse, "Drawing Down the Fire of the Gods: Reflections on the Leo/Aquarius Axis."

43. Allen, "10-Year BYU Study Shows Elevated Suicide Risk from Excess Social Media Time for Young Teen Girls."

CHAPTER 3. SOUL

1. Moore, *Care of the Soul*, xi–xii.

2. Edmonds, "A Lively Afterlife and Beyond," para. 9.

3. Edmonds, "A Lively Afterlife and Beyond" para. 10–11.

4. Huffman, *The Pythagorean conception of the soul from Pythagoras to Philolaus*, 34.

5. Plato, *The Last Days of Socrates*, 107.

6. Plato, *The Republic of Plato*, trans. Allan Bloom, 297.

7. Pakaluk, Aristotle's Nicomachean Ethics: An Introduction, 20.

8. Wasson, et al., *The Road to Eleusis: Unveiling the Secret of the Mysteries*, 51.

9. Muraresku, *The Immortality Key*, 27–31.

10. Robert Thurman (author) in discussion with the author, October 20, 2021.

11. Muraresku, *The Immortality Key*, 24.

12. Muraresku, *The Immortality Key*, 24.

13. Firdos, et al, "The Influence of Greek Classics on Indian Culture in Ancient Era," 196.

14. Krajewksi, "Ancient Wine Culture: Alexander the Great's Most Significant Export?," *Jane Anson: Inside Bordeau*; Klimburg, "Transregional Intoxications: Wine in Buddhist Gandhara and Kafiristan," and Tanabe, "The Transmission of Dionysiac Imagery to Gandhāran Buddhist Art."

15. Dowman, "The Eighty-Four Mahasiddhas and the Path of Tantra" from his website.

16. Tanabe, "The Transmission of Dionysiac Imagery to Gandhāran Buddhist Art."

17. "Guru Padmasambhava; His Provenance," Lokesh Chandra, Sahapedia website, accessed July 20, 2023.

18. Klimburg, "Transregional Intoxications," 277.

19. Filigenzi, "Non-Buddhist Customs of Buddhist People," 53.

20. Mehrtens, "Jung on Soul Tending."

21. Mehrtens, "Jung on Soul Tending."

22. Siegel, *The Developing Mind.* Chap. 1; Goleman and Davidson, *Altered States: Science Reveals How Meditation Changes Your Mind, Brain, and Body.* Chap. 11.

CHAPTER 4. SOLVE ET COAGULA

1. Trismegistus, *Emerald Tablet*, 52–53.

2. Trismegistus, *Emerald Tablet*, 52–53.

3. Silva, *The Lost Art of Resurrection*, 114.

4. Greer and Neale, "John Michael Greer: Esoteric Wisdom, Solve et Coagula and Civilizational Collapse Ep 9 Wisdom Keeper."

5. Tolkien, *The Fellowship of the Ring*, 71.

6. Hancock, *Fingerprints of the Gods*, 343.; and Hancock and Bauval, *The Message of the Sphinx*, 297; West, *Serpent in the Sky*.

7. Schmidt, *"Zuerst kam der Tempel, dann die Stadt,"* 5–41.

8. De Lorenzis and Orofino, "New Possible Astronomic Alignments at the Megalithic Site of Göbekli Tepe, Turkey," 40.

9. Cruttenden, *Lost Star of Myth and Time*, Chap. 2.

10. Kreisberg, *Lost Knowledge of the Ancients*, 79–80.

11. Hesiod, *The Homeric Hymns, and Homerica*, trans. by Hugh G. Evelyn-White, 2.

12. Philolaus and Huffman, *Philolaus of Croton: Pythagorean and Presocratic*, 320.

13. Cruttenden, (2003) The Great Year. The Yuga Project. (film).

14. Tarnas, *Cosmos and Psyche*, 137–38.

15. Tarnas, *Cosmos and Psyche*, 159.

16. Jung, *Jung Letters, Volume 2: 1951–1961*, 463.

17. Siegel and Bryson, *The Whole-Brain Child*, 14.

CHAPTER 5. PILGRIMAGE

1. Campbell & Moyers, *The Power of Myth*, 225.
2. Tolkien, *The Hobbit*, 335.
3. Campbell, *Occidental Mythology (Masks of God)*.
4. Campbell, *The Hero with a Thousand Faces*, chap. 3.
5. Murdock, *The Heroine's Journey*; Miller, "Forget the 'Hero's Journey' and Consider the Heroine's Quest Instead."
6. Vogler, "The Memo That Started It All."
7. Stevens, *Jung: A Very Short Introduction* 93; Dunne, *Carl Jung: Wounded Healer of the Soul*, 15.
8. Dunne, *Carl Jung: Wounded Healer of the Soul*, viii.
9. C. G. Jung, *Psychology and Alchemy*, trans. Gerhard Adler and R. F. C. Hull, 449–71.
10. Jung, *Foreword to the I Ching in Psychology and Religion*, trans. R.F.C. Hull, 589–608.
11. Wilhelm, *The Secret of the Golden Flower*, 18.
12. Thomas Cleary, *The Secret of the Golden Flower* (San Fransisco, CA.: Harper One. 1993), 3–5.
13. Wilhelm, *The Secret of the Golden Flower*, 18.
14. Jung, *Mysterium Coniunctionis*, 546.
15. Jung, *Mysterium Coniunctionis*, 556.
16. Jung, *The Psychology of Kundalini Yoga*, xv.
17. Jung, *Yoga and the West*, 529–537: and C.G. Jung, *The Psychology of Eastern meditation*, 558–575.
18. Jung, *What India Can Teach Us*, 525–530; and Vrajaprana, "Jung and Indian Thought."
19. Meckel & Moore, *Self and Liberation*, 1; and Jung, "Psychological Commentary on The Tibetan Book of the Great Liberation" and "Psychological Commentary on The Tibetan Book of the Dead," 457–508; and 509–26.
20. Mansfield, "Tibetan Buddhism and Jungian Psychology," 18; and Lopez, Jr, *The Tibetan Book of the Dead*, 124.
21. Lopez, Jr, *The Tibetan Book of the Dead*, 124.
22. Jung, *Memories, Dreams, Reflections*, 73.
23. Jung, "The Philosophical Tree," 265.
24. Jung, *Man and His Symbols*, 102.
25. Jung, *Man and His Symbols*, 94.
26. Jung, *Memories, Dream, Reflections*, 209.

27. Thurman, *The Jewel Tree of Tibet*, 10–12.

28. Loizzo, *Sustainable Happiness*, 188.

CHAPTER 6. DEPARTURE

1. Campbell and Moyers, "Ep. 1: Joseph Campbell and the Power of Myth—'The Hero's Adventure.'"

2. Richard, "Thoughts on Happiness and the Mind."

3. Jung, *Memories, Dreams, Reflections*, 158.

4. Jung, *Memories, Dreams, Reflections*, 197.

5. Jung, *Memories, Dreams, Reflections*, 198–99.

6. Genesis 1:26-27; Genesis 2.7; 2:18; Genesis 2:21-23; 2:16-17 (King James Version).

7. Genesis 3:5 (King James Version).

CHAPTER 7. INITIATION

1. Lama Yeshe, *The Bliss of Inner Fire*, 49.

2. Padmasambhava, et al., *The Tibetan Book of the Dead*, 89.

3. Jung, *Memories, Dreams, Reflections*, 492.

4. Burton, "Jung: The Man and His Symbols: Carl Jung in a Nutshell."

5. Jung, *Memories, Dreams, Reflections*, 22–23.

6. Jung, *Memories, Dreams, Reflections*, 51.

7. Jung, *Memories, Dreams, Reflections*, 180.

8. Jung, *Memories, Dreams, Reflections*, 222.

9. Jung, *Memories, Dreams, Reflections*, 224.

10. Jung, *Memories, Dreams, Reflections*, 222.

11. Burton, "Jung: The Man and His Symbols: Carl Jung in a Nutshell."

12. Jung, *Memories, Dreams, Reflections*, 180.

13. Jung, *Memories, Dreams, Reflections*, 181.

14. Jung, *Memories, Dreams, Reflections*, 182.

15. Jung, *Memories, Dreams, Reflections*, 183.

16. Jung, *Memories, Dreams, Reflections*, 183.

17. Burton, "Jung: The Man and His Symbols: Carl Jung in a Nutshell."

18. Jung, *Memories, Dreams, Reflections*, 185.

19. Buddhanet, "The Buddha's First Teachers."

20. Access to Insight "A Sketch of the Buddha's Life: Readings from the Pali Canon."

21. Fernandez, "The Saturn—Pluto Conjunction and the transits for the year 2020."

22. Benton-Banai, *The Mishomis Book*, 91–93.

23. Vandana Shiva, "Bill Gates' Global Agenda and How We Can Resist His War on Life," Resilience (website), September 23, 2020, accessed May 14, 2023.

CHAPTER 8. ORDEAL

1. Jung, *The Red Book*, 241–42.

2. Jung, *Memories, Dreams Reflections*, 171.

3. Jung, *Memories, Dreams, Reflections*, 400.

4. Jung, *Memories, Dreams, Reflections*, 173.

5. Jung, *Memories, Dreams, Reflections*, 174.

6. Jung, *Memories, Dreams, Reflections*, 215.

7. Jung, *Memories, Dreams, Reflections*, 179.

8. Jung, *Memories, Dreams, Reflections*, 179.

9. Corbett, "The Holy Grail of the Unconscious."

10. Jung, *The Red Book*, 290.

11. Meizner, "Revisiting the Tibetan Book of the Dead and The Psychedelic Experience."

12. Woolfe, "How Does Culture Influence a Psychedelic Experience?"

13. Padmasambhava, et al., *The Tibetan Bookof the Dead*, 197–98.

14. Padmasambhava, et al., *The Tibetan Book of the Dead*, 48–49.

15. Padmasambhava, et al., *The Tibetan Book of the Dead*, 251.

16. Bhikkhu, *The Life of the Buddha*, 19.

17. Bhikkhu, *The Life of the Buddha*, 19.

18. Jung, *The Red Book*, 208.

CHAPTER 9. TREASURE

1. Muraresku, *The Immortality Key*, 29.

2. Miksic, *Borobudur: Golden Tales of the Buddhas*, Part II.

3. Sparavigna, "The Zenith Passage of the Sun at Candi Borobudur," 1–5.

4. Jung, *Psychological Types*, 78.

5. Jung, *Psychological Types*, 757.

6. Jung, *Psychological Types*, 762.

7. Jacobi, "The Process of Individuation: A Study in Developmental Psychology," 96.

8. Engler, "Being somebody and being nobody: A Reexamination of the Understanding of Self in Psychoanalysis and Buddhism," 48.

9. Jung Society, "Intro to Jung: What is the Self?"

10. Jung, *Two Essays on Analytical Psychology*, 238.
11. Jung, *Two Essays on Analytical Psychology*, 195.
12. Jung, *Two Essays on Analytical Psychology*, 196.
13. Jung, *Mandala Symbolism*, trans. R.F.C. Hull, 20.
14. Stein, *The Principle of Individuation*, 166.
15. Jung, *Memories, Dreams, Reflections*, 226.
16. Jung, *Memories, Dreams, Reflections*, 225.
17. Jung, *Memories, Dreams, Reflections*, 227.
18. Bhikkhu, "Maha-Saccaka Sutta: The Longer Discourse to Saccaka."
19. Leidy and Thurman, *Mandala*, 127.

CHAPTER 10. RETURN

1. Ross, "The Integration of Transformation: Extending Campbell's Monomyth."
2. Gauthama Nagappan, "After the Seventh Week of Enlightenment: From Bodh Gaya to Isipatana."
3. Bodhi, "Majjhima Nikāya—26. The Noble Search."
4. Horner, "Majjhima Nikaya I (Middle Length Sayings), Ariyapariyesana Sutta," 18–19.
5. Bodhi, "Majjhima Nikāya—26. The Noble Search."
6. Bodhi, "Majjhima Nikāya—26. The Noble Search."
7. Campbell, *Pathways to Bliss*, 119.
8. Ross, "The Integration of Transformation: Extending Campbell's Monomyth," 1–29.
9. Ross, "The Integration of Transformation: Extending Campbell's Monomyth," 1–29.
10. Ross, "The Integration of Transformation: Extending Campbell's Monomyth," 6.
11. Ross, "The Integration of Transformation: Extending Campbell's Monomyth," 10–11.
12. Ross, "The Integration of Transformation: Extending Campbell's Monomyth," 1–29.
13. Jung, *Memories, Dreams, Reflections*, 284.
14. Jung, *Memories, Dreams, Reflections*, 285.
15. Jung, *Memories, Dreams, Reflections*, 344.
16. Davis, "The Primordial Mandalas of East and West," 252.
17. Jung, *Memories, Dreams, Reflections*, 188.
18. Indosphere Culture, "The 9 sacred mountains of Java."
19. Dunn, *The Giza Power Plant: Technologies of Ancient Egypt*, Chapter 8.

20. Indosphere Culture, "The Sabdapalon Prophecy in Java."

21. Guinness Book of World Records, "Angkor Wat."

22. Suamba, Siwa-Buddha di Indonesia, 53.

23. Indosphere Culture, "The Sabdapalon Prophecy in Java."

24. Berzin, "Shambhala: Myths and Reality."

25. Berzin, "Shambhala: Myths and Reality."

26. Berzin, "Taking the Kalachakra Initiation," 33 and Belka, "The Shambhala Myth in Buryatia and Mongolia," 19–30.

27. Hammar, "A History of the Kalacakra in Tibet and a Study of the Concept of Adibuddha, the Fourth Body of the Buddha and the Supreme Unchanging," 82–83.

28. Berzin, "The Kalachakra Prophesies of a Future Invasion."

29. Symmes, "The Kingdom of the Lotus."

CHAPTER 11. THERAPEIA

1. Jung, *Collected Works of CG Jung: Alchemical Studies (Volume 13)*, Para. 54.

2. Aday, et al., "Long-Term Effects of Psychedelic Drugs: A Systematic Review," 179–89; and Reiff, et al., "Psychedelics and Psychedelic-Assisted Psychotherapy," 391–410.

3. Schlag, et al, "Adverse Effects of Psychedelics: From Anecdotes and Misinformation to Systematic Science," 258–272; and Strassman, "Adverse Reactions to Psychedelic Drugs. A Review of the Literature," 577–595.

4. Wasson, Hoffman and Ruck, *The Road to Eleusis: Unveiling the Secret of the Mysteries*, 83–86.

5. Muraresku, *The Immortality Key*, 32.

6. Wasson, et al., *The Road to Eleusis*; and Muraresku, *New-The Immortality Key*, 64.

7. Wasson, et al., *The Road to Eleusis*, 58.

CHAPTER 12. REUNION

1. Jung, *Aion: Researches into the Phenomenology of the Self (Collected Works of C.G. Jung Vol.9 Part 2)*, 92–93.

2. Peterson, *Maps of Meaning*, 268–69.

3. Jung, et al., *Aion: Researches into the Phenomenology of the Self*, 87.

4. Greene, "C.G. Jung's Vision of the Aquarian Age."

5. Swami Sri Yukteswar, *The Holy Science*, 46.

6. Campbell, *Reflections on the Art of Living*, 39.

7. Sheldrake, "Prayer: A Challenge for Science."

8. Gilbert, "Masters of the Net," 2:27.

9. Hancock, *Fingerprints of the Gods: The Evidence of Earth's Lost Civilization*, Part. VI; Bauval. *The Egypt Code*, Chap. 2; West, *Serpent in the Sky: The High Wisdom of Ancient Egypt*. Chap. The Temple of Man.; Silva. *The Divine Blueprint: Temples, Power Places, and the Global Plan to Shape the Human Soul*, Chap.7; Wilcock, *The Source Field Investigations: The Hidden Science and Lost Civilizations Behind the 2012 Prophecies*, Chap. 7.

10. Humas Buddha, "Gerak Cepat Rencana Pemasangan Chattra, Ditjen Bimas Buddha dan BRIN Siapkan Rencana Kunjungan Kelapangan," Ditjen Bimas Buddha Kementerian Agama RI website accessed 1 June, 2024.

11. Peterson and Rogan, The Joe Rogan Experience, Podcast Notes website.

12. Orwell, *Nineteen Eighty-Four*, 165–66; and Aldous Huxley, *A Brave New World*, 297–324.

13. Dalai Lama, *Ethics for the New Millennium*, 24.

14. Pinchbeck, "Planetary Initiation."

Bibliography

Abbott, Daniel. *The Handbook of Fifth-Generation Warfare*. Ann Arbor, MI.: Nimble Books, 2010.

Aday, Jacob S., Cayla M. Mitzkovitz, Emily K. Bloesch, Christopher C. Davoli, and Alan K. Davis. "Long-Term Effects of Psychedelic Drugs: A Systematic Review." *Neuroscience and Biobehavioral Reviews* 113, (2020): 179–189.

Allen, Christie. "10-Year BYU Study Shows Elevated Suicide Risk from Excess Social Media Time for Young Teen Girls." Brigham Young University, University Communication News (website). February 3, 2021. Accessed May 15, 2023.

Beiner, Alexander. "Lost Ways of Knowing." *Medium* (website). February 14, 2020. Accessed July 15, 2008.

Benson, Herbert. *Timeless Healing*. New York, NY.: Fireside, 1996.

Benton-Banai, Edward. *The Mishomis Book*. St. Paul, MN.: Red School House Publishers, 1988.

Berzin, Alexander. "Shambhala: Myths and Reality." Study Buddhism by Berzin Archives (website). Accessed May 16, 2023.

———. "The Kalachakra Prophesies of a Future Invasion." Study Buddhism by Berzin Archives (website). Accessed May 1, 2023.

———. "Taking the Kalachakra Initiation." (1997) and Lubosh Belka. "The Shambhala Myth in Buryatia and Mongolia." In Proceedings of the Ninth Conference of the European Society for Central Asian Studies, Cambridge Scholars Publishing (2009): 19–30.

Bhikkhu, Thanissaro. "Maha-Saccaka Sutta: The Longer Discourse to Saccaka." Translated by Thanissaro Bhikkhu. Access to Insight, BCBS Edition (website), November 30, 2013. Accessed May 14, 2023.

———. "A Sketch of the Buddha's Life: Readings from the Pali Canon." Translated by Thanissaro Bhikkhu. Access to Insight, BCBS Edition (website). November 30, 2013. Accessed May 20, 2023.

Bodhi, Bhikkhu. "Majjhima Nikāya—26. The Noble Search." SuttaCentral (website). Accessed May 20, 2023.

Buddhanet. "The Buddha's First Teachers." Buddhanet (website). Accessed May 19, 2023.

Burton, Neel. "Jung: The Man and His Symbols: Carl Jung in a Nutshell." *Psychology Today* (website). April 8, 2012. Accessed May 21, 2023.

Cain, Benjamin. "John Vervaeke on Wisdom and the Meaning Crisis." *Medium* (website). February 24, 2020. Accessed July 19, 2023.

Campbell, Joseph. *The Hero with a Thousand Faces*. New Jersey: Princeton University Press, 2004.

———. *Occidental Mythology (Masks of God)*. New York, NY.: Penguin Books, 1991.

———. *Pathways to Bliss*. Novato, CA.: New World Library, 2004.

———. *Reflections on the Art of Living*. New York, NY: Harper Collins, 1995.

Campbell, Joseph and Bill Moyers "Ep. 1: Joseph Campbell and the Power of Myth—'The Hero's Adventure.'" Bill Moyers (website). June 21, 1988. Accessed June 21, 1988.

Campbell, Joseph and Bill Moyers. *The Power of Myth*. New York, NY.: Doubleday, 1988.

Carod-Artal, F.J. "Psychoactive Plants in Ancient Greece." *Neurosciences and History* 1, no. 1 (2013): 28–38.

Cleary, Thomas. *The Secret of the Golden Flower*. San Fransisco, CA.: Harper One. 1993.

Corbett, Sara. "The Holy Grail of the Unconscious. *New York Times Magazine* (website). September 16, 2009.

Cruttenden, Walter. *The Great Year Adventures*. Newport Beach, CA: Binary Research Institute, 2011.

———. *Lost Star of Myth and Time*. Pittsburgh, PA: St, Lynn's Press, 2005.

Dalai Lama. *Ethics for the New Millennium*. New York, NY.: Riverhead Books, 2001.

Davis, Judson. "The Primordial Mandalas of East and West." *NeuroQuantology* 14, no. 2 (2016): 252.

De Lorenzis, Alessandro and Vincenzo Orofino. "New Possible Astronomic Alignments at the Megalithic Site of Göbekli Tepe, Turkey." *Archaeological Discovery* 3, no. 1 (2014).

Dillard, Annie. *The Writing Life*. New York, NY.: Harper Perennial, 1990.

Dunne, Claire. *Carl Jung: Wounded Healer of the Soul*. London, UK: Watkins, 2015.

Edmonds III, Radcliffe G. "A Lively Afterlife and Beyond: The Soul in Plato, Homer, and the Orphica." *Études Platoniciennes* 11 (2014).

Engler, Jack. "Being somebody and being nobody: A Reexamination of the Understanding of Self in Psychoanalysis and Buddhism." *Psychoanalysis and Buddhism: An Unfolding dialogue* (2003).

Evelyn, Kenya. "Amazon CEO Jeff Bezos Grows Fortune By $24bn Amid Coronavirus Pandemic." *The Guardian* (website). April 15, 2020. Accessed June 19, 2023.

Fernandez, Maurice. "The Saturn-Pluto Conjunction and the transits for the year 2020." Evolutionary Astrology with Maurice Fernandez (website). Accessed May 16, 2023.

Firdos, Shumaila, Yu Wenjie and Xu Sangyi. "The Influence of Greek Classics on Indian Culture in Ancient Era." *Journal of the Punjab University Historical Society*, 30, no. 1 (Jan–Jun 2017): 195–204.

Filigenzi, A. "Non-Buddhist Customs of Buddhist People: Visual and Archaeological Evidence from North-West Pakistan," In *Buddhism and the Dynamics of Transculturality*, ed. Bridgit Keller. (Berlin, Germany: DeGruyter, 2019), 56.

Firestone, Randall. "Nietzsche's Best Life: The Ten Greatest Attributes of the Ubermensch, & a Comparison to Aristotle's Virtuous Person." *Open Journal of Philosophy*, 7, no. 3 (2017).

Fitzgerald, Robert. *Signs of the Times: The End of the World and the Coming Golden Age*. Fairfields, IA.: 1st World Library, 2005.

Freud, Sigmund. *A General Introduction to Psychoanalysis*. Germany: Horace Liveright, 1920.

Grasse, Ray. "Drawing Down the Fire of the Gods: Reflections on the Leo/Aquarius Axis," *Astrodiens* (website). Accessed May 22, 2023.

———. "Ray Grasse: Uncovering the Lost Tomb of Osiris." Theosophical Society in America (YouTube video). Last modified October 31, 2017. Accessed May 22, 2023.

———. *Signs of the Times: Unlocking the Symbolic Language of World Events*. Charlottesville, VA.: Hampton Roads, 2002.

Greene, Liz. "C.G. Jung's Vision of the Aquarian Age." The Theosophical Society in America (website). Accessed May 15, 2023.

Greer, John Michael and Dr. Miles Neale. "John Michael Greer: Esoteric Wisdom, Solve et Coagula and Civilizational Collapse Ep 9 Wisdom Keeper." Channel Dr. Miles Neale (YouTube video). June 25, 2022. Accessed May 24, 2023.

Guinness Book of World Records. "Angkor Wat." Guinness Book of World Records (website). Accessed May 20, 2024.

Hammar, Urban. "A History of the Kalacakra in Tibet and a Study of the Concept of Adibuddha, the Fourth Body of the Buddha and the Supreme Unchanging." *Studies in the Kalacakra Tantra* (2005), 82–83.

Hancock, Graham. *Fingerprints of the Gods*. New York, NY.: Three River Press, 1996.

———. "The Lament of Hermes, Read by Graham Hancock." Graham Hancock Official Channel. (YouTube video). September 1, 2020. Accessed May 4, 2023.

Hancock Graham and Robert Bauval. *The Message of the Sphinx*. New York, NY.: Three River Press, 1997.

Hegedus, Timothy. *Early Christianity and Ancient Astrology*. Lausanne, Switzerland: Peter Lang Inc., 2007.

Henderson, James (Sákéj) Youngblood. ("*Ayukpachi*: Empowering Aboriginal Thought" in *Reclaiming Indigenous Voice and Vision*, ed. Marie Battitse. (Seattle, WA.: University of Washington Press, 2000), 260.

Hesiod. *The Homeric Hymns, and Homerica*, trans. by Hugh G. Evelyn-White. (New York, NY.: The Macmillan Co), 2.

Hilman, James. *The Dream and the Underworld*. (Manhattan, NY.: Harper & Row, 1979), 12.

Horner, I. B. "Majjhima Nikaya I (Middle Length Sayings), Ariyapariyesana Sutta." *Oxford: The Pali Text Society*. (1967): 18–19.

Huffman, Carl. *The Pythagorean conception of the soul from Pythagoras to Philolaus*. New York, NY.: De Gruyter, 2009.

Huxley, Aldous. *A Brave New World*. London, UK.: Harper Perennial, 1958.

Indosphere Culture. "The 9 sacred mountains of Java." *Medium* (website). December 25, 2019. Accessed May 12, 2023.

Indosphere Culture. "The Sabdapalon Prophecy in Java." *Medium* (website). December 8, 2019. Accessed May 13, 2023.

IPCC Sixth Assessment Report. "IPCC, 2021: Climate Change 2021: The Physical Science Basis." Cambridge, United Kingdom and New York.: Cambridge University Press, 2023. Accessed June 19, 2023.

Jacobi, Jolande. "The Process of Individuation: A Study in Developmental Psychology." *Journal of Analytical Psychology* (1958).

Joseph, Sister Miriam. *The Trivium*. Philadelphia, PA: Paul Dry Books, 2002.

Jung, C. G. *Aion: Researches into the Phenomenology of the Self (Collected Works of C. G. Jung Vol 9 Part 2)*. Translated by R.F.C. Hull. Princeton University Press, 1979.

———. *Foreword to the I Ching in Psychology and Religion*. Translated by R. F. C. Hull. London, UK.: Tourledge, 1950.

———. Man and His Symbols. New York, NY.: Dell Publishing, 1968.

———. *Memories, Dreams, Reflections*. Translated by Richard and Clara Winston. New York, NY.: Vintage Books, 1963.

———. *Mysterium Coniunctionis (Collected Works of C. G. Jung Volume 14)*. Translated by R.F.C. Hull. London, UK: Routledge, 2014.

———. "The Philosophical Tree." *Alchemical Studies*. Translated by R. F. C. Hull. Princeton, NJ.: Princeton University Press, 1967.

———. *Psychological Types*. Translated by R. F. C. Hull. New York, NY: Bollingen Foundation, 1921.

———. *Psychology and Alchemy*. Translated by R. F. C. Hull. Princeton, NJ.: Princeton University Press, 1980.

———. "Psychological Commentary on The Tibetan Book of the Great Liberation" and "Psychological Commentary on The Tibetan Book of the Dead." Translated by R. F. C. Hull. London, UK: Routledge & Kegan Paul, 1958, 457-508.

———. "Psychological Commentary on The Tibetan Book of the Great Liberation" and "Psychological Commentary on The Tibetan Book of the Dead." Translated by R. F. C. Hull. Princeton, NJ.: Princeton University Press, 1969, 509–526.

———. *The Psychology of Eastern Meditation*. Translated by R. F. C. Hull. London, UK.: Routledge & Kegan Paul, 1958, 558–575.

———. *The Psychology of Kundalini Yoga*. Edited by Sonu Shamdasani. London, UK.: Routledge, 1996.

———. *Mandala Symbolism*. Translated by R. F. C. Hull. Princeton, NJ.: Princeton University Press, 1972.

———. *The Red Book*. Edited by Sonu Shamdasani. London, UK.: W. W. Norton, 2012.

———. *Two Essays on Analytical Psychology (Collected Works of C. G. Jung Vol. 7)*. Translated by R. F. C. Hull. Princeton, NJ.: Princeton University Press, 1966.

———. *What India Can Teach Us*. Translated by R. F. C. Hull. London, UK.: Routledge & Kegan Paul, 1970, 525–530.

———. *Yoga and the West*. Translated by R. F. C. Hull. London, UK.: Routledge & Kegan Paul, 1958, 529–537.

Jung Society. "Intro to Jung: What is the Self?" Jung Society of Utah (website). December 29, 2020. Accessed May 24, 2023.

Keynes, Milo. "The Personality of Isaac Newton." *Notes and Records of the Royal Society of London* 49, no. 1 (1995): 1–56.

Klimburg, Max. "Transregional Intoxications: Wine in Buddhist Gandhara and Kafiristan." *Eurasiatica*, 4 (2016): 271–302. doi 10.14277/6969-100-3/ EUR-5-11

Krajewksi, Nicolette. "Ancient Wine Culture: Alexander the Great's Most Significant Export?" Jane Anson: Inside Bordeau (website). November 2022. Accessed April 28, 2023.

Kreisberg, Glenn. *Lost Knowledge of the Ancients*. Rochester, VT: Bear and Company, 2010.

Leidy, D. P and Robert Thurman. *Mandala*. New York, NY.: Asia Society Galleries and Tibet House, 1997.

Loizzo, Joe. *Sustainable Happiness*. London, UK.: Routledge, 2012.

Lopez, Jr, Donald S. *The Tibetan Book of the Dead*. Princeton, NJ.: Princeton University Press, 2011.

Mansfield, Victor. "Tibetan Buddhism and Jungian Psychology." *Department of Physics and Astronomy*, 2006, 18.

Maté, Gabor. *In the Realm of Hungry Ghosts*. Berkeley, CA.: North Atlantic Books, 2010.

Matthews, Dylan. "Are 26 Billionaires Worth More Than Half the Planet? The Debate, Explained." *Vox* (website). January 22, 2019. Accessed June 19, 2023.

McGilchrist, Iain. *The Divided Brain and the Search for Meaning*. New Haven, CT: Yale University Press, 2012.

Meckel, Daniel J. and Robert L. Moore. *Self and Liberation*. Mahwah, NJ.: Paulist Press, 1992.

Mehrtens, Sue. "Jung on Soul Tending." *Jungian Center for the Spiritual Sciences* (website). Accessed May 5, 2023.

Meizner, Ralph. "Revisiting the Tibetan Book of the Dead and The Psychedelic Experience." *MAPS Special Edition: Psychedelics, Death and Dying* (online), 20, no. 1 (2010). Accessed May 20, 2023, 32–33.

Miller, Laura. "Forget the 'Hero's Journey' and Consider the Heroine's Quest Instead." Review of *The Heroine with 1001 Faces* by Maria Tatar. *New York Times* (website). September 29, 2021. Accessed May 10, 2023.

Moore, Thomas. *Care of the Soul*. New York, NY.: HarperCollins, 1992.

Muraresku, Brian C. *The Immortality Key*. New York, NY.: St, Martin's Press, 2020.

Murdock, Maureen. *The Heroine's Journey*. Boulder, CO: Shambhala Publication Inc, 2020.

Ñāṇamoli, Bhikkhu. *The Life of the Buddha*. Kandy, Sri Lanka: Buddhist Publication Society, 1972.

Nagappan, Gauthama Prabhu. "After the Seventh Week of Enlightenment: From Bodh Gaya to Isipatana." BDG Buddhistdoor Global (website). February 26, 2022. Accessed May 22, 2023.

Nietzsche, Friedrich. *The Gay Science*. Leipzig, Germany: Fritzsch 1882.

Nochaiwong, Surapon, Chidchanok Ruengorn, Kednapa Thavorn, Brian Hutton, Ratanaporn Awiphan, Chabaphai Phosuya, Yongyuth Ruanta, Nahathai Wongpakaran and Tinakon Wongpakaran. "Global Prevalence of Mental Health Issues Among the General Population During the Coronavirus Disease-2019 Pandemic: A Systematic Review and Meta-Analysis." *Scientific Reports* no. 11, Article number: 10173 (May 2021).

Orwell, George. *Nineteen Eighty-Four*. New York, NY.: Harcourt Brace & Co, 1949.

Padmasambhava, et al. *The Tibetan Book of the Dead*. Translated by Robert A. F. Thurman. New York, NY.: Bantam Books, 1993.

Pakaluk, Michael. *Aristotle's Nicomachean Ethics: An Introduction*. Cambridge, UK.: Cambridge University Press, 2005, 20.

Peterson, Jordan B. *Maps of Meaning*. London, UK.: Routledge, 1999.

Peterson, Jordan B. and Joe Rogan. "The Joe Rogan Experience." Podcast Notes (website). February 26, 2023. Accessed May 24, 2023.

Pinchbeck, Daniel. *How Soon is Now*, London, UK.: Watkins Media Limited, 2017.

———. "Planetary Initiation." Open Transcripts (website). May 20, 2016. Accessed May 20, 2023.

Plato. *The Last Days of Socrates*. London, UK: Penguin Books, 2010.

———. *The Republic of Plato*, trans. Allan Bloom. New York, NY.: BasicBooks, 1991.

Pratt, Alan. "Nihilism." *Internet Encyclopedia of Philosophy* (website). Accessed May 20, 2023.

Reiff, Collin M., Elon E. Richman, Charles B. Nemeroff, Linda L. Carpenter, Alik S. Widge, Carolyn I Rodriguez, Ned H. Kalin, William M. McDonal. "Psychedelics and Psychedelic-Assisted Psychotherapy." *American Journal of Psychiatry* 177, no. 5 (2020): 391–410.

Richard, Matthieu. "Thoughts on Happiness and the Mind." Matthieu Ricard (website). July 11, 2017. Accessed May 18, 2023.

Ross, Susan L. "The Integration of Transformation: Extending Campbell's Monomyth." *Heroism Science* 4, no. 2, article 7 (2019): 1–29.

Saunders, Hamish. "A Brief Overview of the History of Western Astrology." *Astrology House* (website). (1998).

Schlag, Anne K., Jacob Aday, Iram Salam, Jo C. Neill, and David J. Nutt. "Adverse Effects of Psychedelics: From Anecdotes and Misinformation to Systematic Science." *Journal of Psychopharmacology* 36, no. 3 (2022): 258–272.

Schmidt, Klaus. *"Zuerst kam der Tempel, dann die Stadt." Vorläufiger Bericht zu den Grabungen am Göbekli Tepe und am Gürcütepe 1995–1999."* (Turkey, Istanbuler Mitteilungen, 2000): 5–41.

Siegel, Daniel J. *The Developing Mind.* New York, NY.: The Guilford Press, 2012.

Silva, Freddy. *The Lost Art of Resurrection.* Rochester, VT.: Inner Traditions, 2017.

Sopa, Geshe Lhundup. *The Wheel of Time.* Boulder, UK.: Shambhala Publications, 1991.

Sparavigna, Amelia Carolina. "The Zenith Passage of the Sun at Candi Borobudur." *Philica,* (2017): 1–5.

Stein, Murray. *The Principle of Individuation.* Asheville, NC.: Chiron Publications, 2013.

Stevens, Anthony. *Jung: A Very Short Introduction.* Oxford, UK: Oxford University Press, 2001.

Strassman, R. J. "Adverse Reactions to Psychedelic Drugs. A Review of the Literature." *Journal of Nervous and Mental Disease* 172, no. 10 (1984): 577–595.

Suitt, Thomas Howard III. "High Suicide Rates Among United States Service Members and Veterans Of The Post-9/11 Wars." Watson Institute International & Public Affairs, Brown University. Costs of War (website). June 21, 2021. Accessed June 19, 2023.

Symmes, Patrick. "The Kingdom of the Lotus." Outside (website). Last modified February 24, 2022. Accessed May 4, 2023.

Tanabe, Tadashi. "The Transmission of Dionysiac Imagery to Gandhāran Buddhist Art." In *Proceedings of the Third International Workshop of the Gandhāra Connections Project, University of Oxford, 18th–19th March, 2019.* Archaeopress Archaeology, (2020): 86–101. DOI: 10.32028/9781789696950

Tarnas, Richard. *Cosmos and Psyche.* New York, NY.: Penguin Publishing, 2007.

———. *The Passion of the Western Mind.* London, UK: Pimlico, 2010.

Taylor, Brian Richard. *Metaphysics of the Gods.* CreateSpace Independent Publishing Platform, 2017.

Thurman, Robert. *The Jewel Tree of Tibet*. New York, NY.: Atria, 2006.

Tolkien, J. R. R. *The Hobbit*. New York, NY.: Mariner Books, 2012.

———. *Lord of the Rings*.

Tyndale. *Holy Bible*. Carol Stream, IL: Tyndale House Publisher, 1996, 4–5.

Trismegistus, Hermes. *Emerald Tablet*. Rochester, VT.: Inner Traditions, 2012.

Van der Kolk, Bessel. *The Body Keeps the Score*. London, UK.: Penguin Books, 2014.

Vervaeke, John. "Awakening from the Meaning Crisis." John Vervaeke Channel (YouTube video). January 20, 2019. Accessed May 15, 2023.

Vervaeke, John, Christopher Mastropietro and Filip Miscevic. *Zombies in Western Culture: A Twenty-First Century Crisis*. Cambridge, UK: Open Book Publishers, 2017.

Vogler, Christopher. "The Memo That Started It All." Private blog (website). Accessed May 23, 2023.

Vonnegut, Mark. *The Eden Express*. New York, NY.: Seven Stories Press, 1975, 208.

Vrajaprana, Pravrajika. "Jung and Indian Thought." Infinity Foundation (website). Accessed May 20, 2023.

Wasson, R. Gordon, Albert Hoffman and Carl A. Ruck. *The Road to Eleusis: Unveiling the Secret of the Mysteries*. Berkeley, CA.: North Atlantic Books, 2008.

Wilhelm, Richard. *Secrets of the Golden Flower*. London, UK: Broadway House, 1947.

Woolfe, Sam. "How Does Culture Influence a Psychedelic Experience?" Sam Woolfe (website). June 22, 2020.

World Health Organization (WHO). "Suicide: One Person Dies Every 40 Seconds." World Health Organization (website). September 6, 2019. Accessed May 25, 2023.

Yeshe, Lama Thubten. *The Bliss of Inner Fire*. Somerville, MA.: Wisdom Publication. 1998.

Yukteswar, Swami Sri. *The Holy Science*. Eastford, CT: Martino Publishing, 2013.

Index

Page references in *italics* refer to illustrations.

Abbot, Daniel, 36
accumulation, 292
active imagination, 197
Adam, 157–62
admiration, in Guru-yoga, 275
advantageous suffering, 213
agape, 50
Age of Aquarius-Leo, 63–66
Age of Aries-Libra, 46–47, 48–49, 63
Age of Cancer-Capricorn, 45
Age of Gemini-Sagittarius, 45
Age of Pisces-Virgo, 47–48, 49, 63
Age of Reason, 27, 56–57
Age of Taurus-Scorpio, 45, 63
Ages, Twelve Astrological, 44–48
Agios Athanasios, 278
Ainsworth, Mary, 149
alchemical map, 29
alchemized return, 300
alchemy, 89–90
  East and West, 119–26
  four stages of, 123–26
  methodology of, 29
  psychology and, 124–26
Alexander the Great, 78, 97
allies, 110

altruistic resolve (in Tibetan
  teaching), 272
ambrosia, 74
amrita, xii, 74–75
anatman, 81
anima, 128
anima mundi, 100–102
Anishinaabe people, 204–5
Antikythera Mechanism, 23
appetites, defined, 73
Aquarius, 63
archetypes, 128
Aries, 46–47
"as above, so below," 30, 89, 92, 118,
  239
Asclepius, 4–6, 7–8
Ashoka, 78
Asklepion, 8–10, 41
astrology, 25–27, 42–44, 96–102
  and healing, 102
  qualified astrologers, 99–100
  Twelve Astrological Ages, 44–48
"as within, so without," 357, 369
attachment theory, 149
axial precession, 43
Ayahuasca, 340

Bacon, Roger, 52
Bali, 137–42, 242–43
  asking Bali for permission, 348–49
  waste management in, 370
Bali Mula, 238–39
banjar, 371
bardos, 130, 229–30
  deities of the, *Plate 1*
  described, 355
Bardo Thodol. *See* Tibetan Book of
  the Dead
beginner's mind, 144
Bell, Lynn, 11–12, 19–20, 26, 138,
  243, 283, 333
Belulang, 238–43
Berzin, Alex, 316–17
betrayal, 244–46
Black Lives Matter, 35
Bly, Robert, 377
bodhicitta, 19, 186
  accumulation of, 188
bodhisattva vow, 134–36, 292–93,
  305–6, 366, 369, 374–75
Bollingen Tower, 264–67
Borobudur Mandala, *Plate 9*, 251–55,
  254, 311–12
Brahma, 285–86
brain, right and left, 12, 40–42
Bronze Age, 25, 26
Buddha (Gautama Sakyamuni), ix,
  18, 121–22, 280
  begins teaching, 284–89
  enlightenment of, 267–71
  finds path to awakening, 201–3
  his defiant stance, 145–47
  his departure, 142–47
  life scenes, *268*

ordeal of, 233–35
past lives of, 269
questions reality, 143–45
six-year initiation of, 200–203
Buddha, bodies of a, 130–31
Buddhism, 31, 50. *See also* tantra;
  tantric visualizations
  compassion in, 369
  five paths of integration, 291–93
  Four Noble Truths, 270
  and micro cycles, 28
  as a raft, 155
  taking refuge, 18–19
  twelve-fold cycle, 270
Buddhism-Shaivism merger, 313,
  351–52, 356–57, 365
Buddhist art, 78
Buddhist universities, 54
bull, 45
Butler, Amanda, 260

call to adventure, 109, 139–40
Campbell, Joseph, iv, 3, 15–16, *93*,
  355–56, 380
  biography, 104–5
  on bringing back the boon, 289
  critics of, 112–15
  on Hero's Journey, 3, 129, 141–42, 285
  and Tibetan teachings, 135–36
Cancer, 45
capitalism, 33–34
Capricorn, 45
cave, approaching the, 110
cave dream, 153–54
chakras, 75
chandali, 75
change, constant, 28

Charles, Ray, 381
chatra, 359, 364, 367
Christ, 43, 76, 121–22, 215–17
    baptism of, 50–51
    baptism of Jesus by Saint John,
        Plate 3
    Jung and the, 262–63
    "Stories of the Life of Christ," *Plate 7*
Christ consciousness, 215–17, 233,
    259, 262
Christianity, 49–52, 59, 76–77, 342
civil unrest, 34–35
clarity, 82
Claudius Ptolemy, 97
climate change, 33, 42
coagula, 130
collective unconscious, 13, 116–17, 128
compassion, in Buddhism, 369
complexes, 128
confession stage, 125
conformist return, the, 297–99
coniunctio, 128
consciousness, 2, 27, 76, 83–84, 103,
    132–33, 152, 162–63, 229, 325
    study of, 86
Copernicus, Nicholas, 52, 54–55
cosmological map, 29
cosmology, ancient, 3, *93*
Cousineau, Phil, 20, 112, 377–83
crab, 45
crisis/crises
    convergence of, 32–33, 66, 367–68,
        371
    six crises, 32–42
Cruttenden, Walter, 95–96, 98
cultural confluence, Greece and
    India, 74–76

Dalai Lama, 371
Dark Age, 25
dark night of the soul, iv, x, 113–14,
    124, 247, 264, 304, 355
dark thread, 380–81
Darwin, Charles, 56–57
Davidson, Richard, 86
death and dying, iv, 214
    conscious death, 379
    death-rebirth, 341–42
    to die so as to grow, 377–78
    eight stages of (Tibetan teachings),
        132–36
    and Hero's Journey, 114
    preparing for, 163–64
    and resistance, 235
    stages of dissolution, 167–68
    symbolic death, 163
    in Tibetan teachings, 129–36,
        162–64
death instinct, 151
decentralization, 65–67
defenses, 128
deities, *Plate 1*
Demeter, 148, 339, 341–43
departure phase, 139–42, 145–47,
    168–69
dependent origination, 270
depression, 36–38
dharmakaya, 18, 76, 271, 366
Diamond Throne, 18
Dionysian principle, 57–58
Dionysus, *Plate 6*, 76, 80, 338
disclosure, in Guru-yoga, 275–76
disenchantment, 32
divine pride, 272
dream analysis, 150–57

dreams, 10, 13, 150, 219. *See also under*
    Jung, Carl; Neale, Miles (author)
drive theory, 151, 153
duende, 381
Dunn, Christopher, 311
Dwapara, 25

Echols, Damien, 20–22, 354
economic disparity, 33–34
Edinger, Edwin, 379
education stage, 125–26
ego, 15–16, 73, 127, 140
ego death, 114
Egyptian culture, 70
Eleusinian mysteries, 73–74, 338–39,
    341–44
Eleusis, 341
Eliade, Mircea, 378
Elijah, 198–99
Eliot, T. S., 379
elixir, ix, 8, 31, 374–76
    defined, 29, 31
    Hero's Journey return with, 111,
        296–300
    imbibing the, 68–87
    as immortality, 247
    meaning of, 378, 380
elucidation stage, 125
emptiness, 87, 186, 232, 261, 272, 356
enemies, 110
Engler, Jack, 259
Enlightenment, Western, 56
environmental crisis, 33
"Epiphany of Dionysus," *Plate 6*
Erin, pilgrim, 296–97
eternal return, 73, 378
ethics, 231–32

Eucharist, 342
Evans-Wentz, W. Y., 227–28
Eve, 157–62
evil, 347–48
extremely subtle mind, 83–84

faith, reason and, 55
fall from grace, 157–62
father-drop, 75–76
fear, 235, 355, 368
feminine archetype, 158–60
Fernandez, Maurice, 22, 26, 203–4
fifth generation warfare, 36
Filigenzi, Anna, 80
Fitzgerald, Robert, 44–48
follow your bliss, 300
food production, 370
four jewels, 183
Four Noble Truths, 31, 270, 289
four sights (of the Buddha), 143–45
Four Stages of Transformation, 125–26
Freidell, Matthew, 367
Freud, Sigmund, 73, 85, 149–54,
        152–53, 156, 276
fruition, 31, 237

Galileo, 55
Galla Placidia, 301–4
Gandhara art style, 79–80
Gandhi, Mohandas K., 368
Garden of Eden story, 157–62
Gemini, 45
Gennep, Arnold van, 382
Geshe-la (Geshe Tenzin Zopa), 154,
    248–50, 306, 326–27, 358–60,
    365–66
    on tantric initiations, 191–93

Gilbert, Robert, 363
Gobekli Tepe, 94–95
God, 35–36
    and Garden of Eden, 157–62
"God is Dead," 28, 58–61
Goethe, Johann Wolfgang von, 377
Golden Age, 25
Gradual Path, 250–51
gradual transmutation, 300
Graham, Alison, 250
grammar, 54
Grasse, Ray, 44, 46, 63
Great Year, the, 18, 24–27, 42–44, 66,
    91, 94–102, 98–100, 106, 346
    chart, 101
Greco-Buddhism, 78–79
Greek culture, ancient, 6–11, 70–77
Green, Liz, 348
Griyawan, Made, 313–14
gross level of mind, 83
ground, defined, 1, 31
Gunung Abang mountain, 174–77, 362
Guru yoga, 185, 189–90, 200, 274–77

Hades, 71
Hancock, Graham, 6–7
Harrowing of Hell story, 215–17
healing, mythological dimensions of,
    12–13
Hellenistic zodiac, 49–50
Henry (client), 257–58
Hermes, 143
    "Lament of Hermes, The," 22, 24
Hermes Trismegistus, 90–91, 218
Hermeticism, 90
Hero's Journey, 14, 20, 105–6, 237,
    345, 382

co-opting of, 113–14
critics of, 112–15
and external assimilation, 296
and solve et coagula, 90
twelve stages of, 108–12
Hesiod, 96
Hillman, James, 13, 378–79, 379
Hippocrates, 97
home, 155
    coming home, 111
Homer, 281
humanism, 53
hydrocele, treatment of author's, 328–37

I Ching, 118–20
id, 73
"If you die before you die . . .," iv, 247
ignorance (in Buddhism), 270
incubatio, 9–10
Indian culture, and Greek, 74–76
individualism, 112–13
individuation, 128, 129, 255–60
    analytic movement and synthetic
        movement, 264
    and becoming who we are, 119–20
    defined, 256
    Jung's process of, 115–29
    methods of, 256–60
information age, 63–64
initiation, 170–205. See also Hero's
        Journey; rite-of-passage
    requesting, 191–93
    tantric, 183–85
innocence, the end of, 148–49
integration, 57, 290–93
    and the conformist return, 297–99
    for Joseph Campbell, 295–96

intimacy, 277
Islam, 51, 69
Ithaca, 14–15, 278–84

Jacobi, Jolande, 256
Jakarta, 170–72
James, William, 85
Jaspers, Karl, 47
Jesus. *See* Christ
Jitho, Mangku, 358–60, 366
Joseph, Chief, 9
Joseph, Miriam, 53–54
Judaism, 47, 49–50, 69
Jung, Carl, 3, 27, 87, *93*, 276, 280
    accepting contents of the
        unconscious, 305
    and alchemy, 123–26
    on Antichrist, 214
    anxiety totem of, 195
    on astrology, 101–2
    and Bollingen Tower, 264–67
    and cave with two skulls, 153–54
    on Christ, 49, 262–63
    on collective unconscious, 13, 44
    and departure, 169
    departure from Freud's ideas, 149–54
    descent into the unconscious,
        156–57
    dreams of, 150–54, 198–200, 217–19,
        219–23
    early life of, 194
    and the East, 118–20
    eating child's liver, 226–27
    experience in Ravenna, 301–4
    flood vision, 221
    and Galla Placidia, 344
    and Harrowing of Hell, 215–17
    his confrontation with the
        unconscious, 217–23
    his primordial fire, 194–95
    his return with elixir, 301–4
    house dream, 150–52
    on India's religion, 120–21
    and individuation, 15–16, 115–29,
        255–60
    initiation of, 193–200
    inward journey of, 129–30
    kills his ideal, 197–99
    mandalas and, 153–54, 262–64
    personal pilgrimage of, 117–18
    and Philemon, 199–200
    on Pisces, 43
    portal into the netherworld, 196–97
    and power struggle, 347–48
    on reclaiming our soul, 347–48
    and *The Red Book*, 223–26
    and the Self, 260–62
    significance of his work, 304
    "The Solar Voyage and the Sea
        Monster," *Plate 4*
    and the soul, iv, 84–86, 116, 381
    and spirit guides, 259
    split personality of, 195–96
    themes from his analytic
        psychology, 127–29, *129*
    and Tibetan teachings, 135–36
    and UFOs, 220
    use of astrology, 24
    vision of red crystal, 222–23
    white bird dream, 218
    why study him?, 116–17

Kabbalah, 69
Kalachakra tantra, *Plate 8*, 315–17, 369

Kalki, 314–15
katharsis, 9
Kaufmann, Walter, 60–61
Kepler, Johannes, 54–55
Kierkegaard, Soren, 380
king, return of the, 310–14
Klimberg, Max, 80
knowing, four kinds of, 39–40
knowledge, vs. wisdom, 14–16
Krishna, 143
Krishnamurti, Jiddu, 5–6
Kumbha Mela, 343
kundalini yoga, 120
kykeon, xii

"Lament of Hermes, The," 6–7,
    22, 24
last stand, the, 367–71
left mode (brain), 40–42, 52, 64,
    66–67, 147–48
Levine, Dr., 331–32
liberation, in Tibetan Buddhism, 84
liberation movements, 34–35
Libra, 46–47
life-death cycle, reversing the,
    131–36
logic, 54
logos, 273
Loizzo, Joe, 134, 179–82, 208–12,
    243–44, 247–49
longing, the return of, 377–83
Loom, The, 92–93, 93, 112, 115
Lopez, Donald, 121
Lorca, Federico Garcia, 381
Lord of Death, 230–33
Lumera, 311
lunar quest, 369

magic, following the, 283
Mahabodhi temple, 18, 339–40
Majapahit, 312–13
mandala, 65, 121, 140, 153, 272–73,
    365. See also Borobudur Mandala
    author's visions of, 16–20, 17, 43
    Bali as, 238–39
    Jung's, 262–64
mandala offerings, 189
Mandala of Kalachakra, Plate 8
mantra, 273–74
maps, four, 29–30
Mara, 233–35
masculine, rise of the, 46
masculine archetype, 158–60
materialism, 116, 347
Maya, 303
McGilchrist, Ian, 40–42, 57
meaning crisis, 28, 32, 38–42
medical industrial complex, 370
meditation path, 292
melukat, 206–8, 239–40
mental health crisis, 36–38
mentor, 184
    bonding process with, 134, 274–75
    finding a, 183–84
    meeting the, 109
    and melding of minds, 185
    student's responsibilities with a, 185
metempsychosis, 71–72
#MeToo, 35, 209–10
Metzner, Ralph, 229–30
middle way (Buddhist), 203
Miksic, John, 254
mind, 82, 363
    levels of, 82–84
    luminous nature of, 232

MindStream, founding of, 282
Missing Peace documentary, 367
money, 45–46
monomyth, 31, 104–15
  chart, *111*
monotheistic religions, 49, 51
morphic resonance, 362–63, 364
Moses, 47
movement of therapy, 193
mulaklesha, 303
Muraresku, Brian, 74, 76–77, 342
mystery schools, 341–44
myth, the power of, 14
mythic dimension of life, 15
mythopoetic map, 29
  cartography of myth, 106–8
myth(s), 106–8
  as maps of the soul, 213
  mythologizing one's life, 345

Nabta Playa, 94
Nagarjuna, 52
Nalanda, 81
Nalanda Institute, author at, 208–13
nationalism, 59–62
Neale, Miles, 382. *See also* Wolf,
  Emily (partner of Miles Neale)
  after first pilgrimage to India,
    296–97
  apprenticeship with Joe Loizzo,
    179–82
  in Bali, 172–77, 238–43, 283–84
  biography, x–xii, 415–16
  departure for Bali, 137–42
  father's death, 165–68
  finds cow skull, 333–34, 336
  and Gradual Path, 250–51

  his departure from conventional
    therapy, 11–14
  his need for change, 4
  in Ithaca, 278–84
  in Jakarta, 170–72
  leads group to Kathmandu, 326–27
  meets Patrick Vanhoebrouck, 310–12
  moves to Bali, 283–84
  post ordeal (after Nalanda), 243–51
  propensity for visions, 2
  and psilocybin treatment, 332–37
  psychedelic therapy of, 328–37
  public trial of, 208–13
  rite at Bali spring, 238–43
  search for elixir, 374–75
  three visions before the pandemic,
    14–22
  vision of a mandala, 16–20
  visions of Asclepius, 4–6
nectar (in tantric practice), 305–8
Newton, Isaac, 55
Nietzsche, Friedrich, 28, 57–61, 347
nihilism, 59–62
Ning, Jero, 349–58, 361
no more learning, 292–93
nostos, 14, 282
  and the return of longing, 377–83

Odysseus, 14, 71, 281, 352
offering, in Guru-yoga, 275
Oliver, Mary, 381–82
ordeal, 206–36
  in Hero's Journey, 110
  reflections on, 235–36

Padmasambhava, 78–79, 131
pagan continuity hypothesis, 76–77, 342

pain, 257

Paleolithic era, and soul, 70

Panchen Lama, third, 318

pandemic, 28–29, 363, 368

Paracelsus, 90

Patanjali, 52

path, defined, 31, 103

Pearce, Joseph Chilton, 372

permission, granting the soul, 374

Persephone, 148, 339, 341–43

persona, 127

personal unconscious, 128

Petrarch, 52

Philemon, 199–200

phurba, 21

pilgrimage
  in Buddhism, 321–22
  defined, 320
  nature of the process, 319–28
  as paradigm therapy, 324–28
  purpose of, 322–24
  to a sacred site, 320–21

pilgrimage in Eleusis, 342–43

pilgrimage of purpose, 106

pilgrimage of rebirth (Tibetan), 129–36
  chart, *136*

pilgrimage of wholeness, Jung on
  individuation, 115–29

pilgrimages, 137

pilgrimage to Indonesia, 350–51

pilgrimage to Java, 358–67

Pinchbeck, Daniel, 372–73

Piscean Age, 27, 48–62

Pisces, 47–48

planetary initiation, 203–5, 372–73

planetary rite of passage, 371–76

Plato, 72–73, 97

pleasure principle, 151

pledge, a final, 373–76

Plutonium cave, 343

Power of Myth, The, 105

precession of the equinoxes, 25–26,
  44, 94, 97

preparation for the journey, 290–91

prima materia, 123, 133

principle of correspondences, 30

Prometheus, 227

prostrations (in Tibetan teaching),
  188, 320

psychedelics, 332–37
  shadow of, 337–48
  and subtle-body yoga, 339–40

psychedelic sacraments, 77, 81

psychic integration, 126–29

psychoanalysis (Freudian), 152–53

psychological map, 29

PTSD, 37–38

Puncak Penulisan Temple, 348–50

purification, in Guru-yoga, 276

put one foot in front of the other, 348

pyramids, 362–63

Pythagoras, 71–72, 96

queen, return of the, 310–14

Quetzalcoatl, 143

raft analogy, 155

Raka, Tjokorda, 207

rationalism, 122

reason, 73, 147–48
  faith and, 55
  vs. intuition, 126–29

rebirth, 29. *See also* reincarnation
  as an altruistic avatar, 134–36

chart, *136*
tantric, 304–9
Red Book, The (Jung), 156, 223–26
refuge (in Tibetan teaching), 188
refusal to return, 296–97
reincarnation, 71–72, 86–87, 129–36, 162–64
rejoicing, in Guru-yoga, 276–77
religion, loss of, 59–60
Renaissance, 52–54
renunciation (in Tibetan teachings), 186, 272
requesting the blessing, 305
responsibility, personal, 245–46
resultant vehicle, 360–61
resurrection, in Hero's Journey, 111
return (in Hero's Journey), 278–318
return with elixir, 31, 113–14, 247, 250, 374–76, 378, 380
    forms of, 296–300
    in Hero's Journey, 111
Return with Elixir course, 251
revisioning of the soul, 378
reward, 110
rhetoric, 54
right mode (brain), 40–42
rite-of-passage, 105, 174, 177–79, 322. *See also* Hero's Journey
    planetary, 371–76
Roman Empire, 51–52
Ross, Susan, 295–96, 301
Rudra Kalki, 316–17

Sabdapalon prophecy, 172–73, 312–14, 351–52, 364
Sagittarius, 45
Salome, 198–99

Saturn, vision of, 21–22
Saturn-Jupiter-Pluto conjunction, 203–4
Schmidt, Klaus, 94
scientific materialism, 27, 86, 95
scientific revolution, 54–55
Scorpio, 45–46
Secret of the Golden Flower, The, 118
Sedana, Pak, 348–49, 353, 357
Self, 15–16, 129, 259–60
    Jung on, 260–62
self-denial, 202
separation, initiation, and return, 30, 106, 112, 382
Seven Fires prophecy, 204–5
72 (number), 253–54
shadow, 15–16, 35, 61–62, 128
    and individuation, 257–60
    power of the, 122
Shaivism-Buddhism merger, 313, 348–57
Shambhala prophecy, 314–18, 369
Shankaracharya, 200
Shantideva, 149
Sheldrake, Rupert, 362
Shiva, 78
Shiva, Vandana, 205
Shiva-Buddha, 348–57, 365
sickness of paradigm, 28
Siegel, Dan, 41, 64, 86, 102
Silk Road, 80
Silva, Freddy, 90
snake, 157–62
Socrates, 50, 72
Sol in Zodiac, *Plate 2*
solve et coagula, 31, 106
    can be overlaid on any process, 327, 345, 373

described, 88–91
and healing trauma, 91–92
and the heroic journey, 90
in Joseph Campbell's biography, 104
and The Loom, 92–93
and tantric visualization, 161
soul, 1, 68–69, 87
in Buddhism, 81–82
etymology of, 69–70
granting it permission, 374
in Greek culture, 70–74
and iimbibing the elixir, 68–87
Jung and the, 84–86
legacy of the, 70–84
Paleolithic era and, 70
revisioning of the, 378–80
soul-plasticity, 86–87
soul sculpting, 260
spirit, 69–70, 73
Steinbeck, John, 381
structures, monolithic, 362–63
subtle level of mind, 83
suffering, Buddha's view of, 269–70
suicide, 36–38
Sumerian culture, 96
super-ego, 73
Swat Valley nexus point, 78–81
sword, as immortality, 247

Tank Man, 368
tantra
extraordinary preliminaries, 187–90
outer preliminaries, 187
prerequisites for, 186–93
as resultant vehicle, 192
six ordinary preliminaries, 186–87
Tantric Buddhism, 81–84

tantric initiation, 183–85
tantric rebirth, 304–9
tantric systems, 75, 80–81
tantric visualizations, 75–76, 103,
    161–62, 164, 304–9, 344
Tara, Green, 141, 274
Tarnus, Rick, 26, 32, 98–99, 100
Taurus, 45–46
teacher, appears when student is
    ready, 154
technocratic and memetic warfare,
    35–36
technology, 65–66
Telesterion, 343
test, in Hero's Journey, 110
tests, enemies, and allies in, in
    Tibetan teachings, 190–91
Three Principles of the Path to
    Awakening, 186
threshold, crossing the, 109–10, 139–40
throwing karma, 244
Thurman, Robert, 76, 130, 192, 232
    biography, xiv
Tibetan Book of the Dead, iv, 121,
    130, 131, 133–36, 227–33
    and departure, 169
Tibetan teachings, 3, 93, 115–16
    and Campbell and Jung, 15–16
    completion stage, 272
    on mandala womb, 271–74
    mastering the death process,
    162–64
    pilgrimage of rebirth (Tibetan),
    129–36
    requesting initiation, 191–93
    tantric departure, 164–67
    tantric rebirth, 304–9

tantric treasure, 274–77
tests, enemies, and allies in, 190–91
time, cyclic, 22–24
tirta, 206, 239
Tolkien, J. R. R., 106
transcendence, 48
transformation stage, 126
transitions, planetary, three
    simultaneous, 26–27
transmigration, 86–87, 269
trauma, 36–38
treasure, 238–77, 280
Tree of Knowledge, 157–62
trickster archetype, 157
Tri Hita Karana, 172, 243, 371
Trimurti, 240–41
trishiksha, 81
truth-act, 368
tulku, 130
Tunjai, Dr., 166–67
turning points, 26
twentieth century, gestalt of, 61–62
twins, 45

Übermensch, 60–61
unearned wisdom, 293–95, 294
unus mundus principle, 26, 128
Upaka, 287–88
upaya, 300

vajra, 354
Vajrasattva practice, 189
Vajrayogini, *Plate 5*
Vanhoebrouck, Patrick, 310–13, 358,
    360, 364

Vervaeke, John, 28, 32, 39
vibration, changing the, 357–58
Virgo, 47–48, 50
voidness, 356, 366
    and the Self, 261
volition, 149

waking up culturally, 27–28
war, 46
Western culture, 2, 372–73
Wilhelm, Richard, 118–20
wisdom, 50
    vs. knowledge, 14–16
    as liberation, 232
Wizard of Bali, the (Tjok Gde
    Kerthyasa), 18, 171–77, 206–8,
    238–43, 250–52, 280
Wolf, Emily (partner of Miles Neale),
    xi, xiii, 139, 182, 209, 247–48,
    348–57, 357
    in Ithaca, 278–84
Woodroffe, J. G., 120
Woolf, Sam, 230
Word, in the beginning was the, 361
world soul, 100–102
writing, origin of, 95–96

Yama, 230–33, 271
Yeshe, Lama, 191–92
yoga, subtle-body yoga and
    psychedelics, 339–40
Yuga system, 25, 98–99

Zen Buddhism, 293–94
Zodiac, 43–48